D0891427

THE COMPLETE WORKS OF ROBERT BROWNING, VOLUME X

*Robert Browning in 1871. Photograph by Elliott and Fry of London.
Courtesy of the Armstrong Browning Library.*

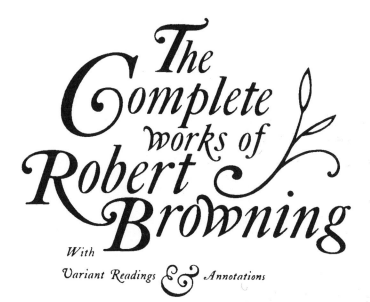

The Complete Works of Robert Browning

With Variant Readings & Annotations

Volume X

EDITED BY

ALLAN C. DOOLEY

SUSAN E. DOOLEY

BAYLOR UNIVERSITY
WACO, TEXAS
OHIO UNIVERSITY PRESS
ATHENS, OHIO
1999

THE COMPLETE WORKS OF ROBERT BROWNING

ALLAN C. DOOLEY, General Editor

JACK W. HERRING, General Editor, Emeritus

PARK HONAN, Founding Editor

ROMA A. KING, Founding Editor

JOHN C. BERKEY

MICHAEL BRIGHT

ASHBY BLAND CROWDER

SUSAN CROWL

SUSAN E. DOOLEY

DAVID EWBANK

RITA S. PATTESON

PAUL TURNER

Ohio University Press, Athens, Ohio 45701
© 1999 by Ohio University Press and Baylor University
Printed in the United States of America
All rights reserved

04 03 02 01 00 99   5 4 3 2 1

Ohio University Press books are printed on acid-free paper ⊗ ™

Library of Congress Cataloging-in-Publication data
(Revised for vol. 10)

Browning, Robert, 1812–1889.
The complete works of Robert Browning, with variant readings & annotations.

Vol. 10 edited by Allan C. Dooley and Susan E. Dooley
Includes bibliographical references and indexes.
I. King, Roma A., 1914–   , ed.
II. Title.
PR4201.K5 1969 821'.8   68-18389
ISBN 0-8214-1300-7 (v. 10)

CONTENTS

I CONTENTS

This edition of the works of Robert Browning is intended to be complete. It will comprise at least seventeen volumes and will contain:

1. The entire contents of the first editions of Browning's works, arranged in their chronological order of publication. (The poems included in *Dramatic Lyrics, Dramatic Romances and Lyrics,* and *Men and Women,* for example, appear in the order of their first publication rather than in the order in which Browning rearranged them for later publication.)

2. All prefaces and dedications which Browning is known to have written for his own works and for those of Elizabeth Barrett Browning.

3. The two prose essays that Browning is known to have published: the review of a book on Tasso, generally referred to as the "Essay on Chatterton," and the preface for a collection of letters supposed to have been written by Percy Bysshe Shelley, generally referred to as the "Essay on Shelley."

4. The front matter and the table of contents of each of the collected editions (1849, 1863, 1865, 1868 [70, 75], 1888-1889) which Browning himself saw through the press.

5. Poems published during Browning's lifetime but not collected by him.

6. Poems not published during Browning's lifetime which have come to light since his death.

7. John Forster's *Thomas Wentworth, Earl of Strafford,* to which Browning contributed significantly, though the precise extent of his contribution has not been determined.

8. Variants appearing in primary and secondary materials as defined in Section II below.

9. Textual emendations.

10. Informational and explanatory notes for each work.

II PRIMARY AND SECONDARY MATERIALS

Aside from a handful of uncollected short works, all of Browning's works but *Asolando* (1889) went through two or more editions during his lifetime. Except for *Pauline* (1833), *Strafford* (1837), and *Sordello*

(1840), all the works published before 1849 were revised and corrected for the 1849 collection. *Strafford* and *Sordello* were revised and corrected for the collection of 1863, as were all the other works in that edition. Though no further poems were added in the collection of 1865, all the works were once again corrected and revised. The 1868 collection added a revised *Pauline* and *Dramatis Personae* (1864) to the other works, which were themselves again revised and corrected. A new edition of this collection in 1870 contained further revisions, and Browning corrected his text again for an 1875 reimpression. The printing of the last edition of the *Poetical Works* over which Browning exercised control began in 1888, and the first eight volumes are dated thus on their title-pages. Volumes 9 through 16 of this first impression are dated 1889, and we have designated them 1889a to distinguish them from the second impression of all 16 volumes, which was begun and completed in 1889. Some of the earlier volumes of the first impression sold out almost immediately, and in preparation for a second impression, Browning revised and corrected the first ten volumes before he left for Italy in late August, 1889. The second impression, in which all sixteen volumes bear the date 1889 on their title-pages, consisted of a revised and corrected second impression of volumes 1-10, plus a second impression of volumes 11-16 altered by Browning in one instance. This impression we term 1889 (see section III below).

Existing manuscripts and editions are classified as either primary or secondary material. The primary materials include the following:

1. The manuscript of a work when such is known to exist.

2. Proof sheets, when known to exist, that contain authorial corrections and revisions.

3. The first and subsequent editions of a work that preserve evidence of Browning's intentions and were under his control.

4. The collected editions over which Browning exercised control:

1849—*Poems.* Two Volumes. London: Chapman and Hall.

1863—*The Poetical Works.* Three Volumes. London: Chapman and Hall.

1865—*The Poetical Works.* Three Volumes. London: Chapman and Hall.

1868—*The Poetical Works.* Six Volumes. London: Smith, Elder and Company.

1870—*The Poetical Works.* Six Volumes. London: Smith, Elder and Company. This resetting constituted a new edition, which was stereotyped and reimpressed several times; the 1875 impression contains revisions by Browning.

1888-1889—*The Poetical Works.* Sixteen Volumes. London: Smith,

Elder and Company. Exists in numerous stereotype impressions, of which two are primary material:

1888-1889a—The first impression, in which volumes 1-8 are dated 1888 and volumes 9-16 are dated 1889.

1889—The corrected second impression of volumes 1-10 and a second impression of volumes 11-16 altered by Browning only as stated in section III below; all dated 1889 on the title pages.

    5. The corrections in Browning's hand in the Dykes Campbell copy of 1888-1889a, and the manuscript list of corrections to that impression in the Brown University Library (see section III below).

    Other materials (including some in the poet's handwriting) that affected the text are secondary. Examples are: the copy of the first edition of *Pauline* which contains annotations by Browning and John Stuart Mill; the copies of the first edition of *Paracelsus* which contain corrections in Browning's hand; a very early manuscript of *A Blot in the 'Scutcheon* which Browning presented to William Macready, but not the one from which the first edition was printed; informal lists of corrections that Browning included in letters to friends, such as the corrections to *Men and Women* he sent to D. G. Rossetti; verbal and punctuational changes Browning essayed in presentation copies of his works or in his own copies, if not used by his printers; Elizabeth Barrett's suggestions for revisions in *A Soul's Tragedy* and certain poems in *Dramatic Romances and Lyrics;* and the edition of *Strafford* by Emily Hickey for which Browning made suggestions.

    The text and variant readings of this edition derive from collation of primary materials as defined above. Secondary materials are occasionally discussed in the notes and sometimes play a part when emendation is required.

III COPY-TEXT

    The copy-text for this edition is Browning's final text: the first ten volumes of 1889 and the last six volumes of 1888-1889a, as described above. For this choice we offer the following explanation.

    Manuscripts used as printer's copy for twenty of Browning's thirty-four book publications are known to exist; others may yet become available. These manuscripts, or, in their absence, the first editions of the works, might be considered as the most desirable copy-text. And this would be the case for an author who exercised little control over his text after the manuscript or first edition stage, or whose text clearly became corrupted in a succession of editions. To preserve the intention of such an author, one would have to choose an early text and emend it as evidence and judgment demanded.

With Browning, however, the situation is different, and our copy-text choice results from that difference. Throughout his life Browning continually revised his poetry. He did more than correct printer's errors and clarify previously intended meanings; his texts themselves remained fluid, subject to continuous alteration. As the manuscript which he submitted to his publisher was no doubt already a product of revision, so each subsequent edition under his control reflects the results of an ongoing process of creating, revising, and correcting. If we were to choose the manuscript (where extant) or first edition as copy-text, preserving Browning's intention would require extensive emendation to capture the additions, revisions, and alterations which Browning demonstrably made in later editions. By selecting Browning's final corrected text as our copy-text, emending it only to eliminate errors and the consequences of changing house-styling, we present his works in the form closest to that which he intended after years of revision and polishing.

But this is true only if Browning in fact exercised extensive control over the printing of his various editions. That he intended and attempted to do so is apparent in his comments and his practice. In 1855, demanding accuracy from the printers, he pointed out to his publisher Chapman, "I attach importance to the mere stops . . ." (DeVane and Knickerbocker, p. 83). There is evidence of his desire to control the details of his text as early as 1835, in the case of *Paracelsus*. The *Paracelsus* manuscript, now in the Forster and Dyce collection in the Victoria and Albert Museum Library, demonstrates a highly unconventional system of punctuation. Of particular note is Browning's unrestrained use of dashes, often in strings of two or three, instead of more precise or orthodox punctuation marks. It appears that this was done for its rhetorical effect. One sheet of Part 1 of the manuscript and all but the first and last sheets of Part 3 have had punctuation revised in pencil by someone other than Browning, perhaps J. Riggs, whose name appears three times in the margins of Part 3. In addition to these revisions, there are analogous punctuation revisions (in both pencil and ink) which appear to be in Browning's hand, and a few verbal alterations obviously in the poet's script.

A collation of the first edition (1835) with the manuscript reveals that a major restyling of punctuation was carried out before *Paracelsus* was published. However, the revisions incorporated into the first edition by no means slavishly follow the example set by the pencilled revisions of Parts 1 and 3 of the manuscript. Apparently the surviving manuscript was not used as printer's copy for the first edition. Browning may have submitted a second manuscript, or he may have revised extensively in proof. The printers may have carried out the revisions to punctuation, with or without the poet's point by point involvement. With the present evidence, we cannot be conclusive about the extent of Browning's control over the first edition of *Paracelsus*. It can be stated, however, in the light of the incompleteness of the pencilled revisions and the frequent lack or correspondence between the pencilled revisions and the lines as printed in 1835, that Browning himself may have been responsible for the punctuation of the first edition of *Paracelsus*. Certainly he was responsible for the frequent instances in the first and subsequent editions where the punctuation defies conventional rules, as in the following examples:

> What though
> It be so?—if indeed the strong desire
> Eclipse the aim in me—if splendour break
> (Part I, ll. 329-331)

> I surely loved them—that last night, at least,
> When we . . . gone! gone! the better: I am saved
> (Part II, ll. 132-133)

> Of the body, even,)—what God is, what we are,
> (Part V, l. 642, 1849 reading)

The manuscripts of *Colombe's Birthday* (1844) and *Christmas-Eve and Easter-Day* (1850) were followed very carefully in the printing of the first editions. There are slight indications of minor house-styling, such as the spellings *colour* and *honour* for the manuscripts' *color* and *honor*. But the unorthodox punctuation, used to indicate elocutionary and rhetorical subtleties as well as syntactical relationships, is carried over almost unaltered from the manuscripts to the first editions. Similar evidence of Browning's painstaking attention to the smallest details in the printing of his poems can be seen in the manuscript and proof sheets of *The Ring and the Book* (1868-69). These materials reveal an interesting and significant pattern. It appears that Browning wrote swiftly, giving primary attention to wording and less to punctuation, being satisfied to use dashes to indicate almost any break in thought, syntax, or rhythm. Later, in the proof sheets for Books 1-6 of the poem and in the manuscript itself for Books 7-12, he changed the dashes to more specific and purposeful punctuation marks. The revised punctuation is what was printed, for the most part, in the first edition of *The Ring and the Book*; what further revisions there are conform to Browning's practice, though hardly to standard rules. Clearly Browning was in control of nearly every aspect of the published form of his works, even to the "mere stops."

Of still greater importance in our choice of copy-text is the substantial evidence that Browning took similar care with his collected editions. Though he characterized his changes for later editions as trivial and few in number, collations reveal thousands of revisions and corrections in each successive text. *Paracelsus,* for example, was extensively revised for the 1849 *Poems;* it was again reworked for the *Poetical Works* of 1863. *Sordello,* omitted in 1849, reappeared in 1863 with 181 new lines and short marginal glosses; Browning admitted only that it was "corrected *throughout*" (DeVane and Knickerbocker, p. 157). The poems of *Men and Women* (1855) were altered in numerous small but meaningful ways for both the 1863 and 1865 editions of the *Poetical Works* (See Allan C. Dooley, "The Textual Significance of Robert Browning's 1865 *Poetical Works,*" *PBSA* 71 [1977], 212-18). Michael Hancher cites evidence of the poet's close supervision of the 1868 collected edition ("Browning and the *Poetical Works* of 1888-1889," *Browning Newsletter,* Spring, 1971, 25-27), and Michael Meredith has traced Browning's attentions to his text in the 1870 edition and an 1875 reimpression of it ("Learning's Crabbed Text," *SBHC* 13 [1985], 97-107); another perspective is offered in Allan C. Dooley's *Author and Printer in Victorian England* (1992), Ch. 4-5. Mrs. Orr, writing of the same period in Browning's life, reports his resentment of those who garbled his text by misplacing his stops (*Life,* pp. 357-58).

There is plentiful and irrefutable evidence that Browning controlled, in the same meticulous way, the text of his last collected edition, that which we term 1888-1889. Hancher has summarized the relevant information:

> The evidence is clear that Browning undertook the 1888-1889 edition of his *Poetical Works* intent on controlling even the smallest minutiae of the text. Though he at one time considered supplying biographical and explanatory notes to the poems, he finally decided against such a scheme, concluding, in his letter to Smith of 12 November 1887, "I am correcting them carefully, and *that* must suffice." On 13 January 1888, he wrote, regarding the six-volume edition of his collected works published in 1868 which was to serve as the printer's copy for the final edition: "I have thoroughly corrected the six volumes of the Works, and can let you have them at once." . . . Browning evidently kept a sharp eye on the production of all sixteen of the volumes, including those later volumes. . . . Browning returned proof for Volume 3 on 6 May 1888, commenting, "I have had, as usual, to congratulate myself on

the scrupulous accuracy of the Printers"; on 31 December he returned proofs of Volume 11, "corrected carefully"; and he returned "the corrected Proofs of Vol. XV" on 1 May 1889.

Throughout his long career, then, Browning continuously revised and corrected his works. Furthermore, his publishers took care to follow his directions exactly, accepting his changes and incorporating them into each successive edition. This is not to say that no one else had any effect whatsoever on Browning's text: Elizabeth Barrett made suggestions for revisions to *A Soul's Tragedy* and *Dramatic Romances and Lyrics*. Browning accepted some suggestions and rejected others, and those which he accepted we regard as his own. Mrs. Orr reports that Browning sent proof sheets to Joseph Milsand, a friend in France, for corrections (*Life,* p. 183), and that Browning accepted suggestions from friends and readers for the corrections of errors in his printed works. In some of the editions, there are slight evidences of minor house-styling in capitalization and the indication of quotations. But the evidence of Browning's own careful attention to revisions and corrections in both his manuscripts and proof sheets assures us that other persons played only a very minor role in the development of his text. We conclude that the vast majority of the alterations in the texts listed above as Primary Materials are Browning's own, and that only Browning's final corrected text, the result of years of careful work by the poet himself, reflects his full intentions.

The first impression of Browning's final collected edition (i.e., 1888-1889a) is not in and of itself the poet's final corrected text. By the spring of 1889 some of the early volumes of the first impression were already sold out, and by mid-August it was evident that a new one would be required. About this time James Dykes Campbell, Honorary Secretary of the London Browning Society, was informed by Browning that he was making further corrections to be incorporated into the new impression. According to Dykes Campbell, Browning had corrected the first ten volumes and offered to transcribe the corrections into Dykes Campbell's copy of 1888-1889a before leaving for Italy. The volumes altered in Browning's hand are now in the British Library and contain on the flyleaf of Volume I Dykes Campbell's note explaining precisely what happened. Of course, Dykes Campbell's copy was not the one used by the printer for the second impression. Nevertheless, these changes are indisputably Browning's and are those which, according to his own statement, he proposed to make in the new impression. This set of corrections carries, therefore, great authority.

Equally authoritative is a second set of corrections, also in Browning's hand, for part of 1888-1889a. In the poet's possession at the time of his death, this handwritten list was included in lot 179 of Sotheby, Wilkinson, and Hodge's auction of Browning materials in 1913; it is today located in the Brown University Library. The list contains corrections only to Volumes 4-10 of 1888-1889a. We know that Browning, on 26 July 1889, had completed and sent to Smith "the corrections for Vol. III in readiness for whenever you need them." By the latter part of August, according to Dykes Campbell, the poet had finished corrections for Volumes 1-10. Browning left for Italy on 29 August. The condition of the Brown University list does not indicate that it was ever used by the printer. Thus we surmise that the Brown list (completing the corrections through volume 10) may be the poet's copy of another list sent to his publisher. Whatever the case, the actual documents used by the printers—a set of marked volumes or handwritten lists—are not known to exist. A possible exception is a marked copy of *Red Cotton Night-Cap Country* (now in the Berg Collection of the New York Public Library) which seems to have been used by printers. Further materials used in preparing Browning's final edition may yet appear.

The matter is complicated further because neither set of corrections of 1888-1889a corresponds exactly to each other nor to the 1889 second impression. Each set contains corrections the other omits, and in a few cases the sets present alternative corrections of the same error. Our study of the Dykes Campbell copy of 1888-1889a reveals fifteen discrepancies between its corrections and the 1889 second impression. The Brown University list, which contains far fewer corrections, varies from the second impression in thirteen instances. Though neither of these sets of corrections was used by the printers, both are authoritative; we consider them legitimate textual variants, and record them as such. The lists are, of course, useful when emendation of the copy-text is required.

The value of the Dykes Campbell copy of 1888-1889a and the Brown University list is not that they render Browning's text perfect. The corrections to 1888-1889a must have existed in at least one other, still more authoritative form: the documents which Browning sent to his publisher. That this is so is indicated by the presence of required corrections in the second impression which neither the Dykes Campbell copy nor the Brown University list calls for. The significance of the existing sets of corrections is that they clearly indicate two important points: Browning's direct and active interest in the preparation of a corrected second impression of his final collected edition; and, given the high degree of correspondence between the two sets of corrections and the affected lines of the second impression, the concern of the printers to follow the poet's directives.

The second impression of 1888-1889 incorporated most of Browning's corrections to the first ten volumes of the first impression. There is no evidence whatever that any corrections beyond those which Browning sent to his publisher in the summer of 1889 were ever made. We choose, therefore, the 1889 corrected second impression of volumes 1-10 as copy-text for the works in those volumes. Corrections to the first impression were achieved by cutting the affected letters or punctuation out of the stereotype plates and pressing or soldering in the correct pieces of type. The corrected plates were then used for many copies, without changing the date on the title pages (except, of course, in volumes 17 [*Asolando*] and 18 [*New Poems*], added to the set by the publishers in 1894 and 1914 respectively). External evidence from publishers' catalogues and the advertisements bound into some volumes of 1889 indicate that copies of this impression were produced as late as 1913, although the dates on the title pages of volumes 1-16 remained 1889. Extensive plate deterioration is characteristic of the later copies, and use of the Hinman collator on early and late examples of 1889 reveals that the inserted corrections were somewhat fragile, some of them having decayed or disappeared entirely as the plates aged. (See Allan C. Dooley, "Browning's *Poetical Works* of 1888-1889," *SBHC* 7:1 [1978], 43-69.)

We do not use as copy-text volumes 11-16 of 1889, because there is a no present evidence indicating that Browning exercised substantial control over this part of the second impression of 1888-1889. We do know that he made one correction, which he requested in a letter to Smith quoted by Hancher:

> I have just had pointed out to [me] that an error, I supposed corrected, still is to be found in the 13th Volume—(Aristophanes' Apology) page 143, line 9, where the word should be Opora—without an i. I should like it altered, if that may be possible.

This correction was indeed made in the second impression. Our collations of copies of volumes 11-16 of 1889a and 1889 show no other intentional changes. The later copies do show, however, extensive type batter, numerous scratches, and irregular inking. Therefore our copy-text for the works in the last six volumes of 1888-1889 is volumes 11-16 of 1888-1889a.

IV VARIANTS

In this edition we record, with a very few exceptions discussed below, all variants from the copy-text appearing in the manuscripts and in the editions under Browning's control. Our purpose in doing this is two-fold.

1. We enable the reader to reconstruct the text of a work as it stood at the various stages of its development.

2. We provide the materials necessary to an understanding of how Browning's growth and development as an artist are reflected in his successive revisions to his works.

As a consequence of this policy our variant listings inevitably contain some variants that were not created by Browning; printer's errors and readings that may result from house-styling will appear occasionally. But the evidence that Browning assumed responsibility for what was printed, and that he considered and used unorthodox punctuation as part of his meaning, is so persuasive that we must record even the smallest and oddest variants. The following examples, characteristic of Browning's revisions, illustrate the point:

> *Pauline,* l. 700:
>> 1833: I am prepared—I have made life my own—
>> 1868: I am prepared: I have made life my own.
> "Evelyn Hope," l. 41:
>> 1855: I have lived, I shall say, so much since then,
>> 1865: I have lived (I shall say) so much since then,
> "Bishop Blougram's Apology," l. 267:
>> 1855: That's the first cabin-comfort I secure—
>> 1865: That's the first-cabin comfort I secure:
> *The Ring and the Book,* Book 11 ("Guido"), l. 1064:
>> 1869: What if you give up boys' and girls' fools'-play
>> 1872: What if you give up boy and girl fools'-play
>> 1889a: What if you give up boy-and-girl-fools' play

We have concluded that Browning himself is nearly always responsible for such changes. But even if he only accepted these changes (rather than originating them), their effect on syntax, rhythm, and meaning is so significant that they must be recorded in our variant listings.

The only variants we do not record are those which strongly appear to result from systematic house-styling. For example, Browning nowhere indicated that he wished to use typography to influence meaning, and our inference is that any changes in line-spacing, depth of paragraph indentation, and the like, were the responsibility of the printers of the various editions, not the poet himself. House-styling was also very probably the cause of certain variants in the apparatus of Browning's plays, including variants in stage directions which involve a change only in manner of statement, such as *Enter Hampden* instead of

Hampden enters; variants in the printing of stage directions, such as *Aside* instead of *aside,* or [*Aside.*] instead of [*Aside*], or [*Strafford.*] instead of [*Strafford*]; variants in character designations, such as *Lady Carlisle* instead of *Car* or *Carlisle.* Browning also accepted current convention for indicating quotations (see section V below). Neither do we list changes in type face (except when used for emphasis), nor the presence or absence of a period at the end of the title of a work.

V ALTERATIONS TO THE COPY-TEXT

We have rearranged the sequence of works in the copy-text, so that they appear in the order of their first publication. This process involves the restoration to the original order of the poems included in *Dramatic Lyrics, Dramatic Romances and Lyrics,* and *Men and Women.* We realize, of course, that Browning himself was responsible for the rearrangement of these poems in the various collected editions; in his prefatory note for the 1888-1889 edition, however, he indicates that he desired a chronological presentation:

> The poems that follow are again, as before, printed in chronological order; but only so far as proves compatible with the prescribed size of each volume, which necessitates an occasional change in the distribution of its contents.

We would like both to indicate Browning's stated intentions about the placement of his poems and to present the poems in the order which suggests Browning's development as a poet. We have chosen, therefore, to present the poems in order of their first publication, with an indication in the notes as to their respective subsequent placement. We also include the tables of contents of the editions listed as Primary Materials above.

We have regularized or modernized the copy-text in the following minor ways:

1. We do not place a period at the end of the title of a work, though the copy-text does.

2. In some of Browning's editions, including the copy-text, the first word of each work is printed in capital letters. We have used the modern practice of capitalizing only the first letter.

3. The inconsistent use of both an ampersand and the word *and* has been regularized to the use of *and.*

4. We have eliminated the space between the two parts of a contraction; thus the copy-text's *it 's* is printed as *it's,* for example.

5. We uniformly place periods and commas within closing quotation marks.

6. We have employed throughout the modern practice of indicating quoted passages with quotation marks only at the beginning and end of the quotation. Throughout Browning's career, no matter which publisher or printer was handling his works, this matter was treated very inconsistently. In some of the poet's manuscripts and in most of his first editions, quotations are indicated by quotation marks only at the beginning and end. In the collected editions of 1863 and 1865, issued by Chapman and Hall, some quoted passages have quotation marks at the beginning of each line of the quotation, while others follow modern practice. In Smith, Elder's collected editions of 1868 and 1888-1889, quotation marks usually appear at the beginning of each line of a quotation. We have regularized and modernized what seems a matter of house-styling in both copy-text and variants.

The remaining way in which the copy-text is altered is by emendation. Our policy is to emend the copy-text to eliminate apparent errors of either Browning or his printers. It is evident that Browning did make errors and overlook mistakes, as shown by the following example from "One Word More," the last poem in *Men and Women*. Stanza sixteen of the copy-text opens with the following lines:

> What, there's nothing in the moon noteworthy?
> Nay: for if that moon could love a mortal,
> Use, to charm him (so to fit a fancy,
> All her magic ('tis the old sweet mythos)
> She . . .

Clearly the end punctuation in the third line is incorrect. A study of the various texts is illuminating. Following are the readings of the line in each of the editions for which Browning was responsible:

MS:	fancy)	1855:	fancy)	1865:	fancy)	1888:	fancy
P:	fancy)	1863:	fancy)	1868:	fancy)	1889:	fancy,

The omission of one parenthesis in 1888 was almost certainly a printer's error. Browning, in the Dykes Campbell copy corrections to 1888-1889a, missed or ignored the error. However, in the Brown University list of corrections, he indicated that *fancy* should be followed by a comma. This is the way the line appears in the corrected second impression of Volume 4, but the correction at best satisfies the demands of syntax only partially. Browning might have written the line:

Use, to charm him, so to fit a fancy,

or, to maintain parallelism between the third and fourth lines:

Use, to charm him (so to fit a fancy),

or he might simply have restored the earlier reading. Oversights of this nature demand emendation, and our choice would be to restore the punctuation of the manuscript through 1868. All of our emendations will be based, as far as possible, on the historical collation of the passage involved, the grammatical demands of the passage in context, and the poet's treatment of other similar passages. Fortunately, the multiple editions of most of the works provide the editor with ample textual evidence to make an informed and useful emendation.

All emendations to the copy-text are listed at the beginning of the Editorial Notes for each work. The variant listings for the copy-text also incorporate the emendations, which are preceded and followed there by the symbol indicating an editor's note.

VI APPARATUS

1. *Variants.* In presenting the variants from the copy-text, we list at the bottom of each page readings from the known manuscripts, proof sheets of the editions when we have located them, and the first and subsequent editions.

A variant is generally preceded and followed by a pickup and a drop word (example a). No note terminates with a punctuation mark unless the punctuation mark comes at the end of the line; if a variant drops or adds a punctuation mark, the next word is added (example b). If the normal pickup word has appeared previously in the same line, the note begins with the word preceding it. If the normal drop word appears subsequently in the line, the next word is added (example c). It a capitalized pickup word occurs within the line, it is accompanied by the preceding word (example d). No pickup or drop words, however, are used for any variant consisting of an internal change, for example a hyphen in a compounded word, an apostrophe, a tense change or a spelling change (example e). A change in capitalization within a line of poetry will be preceded by a pickup word, for which, within an entry containing other variants, the < > is suitable (example f). No drop word is used when the variant comes at the end of a line (example g). Examples):

a. [611] *1840*:but that appeared   *1863*:but this appeared
b. variant at end of line: [109] *1840*:intrigue:"   *1863*:intrigue.
   variant within line: [82] *1840*:forests like   *1863*:forests, like
c. [132] *1840*:too sleeps; but   *1863*:too sleeps: but   [77] *1840*:that night
   by   *1863*:that, night by night,   *1888*:by night
d. [295] *1840*:at Padua to repulse the   *1863*:at Padua who repulsed the
e. [284] *1840*:are   *1863*:were
   [344] *1840*:dying-day,   *1863*:dying day,
f. capitalization change with no other variants: [741] *1840*:
   retaining Will,   *1863*:will,
   with other variants: [843] *1840*:Was < > Him back! Why   *1863*:Is
   < > back!" Why   *1865*:him
g. [427] *1840*:dregs: *1863*:dregs.

Each recorded variant will be assumed to be incorporated in the next edition if there is no indication otherwise. This rule applies even in cases where the only change occurs in 1888-1889, although it means that the variant note duplicates the copy-text. A variant listing, then, traces the history of a line and brings it forward to the point where it matches the copy-text.

With regard to manuscript readings, our emphasis is on the textual development and sequence of revisions; visual details of the manuscripts are kept to a minimum. For economy of space, we use formulae such as §crossed out and replaced above by§, but these often cannot report fine details such as whether, when two words were crossed out, the accompanying punctuation was precisely cancelled also. Our MS entries provide enough information to reconstruct with reasonable accuracy B's initial and revised manuscript readings, but they cannot substitute for direct scrutiny of the documents themselves.

It should be noted that we omit drop words in manuscript entries where the final reading is identical to the printed editons—thus

> MS:Silence, and all that ghastly §crossed out and replaced above by§ tinted pageant, base
>
> Printed editions: Silence, and all that tinted pageant, base

is entered as

> MS:that ghastly §crossed out and replaced above by§ tinted

in our variant listings.

An editor's note always refers to the single word or mark of punctuation immediately preceding or following the comment, unless otherwise specified.

In Browning's plays, all character designations which happen to occur in variant listings are standardized to the copy-text reading. In listing variants in the plays, we ignore character designations unless the designation comes within a numbered line. In such a case, the character designation is treated as any other word, and can be used as a pickup or drop word. When a character designation is used as a pickup word, however, the rule excluding capitalized pickup words (except at the beginning of a line) does not apply, and we do not revert to the next earliest uncapitalized pickup word.

2. *Line numbers.* Poetic lines are numbered in the traditional manner, taking one complete poetic line as one unit of counting. In prose passages the unit of counting is the type line of this edition.

3. *Table of signs in variant listings.* We have avoided all symbols and signs used by Browning himself. The following is a table of the signs used in the variant notes:

§ . . . §	Editor's note
< >	Words omitted
/	Line break
/ / , / / / , . . .	Line break plus one or more lines without internal variants

4 *Annotations.* In general principle, we have annotated proper names, phrases that function as proper names, and words or groups of words the full meaning of which requires factual, historical, or literary background. Thus we have attempted to hold interpretation to a minimum, although we realize that the act of selection itself is to some extent interpretive.

Notes, particularly on historical figures and events, tend to fullness and even to the tangential and unessential. As a result, some of the information provided may seem unnecessary to the scholar. On the other hand, it is not possible to assume that all who use this edition are fully equipped to assimilate unaided all of Browning's copious literary, historical, and mythological allusions. Thus we have directed our efforts toward a diverse audience.

TABLES

1. *Manuscripts.* We have located manuscripts for the following of Browning's works; the list is chronological.

Paracelsus
 Forster and Dyce Collection,
 Victoria and Albert Museum, London
Colombe's Birthday
 New York Public Library
Christmas-Eve and Easter-Day
 Forster and Dyce Collection,
 Victoria and Albert Museum, London
"Love Among the Ruins"
 Lowell Collection,
 Houghton Library, Harvard University
"The Twins"
 Pierpont Morgan Library, New York
"One Word More"
 Pierpont Morgan Library, New York
"James Lee's Wife," ll. 244-69
 Armstrong Browning Library, Baylor University
"May and Death"
 Armstrong Browning Library, Baylor University
"A Face"
 Armstrong Browning Library, Baylor University
Dramatis Personae
 Pierpont Morgan Library, New York
The Ring and the Book
 British Library, London
Balaustion's Adventure
 Balliol College Library, Oxford
Prince Hohenstiel-Schwangau
 Balliol College Library, Oxford
Fifine at the Fair
 Balliol College Library, Oxford
Red Cotton Night-Cap Country
 Balliol College Library, Oxford
Aristophanes' Apology
 Balliol College Library, Oxford
The Inn Album
 Balliol College Library, Oxford
Of Pacchiarotto, and How He Worked in Distemper
 Balliol College Library, Oxford
"Hervé Riel"
 Pierpont Morgan Library, New York

The Agamemnon of Aeschylus
    Balliol College Library, Oxford
La Saisiaz and The Two Poets of Croisic
    Balliol College Library, Oxford
Dramatic Idylls
    Balliol College Library, Oxford
Dramatic Idylls, Second Series
    Balliol College Library, Oxford
Jocoseria
    Balliol College Library, Oxford
Ferishtah's Fancies
    Balliol College Library, Oxford
Parleyings With Certain People of Importance in Their Day
    Balliol College Library, Oxford
Asolando
    Pierpont Morgan Library, New York

We have been unable to locate manuscripts for the following works, and request that persons with information about any of them communicate with us.

Pauline	*The Return of the Druses*
Strafford	*A Blot in the 'Scutcheon*
Sordello	*Dramatic Romances and Lyrics*
Pippa Passes	*Luria*
King Victor and King Charles	*A Soul's Tragedy*
"Essay on Chatterton"	"Essay on Shelley"
Dramatic Lyrics	*Men and Women*

2. *Editions referred to in Volume X.* The following editions have been used in preparing the text and variants presented in this volume. The dates given below are used as symbols in the variant listings at the foot of each page.

1871a   *Balaustion's Adventure; Including a Transcript from Euripides.*
         London: Smith, Elder and Company.

1871b   *Prince Hohenstiel-Schwangau, Saviour of Society.*
         London: Smith, Elder and Company.

1872   *Balaustion's Adventure; Including a Transcript from Euripides.*
         Second Edition. London: Smith, Elder and Company.
         (corrected impression of 1871a)

1881   *Balaustion's Adventure; Including a Transcript from Euripides.*
        Third Edition. London: Smith, Elder and Company.

1889a   *The Poetical Works.*
        Volumes 9-16. London: Smith, Elder and Company.

3. *Short titles and abbreviations.* The following short forms of reference have been used in the Editorial Notes:

Alcestis	*Alcestis,* in *Euripides,* Vol. 4 (Loeb Classical Library), ed. and tr. A. S. Way. London, 1912.
Alciphron	*The Letters of Alciphron, Aelian, and Philostratus* (Loeb Classical Library), ed. and tr. A. R. Benner and F. H. Fobes. London, 1949.
B	Browning
Correspondence	*The Brownings' Correspondence,* ed. P. Kelley and R. Hudson. Winfield, KS, 1984-.
DeVane, *Hbk.*	W. C. DeVane. *A Browning Handbook,* 2nd ed. New York, 1955.
DeVane and Knickerbocker	*New Letters of Robert Browning,* ed W. C. DeVane and K. L. Knickerbocker. New Haven, CT, 1950.
EBB	Elizabeth Barrett Browning
Griffin and Minchin	W. H. Griffin and H. C. Minchin. *The Life of Robert Browning.* Hamden, CT, 1966.
Herodotus	*The Histories,* tr. A. de Selincourt. Rev. ed. by A. R. Burn, Harmondsworth, 1972.
Hood	*Letters of Robert Browning Collected by Thomas J. Wise,* ed. T. L. Hood. New Haven, CT, 1933.
Hudson	*Browning to His American Friends,* ed. G. R. Hudson. New York, 1965.
Iliad	Homer. *The Iliad,* tr. R. Fagles. New York, 1990.
Irvine and Honan	W. Irvine and P. Honan. *The Book, the Ring, and the Poet.* New York, 1974.
Landis and Freeman	*Letters of the Brownings to George Barrett,* ed. P. Landis and R. E. Freeman. Urbana, IL, 1958.
Letters of EBB	*The Letters of Elizabeth Barrett Browning,* ed. F. G. Kenyon. New York, 1897.
Maynard	J. Maynard, *Browning's Youth.* Cambridge, MA, 1977.
McAleer	*Dearest Isa: Robert Browning's Letters to Isabella Blagden,* ed. E. C. McAleer. Austin, TX, 1951.

Odyssey	Homer. *The Odyssey*, tr. R. Fagles. New York, 1996.
OED	*The Oxford English Dictionary*, 2nd ed. Oxford, 1989.
Orr	Mrs. Sutherland Orr. *A Handbook to the Works of Robert Browning*, 6th ed. London, 1892.
Pausanias	*Guide to Greece*, Vol. 1, tr. P. Levi. Harmondsworth, 1971.
P-C	*The Works of Robert Browning*, ed. C. Porter and H. A. Clarke. New York, 1910.
Plutarch	*The Rise & Fall of Athens: Nine Greek Lives*, tr. I. Scott-Kilvert. Harmondsworth, 1960.
Thucydides	*History of the Peloponnesian War*, tr. Rex Warner. Rev. ed. by M. I. Finley, Harmondsworth, 1972.

Citations and quotations from the Bible refer to the King James Version.

Citations and quotations from Shakespeare refer to T*he Riverside Shakespeare*, 2nd ed. G.B. Evans, et al. Boston, 1997.

ACKNOWLEDGMENTS

For providing services and money which have made it possible for us to prepare this volume, the following institutions have our gratitude: the Ohio University Press; Baylor University and the Armstrong Browning Library of Baylor University; Kent State University Library and the Institute for Bibliography and Editing.

For making available to us materials under their care we thank the Armstrong Browning Library; the Balliol College Library, Oxford; the British Library; the John Hay Library, Brown University; Philip Kelley; the Ohio University Library.

For scholarly and material assistance in preparing this volume, we particularly thank the following: Nancy Birk of the Kent State University Library; James F. Bouchard and Scott Shafer of the Lima, Ohio, Public Library; Philip Kelley; S. W. Reid; John Willoughby at Wedgestone Press.

The frontispiece is reproduced by permission of the Armstrong Browning Library.

BALAUSTION'S ADVENTURE; INCLUDING A TRANSCRIPT
FROM EURIPIDES

PRINCE HOHENSTIEL-SCHWANGAU, SAVIOUR OF SOCIETY

Edited by Allan C. Dooley and Susan E. Dooley

BALAUSTION'S ADVENTURE; Including a Transcript from
Euripides

Edited by Allan C. Dooley and Susan E. Dooley

BALAUSTION'S ADVENTURE; INCLUDING A TRANSCRIPT FROM EURIPIDES

MS:Adventure: including   *1889a*:ADVENTURE; INCLUDING

TO THE COUNTESS COWPER.

If I mention the simple truth: that this poem absolutely owes its existence to you,—who not only suggested, but imposed on me as a task, what has proved the most delightful of May-month amusements—I shall seem honest, indeed, but
5 *hardly prudent; for, how good and beautiful ought such a poem to be!*

Euripides might fear little; but I, also, have an interest in the performance; and what wonder if I beg you to suffer that it make, in another and far easier sense, its nearest possible approach to those Greek qualities of goodness and beauty, by laying itself gratefully at your feet?

                                                                                                R. B.

LONDON: July 23, 1871.

---

²| MS:this Poem   *1871a:*poem   ⁴| MS:amusements,—I   *1871a:*amusements—I
⁶⁻⁷| MS:performance:and   *1889a:*performance; and   ⁸| MS:neares   *1871a:*nearest

OUR EURIPIDES, THE HUMAN,
   WITH HIS DROPPINGS OF WARM TEARS,
AND HIS TOUCHES OF THINGS COMMON
   TILL THEY ROSE TO TOUCH THE SPHERES.

BALAUSTION'S ADVENTURE

1871

About that strangest, saddest, sweetest song
I, when a girl, heard in Kameiros once,
And, after, saved my life by? Oh, so glad
To tell you the adventure!
                                    Petalé,
5   Phullis, Charopé, Chrusion! You must know,
This "after" fell in that unhappy time
When poor reluctant Nikias, pushed by fate,
Went falteringly against Syracuse;
And there shamed Athens, lost her ships and men,
10 And gained a grave, or death without a grave.
I was at Rhodes—the isle, not Rhodes the town,
Mine was Kameiros—when the news arrived:
Our people rose in tumult, cried "No more
Duty to Athens, let us join the League
15 And side with Sparta, share the spoil,—at worst,
Abjure a headship that will ruin Greece!"
And so, they sent to Knidos for a fleet
To come and help revolters. Ere help came,—
Girl as I was, and never out of Rhodes
20 The whole of my first fourteen years of life,
But nourished with Ilissian mother's-milk,—
I passionately cried to who would hear
And those who loved me at Kameiros—"No!
Never throw Athens off for Sparta's sake—
25 Never disloyal to the life and light

---

§MS in Balliol College Library, Oxford. Ed. *1871a, 1872, 1881, 1889a*§   ²| MS:in our
city §last two words crossed out and replaced above by§ Kameiros   ⁵| MS:Phullis,
Charopé, Chrusion!—You *1871a*:Phullis, Charopé, Chrusion! You   ⁸| MS:faulteringly
<> Syracuse *1871a*:against Syracuse; *1889a*:falteringly   ¹⁷| MS:so they *1871a*:so,
they   ²⁰| MS:my long §crossed out and replaced above by§ first   ²³| MS:And all
who §last two words crossed out and replaced above by two words§ those that §crossed out,
with *who* marked for retention§   ²⁵| MS:the light and light *1871a*:the life and light

Of the whole world worth calling world at all!
Rather go die at Athens, lie outstretched
For feet to trample on, before the gate
Of Diomedes or the Hippadai,
30 Before the temples and among the tombs,
Than tolerate the grim felicity
Of harsh Lakonia! Ours the fasts and feasts,
Choës and Chutroi; ours the sacred grove,
Agora, Dikasteria, Poikilé,
35 Pnux, Keramikos; Salamis in sight,
Psuttalia, Marathon itself, not far!
Ours the great Dionusiac theatre,
And tragic triad of immortal fames,
Aischulos, Sophokles, Euripides!
40 To Athens, all of us that have a soul,
Follow me!" And I wrought so with my prayer,
That certain of my kinsfolk crossed the strait
And found a ship at Kaunos; well-disposed
Because the Captain—where did he draw breath
45 First but within Psuttalia? Thither fled
A few like-minded as ourselves. We turned
The glad prow westward, soon were out at sea,
Pushing, brave ship with the vermilion cheek,
Proud for our heart's true harbour. But a wind

26| MS:Of all §inserted above and cancelled§ the whole §inserted above§   27| MS:Better
§crossed out and replaced in margin by§ Rather < > Athens—lie   *1871a*:at Athens, lie
28| MS:on before   *1871a*:on, before   30| MS:Among the tombs, before §altered to§
Before the temples there, §last word crossed out; preceding three words marked for
transposition to beginning of line; *and* added in margin§   33| MS:and Chutroi, ours
1871a:and Chutroi; ours   34| MS:The §crossed out§ Agora the§crossed out§ Dikasteria,
too, §crossed out§ Poikile,   *1871a*:Poikilé,   35| MS:Pnux, Keramikos,—Salamis in
sight,—   *1871a*:Pnux, Keramikos; Salamis in sight,   36| The neighbourhood of §last
three words crossed out and replaced in margin by one word§ Psuttalia, Marathon be ours
§last two words crossed out and replaced above by one word§ itself, not   37| MS:theatre
1871a:theatre,   38| MS:§line added§   39| MS:Aischulos, Sophokles, Euripides—
1871a:Aischulos, Sophokles, Euripides!   40| MS:us who §crossed out and replaced
above by§ that   41| MS:prayer   *1871a*:prayer,   43| MS:at Kaunos—well disposed
1871a:at Kaunos; well-disposed   46| MS:ourselves: we   *1871a*:ourselves. We
48| MS:cheeks, §altered to§ cheek,   49| MS:a storm §crossed out and replaced by§ wind

⁵⁰ Lay ambushed by Point Malea of bad fame,
And leapt out, bent us from our course. Next day
Broke stormless, so broke next blue day and next.
"But whither bound in this white waste?" we plagued
The pilot's old experience: "Cos or Crete?"
⁵⁵ Because he promised us the land ahead.
While we strained eyes to share in what he saw,
The Captain's shout startled us; round we rushed:
What hung behind us but a pirate-ship
Panting for the good prize! "Row! harder row!
⁶⁰ Row for dear life!" the Captain cried: "'tis Crete,
Friendly Crete looming large there! Beat this craft
That's but a keles, one-benched pirate-bark,
Lokrian, or that bad breed off Thessaly!
Only, so cruel are such water-thieves,
⁶⁵ No man of you, no woman, child, or slave,
But falls their prey, once let them board our boat!"
So, furiously our oarsmen rowed and rowed;
And when the oars flagged somewhat, dash and dip,
As we approached the coast and safety, so
⁷⁰ That we could hear behind us plain the threats
And curses of the pirate panting up
In one more throe and passion of pursuit,—
Seeing our oars flag in the rise and fall,
I sprang upon the altar by the mast
⁷⁵ And sang aloft,—some genius prompting me,—
That song of ours which saved at Salamis:
"O sons of Greeks, go, set your country free,
Free your wives, free your children, free the fanes
O' the Gods, your fathers founded,—sepulchres
⁸⁰ They sleep in! Or save all, or all be lost!"

---

⁵⁰| MS:by Point §inserted above§   ⁵²| stormless, and so next <> next:
1871a:day and next. *1889a*:stormless, so broke next blue   ⁵³| MS:waste?" I plagued
1871a:waste?" we plagued   ⁵⁹| MS:prize! "Row—harder row— *1871a*:prize!
"Row! harder row!   ⁶⁰| MS:cried—"'tis *1871a*:cried: "'tis
⁶¹| MS:there: beat *1871a*:there! Beat   ⁶²| MS:§line added§ breed by §crossed out
and replaced above by§ off Thessaly, *1871a*:off Thessaly!   ⁷⁰| MS:That you §crossed
out and replaced above by§ we   ⁷⁶| MS:at Salamis— *1871a*:at Salamis:

Then, in a frenzy, so the noble oars
Churned the black water white, that well away
We drew, soon saw land rise, saw hills grow up,
Saw spread itself a sea-wide town with towers,
85 Not fifty stadia distant; and, betwixt
A large bay and a small, the islet-bar,
Even Ortugia's self—oh, luckless we!
For here was Sicily and Syracuse:
We ran upon the lion from the wolf.
90 Ere we drew breath, took counsel, out there came
A galley, hailed us. "Who asks entry here
In war-time? Are you Sparta's friend or foe?"
"Kaunians"—our Captain judged his best reply,
"The mainland-seaport that belongs to Rhodes;
95 Rhodes that casts in her lot now with the League,
Forsaking Athens,—you have heard belike!"
"Ay, but we heard all Athens in one ode
Just now! we heard her in that Aischulos!
You bring a boatful of Athenians here,
100 Kaunians although you be: and prudence bids,
For Kaunos' sake, why, carry them unhurt
To Kaunos, if you will: for Athens' sake,
Back must you, though ten pirates blocked the bay!
We want no colony from Athens here,
105 With memories of Salamis, forsooth,
To spirit up our captives, that pale crowd
I' the quarry, whom the daily pint of corn
Keeps in good order and submissiveness."

---

[81] MS:Then in a frenzy so *1871a:*Then, in a frenzy, so   [82] MS:the sea §crossed out
and replaced above by§ black   [83] MS:drew, and §crossed out and replaced above by§
soon <> rise, with §crossed out and replaced above by§ saw hills behind, §crossed out and
replaced above by two words and punctuation§ grow up,   [85] MS:distant, and *1871a:*distant;
and   [88] MS:and Syracuse,— *1871a:*and Syracuse: [93] MS:"Kaunians"—the
§crossed out and replaced above by§ our   [98] MS:now—we *1871a:*now! we
[101] MS:sake, go §crossed out and replaced above by§ why,   [102] MS:will,—for
*1871a:*will: for   [103] MS:the way! §altered to§ bay!   [104] MS:We need §crossed out
and replaced above by§ want <> Athens now §crossed out and replaced by§ here
*1871a:*here,   [105] MS:§line added§   [106] MS:pale §crossed out and then marked
for retention§   [107] MS:daily §inserted above§ <> corn a day §last two words crossed out§

Then the grey Captain prayed them by the Gods,
110 And by their own knees, and their fathers' beards,
They should not wickedly thrust suppliants back,
But save the innocent on traffic bound—
Or, may be, some Athenian family
Perishing of desire to die at home,—
115 From that vile foe still lying on its oars,
Waiting the issue in the distance. Vain!
Words to the wind! And we were just about
To turn and face the foe, as some tired bird
Barbarians pelt at, drive with shouts away
120 From shelter in what rocks, however rude,
She makes for, to escape the kindled eye,
Split beak, crook'd claw o' the creature, cormorant
Or ossifrage, that, hardly baffled, hangs
Afloat i' the foam, to take her if she turn.
125 So were we at destruction's very edge,
When those o' the galley, as they had discussed
A point, a question raised by somebody,
A matter mooted in a moment,—"Wait!"
Cried they (and wait we did, you may be sure).
130 "That song was veritable Aischulos,
Familiar to the mouth of man and boy,
Old glory: how about Euripides?
The newer and not yet so famous bard,
He that was born upon the battle-day
135 While that song and the salpinx sounded him
Into the world, first sound, at Salamis—
Might you know any of his verses too?"

Now, some one of the Gods inspired this speech:

---

¹¹²| MS:innocent mere §crossed out and replaced above by§ on traffic §followed by illegible erasure§   ¹¹³⁻¹⁴| MS:§lines added§   ¹²⁰| MS:in some §crossed out and replaced above by§ what rock < > rude   *1871a*:rocks < > rude,   *1872*:rock   *1881*:rocks
¹²⁴| MS:turn,—   *1871a*:turn.   ¹²⁵| MS:edge,—   *1871a*:edge,   ¹²⁶| MS:raised by §inserted above§ somebody, found come, §last two words crossed out§   ¹²⁹| MS:they— and < > sure: *1871a*:they (and < > sure)   *1889a*:sure).   ¹³⁰| MS:veritable Aischulos— *1871a*:veritable Aischulos,   ¹³¹| MS:§line added§   ¹³²| MS:about Euripides?— *1871a*:about Euripides?   ¹³³| §line added§   ¹³⁸| MS:the Gods gave §crossed out and replaced above by§ inspired this great §crossed out§ thought: *1871a*:this speech:

Since ourselves knew what happened but last year—
140 How, when Gulippos gained his victory
Over poor Nikias, poor Demosthenes,
And Syracuse condemned the conquered force
To dig and starve i' the quarry, branded them—
Freeborn Athenians, brute-like in the front
145 With horse-head brands,—ah, "Region of the Steed"!—
Of all these men immersed in misery,
It was found none had been advantaged so
By aught in the past life he used to prize
And pride himself concerning,—no rich man
150 By riches, no wise man by wisdom, no
Wiser man still (as who loved more the Muse)
By storing, at brain's edge and tip of tongue,
Old glory, great plays that had long ago
Made themselves wings to fly about the world,—
155 Not one such man was helped so at his need
As certain few that (wisest they of all)
Had, at first summons, oped heart, flung door wide
At the new knocking of Euripides,
Nor drawn the bolt with who cried "Decadence!
160 And, after Sophokles, be nature dumb!"
Such,—and I see in it God Bacchos' boon
To souls that recognized his latest child,
He who himself, born latest of the Gods,
Was stoutly held impostor by mankind,—
165 Such were in safety: any who could speak

139| MS:Since we all §inserted above§ §last two words crossed out and replaced above by one word§ ourselves knew the story of §last three words crossed out and replaced above by three words§ what happened but   141| MS:poor Nikias, and §crossed out and replaced above by§ poor   146| MS:§line added between present line 147 and 148, marked for transposition with 147§   151| MS:still, as loving §crossed out and replaced above by two words§ who loved <> Muse,   *1871a*:still (as <> Muse)   152| MS:By having §crossed out and replaced above by§ storing at heart's §crossed out and replaced above by§ brain's <> tongue   *1871a*:storing, at <> tongue,   153| MS:The §crossed out§ old §altered to§ Old   156| MS:that—wisest <> all—   *1871a*:that (wisest <> all)   157| MS:opened §altered to§ oped <> door §inserted above§   161| MS:and I think §crossed out and replaced above by two words§ see in it was §crossed out§ God   162| MS:To those who §last two words crossed out and replaced above by two words§ souls that

14

A chorus to the end, or prologize,
Roll out a rhesis, wield some golden length
Stiffened by wisdom out into a line,
Or thrust and parry in bright monostich,
¹⁷⁰ Teaching Euripides to Syracuse—
Any such happy man had prompt reward:
If he lay bleeding on the battle-field
They staunched his wounds and gave him drink and food;
If he were slave i' the house, for reverence
¹⁷⁵ They rose up, bowed to who proved master now,
And bade him go free, thank Euripides!
Ay, and such did so: many such, he said,
Returning home to Athens, sought him out,
The old bard in the solitary house,
¹⁸⁰ And thanked him ere they went to sacrifice.
I say, we knew that story of last year!—

Therefore, at mention of Euripides,
The Captain crowed out "Euoi, praise the God!
Oöp, boys, bring our owl-shield to the fore!
¹⁸⁵ Out with our Sacred Anchor! Here she stands,
Balaustion! Strangers, greet the lyric girl!
Euripides? Babai! what a word there 'scaped
Your teeth's enclosure, quoth my grandsire's song!
Why, fast as snow in Thrace, the voyage through,
¹⁹⁰ Has she been falling thick in flakes of him!
Frequent as figs at Kaunos, Kaunians said.
Balaustion, stand forth and confirm my speech!

---

¹⁶⁷⁻⁶⁸| MS:§lines added§ ¹⁶⁷| MS:wield some §inserted above two words illegibly crossed out§ ¹⁷⁰| MS:And §crossed out§ teach §altered to§ Teaching ¹⁷¹| MS:§line added§ ¹⁷³| MS:food,— *1871a*:food; ¹⁷⁷| MS:and they §crossed out and replaced above by§ such ¹⁸¹| MS:say, all §crossed out and replaced above by§ we ¹⁸²| MS:Therefore at <> Euripides *1871a*:Therefore, at <> Euripides, ¹⁸³| MS:The Captain laughed loud §last two words crossed out and replaced above by two words§ crowed out: "Euoi *1871a*:out "Euoi ¹⁸⁴| MS:boys, §inserted above§ <> our beauty §crossed out and replaced above by§ owl-shield to the front, §crossed out and replaced above by§ fore! ¹⁸⁵| MS:our Sacred Anchor! See her §last two words crossed out and replaced above by two words§ Here she stand §altered to§ stands, ¹⁸⁷| MS:Euripides? Why, §crossed out and replaced above by§ Babai!

Now it was some whole passion of a play;
Now, peradventure, but a honey-drop
195 That slipt its comb i' the chorus. If there rose
A star, before I could determine steer
Southward or northward—if a cloud surprised
Heaven, ere I fairly hollaed 'Furl the sail!—'
She had at fingers' end both cloud and star;
200 Some thought that perched there, tame and tuneable,
Fitted with wings; and still, as off it flew,
'So sang Euripides,' she said, 'so sang
The meteoric poet of air and sea,
Planets and the pale populace of heaven,
205 The mind of man, and all that's made to soar!'
And so, although she has some other name,
We only call her Wild-pomegranate-flower,
Balaustion; since, where'er the red bloom burns
I' the dull dark verdure of the bounteous tree,
210 Dethroning, in the Rosy Isle, the rose,
You shall find food, drink, odour, all at once;
Cool leaves to bind about an aching brow,
And, never much away, the nightingale.
Sing them a strophe, with the turn-again,
215 Down to the verse that ends all, proverb-like,
And save us, thou Balaustion, bless the name!"

But I cried "Brother Greek! better than so,—
Save us, and I have courage to recite

---

^{193|} MS:play, *1871a*:play; ^{195|} MS:chorus: if *1871a*:chorus. If ^{196|} MS:star—
before *1871a*:star, before ^{198|} MS:hollaed "Furl the Sail!—" *1871a*:hollaed 'Furl the
sail!—' ^{199|} MS:star— *1871a*:star; ^{200|} MS:§line added§ ^{201|} MS:wings,
and <> off they §crossed out and replaced below by§ it *1871a*:wings; and
^{202|} MS:"So sang of these §last two words crossed out§ Euripides," she said, "So *1871a*:'So
<> Euripides,' she said, 'so ^{205|} MS:And §crossed out§ the §altered to§ The <> soar!"
1871a:soar!' ^{208|} MS:Balaustion,—since where'er *1871a*:Balaustion; since, where'er
^{210|} MS:in the Rosy Isle, §last four words and punctuation inserted above§
^{211|} MS:once, *1871a*:once; ^{213|} MS:never far §crossed out and replaced above by§
much ^{214|} MS:strophe and §crossed out and replaced above by§ with *1871a*:strophe,
with ^{216|} MS:us, all, §crossed out and replaced above by§ thou
^{217|} MS:cried, "Brother Greek, better *1871a*:cried "Brother Greek! better

The main of a whole play from first to last;
220   That strangest, saddest, sweetest song of his,
ALKESTIS; which was taught, long years ago
At Athens, in Glaukinos' archonship,
But only this year reached our Isle o' the Rose.
I saw it, at Kameiros, played the same,
225   They say, as for the right Lenean feast
In Athens; and beside the perfect piece—
Its beauty and the way it makes you weep,—
There is much honour done your own loved God
Herakles, whom you house i' the city here
230   Nobly, the Temple wide Greece talks about!
I come a suppliant to your Herakles!
Take me and put me on his temple-steps
To tell you his achievement as I may,
And, that told, he shall bid you set us free!"

235   Then, because Greeks are Greeks, and hearts are hearts,
And poetry is power,—they all outbroke
In a great joyous laughter with much love:
"Thank Herakles for the good holiday!
Make for the harbour! Row, and let voice ring,
240   'In we row, bringing more Euripides!'"
All the crowd, as they lined the harbour now,
"More of Euripides!"—took up the cry.
We landed; the whole city, soon astir,
Came rushing out of gates in common joy

---

[219] MS:last— *1871a*:last;   [220] MS:strangest saddest sweetest   *1871a*:strangest, saddest, sweetest   [221] MS:Alkestis §double-underlined§; which he §crossed out and replaced above by§ he   [223] MS:reached the §crossed out and replaced above by§ our <> Rose;   *1871a*:the Rose.   [224] MS:it at   *1871a*:at Kameiros; played   *1889a*:it, at Kameiros, played   [225] MS:say as at §crossed out and replaced above by§ for   *1871a*:say, as   [228] MS:honor   *1889a*:honour   [230] MS:Nobly, in §erased§ [232] MS:temple-steps,   *1889a*:temple-steps   [233] MS:achievement §letters *em* inserted above§   [235] MS:are Greeks and   *1871a*:are Greeks, and   [237] MS:love— *1871a*:love: [238] MS:Thank   *1871a*: "Thank   [239] MS:ring §punctuation erased§ *1871a*:ring,   [240] MS:more Euripides!'   *1872*:more Euripides!'"   [242] MS:'More of Euripides!'—took   *1872:* "More of Euripides!"—took   [243] MS:landed; all §crossed out§ the whole §inserted above§ city was §crossed out and replaced above by§ soon   *1871a*:city, soon

²⁴⁵ To the suburb temple; there they stationed me
O' the topmost step: and plain I told the play,
Just as I saw it; what the actors said,
And what I saw, or thought I saw the while,
At our Kameiros theatre, clean-scooped
²⁵⁰ Out of a hill-side, with the sky above
And sea before our seats in marble row:
Told it, and, two days more, repeated it,
Until they sent us on our way again
With good words and great wishes.

Oh, for me—

²⁵⁵ A wealthy Syracusan brought a whole
Talent and bade me take it for myself:
I left it on the tripod in the fane,
—For had not Herakles a second time
Wrestled with Death and saved devoted ones?—
²⁶⁰ Thank-offering to the hero. And a band
Of captives, whom their lords grew kinder to
Because they called the poet countryman,
Sent me a crown of wild-pomegranate-flower:
So, I shall live and die Balaustion now.
²⁶⁵ But one—one man—one youth,—three days, each day,—
(If, ere I lifted up my voice to speak,
I gave a downward glance by accident)
Was found at foot o' the temple. When we sailed,
There, in the ship too, was he found as well,
²⁷⁰ Having a hunger to see Athens too.
We reached Peiraieus; when I landed—lo,
He was beside me. Anthesterion-month

---

²⁴⁶| MS:and so §crossed out and replaced above by§ plain <> play,— *1871a*:play,
²⁴⁷| MS:it, what *1871a*:it; what   ²⁴⁸| MS:saw—or *1871a*:saw, or
²⁴⁹| MS:theatre clean-scooped *1871a*:theatre, clean-scooped   ²⁵⁰| MS:hill-side with
1871a:hill-side, with   ²⁵¹| MS:row,— *1871a*:row: ²⁵³| MS:And so §last two words
crossed out and replaced above by one word§ Until   ²⁵⁸⁻⁵⁹| MS:§lines added§
²⁶⁰| MS:the Hero: and *1871a*:hero. And   ²⁶³| MS:Gave §crossed out and replaced
above by§ Sent <> wild-pomegranate-flower, *1871a*:wild-pomegranate-flower:
²⁶⁴| MS:So I *1871a*:So, I   ²⁶⁶⁻⁶⁷| MS:§lines added§
²⁶⁶| MS:—If, ere *1871a*:(If, ere   ²⁶⁷| MS:accident— *1871a*:accident)

18

Is just commencing: when its moon rounds full,
We are to marry. O Euripides!

275 I saw the master: when we found ourselves
(Because the young man needs must follow me)
Firm on Peiraieus, I demanded first
Whither to go and find him. Would you think?
The story how he saved us made some smile:
280 They wondered strangers were exorbitant
In estimation of Euripides.
He was not Aischulos nor Sophokles:
—"Then, of our younger bards who boast the bay,
Had I sought Agathon, or Iophon,
285 Or, what now had it been Kephisophon?
A man that never kept good company,
The most unsociable of poet-kind,
All beard that was not freckle in his face!"

I soon was at the tragic house, and saw
290 The master, held the sacred hand of him
And laid it to my lips. Men love him not:
How should they? Nor do they much love his friend
Sokrates: but those two have fellowship:
Sokrates often comes to hear him read,
295 And never misses if he teach a piece.
Both, being old, will soon have company,
Sit with their peers above the talk. Meantime,
He lives as should a statue in its niche;

273| MS:moon is §crossed out and replaced above by§ rounds full   *1871a*:full,
274| MS:We shall §crossed out and replaced above by§ are   274-75| *1871a*:§¶ lost in paging§   *1889a*:§¶ restored§   275| MS:the poet §crossed out and replaced above by§ master   281| MS:of Euripides: *1871a*:of Euripides.   283| MS:—"Then of   *1871a*:—"Then, of   285| MS:Or what   *1871a*:Or, what   286| MS:§line added§ The most §over illegible erasure§   288| MS:§line added after 287§   290| MS:the noble   *1871a*:the sacred   294| MS:two keep company— §last two words crossed out and replaced above by two words and punctuation§ have fellowship: 295| MS:And always goes to hear him §last five words crossed out and replaced above by four words§ never misses if he   296| MS:He §crossed out and replaced in margin by§ Both <> soon find §crossed out and replaced above by§ have   297| MS:with his §crossed out and replaced above by§ their <> the world §crossed out and replaced above by§ talk. Meantime   *1871a*:talk. Meantime,

Cold walls enclose him, mostly darkness there,
300 Alone, unless some foreigner uncouth
Breaks in, sits, stares an hour, and so departs,
Brain-stuffed with something to sustain his life,
Dry to the marrow mid much merchandise.
How should such know and love the man?
Why, mark!
305 Even when I told the play and got the praise,
There spoke up a brisk little somebody,
Critic and whippersnapper, in a rage
To set things right: "The girl departs from truth!
Pretends she saw what was not to be seen,
310 Making the mask of the actor move, forsooth!
'Then a fear flitted o'er the wife's white face,'—
'Then frowned the father,'—'then the husband shook,'—
'Then from the festal forehead slipt each spray,
'And the heroic mouth's gay grace was gone;'—
315 As she had seen each naked fleshly face,
And not the merely-painted mask it wore!"
Well, is the explanation difficult?
What's poetry except a power that makes?
And, speaking to one sense, inspires the rest,
320 Pressing them all into its service; so
That who sees painting, seems to hear as well

299| MS:enclosing §altered to§ enclose him, §inserted above§   301| MS:Break in, to
§crossed out§ sit §altered to§ sits, and §crossed out§ stares an hour, §last two words inserted
above§   *1871a*:Breaks   302| MS:something shall §crossed out and replaced above by§ to
303| MS:Dwindling and dry §last three words crossed out and replaced above by four words§
Dry to the marrow < > merchandize.   *1889a*:merchandise.   305| MS:when I spoke
§crossed out and replaced above by§ told   307| MS:§line added§   308| MS:truth;
1871a:truth!   310| MS:forsooth,—   *1871a*:forsooth!   311| MS:a change §crossed
out and replaced above by§ fear   312| MS:husband wept'— §crossed out and replaced
above by§ shook'—   *1871a*:shook,'—   313| MS:festal §over illegible erasure§ forehead
fell the §last two words crossed out and replaced above by two words§ slipt each sprays
§altered to§ spray,   314| MS:Of myrtle, §crossed out§ and §altered to§ And the heroic
§inserted above§ < > gone'—   *1871a*:gone;'—   315| MS:face   *1871a*:face,
317| MS:§line of ten words, ending with *explain you poetry!* entirely crossed out; present line
added in margin§   318| MS:except the §crossed out and replaced above by§ a < >
makes?—   *1871a*:makes?   319| MS:That, speaking   *1871a*:And, speaking

The speech that's proper for the painted mouth;
And who hears music, feels his solitude
Peopled at once—for how count heart-beats plain
325 Unless a company, with hearts which beat,
Come close to the musician, seen or no?
And who receives true verse at eye or ear,
Takes in (with verse) time, place, and person too,
So, links each sense on to its sister-sense,
330 Grace-like: and what if but one sense of three
Front you at once? The sidelong pair conceive
Thro' faintest touch of finest finger-tips,—
Hear, see and feel, in faith's simplicity,
Alike, what one was sole recipient of:
335 Who hears the poem, therefore, sees the play.

Enough and too much! Hear the play itself!
Under the grape-vines, by the streamlet-side,
Close to Baccheion; till the cool increase,
And other stars steal on the evening-star,
340 And so, we homeward flock i' the dusk, we five!
You will expect, no one of all the words

322| MS:What words are §last three words crossed out and replaced above by three words§ The speech so proper <> mouth, *1871a*:speech that's proper <> mouth; 323| MS:music feels a §altered to§ his *1871a*:music, feels 324| MS:for §inserted above§ how hear §crossed out and replaced above by§ count the §crossed out§ heart-beats 325| MS:Unless the §crossed out and replaced above by§ a company with hearts that beat *1871a*:company, with hearts which beat, 327| MS:ear *1871a*:ear, 328| MS:in, with it §crossed out and replaced above by§ verse, time *1871a*:in (with verse) time 329| MS:So does §crossed out and replaced above by§ links <> sense link §crossed out§ <> its §inserted above§ *1871a*:So, links 330| MS:if only one of *1871a*:if but one sense of 332| MS:touching §altered to§ touch of those §crossed out and replaced above by§ fine 336| MS:much! Let me tell §last three words crossed out and replaced above by one word§ Hear <> itself *1871a*:itself! 337| MS:the trees here §last two crossed out and replaced above by one word§ grape-vines, by the river-§crossed out§ side, *1871a*:the streamlet-side, 338| MS:Close by §crossed out and replaced above by§ to Baccheion where the feasters come. §last four words crossed out and replaced above by four words§ till the cool begins §last two words crossed out and replaced above by one word§ cool increase, *1871a*:to Baccheion; till 339-40| MS:§lines added§ 339| MS:And we will homeward with an §last five words crossed out and replaced above by seven words§ other §two words illegibly crossed out§ stars steal on the 340| MS:so we <> go §crossed out and replaced above by§ flock <> cool §crossed out and replaced above by§ dusk, *1871a*:so, we 341| MS:You may believe §last two words crossed out and replaced below by two words and punctuation§ will expect,

O' the play but is grown part now of my soul,
Since the adventure. 'Tis the poet speaks:
But if I, too, should try and speak at times,
345 Leading your love to where my love, perchance,
Climbed earlier, found a nest before you knew—
Why, bear with the poor climber, for love's sake!
Look at Baccheion's beauty opposite,
The temple with the pillars at the porch!
350 See you not something beside masonry?
What if my words wind in and out the stone
As yonder ivy, the God's parasite?
Though they leap all the way the pillar leads,
Festoon about the marble, foot to frieze,
355 And serpentiningly enrich the roof,
Toy with some few bees and a bird or two,—
What then? The column holds the cornice up.

———

There slept a silent palace in the sun,
With plains adjacent and Thessalian peace—
360 Pherai, where King Admetos ruled the land.

Out from the portico there gleamed a God,
Apollon: for the bow was in his hand,
The quiver at his shoulder, all his shape
One dreadful beauty. And he hailed the house

342| MS:the poet §crossed out and replaced above by§ play <> grown §inserted above§   <> soul
*1871a:*soul,   343| MS:adventure. Tis <> speaks—   *1871a:*adventure. 'Tis <> speaks:
347| MS:poor speaker §crossed out and replaced above by§ climber   350| MS:§line added§ Is
not there §last three words crossed out and replaced above by three words§ See not you §*See* in
margin§ something beside marble there? §last two words crossed out§ masonry?   *1871a:*See you
not something   352| MS:As ivy, yonder §last two words marked for transposition§
353| MS:Tho'   *1871a:*Though   354| MS:§line added§   356| MS:Harbour §crossed out
and replaced above by two words§ Toy with some few §inserted above§ <> a stray §crossed
out§ bird or two,   *1871a:*two,—   357| MS:then?   The hard stone §last three words
crossed out and replaced above by two words§ 'Tis marble §last two words crossed out and
replaced below by two words§ The column hold §altered to§ holds <> up!   *1889a:*up.
364| MS:beauty: and <> house—   *1871a:*beauty. And <> house,   *1889a:*house

365 As if he knew it well and loved it much:
"O Admeteian domes, where I endured,
Even the God I am, to drudge awhile,
Do righteous penance for a reckless deed,
Accepting the slaves' table thankfully!"
370 Then told how Zeus had been the cause of all,
Raising the wrath in him which took revenge
And slew those forgers of the thunderbolt
Wherewith Zeus blazed the life from out the breast
Of Phoibos' son Asklepios (I surmise,
375 Because he brought the dead to life again)
And so, for punishment, must needs go slave,
God as he was, with a mere mortal lord:
—Told how he came to King Admetos' land,
And played the ministrant, was herdsman there,
380 Warding all harm away from him and his
Till now; "For, holy as I am," said he,
"The lord I chanced upon was holy too:
Whence I deceived the Moirai, drew from death
My master, this same son of Pheres,—ay,
385 The Goddesses conceded him escape
From Hades, when the fated day should fall,
Could he exchange lives, find some friendly one
Ready, for his sake, to content the grave.
But trying all in turn, the friendly list,
390 Why, he found no one, none who loved so much,
Nor father, nor the aged mother's self
That bore him, no, not any save his wife,

365| MS:much— *1871a*:much: 368-69| MS:§lines transposed§   368| MS:deed."
1889a:deed,   369| MS:slave's <> thankfully, *1889a*:slaves' <> thankfully!"
370| MS:And §crossed out and replaced in margin by§ Then
374| MS:Of the God's son Asklepios—I *1871a*:Of Phoibos' son Asklepios (I
375| MS:again— *1871a*:again)   376| MS:slave *1872*:slave,   378| MS:land
1871a:land,   379| MS:there *1871a*:there,   380| MS:Warding from him and his all
harm away *1889a*:Warding all harm away from him and his   381| MS:now, "for holy
1871a:now; "For, holy   382| MS:The *1871a*:"The   385| MS:conceded him
§crossed out and replaced above by§ me escape *1871a*:conceded him escape
386| MS:fall; *1871a*:fall,   391| MS:father nor the very §crossed out and replaced above
by§ aged *1871a*:father, nor   392| MS:no not <> wife *1871a*:no, not <> wife,

Willing to die instead of him and watch
Never a sunrise nor a sunset more:
395 And she is even now within the house,
Upborne by pitying hands, the feeble frame
Gasping its last of life out; since to-day
Destiny is accomplished, and she dies,
And I, lest here pollution light on me,
400 Leave, as ye witness, all my wonted joy
In this dear dwelling. Ay,—for here comes Death
Close on us of a sudden! who, pale priest
Of the mute people, means to bear his prey
To the house of Hades. The symmetric step!
405 How he treads true to time and place and thing,
Dogging day, hour and minute, for death's-due!"

And we observed another Deity,
Half in, half out the portal,—watch and ward,—
Eyeing his fellow: formidably fixed,
410 Yet faltering too at who affronted him,
As somehow disadvantaged, should they strive.
Like some dread heapy blackness, ruffled wing,
Convulsed and cowering head that is all eye,
Which proves a ruined eagle who, too blind
415 Swooping in quest o' the quarry, fawn or kid,
Descried deep down the chasm 'twixt rock and rock,
Has wedged and mortised, into either wall
O' the mountain, the pent earthquake of his power;
So lies, half hurtless yet still terrible,

395| MS:She who is <> house *1871a*:And she is <> house, 396| MS:hands,—the
1871a:hands, the 397| MS:Breathing §crossed out and replaced above by§ Gasping <>
of breath §crossed out and replaced above by§ life out, since *1871a*:out; since
399| MS:lest a §crossed out and replaced above by§ here 402| MS:sudden!—who
1871a:sudden! who 406| MS:hour, and minute for *1871a*:hour and minute, for
406-7| *1871a*:§¶ lost in paging§ *1889a*:§¶ restored§ 407| MS:And you observed
1871a:And we observed 410| MS:faultering *1889a*:faltering 413| MS:Convulsed
claw, §crossed out and replaced above by§ and 414| MS:That §crossed out and replaced
above by§ Which 417| MS:Hath <> mortised into *1871a*:Has <> mortised, into
418| MS:mountain the <> power, *1871a*:mountain, the <> power;

24

420   Just when—who stalks up, who stands front to front,
      But the great lion-guarder of the gorge,
      Lord of the ground, a stationed glory there?
      Yet he too pauses ere he try the worst
      O' the frightful unfamiliar nature, new
425   To the chasm, indeed, but elsewhere known enough,
      Among the shadows and the silences
      Above i' the sky: so each antagonist
      Silently faced his fellow and forbore.
      Till Death shrilled, hard and quick, in spite and fear:

430   "Ha ha, and what mayst thou do at the domes,
      Why hauntest here, thou Phoibos? Here again
      At the old injustice, limiting our rights,
      Baulking of honour due us Gods o' the grave?
      Was't not enough for thee to have delayed
435   Death from Admetos,—with thy crafty art
      Cheating the very Fates,—but thou must arm
      The bow-hand and take station, press 'twixt me
      And Pelias' daughter, who then saved her spouse,—
      Did just that, now thou comest to undo,—
440   Taking his place to die, Alkestis here?"

      But the God sighed "Have courage! All my arms,

420| MS:when who   *1872*:when—who   421| MS:of the pass §crossed out§ gorge,
422| MS:there!   *1889a*:there?   423| MS:While he   *1871a*:Yet he   425| MS:enough
1871a:enough,   428| MS:forbore,   *1871a*:forbore.   429| MS:fear—   *1871a*:fear:
430| MS:Ha, ha, ha, §crossed out§ and what dost §inserted above, then crossed out and
replaced above by§ mayst thou do §inserted above§   *1871a*: "Ha   *1889a*:"Ha ha
431| MS:thou Phoibos?   Art §crossed out and replaced above by§ Here
432| MS:injustice, harrying up and down §last four words crossed out and replaced above by
three words§ limiting our rights,   432-33| MS:§line added: *With limitation thou must needs
prescribe,*§ §entire line crossed out§   433| MS:Hindering §crossed out and replaced below
by§ Baulking   434| MS:to deny the death §last three words crossed out and replaced
above by two words§ have delayed   435| MS:Of my §last two words crossed out and
replaced above by two words§ Death from Admetos, with   *1871a*:from Admetos,—with
439| §line added§   440| MS:here?   *1871a*:here?"   440-41| MS:§no¶§   *1889a*:§¶§

This time, are simple justice and fair words."

Then each plied each with rapid interchange:

"What need of bow, were justice arms enough?"

445   "Ever it is my wont to bear the bow."

"Ay, and with bow, not justice, help this house!"

"I help it, since a friend's woe weighs me too."

"And now,—wilt force from me this second corpse?"

"By force I took no corpse at first from thee."

450   "How then is he above ground, not beneath?"

"He gave his wife instead of him, thy prey."

"And prey, this time at least, I bear below!"

"Go take her!—for I doubt persuading thee . . ."

"To kill the doomed one? What my function else?"

455   "No! Rather, to despatch the true mature."

"Truly I take thy meaning, see thy drift!"

442| MS:fair speech." §crossed out and replaced above by§ words."   443| MS:§¶ called for in margin§   *1871a:*§no ¶§   444-468| MS:§no quotation marks in this passage; see Editorial Notes§   444| MS:bow were   *1872:*bow, were   453| MS:Go §added in margin§ Take her! and go! then! How shall prayer persuade . . . §last seven words and punctuation crossed out and replaced above by five words and punctuation§ —for I doubt persuading thee . . .   *1871a:*take   454| MS:That I §last two words crossed out and replaced above by one word§ To kill the §inserted above§ <> ones §altered to§ one   455| MS:No! §added in margin§ Rather to strike the old, §last three words and punctuation crossed out and replaced above by one word§ despatch   *1871a:*No! Rather, to

26

"Is there a way then she may reach old age?"

"No way! I glad me in my honours too!"

"But, young or old, thou tak'st one life, no more!"

460 "Younger they die, greater my praise redounds!"

"If she die old,—the sumptuous funeral!"

"Thou layest down a law the rich would like."

"How so? Did wit lurk there and 'scape thy sense?"

"Who could buy substitutes would die old men."

465 "It seems thou wilt not grant me, then, this grace?"

"This grace I will not grant: thou know'st my ways."

"Ways harsh to men, hateful to Gods, at least!"

"All things thou canst not have: my rights for me!"

457| MS:Shall she go on to age then ere she die? §entire line crossed out and replaced above by new line§ Is there a way than she may reach old age? 458| MS:Nowise §last four letters crossed out and replaced above by way:§ I too have §last two words crossed out and replaced above by four words§ glad me in my honours too! §inserted above§ that make glad. §last three words and punctuation crossed out§ *1871a:*way! I 459| MS:But, §added in margin§ Young or old, but §crossed out and replaced above by§ you §crossed out and replaced above by§ thou tak'st §inserted above§ one life, is death's to take! §last four words crossed out and replaced above by two words§ no more! *1871a:*young 460| MS:The §crossed out§ younger §altered to§ Younger grasped, the §last two words crossed out and replaced above by two words§ they die, greater glory mine! §last two words crossed out and replaced above by three words§ the praise redounds! *1871a:*greater my praise
461| MS:Nay, §crossed out§ if §altered to§ If <> old, richer prove the rites. §last four words crossed out and replaced above by three words§ the splendid §crossed out and replaced above by§ sumptuous funeral! *1871a:*old,—the 464| MS:would see old friends. §last three words crossed out and replaced above by three words§ die old men. 465| MS:This is a grace, §last four words crossed out§ It seems, §inserted above§ thou <> grant, in fine? § last two words and punctuation crossed out and replaced above by four words and punctuation§ me, then, this grace? 466| MS:This §added in margin§ A §crossed out§ grace

And then Apollon prophesied,—I think,
470 More to himself than to impatient Death,
Who did not hear or would not heed the while,—
For he went on to say "Yet even so,
Cruel above the measure, thou shalt clutch
No life here! Such a man do I perceive
475 Advancing to the house of Pheres now,
Sent by Eurustheus to bring out of Thrace,
The winter world, a chariot with its steeds!
He indeed, when Admetos proves the host,
And he the guest, at the house here,—he it is
480 Shall bring to bear such force, and from thy hands
Rescue this woman. Grace no whit to me
Will that prove, since thou dost thy deed the same,
And earnest too my hate, and all for nought!"

But how should Death or stay or understand?
485 Doubtless, he only felt the hour was come,
And the sword free; for he but flung some taunt—
"Having talked much, thou wilt not gain the more!
This woman, then, descends to Hades' hall
Now that I rush on her, begin the rites

469| MS:think *1871a*:think,   470| MS:than to §altered to§ that impatient Death
1871a:than to impatient Death,   475| MS:Come striding §last two words crossed out and
replaced above by one word§ Advancing   477| MS:And snow storm §last three words
crossed out and replaced above by two words and punctuation§ The winter-world, a famed
§crossed out§ chariot <> steeds: *1871a*:winter world <> steeds!   478| MS:indeed
when <> host *1871a*:indeed, when <> host,   479| MS:the glad §crossed out§ guest at
the kindly hearth, §last two words and punctuation crossed out and replaced above by five
words and punctuation§ house here,—he it is *1871a*:guest, at   480| MS:He it is that
§last four words crossed out§ shall §altered to§ Shall <> bear the force *1871a*:bear such
force   481| MS:woman! from thee! §last two words and punctuation crossed out§ Grace
1889a:woman. Grace   482| MS:To me, §last two words crossed out and replaced above by
three words§ Shall that prove, <> thou hast done §last two words crossed out and replaced
above by one word§ dost thy *1871a*:Will that   483| MS:too §inserted above§ my hate,
moreover §crossed out and replaced above by§ and <> nought! *1871a*:nought!"
485| MS:come *1871a*:come,   486| MS:free, for <> taunt *1871a*:free; for <> taunt—
487| MS:"Much §crossed out and replaced above by§ "Having talking §altered to§ talked here,
and all the profit—this! §last six words and punctuation crossed out and replaced above by
seven words and punctuation§ much, thou woulds't not gain the more! *1871a*:thou wilt not
488| MS:woman, shall §crossed out and replaced above by§ then, <> Hades §altered to§
Hades' now— §crossed out and replaced above by§ hall

490　O' the sword; for sacred, to us Gods below,
　　That head whose hair this sword shall sanctify!"

　　And, in the fire-flash of the appalling sword,
　　The uprush and the outburst, the onslaught
　　Of Death's portentous passage through the door,
495　Apollon stood a pitying moment-space:
　　I caught one last gold gaze upon the night
　　Nearing the world now: and the God was gone,
　　And mortals left to deal with misery,
　　As in came stealing slow, now this, now that
500　Old sojourner throughout the country-side,
　　Servants grown friends to those unhappy here:
　　And, cloudlike in their increase, all these griefs
　　Broke and began the over-brimming wail,
　　Out of a common impulse, word by word.

505　"What now may mean the silence at the door?
　　Why is Admetos' mansion stricken dumb?
　　Not one friend near, to say if we should mourn
　　Our mistress dead, or if Alkestis lives
　　And sees the light still, Pelias' child—to me,
510　To all, conspicuously the best of wives
　　That ever was toward husband in this world!
　　Hears anyone or wail beneath the roof,
　　Or hands that strike each other, or the groan
　　Announcing all is done and nought to dread?
515　Still not a servant stationed at the gates!
　　O Paian, that thou wouldst dispart the wave

490| MS:sword, for sacred to <> below　*1871a:*sword; for <> below,　*1889a:*sacred, to
492| MS:And in <> sword—　*1871a:*And, in <> sword,　497| MS:Left in §last two words
crossed out and replaced above by one word§ Nearing <> now, and　*1871a:*now: and
498| MS:mortals had §crossed out and replaced above by§ left　499| MS:slow now this now
*1871a:*slow, now this, now　502| MS:And cloudlike　*1871a:*And, cloudlike
503| MS:wail　*1871a:*wail,　504| MS:by word—　*1871a:*by word.　505| MS:Whatever
means the silence　*1871a:* "Whatever　*1889a:* "What now may mean the silence
507| MS:near to　*1871a:*near, to　508| MS:or still Alkestis live　*1889a:*or if Alkestis lives
509| MS:see the light here, Pelias'　*1889a:*sees the light still, Pelias'　513| MS:or that
§altered to§ the　514| MS:Announcing there §crossed out and replaced above by§ all

O' the woe, be present! Yet, had woe o'erwhelmed
The housemates, they were hardly silent thus:
It cannot be, the dead is forth and gone.
520 Whence comes thy gleam of hope? I dare not hope:
What is the circumstance that heartens thee?
How could Admetos have dismissed a wife
So worthy, unescorted to the grave?
Before the gates I see no hallowed vase
525 Of fountain-water, such as suits death's door;
Nor any clipt locks strew the vestibule,
Though surely these drop when we grieve the dead,
Nor hand sounds smitten against youthful hand,
The women's way. And yet—the appointed time—
530 How speak the word?—this day is even the day
Ordained her for departing from its light.
O touch calamitous to heart and soul!
Needs must one, when the good are tortured so,
Sorrow,—one reckoned faithful from the first."

535 Then their souls rose together, and one sigh
Went up in cadence from the common mouth:
How "Vainly—anywhither in the world
Directing or land-labour or sea-search—
To Lukia or the sand-waste, Ammon's seat—
540 Might you set free their hapless lady's soul
From the abrupt Fate's footstep instant now.

517| MS:present! Yet had *1871a*:present! Yet, had   518| MS:housemates they
1871a:housemates, they   519| MS:be the   *1871a*:be, the   520| MS:not hope—
1871a:not hope: 521| MS:is it §crossed out and replaced above by three words§ the
circumstance that   524| MS:no water §crossed out and replaced above by§ hallowed
525| MS:Such as is set by door the dead must §last nine words crossed out and replaced above
by seven words and punctuation§ Of fountain-water such as suits death's door;
1871a:fountain-water, such   527| MS:these fall §crossed out and replaced above by§
drop < > dead: *1889a*:dead,   528| MS:Nor sounds hand smitten   *1889a*:Nor hand
sounds smitten   534| MS:one ever §crossed out and replaced above by§ reckoned < >
first.   *1871a*:first."   535| MS:together and   *1871a*:together, and   536| MS:mouth
1871a:mouth: 537| MS:How vainly   *1871a*:How "Vainly—any whither
1889a:anywhither   540| MS:you release §crossed out and replaced above by two words§
set free   541| MS:now.   *1889a*:now §emended to§ now. §see Editorial Notes§

Not a sheep-sacrificer at the hearths
Of Gods had they to go to: one there was
Who, if his eyes saw light still,—Phoibos' son,—
545   Had wrought so she might leave the shadowy place
And Hades' portal; for he propped up Death's
Subdued ones till the Zeus-flung thunder-flame
Struck him; and now what hope of life were hailed
With open arms? For, all the king could do
550   Is done already,—not one God whereof
The altar fails to reek with sacrifice:
And for assuagement of these evils—nought!"

But here they broke off, for a matron moved
Forth from the house: and, as her tears flowed fast,
555   They gathered round. "What fortune shall we hear?
For mourning thus, if aught affect thy lord,
We pardon thee: but lives the lady yet
Or has she perished?—that we fain would know!"

"Call her dead, call her living, each style serves,"
560   The matron said: "though grave-ward bowed, she breathed;
Nor knew her husband what the misery meant
Before he felt it: hope of life was none:
The appointed day pressed hard; the funeral pomp
He had prepared too."
            When the friends broke out:

542| MS:Not one §crossed out and replaced above by§ a   545| MS:so, she had left §last two words crossed out and replaced above by two words§ might leave   *1889a:*so she
546| MS:he raised the dead again— §last four words and punctuation crossed out and replaced above by three words§ propped up Death's   547| MS:ones, till   *1889a:*ones till
548| MS:him: and <> life to hail   *1881:*him; and   *1889a:*life were hailed
549| MS:arms? For all   *1871a:*arms? For, all   551| MS:sacrifice,—   *1871a:*sacrifice:
552| MS:nought!   *1871a:*nought!"   554| MS:tears fell §crossed out and replaced above by§ flowed   555| MS:round "What   *1871a:*round. "What   556| MS:To mourn indeed, if <> affect your lord,   *1871a:*affect thy lord,   *1889a:*For mourning thus, if
557| Is pardonable: §last two words crossed out and replaced above by four words§ We pardon you: but, lives the woman yet   *1871a:*pardon thee <> the lady yet   *1889a:*but lives
558| MS:perished,—that   *1871a:*perished?—that   560| MS:grave-wards bent §crossed out and replaced above by§ bowed, she breathed,   *1871a:*breathed;   *1889a:*grave-ward
563| MS:hard, the   *1871a:*hard; the   564| MS:That was §last two words crossed out and replaced above by two words§ He had <> out   *1889a:*out:

565 "Let her in dying know herself at least
Sole wife, of all the wives 'neath the sun wide,
For glory and for goodness!"—"Ah, how else
Than best? who controverts the claim?" quoth she:
"What kind of creature should the woman prove
570 That has surpassed Alkestis?—surelier shown
Preference for her husband to herself
Than by determining to die for him?
But so much all our city knows indeed:
Hear what she did indoors and wonder then!
575 For, when she felt the crowning day was come,
She washed with river-waters her white skin,
And, taking from the cedar closets forth
Vesture and ornament, bedecked herself
Nobly, and stood before the hearth, and prayed:
580 'Mistress, because I now depart the world,
Falling before thee the last time, I ask—
Be mother to my orphans! wed the one
To a kind wife, and make the other's mate
Some princely person: nor, as I who bore
585 My children perish, suffer that they too
Die all untimely, but live, happy pair,
Their full glad life out in the fatherland!'
And every altar through Admetos' house
She visited and crowned and prayed before,
590 Stripping the myrtle-foliage from the boughs,
Without a tear, without a groan,—no change
At all to that skin's nature, fair to see,
Caused by the imminent evil. But this done—
Reaching her chamber, falling on her bed,
595 There, truly, burst she into tears and spoke:
'O bride-bed, where I loosened from my life

568| MS:best—who *1871a*:best? who 571| MS:her lord §crossed out and replaced
above by§ husband 575| MS:For when *1871a*:For, when
579| MS:prayed— *1871a*:prayed: 580| MS:I go ben §last word and syllable crossed
out and replaced above by one word§ now 581| MS:ask,— *1871a*:ask,
586| MS:all-untimely *1871a*:all untimely 587| MS:fatherland!" *1871a*:fatherland!'
593| MS:evil: but *1871a*:evil. But 596| MS:O *1871a*:'O

Virginity for that same husband's sake
Because of whom I die now—fare thee well!
Since nowise do I hate thee: me alone
600 Hast thou destroyed; for, shrinking to betray
Thee and my spouse, I die: but thee, O bed,
Some other woman shall possess as wife—
Truer, no! but of better fortune, say!'
—So falls on, kisses it till all the couch
605 Is moistened with the eyes' sad overflow.
But, when of many tears she had her fill,
She flings from off the couch, goes headlong forth,
Yet,—forth the chamber,—still keeps turning back
And casts her on the couch again once more.
610 Her children, clinging to their mother's robe,
Wept meanwhile: but she took them in her arms,
And, as a dying woman might, embraced
Now one and now the other: 'neath the roof,
All of the household servants wept as well,
615 Moved to compassion for their mistress; she
Extended her right hand to all and each,
And there was no one of such low degree
She spoke not to nor had an answer from.
Such are the evils in Admetos' house.
620 Dying,—why, he had died; but, living, gains
Such grief as this he never will forget!"

And when they questioned of Admetos, "Well—
Holding his dear wife in his hands, he weeps;
Entreats her not to give him up, and seeks

---

⁵⁹⁹| MS:Since §added in margin§ For §crossed out§ nowise   ⁶⁰⁵| MS:sad §crossed out and then marked for retention§   ⁶⁰⁶| MS:But when <> fill   *1871a*:But, when <> fill,
⁶¹⁰| MS:robe   *1871a*:robe,   ⁶¹³| MS:other. 'Neath   *1871a*:other: 'neath
⁶¹⁵| MS:mistress,—she   *1871a*:mistress; she   ⁶¹⁶| MS:Stretched, out §last two words crossed out and replaced above by§ Extended to each one of them, her right hand out, §last ten words crossed out§ Extended her right hand to all and each,   ⁶²¹| MS:forget!
1871a:forget!"   ⁶²¹⁻²²| *1871a*:§¶ lost in paging§   *1889a*:§¶ restored§   ⁶²²| MS:of
Admetos,—"Well—   *1871a*:of Admetos, "Well—   ⁶²³| MS:weeps—   *1871a*:weeps;
⁶²⁴| MS:Implores §crossed out and replaced above by§ Entreats

625   The impossible, in fine: for there she wastes
        And withers by disease, abandoned now,
        A mere dead weight upon her husband's arm.
        Yet, none the less, although she breathe so faint,
        Her will is to behold the beams o' the sun:
630   Since never more again, but this last once,
        Shall she see sun, its circlet or its ray.
        But I will go, announce your presence,—friends
        Indeed; since 'tis not all so love their lords
        As seek them in misfortune, kind the same:
635   But you are the old friends I recognise."

        And at the word she turned again to go:
        The while they waited, taking up the plaint
        To Zeus again: "What passage from this strait?
        What loosing of the heavy fortune fast
640   About the palace? Will such help appear,
        Or must we clip the locks and cast around
        Each form already the black peplos' fold?
        Clearly the black robe, clearly! All the same,
        Pray to the Gods!—like Gods' no power so great!
645   O thou king Paian, find some way to save!
        Reveal it, yea, reveal it! Since of old
        Thou found'st a cure, why, now again become
        Releaser from the bonds of Death, we beg,
        And give the sanguinary Hades pause!"
650   So the song dwindled into a mere moan,
        How dear the wife, and what her husband's woe;

625| MS:What may not §last three words crossed out and replaced above by two words and punctuation§ The impossible,   627| MS:weight on his §last two words crossed out and replaced above by three words§ upon her husband's   629| MS:sun—   *1871a:*sun:
631| MS:sun, the §crossed out and replaced above by§ its < > or the §crossed out and replaced above by§ its   633| MS:all are §crossed out and replaced above by§ so
634| MS:They §crossed out and replaced above by§ As   635| MS:recognize.
*1871a:*recognize."   *1889a:*recognise."   637| MS:the wail   *1871a:*the plaint
640| MS:palace? Would such   *1871a:*palace? Will such   641| MS:must they clip the hair §crossed out and replaced above by§ locks   *1871a:*must we clip   643| MS:same
*1872:*same,   646| MS:reveal it! Since before §crossed out§ of
647| MS:become   *1889a:*becom §emended to§ become §see Editorial Notes§
650| MS:moan—   *1871a:*moan;   *1889a:*moan,   651| MS:woe,   *1871a:*woe;

When suddenly—
            "Behold, behold!" breaks forth:
"Here is she coming from the house indeed!
Her husband comes, too! Cry aloud, lament,
655 Pheraian land, this best of women, bound—
So is she withered by disease away—
For realms below and their infernal king!
Never will we affirm there's more of joy
Than grief in marriage; making estimate
660 Both from old sorrows anciently observed,
And this misfortune of the king we see—
Admetos who, of bravest spouse bereaved,
Will live life's remnant out, no life at all!"

So wailed they, while a sad procession wound
665 Slow from the innermost o' the palace, stopped
At the extreme verge of the platform-front:
There opened, and disclosed Alkestis' self,
The consecrated lady, borne to look
Her last—and let the living look their last—
670 She at the sun, we at Alkestis.
                                    We!
For would you note a memorable thing?
We grew to see in that severe regard,—
Hear in that hard dry pressure to the point,
Word slow pursuing word in monotone,—
675 What Death meant when he called her consecrate
Henceforth to Hades. I believe, the sword—

652| MS:behold!" They cried: §last two words crossed out§ breaks   656| MS:§line added§   659| MS:Than sorrow §crossed out and replaced above by§ grief in a §crossed out§ marriage—making   *1871a*:marriage; making   662| MS:The King §last two words crossed out and replaced above by one word§ Admetos who, of this §crossed out§ bravest wife §crossed out and replace above by§ spouse   666| MS:platform-front,   *1871a*:platform-front: 669| MS:the living look §last three words inserted above§   670| MS:§¶§ Ay §crossed out§ We!   *1871a*:§¶§ We   *1872*:§¶§ We!   671| MS:would §over perhaps *will*§   673| MS:And in that §last three words crossed out and replaced above by three words§ Hear in that hard hollow §crossed out and replaced above by§ dry <> point   *1871a*:point,   674| MS:Of word pursuing   *1871a*:Word slow pursuing   676| MS:believe his §crossed out and replaced above by§ the   *1871a*:believe, the

Its office was to cut the soul at once
From life,—from something in this world which hides
Truth, and hides falsehood, and so lets us live
680   Somehow. Suppose a rider furls a cloak
About a horse's head; unfrightened, so,
Between the menace of a flame, between
Solicitation of the pasturage,
Untempted equally, he goes his gait
685   To journey's end: then pluck the pharos off!
Show what delusions steadied him i' the straight
O' the path, made grass seem fire and fire seem grass,
All through a little bandage o'er the eyes!
As certainly with eyes unbandaged now
690   Alkestis looked upon the action here,
Self-immolation for Admetos' sake;
Saw, with a new sense, all her death would do,
And which of her survivors had the right,
And which the less right, to survive thereby.
695   For, you shall note, she uttered no one word
Of love more to her husband, though he wept
Plenteously, waxed importunate in prayer—
Folly's old fashion when its seed bears fruit.
I think she judged that she had bought the ware
700   O' the seller at its value,—nor praised him
Nor blamed herself, but, with indifferent eye,
Saw him purse money up, prepare to leave
The buyer with a solitary bale—

677| MS:With its fire-flash divided her §last five words crossed out and replaced above by seven words§ Its office was to cut the soul   680| MS:Somehow: suppose a man that furls *1871a*:Somehow. Suppose a rider furls   681| MS:head,—unfrightened   *1871a*:head; unfrightened   683| MS:pasturage   *1871a*:pasturage,   685| MS:off—   *1871a*:off!   689| MS:For certainly   *1872*:As certainly   692| MS:Saw with a §inserted above§ new eyes now §last two words crossed out and replaced above by one word§ sense all   *1871a*:Saw, with <> sense, all   695| MS:For you <> note she   *1871a*:For, you <> note, she   698| MS:fruit: *1871a*:fruit.   701| MS:but with indifferent air §crossed out§ eye *1871a*:but, with <> eye,   702| MS:purse coin §crossed out and replaced above by§ money up, and §crossed out§   703| MS:with his §crossed out and replaced above by§ a

True purple—but in place of all that coin,
705   Had made a hundred others happy too,
If so willed fate or fortune! What remained
To give away, should rather go to these
Than one with coin to clink and contemplate.
Admetos had his share and might depart,
710   The rest was for her children and herself.
(Charopé makes a face: but wait awhile!)
She saw things plain as Gods do: by one stroke
O' the sword that rends the life-long veil away.
(Also Euripides saw plain enough:
715   But you and I, Charopé!—you and I
Will trust his sight until our own grow clear.)

"Sun, and thou light of day, and heavenly dance
O' the fleet cloud-figure!" (so her passion paused,
While the awe-stricken husband made his moan,
720   Muttered now this now that ineptitude:
"Sun that sees thee and me, a suffering pair,
Who did the Gods no wrong whence thou shouldst die!")
Then, as if caught up, carried in their course,
Fleeting and free as cloud and sunbeam are,
725   She missed no happiness that lay beneath:
"O thou wide earth, from these my palace roofs,
To distant nuptial chambers once my own
In that Iolkos of my ancestry!"—
There the flight failed her. "Raise thee, wretched one!

704| MS:coin   *1871a:*coin,   705| MS:made so many §last two words crossed out and replaced above by two words§ a hundred   707| MS:away should <> these §punctuation, possible colon, scraped off§ *1871a:*away, should   708| MS:§line added§ 710| MS:herself,— *1871a:*herself.   711| MS:face,—but *1871a:*face: but 712| MS:as Gods see §crossed out and replaced above by§ do—by *1871a:*do: by 713| MS:away: *1871a:*away.   714| MS:enough— *1871a:*enough: 715-16| §lines added§   715| MS:and I, Charope!—You *1871a:*and I, Charopé!—you 718| MS:cloud-figure!"—so *1871a:*cloud-figure!" (so   720| MS:ineptitude— *1871a:*ineptitude: 722| MS:die!" *1871a:*should'st die!") *1889a:*shouldst 725| MS:beneath,— *1871a:*beneath: 726| MS:earth—from *1871a:*earth, from

730   Give us not up! Pray pity from the Gods!"

Vainly Admetos: for "I see it—see
The two-oared boat! The ferryer of the dead,
Charon, hand hard upon the boatman's-pole,
Calls me—even now calls—'Why delayest thou?
735   Quick! Thou obstructest all made ready here
For prompt departure: quick, then!'"
                                        "Woe is me!

A bitter voyage this to undergo,
Even i' the telling! Adverse Powers above,
How do ye plague us!"
                            Then a shiver ran:
740   "He has me—seest not?—hales me,—who is it?—
To the hall o' the Dead—ah, who but Hades' self,
He, with the wings there, glares at me, one gaze
All that blue brilliance, under the eyebrow!
What wilt thou do? Unhand me! Such a way
745   I have to traverse, all unhappy one!"

"Way—piteous to thy friends, but, most of all,
Me and thy children: ours assuredly
A common partnership in grief like this!"

Whereat they closed about her; but "Let be!
750   Leave, let me lie now! Strength forsakes my feet.
Hades is here, and shadowy on my eyes
Comes the night creeping. Children—children, now
Indeed, a mother is no more for you!
Farewell, O children, long enjoy the light!"

730·31| MS:§no ¶ called for§   *1871a*:§¶§   732| MS:boat, the   *1871a*:boat! The
734| MS:now I hear §last two words crossed out and replaced above by one word§ calls
739| MS:ran—   *1871a*:ran: 743| MS:eye-brow—   *1871a*:eye-brow!   *1889a*:eyebrow!
744| MS:me! What §crossed out and replaced above by§ Such   745| MS:Have I §last two
words marked for transposition§ <> all-unhappy   *1871a*:all unhappy   746| MS:but
most of all   *1871a*:but, most of all,   747| MS:children—ours   *1871a*:children: ours
749| MS:her, but   *1871a*:her; but   751| MS:is nigh §crossed out and replaced above by§
here   752| MS:children, you! §crossed out§ now   754| MS:light!   *1871a*:light!"

⁷⁵⁵ "Ah me, the melancholy word I hear,
Oppressive beyond every kind of death!
No, by the Deities, take heart nor dare
To give me up—no, by our children too
Made orphans of! But rise, be resolute,
⁷⁶⁰ Since, thou departed, I no more remain!
For in thee are we bound up, to exist
Or cease to be—so we adore thy love!"

—Which brought out truth to judgment. At this word
And protestation, all the truth in her
⁷⁶⁵ Claimed to assert itself: she waved away
The blue-eyed black-wing'd phantom, held in check
The advancing pageantry of Hades there,
And, with no change in her own countenance,
She fixed her eyes on the protesting man,
⁷⁷⁰ And let her lips unlock their sentence,—so!

"Admetos,—how things go with me thou seest,—
I wish to tell thee, ere I die, what things
I will should follow. I—to honour thee,
Secure for thee, by my own soul's exchange,
⁷⁷⁵ Continued looking on the daylight here—
Die for thee—yet, if so I pleased, might live,
Nay, wed what man of Thessaly I would,
And dwell i' the dome with pomp and queenliness.
I would not,—would not live bereft of thee,

---

⁷⁵⁴⁻⁵⁵| *1871a*:§¶ lost in paging§   *1889a*:§¶ restored§   ⁷⁵⁶| MS:beyond any kind
1871a:beyond every kind   ⁷⁵⁷| MS:deities   *1871a*:the Deities   ⁷⁵⁸| MS:by the
children   *1871a*:by our children   ⁷⁵⁹| MS:be brave again, §last two words crossed out
and replaced above by one word and punctuation§ resolute!   *1889a*:resolute,
⁷⁶⁰| MS:more should be! §last two words crossed out and replaced above by one word§
remain!   ⁷⁶¹| MS:up, live or §last two words crossed out§ to   ⁷⁶⁶| MS:black-winged
§altered to§ black-wing'd spectre §crossed out and replaced above by§ phantom
⁷⁶⁸| MS:in that white §last two words crossed out and replaced above by two words§ her own
⁷⁶⁹| MS:on who §crossed out and replaced above by§ the protested §altered to§ protesting
thus, §crossed out§ man,   ⁷⁷⁰| MS:let the §crossed out and replaced above by§ her
⁷⁷⁰⁻⁷¹| *1871a*:§¶ lost in paging§   *1889a*:§¶ restored§   ⁷⁷¹| MS:Admetos   *1871a*:
"Admetos   ⁷⁷⁶| MS:thee—who, if   *1871a*:thee—yet, if   ⁷⁷⁹| MS:thee   *1871a*:thee,

780 With children orphaned, neither shrank at all,
Though having gifts of youth wherein I joyed.
Yet, who begot thee and who gave thee birth,
Both of these gave thee up; no less, a term
Of life was reached when death became them well,
785 Ay, well—to save their child and glorious die:
Since thou wast all they had, nor hope remained
Of having other children in thy place.
So, I and thou had lived out our full time,
Nor thou, left lonely of thy wife, wouldst groan
790 With children reared in orphanage: but thus
Some God disposed things, willed they so should be.
Be they so! Now do thou remember this,
Do me in turn a favour—favour, since
Certainly I shall never claim my due,
795 For nothing is more precious than a life:
But a fit favour, as thyself wilt say,
Loving our children here no less than I,
If head and heart be sound in thee at least.
Uphold them, make them masters of my house,
800 Nor wed and give a step-dame to the pair,
Who, being a worse wife than I, thro' spite
Will raise her hand against both thine and mine.
Never do this at least, I pray to thee!
For hostile the new-comer, the step-dame,
805 To the old brood—a very viper she
For gentleness! Here stand they, boy and girl;

780| MS:orphaned,—neither *1871a:*orphaned, neither 783| MS:up,—for all, a
*1871a:*up; for *1889a:*up; no less, a 787| MS:place: *1871a:*place. 788| MS:So I
<> full life, §crossed out and replaced above by§ time *1871a:*So, I 789| MS:thou,
been §crossed out and replaced above by§ wert §crossed out§ left to groan with in §last four
words crossed out and replaced above by four words and punctuation§ lonely of thy wife,
791| MS:things—willed *1871a:*things, willed 793| MS:And what shall prove the
appropriate grace—mere grace, §entire line crossed out and replaced above by new line§ Do
me in turn a favour—favour, since *1871a:*favor—favor *1889a:*favour—favour
794| MS:Since §crossed out and replaced above by§ Certainly <> claim its §inserted above§
the §crossed out§ due; thereof—§crossed out§ due, *1871a:*claim my due, 796| *1871a:*favor
*1889a:*favour 797| MS:Loving the children *1871a:*Loving our children
805| MS:viper's §altered to§ viper self §crossed out§ she
806| MS:gentleness! here <> girl— *1871a:*gentleness! Here <> girl;

The boy has got a father, a defence
Tower-like, he speaks to and has answer from:
But thou, my girl, how will thy virginhood
810   Conclude itself in marriage fittingly?
Upon what sort of sire-found yoke-fellow
Art thou to chance? with all to apprehend—
Lest, casting on thee some unkind report,
She blast thy nuptials in the bloom of youth.
815   For neither shall thy mother watch thee wed,
Nor hearten thee in childbirth, standing by
Just when a mother's presence helps the most!
No, for I have to die: and this my ill
Comes to me, nor to-morrow, no, nor yet
820   The third day of the month, but now, even now,
I shall be reckoned among those no more.
Farewell, be happy! And to thee, indeed,
Husband, the boast remains permissible
Thou hadst a wife was worthy! and to you,
825   Children; as good a mother gave you birth."

"Have courage!" interposed the friends, "For him
I have no scruple to declare—all this
Will he perform, except he fail of sense."

"All this shall be—shall be!" Admetos sobbed:
830   "Fear not! And, since I had thee living, dead
Alone wilt thou be called my wife: no fear
That some Thessalian ever styles herself
Bride, hails this man for husband in thy place!
No woman, be she of such lofty line

807| MS:has yet a   *1871a:*has got a   808| MS:Tower-like,—he <> and is answered by:
*1871a:*Tower-like, he <> and has answer from: 809| girl, wh §last two letters crossed
out§ how   810| MS:In §altered to§ Upon   813| MS:Lest casting <> report
*1871a:*Lest, casting <> report,   818| MS:die—and   *1871a:*die: and
819| MS:me nor   *1871a:*me, nor   824| MS:worthy—as to   *1871a:*worthy! and to
825| MS:Children, as <> birth.   *1871a:*Children; as <> birth."
826| MS:friends—"for him.   *1871a:*friends, "For him   828| MS:perform, unless §crossed
out and replaced above by§ except <> sense.   *1871a:*sense."
829| MS:sobbed—   *1871a:*sobbed: 831| MS:nor   *1871a:*no

835 Or such surpassing beauty otherwise!
Enough of children: gain from these I have,
Such only may the Gods grant! since in thee
Absolute is our loss, where all was gain.
And I shall bear for thee no year-long grief,
840 But grief that lasts while my own days last, love!
Love! For my hate is she who bore me, now:
And him I hate, my father: loving-ones
Truly, in word not deed! But thou didst pay
All dearest to thee down, and buy my life,
845 Saying me so! Is there not cause enough
That I who part with such companionship
In thee, should make my moan? I moan, and more:
For I will end the feastings—social flow
O' the wine friends flock for, garlands and the Muse
850 That graced my dwelling. Never now for me
To touch the lyre, to lift my soul in song
At summons of the Lybian flute; since thou
From out my life hast emptied all the joy!
And this thy body, in thy likeness wrought
855 By some wise hand of the artificers,
Shall lie disposed within my marriage-bed:
This I will fall on, this enfold about,
Call by thy name,—my dear wife in my arms

836| MS:children—gain *1871a*:children: gain   837| MS:Such §added in margin§ That §crossed out§ <> grant—since *1871a*:grant! since   838| MS:All §crossed out and replaced above by§ Absolute <> loss, now! §crossed out§ where <> gain! *1871a*:gain.
839| MS:And §added in margin§ But §crossed out§   841| MS:bore an §crossed out and replaced above by§ me, now— *1871a*:now: 842| MS:father—loving-ones *1871a*:father: loving-ones   844| MS:down and *1871a*:down, and   847| MS:In thee, §added in margin§ Should <> I moan and *1871a*:should <> I moan, and
849| MS:friends come §crossed out and replaced above by§ flock <> muse *1871a*:the Muse
850| MS:Which graced my dwelling: never *1871a*:That graced my dwelling. Never
852| MS:the Lybian *1889a*:the Lydian §emended to§ Lybian §see Editorial Notes§
853| MS:Hast taken out of life its joy of §entire line crossed out and replaced above by new line§ hast emptied all the joy. From out my life §last four words marked for transposition to beginning of line§ *1871a*:joy!   854| MS:Nay, §crossed out and replaced above by§ And
856| MS:disposed upon §crossed out and replaced above by§ within
857| MS:on and enfold *1871a*:on, this enfold   858| MS:Calling §altered to§ Call by §inserted above§ thy name,—O I shall seem to have §last six words crossed out and replaced above by five words§ my dear wife in my

Even though I have not, I shall seem to have—
⁸⁶⁰ A cold delight, indeed, but all the same
So should I lighten of its weight my soul!
And, wandering my way in dreams perchance,
Thyself wilt bless me: for, come when they will,
Even by night our loves are sweet to see.
⁸⁶⁵ But were the tongue and tune of Orpheus mine,
So that to Koré crying, or her lord,
In hymns, from Hades I might rescue thee—
Down would I go, and neither Plouton's dog
Nor Charon, he whose oar sends souls across,
⁸⁷⁰ Should stay me till again I made thee stand
Living, within the light! But, failing this,
There, where thou art, await me when I die,
Make ready our abode, my house-mate still!
For in the self-same cedar, me with thee
⁸⁷⁵ Will I provide that these our friends shall place,
My side lay close by thy side! Never, corpse
Although I be, would I division bear
From thee, my faithful one of all the world!"

So he stood sobbing: nowise insincere,
⁸⁸⁰ But somehow child-like, like his children, like
Childishness the world over. What was new
In this announcement that his wife must die?
What particle of pain beyond the pact
He made, with eyes wide open, long ago—
⁸⁸⁵ Made and was, if not glad, content to make?
Now that the sorrow, he had called for, came,
He sorrowed to the height: none heard him say,
However, what would seem so pertinent,

---

^{859|} MS:shall then §crossed out§ seem   ^{861|} MS:soul: *1871a*:soul!
^{865|} MS:But §added in margin§ Were the §inserted above§   *1871a*:were
^{870|} MS:again §inserted above§ <> stand once more §last two words crossed out§
^{876|} MS:lay close §last two words inserted above§ <> side!—close §crossed out§ ever §altered
to§ never, corpse §crossed out and restored above§   *1871a*:thy side! Never
^{878|} MS:thee, the §crossed out§ found §crossed out and replaced above by§ my faithful out
§crossed out and replaced above by§ one <> world! *1871a*:world!"   ^{880|} MS:somehow
§inserted above§   ^{884|} MS:made with <> open long   *1871a*:made, with <> open, long
^{887|} MS:height: but §crossed out§ none   ^{888|} MS:pertinent— *1871a*:pertinent,

43

"To keep this pact, I find surpass my power:
890   Rescind it, Moirai! Give me back her life,
And take the life I kept by base exchange!
Or, failing that, here stands your laughing-stock
Fooled by you, worthy just the fate o' the fool
Who makes a pother to escape the best
895   And gain the worst you wiser Powers allot!"
No, not one word of this: nor did his wife
Despite the sobbing, and the silence soon
To follow, judge so much was in his thought—
Fancy that, should the Moirai acquiesce,
900   He would relinquish life nor let her die.
The man was like some merchant who, in storm,
Throws the freight over to redeem the ship:
No question, saving both were better still.
As it was,—why, he sorrowed, which sufficed.
905   So, all she seemed to notice in his speech
Was what concerned her children. Children, too,
Bear the grief and accept the sacrifice.
Rightly rules nature: does the blossomed bough
O' the grape-vine, or the dry grape's self, bleed wine?

910   So, bending to her children all her love,
She fastened on their father's only word
To purpose now, and followed it with this.
"O children, now yourselves have heard these things—
Your father saying he will never wed
915   Another woman to be over you,
Nor yet dishonour me!"

               "And now at least
I say it, and I will accomplish too!"

889| MS:pact I   *1871a:*pact, I   890| MS:it, Moirai; give <> life   *1871a:*it, Moirai! Give
<> life,   891| MS:exchange—   *1871a:*exchange!   897| MS:sobbing and
*1871a:*sobbing, and   900| MS:die: *1871a:*die.   901| MS:who in storm
*1871a:*who, in storm,   903| MS:still: *1871a:*still.   905| MS:So all *1871a:*So, all
907| MS:and made §crossed out and replaced above by§ accept the sacrifice: *1871a:*sacrifice.
909| MS:self bleed   *1871a:*self, bleed   909-10| MS:§¶§   *1889a:*§¶ lost in paging.
Emended to restore ¶; see Editorial Notes§   917| MS:say them, and   *1871a:*say it, and

"Then, for such promise of accomplishment,
Take from my hand these children!"

"Thus I take—
⁹²⁰ Dear gift from the dear hand!"

"Do thou become
Mother, now, to these children in my place!"

"Great the necessity I should be so,
At least, to these bereaved of thee!"

"Child—child!
Just when I needed most to live, below
⁹²⁵ Am I departing from you both!"

"Ah me!
And what shall I do, then, left lonely thus?"

"Time will appease thee: who is dead is nought."

"Take me with thee—take, by the Gods below!"

"We are sufficient, we who die for thee."

⁹³⁰ "Oh, Powers, ye widow me of what a wife!"

"And truly the dimmed eye draws earthward now!"

"Wife, if thou leav'st me, I am lost indeed!"

"She once was—now is nothing, thou mayst say."

"Raise thy face nor forsake thy children thus!"

---

⁹²⁸| MS:the Gods, below!" *1871a*:the Gods below!" ⁹³³| MS:nothing, you may
§last two words crossed out and replaced above by two words§ thou may'st
1889a:mayst ⁹³⁴| MS:face—nor *1871a*:face nor

45

935   "Ah, willingly indeed I leave them not!
But—fare ye well, my children!"

                           "Look on them—
Look!"

             "I am nothingness."

                   "What dost thou? Leav'st . . ."

"Farewell!"
            And in the breath she passed away.
"Undone—me miserable!" moaned the king,
940   While friends released the long-suspended sigh
"Gone is she: no wife for Admetos more!"

Such was the signal: how the woe broke forth,
Why tell?—or how the children's tears ran fast
Bidding their father note the eyelids' stare
945   Hands' droop, each dreadful circumstance of death.

"Ay, she hears not, she sees not: I and you,
'Tis plain, are stricken hard and have to bear!"
Was all Admetos answered; for, I judge,
He only now began to taste the truth:
950   The thing done lay revealed, which undone thing,
Rehearsed for fact by fancy, at the best,
Never can equal. He had used himself
This long while (as he muttered presently)
To practise with the terms, the blow involved
955   By the bargain, sharp to bear, but bearable

940| MS:sigh—   *1871a*:sigh   941| MS:she, —no   *1871a*:she: no   943| MS:childrens
1871a:children's   944| MS:eye-lids'   *1871a*:stare,   *1881*:stare   *1889a*:eyelids'
945| MS:droop, and §crossed out§ each sad §crossed out and replaced above by§ dreadful
947| MS:bear—"   *1871a*:bear!"   948| MS:answered,—for   *1871a*:answered; for
950| MS:revealed, as undone thing   *1871a*:revealed, which < > thing,
953| MS:while—, as < > presently,—   *1871a*:while (as < > presently)
954| MS:terms, try blows §altered to§ blow   *1871a*:terms, the blow

Because of plain advantage at the end.
Now that, in fact not fancy, the blow fell—
Needs must he busy him with the surprise.

"Alkestis—not to see her nor be seen,
960   Hear nor be heard of by her, any more
To-day, to-morrow, to the end of time—
Did I mean this should buy my life?" thought he.

So, friends came round him, took him by the hand,
Bade him remember our mortality,
965   Its due, its doom: how neither was he first,
Nor would be last, to thus deplore the loved.

"I understand" slow the words came at last.
"Nor of a sudden did the evil here
Fly on me: I have known it long ago,
970   Ay, and essayed myself in misery;
Nothing is new. You have to stay, you friends,
Because the next need is to carry forth
The corpse here: you must stay and do your part,
Chant proper pæan to the God below;
975   Drink-sacrifice he likes not. I decree
That all Thessalians over whom I rule
Hold grief in common with me; let them shear
Their locks, and be the peplos black they show!
And you who to the chariot yoke your steeds,
980   Or manage steeds one-frontleted,—I charge,
Clip from each neck with steel the mane away!
And through my city, nor of flute nor lyre
Be there a sound till twelve full moons succeed.
For I shall never bury any corpse

---

⁹⁵⁹| MS:seen— *1871a*:seen,   ⁹⁶⁰| MS:her any *1871a*:her, any
⁹⁶³| MS:So friends *1871a*:So, friends   ⁹⁶⁵| MS:first *1871a*:first,
⁹⁷¹| MS:new: you *1871a*:new. You   ⁹⁷⁴| MS:below— *1871a*:below;
⁹⁷⁸| MS:peplus <> show; *1871a*:peplos <> show!   ⁹⁸⁰| MS:And manage *1871a*:Or
manage   ⁹⁸²| MS:flute nor harp §crossed out§ lyre

47

985 Dearer than this to me, nor better friend:
One worthy of all honour from me, since
Me she has died for, she and she alone."

With that, he sought the inmost of the house,
He and his dead, to get grave's garniture,
990 While the friends sang the pæan that should peal.
"Daughter of Pelias, with farewell from me,
I' the house of Hades have thy unsunned home!
Let Hades know, the dark-haired deity,—
And he who sits to row and steer alike,
995 Old corpse-conductor, let him know he bears
Over the Acherontian lake, this time,
I' the two-oared boat, the best—oh, best by far
Of womankind! For thee, Alkestis Queen!
Many a time those haunters of the Muse
1000 Shall sing thee to the seven-stringed mountain-shell,
And glorify in hymns that need no harp,
At Sparta when the cycle comes about,
And that Karneian month wherein the moon
Rises and never sets the whole night through:
1005 So too at splendid and magnificent
Athenai. Such the spread of thy renown,
And such the lay that, dying, thou hast left
Singer and sayer. O that I availed
Of my own might to send thee once again
1010 From Hades' hall, Kokutos' stream, by help
O' the oar that dips the river, back to day!"

So, the song sank to prattle in her praise:
"Light, from above thee, lady, fall the earth,

986| MS:honor *1871a:*honour   994| MS:steer, that old §punctuation and last two words
crossed out§ alike,   995| MS:Corpse-carrier, he §last two words crossed out and replaced
above by two words§ Old corpse-conductor,   1001| MS:harp *1871a:*harp,
1005| MS:at Athens, rich, §last two words and punctuation crossed out and replaced above by
two words§ splendid and   1006| §line added§ Athenai.—such *1871a:*Athenai. Such
1007| MS:And §added in margin§ Such is §crossed out§ the   *1871a:*such
1009| MS:thee back §crossed out§ again   1012| MS:So the *1871a:*So, the

48

Thou only one of womankind to die,
1015 Wife for her husband! If Admetos take
Anything to him like a second spouse—
Hate from his offspring and from us shall be
His portion, let the king assure himself!
No mind his mother had to hide in earth
1020 Her body for her son's sake, nor his sire
Had heart to save whom he begot,—not they,
The white-haired wretches! only thou it was,
I' the bloom of youth, didst save him and so die!
Might it be mine to chance on such a mate
1025 And partner! For there's penury in life
Of such allowance: were she mine at least,
So wonderful a wife, assuredly
She would companion me throughout my days
And never once bring sorrow!"
                                A great voice—
1030 "My hosts here!"
                    Oh, the thrill that ran through us!
Never was aught so good and opportune
As that great interrupting voice! For see!
Here maundered this dispirited old age
Before the palace; whence a something crept
1035 Which told us well enough without a word
What was a-doing inside,—every touch
O' the garland on those temples, tenderest
Disposure of each arm along its side,
Came putting out what warmth i' the world was left.
1040 Then, as it happens at a sacrifice
When, drop by drop, some lustral bath is brimmed:
Into the thin and clear and cold, at once
They slaughter a whole wine-skin: Bacchos' blood

1022| MS:was   *1871a:*was,   1026| MS:least   *1871a:*least,   1027| MS:The wonder of a
woman, sure am I §last four words crossed out and replaced above by two words§ wife,
assuredly   *1871a:*So wonderful a   1032| MS:see: *1871a:*see!   1034| MS:palace
whence   *1871a:*palace; whence   1035| MS:told you well   *1871a:*told us well
1039| MS:left: *1871a:*left.   1040| MS:When §altered to§ Then   1041| MS:Then
§altered to§ When < > brimmed,   *1871a:*brimmed: 1043| MS:wineskin, Bacchos'
blood,   *1871a:*wine-skin; Bacchos' blood   *1889a:*wine-skin: Bacchos'

49

Sets the white water all a-flame; even so,
1045 Sudden into the midst of sorrow, leapt
Along with the gay cheer of that great voice,
Hope, joy, salvation: Herakles was here!
Himself, o' the threshold, sent his voice on first
To herald all that human and divine
1050 I' the weary happy face of him,—half God,
Half man, which made the god-part God the more.

"Hosts mine," he broke upon the sorrow with,
"Inhabitants of this Pheraian soil,
Chance I upon Admetos inside here?"

1055 The irresistible sound wholesome heart
O' the hero,—more than all the mightiness
At labour in the limbs that, for man's sake,
Laboured and meant to labour their life long,—
This drove back, dried up sorrow at its source.
1060 How could it brave the happy weary laugh
Of who had bantered sorrow "Sorrow here?
What have you done to keep your friend from harm?
Could no one give the life I see he keeps?
Or, say there's sorrow here past friendly help,
1065 Why waste a word or let a tear escape
While other sorrows wait you in the world,
And want the life of you, though helpless here?"
Clearly there was no telling such an one
How, when their monarch tried who loved him more
1070 Than he loved them, and found they loved, as he,
Each man, himself, and held, no otherwise,

1044| MS:Set <> aflame,—even so   1871a:Sets <> a-flame: even so,   1889a:a-flame; even
1045| MS:sorrow leapt,   1871a:sorrow, leapt   1047| MS:here,   1871a:here!
1048| MS:Himself o'   1872:Himself, o'   1052| MS:the solemn §crossed out§ sorrow
1054| MS:inside there?"   1871a:inside here?"   1054-55| MS:§¶§   1889a:§¶ lost in paging.
Emended to restore ¶; see Editorial Notes§   1057| MS:that for man's sake   1871a:that,
for man's sake,   1059| MS:Drove <> up the sorrow   1871a:This drove <> up sorrow
1061| MS:sorrow—"Sorrow   1871a:sorrow "Sorrow   1064| MS:Or say <> help—
1871a:Or, say <> help,   1070| MS:found all §crossed out and replaced above by§ they

That, of all evils in the world, the worst
Was—being forced to die, whate'er death gain:
How all this selfishness in him and them
1075   Caused certain sorrow which they sang about,—
I think that Herakles, who held his life
Out on his hand, for any man to take—
I think his laugh had marred their threnody.

"He is in the house" they answered. After all,
1080   They might have told the story, talked their best
About the inevitable sorrow here,
Nor changed nor checked the kindly nature,—no!
So long as men were merely weak, not bad,
He loved men: were they Gods he used to help?
1085   "Yea, Pheres' son is in-doors, Herakles.
But say, what sends thee to Thessalian soil,
Brought by what business to this Pherai town?"

"A certain labour that I have to do
Eurustheus the Tirunthian," laughed the God.

1090   "And whither wendest—on what wandering
Bound now?" (they had an instinct, guessed what meant
Wanderings, labours, in the God's light mouth.)

"After the Thrakian Diomedes' car
With the four horses."

            "Ah, but canst thou that?
1095   Art inexperienced in thy host to be?"

1073| MS:death's gain—   *1871a*:death gain: 1076| MS:Clearly he had not joined the threnody. §entire line crossed out and replaced above by new line§ I think that Herakles, who held his life   1079| MS:i' the house—" they   *1871a*:house" they   *1872*:in
1083| MS:weak not bad   *1871a*:weak, not bad,   1084| MS:men—were   *1871a*:men: were
1085| MS:doors, Herakleis: *1889a*:doors, Herakles.   1088| MS:that I have to §last two words inserted above§ do my lord §last two words crossed out§   1091| MS:now?" They had experience, knew §last two words crossed out and replaced above by three words§ an inkling §crossed out and replaced above by§ instinct, guessed   *1871a*:now?" (they
1092| MS:mouth.   *1871a*:mouth.)   1093| MS:the Thracian   *1889a*:the Thrakian

"All-inexperienced: I have never gone
As yet to the land o' the Bistones."

        "Then, look

By no means to be master of the steeds
Without a battle!"
      "Battle there may be:
1100 I must refuse no labour, all the same."

"Certainly, either having slain a foe
Wilt thou return to us, or, slain thyself,
Stay there!"
    "And, even if the game be so,
The risk in it were not the first I run."

1105 "But, say thou overpower the lord o' the place,
What more advantage dost expect thereby?"

"I shall drive off his horses to the king."

"No easy handling them to bit the jaw!"

"Easy enough; except, at least, they breathe
1110 Fire from their nostrils!"
      "But they mince up men
With those quick jaws!"
     "You talk of provender
For mountain-beasts, and not mere horses' food!"

"Thou mayst behold their mangers caked with gore!"
"And of what sire does he who bred them boast

1102| MS:Will you return <> slain yourself, *1871a:*Wilt thou return <> slain thyself,
1103| MS:§¶§ "And even *1871a:*§¶§ "And, even 1104| MS:But say you over-power
1871a:"But, say thou over-power *1889a:*overpower 1106| MS:more do
you expect *1871a:*more advantage dost expect 1107| MS:king. Tirunthian—"
§last word and dash crossed out§ 1109| MS:enough—except at least they
*1871a:*enough; except, at least, they 1112| MS:food." *1871a:*food!"
1113| MS:"You may behold *1871a:*"Thou may'st behold *1889a:*mayst

¹¹¹⁵ Himself the son?"

                   "Of Ares, king o' the targe—

Thrakian, of gold throughout."

                            Another laugh.

"Why, just the labour, just the lot for me

Dost thou describe in what I recognize!

Since hard and harder, high and higher yet,

¹¹²⁰ Truly this lot of mine is like to go

If I must needs join battle with the brood

Of Ares: ay, I fought Lukaon first,

And again, Kuknos: now engage in strife

This third time, with such horses and such lord.

¹¹²⁵ But there is nobody shall ever see

Alkmené's son shrink foemen's hand before!"

—"Or ever hear him say" (the Chorus thought)

"That death is terrible; and help us so

To chime in—'terrible beyond a doubt,

¹¹³⁰ And, if to thee, why, to ourselves much more:

Know what has happened, then, and sympathise'!"

Therefore they gladly stopped the dialogue,

Shifted the burthen to new shoulder straight,

As, "Look where comes the lord o' the land, himself,

¹¹³⁵ Admetos, from the palace!" they outbroke

In some surprise, as well as much relief.

What had induced the king to waive his right

And luxury of roe in loneliness?

Out he came quietly; the hair was clipt,

---

¹¹¹⁶| MS:The Thracian, gold <> laugh—   *1871a:*Thracian, of gold <> laugh.
*1889a:*Thrakian   ¹¹²³| MS:again, Kuknos, and engage   *1871a:*again, Kuknos: now
engage   ¹¹²⁴| MS:and their §crossed out and replaced above by§ such
¹¹²⁶| MS:Alkmene's son shrink, foemen's   *1871a:*Alkmené's   *1889a:*shrink foemen's
¹¹²⁷| MS:say," the chorus thought   *1871a:*say (the <> thought)   *1889a:*the Chorus
¹¹²⁸| MS:terrible, and   *1871a:*terrible; and   ¹¹³⁰| MS:And if <> why to <> more—
*1871a:*And, if <> why, to <> more: ¹¹³¹| MS:Hear §crossed out and replaced above
by§ Know   ¹¹³³| MS:straight   *1871a:*straight,   ¹¹³⁴| MS:As "Look <> land
*1871a:*As, "Look <> land, himself   ¹¹³⁵| MS:out-broke—   *1871a:*out-broke
¹¹³⁶| MS:surprise as well <> relief: *1871a:*surprise, as well <> relief.
¹¹³⁷| MS:the man to   *1871a:*the king to   ¹¹³⁸⁻³⁹| MS:§no ¶§   *1889a:*§¶§

¹¹⁴⁰ And the garb sable; else no outward sign
Of sorrow as he came and faced his friend.
Was truth fast terrifying tears away?
"Hail, child of Zeus, and sprung from Perseus too!"
The salutation ran without a fault.

¹¹⁴⁵ "And thou, Admetos, King of Thessaly!"

"Would, as thou wishest me, the grace might fall!
But my good-wisher, that thou art, I know."

"What's here? these shorn locks, this sad show of thee?"

"I must inter a certain corpse to-day."

¹¹⁵⁰ "Now, from thy children God avert mischance!"

"They live, my children; all are in the house!"

"Thy father—if 'tis he departs indeed,
His age was ripe at least."

"My father lives,
And she who bore me lives too, Herakles."

¹¹⁵⁵ "It cannot be thy wife Alkestis gone?"

"Two-fold the tale is, I can tell of her."

"Dead dost thou speak of her, or living yet?"

"She is—and is not: hence the pain to me!"

---

^{1140|} MS:sable, else   *1871a:*sable; else   ^{1147|} MS:good-wisher that <> art I
*1871a:*good-wisher, that <> art, I   ^{1148|} MS:here—these   *1871a:*here? these
^{1150|} MS:"Now from   *1871a:* "Now, from   ^{1151|} MS:house."   *1871a:*house!"
^{1154|} MS:Herakleis."   *1871a:*Herakles."   ^{1156|} MS:is I   *1871a:*is, I
^{1157|} MS:thou say §crossed out and replaced above by§ speak of her or   *1871a:*her, or
^{1158|} MS:She is—and §crossed out and then marked for retention§ yet §crossed out§ is not,—

"I learn no whit the more, so dark thy speech!"

1160   "Know'st thou not on what fate she needs must fall?"

"I know she is resigned to die for thee."

"How lives she still, then, if submitting so?"

"Eh, weep her not beforehand! wait till then!"

"Who is to die is dead; doing is done."

1165   "To be and not to be are thought diverse."

"Thou judgest this—I, that way, Herakles!"

"Well, but declare what causes thy complaint!
Who is the man has died from out thy friends?"

"No man: I had a woman in my mind."

1170   "Alien, or someone born akin to thee?"

"Alien: but still related to my house."

"How did it happen then that here she died?"

"Her father dying left his orphan here."

---

and the grief is there §last five words crossed out and replaced above by five words and
punctuation§ hence the pain to me!   *1871a:* "She < > not: hence < > me!"
1163| MS:"Eh—weep < > beforehand—wait   *1871a:* "Eh, weep < > beforehand! wait
1165| MS:are judged §crossed out and replaced above by§ thought
1166| MS:"You judge §inserted above§ this way, I judge §crossed out§ that way, Herakleis!"
1871a: "Thou judgest this—I, that way, Herakles!"   1167| MS:complaint—
1871a: complaint!   1168| MS:friends?   *1871a:* friends?"   1168-69| MS:§between lines,
one word§ What §crossed out§   1169| MS:man—I   *1871a:* man: I
1172| MS:that she died here?" §last word marked for transposition to follow *that*§

"Alas, Admetos—would we found thee gay,
1175 Not grieving!"

"What as if about to do
Subjoinest thou that comment?"

"I shall seek
Another hearth, proceed to other hosts."

"Never, O king, shall that be! No such ill
Betide me!"

"Nay, to mourners should there come
1180 A guest, he proves importunate!"
"The dead—
Dead are they: but go thou within my house!"

"'Tis base carousing beside friends who mourn."

"The guest-rooms, whither we shall lead thee, lie
Apart from ours."
"Nay, let me go my way!
1185 Ten thousandfold the favour I shall thank!"

"It may not be thou goest to the hearth
Of any man but me!" so made an end
Admetos, softly and decisively,
Of the altercation. Herakles forbore:
1190 And the king bade a servant lead the way,
Open the guest-rooms ranged remote from view
O' the main hall; tell the functionaries, next,

1177| MS:hearth—proceed   *1871a*:hearth, proceed   1178| MS:"Never, O King, §last two
words inserted above§ <> be! no   *1871a*:be! No   1179| MS:mourners, should
1889a:mourners should   1181| MS:within the §crossed out and replaced above by§ my
1185| MS:Then §crossed out and replaced above by§ Ten thousand fold <> favor
1871a:tenthousandfold   *1889a*:favour   1187| MS:me!"—so   *1871a*:me!" so
1188| MS:decisively   *1871a*:decisively,   1189| MS:altercation: Herakles forbore,
1871a:altercation. Herakles forbore: 1192| MS:hall, tell the functionaries too
1871a:functionaries, too,   *1889a*:hall; tell the functionaries, next,

They had to furnish forth a plenteous feast,
And then shut close the doors o' the hall, midway,
1195   "Because it is not proper friends who feast
Should hear a groaning or be grieved," quoth he.

Whereat the hero, who was truth itself,
Let out the smile again, repressed awhile
Like fountain-brilliance one forbids to play.
1200   He did too many grandnesses, to note
Much in the meaner things about his path:
And stepping there, with face towards the sun,
Stopped seldom to pluck weeds or ask their names.
Therefore he took Admetos at the word:
1205   This trouble must not hinder any more
A true heart from good will and pleasant ways.
And so, the great arm, which had slain the snake,
Strained his friend's head a moment in embrace
On that broad breast beneath the lion's hide,
1210   Till the king's cheek winced at the thick rough gold;
And then strode off, with who had care of him,
To the remote guest-chamber: glad to give
Poor flesh and blood their respite and relief
In the interval 'twixt fight and fight again—
1215   All for the world's sake. Our eyes followed him,
Be sure, till those mid-doors shut us outside.

---

¹¹⁹³| *1871a:*feast: *1889a:*feast,   ¹¹⁹⁵| MS:friends that §crossed out and replaced above by§ who   ¹¹⁹⁶| MS:§following this line are cancelled versions of what became ll. 1217-18§ The while he §last three words crossed out and replaced above by three words§ The king too watched great Herakles go in, / All faith and trust, obedient to his friend
¹¹⁹⁷⁻¹²¹⁸| MS:§these lines composed on verso of leaf bearing ll. 1192-97 and 1219-39, with instructions to insert passage between ll. 1196 and 1219§   ¹¹⁹⁷| MS:hero who *1871a:*hero, who   ¹¹⁹⁸| MS:again repressed   *1871a:*again, repressed
¹²⁰¹| MS:path,   *1871a:*path: ¹²⁰²| MS:there with   *1871a:*there, with
¹²⁰³| MS:pluck flowers or <> names: *1871a:*pluck weeds or <> names.
¹²⁰⁴| MS:word—   *1871a:*word: ¹²⁰⁶| MS:from the goodwill and free ways,   *1871a:*from good will and pleasant ways.   ¹²⁰⁷| MS:so the <> arm that §crossed out and replaced above by§ which had grasped §crossed out and replaced above by§ slain the snake   *1871a:*so, the <> arm, which <> snake,   ¹²⁰⁹| MS:lion's-hide   *1871a:*lion's-hide,   *1889a:*lion's hide,
¹²¹⁰| MS:gold,   *1871a:*gold;   ¹²¹¹| MS:who preceded §crossed out and replaced above by three words§ had care of   ¹²¹²| MS:guest-chamber,—glad   *1871a:*guest-chamber: glad   ¹²¹⁴| MS:twixt   *1871a:*'twixt   ¹²¹⁶| MS:us away.   *1871a:*us outside.

The king, too, watched great Herakles go off
All faith, love, and obedience to a friend.

And when they questioned him, the simple ones,
1220 "What dost thou? Such calamity to face,
Lies full before thee—and thou art so bold
As play the host, Admetos? Hast thy wits?"
He replied calmly to each chiding tongue:
"But if from house and home I forced away
1225 A coming guest, wouldst thou have praised me more?
No, truly! since calamity were mine,
Nowise diminished; while I showed myself
Unhappy and inhospitable too:
So adding to my ills this other ill,
1230 That mine were styled a stranger-hating house.
Myself have ever found this man the best
Of entertainers when I went his way
To parched and thirsty Argos."
                                        "If so be—
Why didst thou hide what destiny was here,
1235 When one came that was kindly, as thou say'st?"

"He never would have willed to cross my door
Had he known aught of my calamities.
And probably to some of you I seem
Unwise enough in doing what I do;

---

¹²¹⁷| MS:king too watched   *1871a*:king, too, watched   ¹²¹⁸| MS:faith, trust, and
1871a:faith, love, and §followed by instruction to return to l. ¹²¹⁹§   ¹²²⁰| MS:thou?
Such misfortune is §last two words crossed out and replaced above by one word§ calamity
¹²²¹| MS:Lies there before   *1871a*:Lies full before   ¹²²³| MS:to the §crossed out and
replaced above by§ each chiding band §crossed out and replaced above by§ tongue:
¹²²⁶| MS:mine   *1871a*:more,   ¹²²⁷| MS:All soon §last two words crossed out and
replaced above by one word§ Nowise diminished, while   *1871a*:diminished; while
¹²²⁸| MS:too—   *1871a*:too: ¹²³⁰| MS:Mine should be styled the §crossed out and
replaced above by§ a   *1871a*:That mine were styled   ¹²³⁵| MS:When he who §last two
words crossed out and replaced above by one illegible word§ came that §inserted above§
1871a:When one came   ¹²³⁶| MS:to enter here §last two words crossed out§ cross my
door   ¹²³⁷| MS:calamities: *1871a*:calamities.   ¹²³⁸| MS:And probably §inserted
above§ to some people, I suppose I seem §last three words crossed out and replaced above by
two words§ perchance appear §last two words and preceding two words crossed out and
replaced above by four words§ of you I seem   ¹²³⁹| MS:do—   *1871a*:do;

¹²⁴⁰ Such will scarce praise me: but these halls of mine
Know not to drive off and dishonour guests."

And so, the duty done, he turned once more
To go and busy him about his dead.
As for the sympathisers left to muse,
¹²⁴⁵ There was a change, a new light thrown on things,
Contagion from the magnanimity
O' the man whose life lay on his hand so light,
As up he stepped, pursuing duty still
"Higher and harder," as he laughed and said.
¹²⁵⁰ Somehow they found no folly now in the act
They blamed erewhile: Admetos' private grief
Shrank to a somewhat pettier obstacle
I' the way o' the world: they saw good days had been,
And good days, peradventure, still might be,
¹²⁵⁵ Now that they overlooked the present cloud
Heavy upon the palace opposite.
And soon the thought took words and music thus.

"Harbour of many a stranger, free to friend,
Ever and always, O thou house o' the man
¹²⁶⁰ We mourn for! Thee, Apollon's very self,
The lyric Puthian, deigned inhabit once,
Become a shepherd here in thy domains,
And pipe, adown the winding hill-side paths,
Pastoral marriage-poems to thy flocks
¹²⁶⁵ At feed: while with them fed in fellowship,
Through joy i' the music, spot-skin lynxes; ay,

---

^{1240|} MS:will not §crossed out and replaced above by§ scarce   ^{1244|} MS:As §over
illegible erasure§ <> left outside §crossed out§   ^{1247|} MS:light   *1871a*:light,
^{1248|}   *1881*:And up   *1889a*:As up   ^{1252|} MS:pettier circumstance, §crossed out and
replaced above by§ obstacle,   *1871a*:obstacle   ^{1254|} MS:be   *1871a*:be;   *1889a*:be,
^{1255|} MS:over-looked   *1889a*:overlooked   ^{1256|} MS:opposite,   *1871a*:opposite.
^{1257|} MS:thus—   *1871a*:thus.   ^{1258|} MS:friend   *1871a*:friend,   ^{1260|} MS:for!
Thee Apollon's <> self   *1871a*:for! Thee, Apollon's <> self,   ^{1261|} MS:The §added in
margin§ Lyrical §altered to§ lyric Pythian   *1871a*:lyric Puthian   ^{1263|} MS:pipe adown
<> hill-side ways   *1871a*:pipe, adown <> hill-side paths,   ^{1265|} MS:feed, while
1871a:feed: while   ^{1266|} MS:in §altered to§ i' <> lynxes, ay—   *1871a*:lynxes; ay,

And lions too, the bloody company,
Came, leaving Othrus' dell; and round thy lyre,
Phoibos, there danced the speckle-coated fawn,
1270   Pacing on lightsome fetlock past the pines
Tress-topped, the creature's natural boundary,
Into the open everywhere; such heart
Had she within her, beating joyous beats,
At the sweet reassurance of thy song!
1275   Therefore the lot o' the master is, to live
In a home multitudinous with herds,
Along by the fair-flowing Boibian lake,
Limited, that ploughed land and pasture-plain,
Only where stand the sun's steeds, stabled west
1280   I' the cloud, by that mid-air which makes the clime
Of those Molossoi: and he rules as well
O'er the Aigaian, up to Pelion's shore,—
Sea-stretch without a port! Such lord have we:
And here he opens house now, as of old,
1285   Takes to the heart of it a guest again:
Though moist the eyelid of the master, still
Mourning his dear wife's body, dead but now!"

And they admired: nobility of soul
Was self-impelled to reverence, they saw:
1290   The best men ever prove the wisest too:
Something instinctive guides them still aright.

1268| MS:lyre   *1871a:*lyre,   1270| MS:Stepping §crossed out and replaced above by§
Pacing   1272| MS:everywhere, such   *1871a:*everywhere; such   1273| MS:Beat
joyously within §last three words crossed out and replaced above by five words§ Had she
within her beating joyously   *1871a:*her, beating joyous beats,   1275| MS:is to   *1871a:*is,
to   1279| MS:stabled there §crossed out and replaced above by§ west
1283| MS:That stretch   *1871a:*Sea-stretch   1284| MS:now as   *1871a:*now, as
1285| MS:again,   *1871a:*again: 1287| MS:Mourning the §crossed out and replaced above
by§ his <> now!   *1871a:*now!"   1288| MS:admired how nobleness §colon inserted; last
two words crossed out and replaced above by one word§ nobility   1289| MS:Was ever
§crossed out§ self-impelled to reverence,—they   *1871a:*reverence, they
1290| MS:How §crossed out§ the §altered to§ The <> ever §inserted above§ prove still
§crossed out§ the <> too,—   *1871a:*too: 1291| MS:them the §crossed out and replaced
above by§ still right §altered to§ aright way. §crossed out, retaining punctuation§

And on each soul this boldness settled now,
That one, who reverenced the Gods so much,
Would prosper yet: (or—I could wish it ran—
1295   Who venerates the Gods, i' the main will still
Practise things honest though obscure to judge).

They ended, for Admetos entered now;
Having disposed all duteously indoors,
He came into the outside world again,
1300   Quiet as ever: but a quietude
Bent on pursuing its descent to truth,
As who must grope until he gain the ground
O' the dungeon doomed to be his dwelling now.
Already high o'er head was piled the dusk,
1305   When something pushed to stay his downward step,
Pluck back despair just reaching its repose.
He would have bidden the kind presence there
Observe that,—since the corpse was coming out,
Cared for in all things that befit the case,
1310   Carried aloft, in decency and state,
To the last burial place and burning pile,—

---

¹²⁹²| MS:this confidence sat §last two words crossed out and replaced above by two words§
boldness settled now   *1871a*:now,   ¹²⁹³| MS:The man who <> gods so much
1871a:That one, who <> Gods so much,   ¹²⁹⁴| MS:yet—(or   *1871a*:yet: (or
¹²⁹⁵| MS:gods i' the main, will   *1871a*:the Gods   *1889a*:the Gods, i' the main will
¹²⁹⁶| MS:judge.)   *1889a*:judge).   ¹²⁹⁶⁻⁹⁷| MS:§¶§   *1889a*:§¶ lost in paging. Emended to
restore ¶; see Editorial Notes§   ¹²⁹⁸| MS:all duly in the house, §last four words crossed out
and replaced above by two words§ duteously indoors,   ¹²⁹⁹| MS:came §inserted above§
¹³⁰⁰| MS:but in quietude   *1871a*:but a quietude   ¹³⁰¹| MS:He was §last two words
crossed out and replaced above by two words§ Bent on pursuing his §crossed out and
replaced above by§ the descent   *1871a*:pursuing its descent   ¹³⁰²| MS:gained
1871a:gain   ¹³⁰³| MS:dwelling place: §crossed out and replaced above by§ now.
¹³⁰⁴| MS:high above §crossed out and replaced above by two words§ o'er head <> dark,
§altered to§ dusk,   ¹³⁰⁵| MS:something interposed §crossed out and replaced above by§
pushed <> downward §inserted above§   ¹³⁰⁶| MS:its repose. §crossed out and then
marked for retention§ §word illegibly crossed out, perhaps *constant*.§   ¹³⁰⁷| MS:He came
to §last two words crossed out and replaced above by two words§ would have bid §altered to§
bidden the kindly §altered to§ kind   ¹³⁰⁸| MS:that, now §crossed out and replaced
above by punctuation and word§ —since <> coming forth, §crossed out and replaced above
by§ out,   ¹³⁰⁹| MS:befit a Queen, §last two words crossed out and replaced above by two
words§ the case,   ¹³¹⁰| MS:And borne §last two words crossed out and replaced above by
one word§ Carried   ¹³¹¹| MS:the last §last two words inserted above§

'Twere proper friends addressed, as custom prompts,
Alkestis bound on her last journeying.

"Ay, for we see thy father" they subjoined
1315   "Advancing as the aged foot best may;
His servants, too: each bringing in his hand
Adornments for thy wife, all pomp that's due
To the downward-dwelling people." And in truth,
By slow procession till they filled the stage,
1320   Came Pheres, and his following, and their gifts.
You see, the worst of the interruption was,
It plucked back, with an over-hasty hand,
Admetos from descending to the truth,
(I told you)—put him on the brink again,
1325   Full i' the noise and glare where late he stood:
With no fate fallen and irrevocable,
But all things subject still to chance and change:
And that chance—life, and that change—happiness.
And with the low strife came the little mind:
1330   He was once more the man might gain so much,
Life too and wife too, would his friends but help!
All he felt now was that there faced him one
Supposed the likeliest, in emergency,
To help: and help, by mere self-sacrifice
1335   So natural, it seemed as if the sire
Must needs lie open still to argument,

1312| MS:journeying—   *1871a*:journeying.   1315| MS:may,—   *1871a*:may;
1316| MS:too—each   *1871a*:too: each   1317| MS:wife, all §crossed out and replaced
above by§ nor §crossed out; *all* marked for retention§ they §crossed out§ pomp
1320| MS:Came Pheres and his following and   *1871a*:Came Pheres, and his following, and
1321| MS:was   *1871a*:was,   1322| MS:back with < > hand   *1871a*:back, with < > hand,
1323| MS:truth—   *1871a*:truth,   1324| MS:I told you,—put   *1871a*:(I told you)—put
1325| MS:stood,   *1871a*:stood: 1327| MS:change—   *1871a*:change:
1328| MS:chance,—life < > change,—happiness.   *1889a*:chance—life < > change—happiness.
1329| MS:mind—   *1871a*:mind: 1332| MS:was—that §inserted above§ there stood
§crossed out and replaced above by§ faced   *1871a*:was, that   *1889a*:was that
1333| MS:likliest in emergency   *1871a*:likliest, in emergency,   1334| MS:help,
that §crossed out and replaced above by§ and §*that* marked for retention§
way by §last two words crossed out and replaced above by one word§ by §crossed out;
first *by* marked for retention§ mere self-sacrifice. §punctutation partially erased§
1871a:help: and help, by < > self-sacrifice   1335| MS:the man   *1871a*:the sire

Withdraw the rash decision, not to die
But rather live, though death would save his son:—
Argument like the ignominious grasp
1340   O' the drowner whom his fellow grasps as fierce,
Each marvelling that the other needs must hold
Head out of water, though friend choke thereby.

And first the father's salutation fell.
Burthened, he came, in common with his child,
1345   Who lost, none would gainsay, a good chaste spouse:
Yet such things must be borne, though hard to bear.
"So, take this tribute of adornment, deep
In the earth let it descend along with her!
Behoves we treat the body with respect
1350   —Of one who died, at least, to save thy life,
Kept me from being childless, nor allowed
That I, bereft of thee, should peak and pine
In melancholy age! she, for the sex,
All of her sisters, put in evidence,
1355   By daring such a feat, that female life
Might prove more excellent than men suppose.
O thou Alkestis!" out he burst in fine,
"Who, while thou savedst this my son, didst raise
Also myself from sinking,—hail to thee!
1360   Well be it with thee even in the house
Of Hades! I maintain, if mortals must
Marry, this sort of marriage is the sole
Permitted those among them who are wise!"

So his oration ended. Like hates like:
1365   Accordingly Admetos,—full i' the face

---

¹³³⁷| MS:decision not   *1871a:*decision, not   ¹³³⁸| MS:live though   *1871a:*live, though
¹³⁴²| MS:water though   *1871a:*water, though   ¹³⁴⁴| MS:he came, §last two words and
punctuation inserted above§ <> child   *1871a:*child,   ¹³⁴⁷| MS:"So take   *1871a:*"So,
take   ¹³⁴⁸| MS:with thee!   *1871a:*with her!   ¹³⁵²| MS:That I bereft of thee should
*1871a:*That I, bereft of thee, should   ¹³⁵³| MS:age; but for   *1871a:*age; she, for
*1881:*age! she   ¹³⁵⁴| MS:evidence   *1871a:*evidence,   ¹³⁵⁷| MS:fine   *1871a:*fine,
¹³⁵⁸| MS:"Who while <> saved'st   *1871a:*"Who, while <> savedst   ¹³⁶⁰| MS:the House
*1871a:*house   ¹³⁶¹| MS:maintain, such marriages §last two words crossed out§ if

Of Pheres, his true father, outward shape
And inward fashion, body matching soul,—
Saw just himself when years should do their work
And reinforce the selfishness inside
1370   Until it pushed the last disguise away:
As when the liquid metal cools i' the mould,
Stands forth a statue: bloodless, hard, cold bronze.
So, in old Pheres, young Admetos showed,
Pushed to completion: and a shudder ran,
1375   And his repugnance soon had vent in speech:
Glad to escape outside, nor, pent within,
Find itself there fit food for exercise.

"Neither to this interment called by me
Comest thou, nor thy presence I account
1380   Among the covetable proofs of love.
As for thy tribute of adornment,—no!
Ne'er shall she don it, ne'er in debt to thee
Be buried! What is thine, that keep thou still!
Then it behoved thee to commiserate
1385   When I was perishing: but thou—who stood'st
Foot-free o' the snare, wast acquiescent then
That I, the young, should die, not thou, the old—
Wilt thou lament this corpse thyself hast slain?
Thou wast not, then, true father to this flesh;
1390   Nor she, who makes profession of my birth
And styles herself my mother, neither she
Bore me: but, come of slave's blood, I was cast

1372| MS:forth the §crossed out and replaced above by§ a statue, bloodless hard cold bronze. *1871a:*statue: bloodless, hard, cold bronze.   1373| MS:So in old Pheres young Admetos stood §crossed out§ showed,   *1871a:*So, in old Pheres, young   1375| MS:soon found §crossed out and replaced above by§ had   1376| MS:Better escape outside than, pent *1871a:*Glad to escape outside, nor, pent   1377-78| MS: §leaf ends§ *1871a:*§no ¶§ *1889a:*§¶§   1382| MS:it—ne'er *1871a:*it, ne'er   1385| MS:who §inserted above§ stand'st §altered to§ stood'st   1386| MS:snare, and acquiescent *1871a:*snare, wast acquiescent   1387| MS:That I the young should <> thou the *1871a:*That I, the young, should <> thou, the   1389| MS:father of §crossed out and replaced above by§ to this flesh, *1871a:*flesh;   1390| MS:profession to have borne §last three words crossed out and replaced above by three words§ of my birth   1391| MS:mother,—neither *1871a:*mother, neither   1392| MS:me, but *1871a:*me: but

Stealthily 'neath the bosom of thy wife!
Thou showedst, put to touch, the thing thou art,
1395 Nor I esteem myself born child of thee!
Otherwise, thine is the preëminence
O'er all the world in cowardice of soul:
Who, being the old man thou art, arrived
Where life should end, didst neither will nor dare
1400 Die for thy son, but left the task to her,
The alien woman, whom I well might think
Own, only mother both and father too!
And yet a fair strife had been thine to strive,
—Dying for thy own child; and brief for thee
1405 In any case, the rest of time to live;
While I had lived, and she, our rest of time,
Nor I been left to groan in solitude.
Yet certainly all things which happy man
Ought to experience, thy experience grasped.
1410 Thou wast a ruler through the bloom of youth,
And I was son to thee, recipient due
Of sceptre and demesne,—no need to fear
That dying thou shouldst leave an orphan house
For strangers to despoil. Nor yet wilt thou
1415 Allege that as dishonouring, forsooth,
Thy length of days, I gave thee up to die,—
I, who have held thee in such reverence!
And in exchange for it, such gratitude

1397| MS:all §inserted above§ the whole §crossed out§ world <> soul. *1871a*:soul:
1399| MS:end, yet neither willed nor dared *1871a*:end, didst neither will nor dare
1400| MS:her *1871a*:her, 1404| MS:thine §altered to§ thy 1405| MS:live,
1871a:live; 1407| MS:Nor been *1871a*:Nor I been 1408| MS:Yet §added in margin§ Certainly §altered to§ certainly <> which the §crossed out§ happy
1409| MS:thy experience knew §crossed out§ grasped. 1410| MS:ruler in §crossed out and replaced above by§ through 1411| MS:was son to thee §last four words crossed out and replaced above by three words illegibly crossed out; original reading marked for retention§ 1412| MS:need at all §last two words crossed out§ to fear
1413| MS:*1871a*:should'st have an *1889a*:shouldst leave an 1415| MS:Allege, at least, §last two words and punctuation crossed out§ 1416| MS:the thus §crossed out and replaced above by§ up 1417| MS:I,— §dash cancelled§ <> reverence!
1889a:reverence §emended to§ reverence! §see Editorial Notes§ 1418| MS:for this, such your §last three words crossed out and replaced above by two words§ it, such

Thou, father,—thou award'st me, mother mine!
1420 Go, lose no time, then, in begetting sons
Shall cherish thee in age, and, when thou diest,
Deck up and lay thee out as corpses claim!
For never I, at least, with this my hand
Will bury thee: it is myself am dead
1425 So far as lies in thee. But if I light
Upon another saviour, and still see
The sunbeam,—his, the child I call myself,
His, the old age that claims my cherishing.
How vainly do these aged pray for death,
1430 Abuse the slow drag of senility!
But should death step up, nobody inclines
To die, nor age is now the weight it was!"

You see what all this poor pretentious talk
Tried at,—how weakness strove to hide itself
1435 In bluster against weakness,—the loud word
To hide the little whisper, not so low
Already in that heart beneath those lips!
Ha, could it be, who hated cowardice
Stood confessed craven, and who lauded so
1440 Self-immolating love, himself had pushed
The loved one to the altar in his place?
Friends interposed, would fain stop further play
O' the sharp-edged tongue: they felt love's champion here
Had left an undefended point or two,
1445 The antagonist might profit by; bade "Pause!
Enough the present sorrow! Nor, O son,
Whet thus against thyself thy father's soul!"

1419| MS:Thus §crossed out§ you §altered to§ You, father,—you §last two words inserted
above§ award me, father, §crossed out§ mother   *1871a:*Thou, father,—thou award'st me
1421| MS:cherish you §crossed out and replaced above by§ thee <> when you   §crossed out
and replaced above by§ thou   1422| MS:lay you §crossed out and replaced above by§
thee   1426| MS:saviour and   *1871a:*saviour, and   1427| MS:The day-beam,—
§altered to§ sunbeam,—his the   *1871a:*his, the   1428| MS:His the   *1871a:*His, the
1430| MS:Abusing §altered to§ Abuse <> dragged §altered to§ drag of §inserted above§
1432-33| *1871a:*§¶ lost in paging§   *1889a:*§¶ restored§   1438| MS:be—who   *1871a:*be, who

66

Ay, but old Pheres was the stouter stuff!
Admetos, at the flintiest of the heart,
1450 Had so much soft in him as held a fire:
The other was all iron, clashed from flint
Its fire, but shed no spark and showed no bruise.
Did Pheres crave instruction as to facts?
He came, content, the ignoble word, for him,
1455 Should lurk still in the blackness of each breast,
As sleeps the water-serpent half surmised:
Not brought up to the surface at a bound,
By one touch of the idly-probing spear,
Reed-like against unconquerable scale.
1460 He came pacific, rather, as strength should,
Bringing the decent praise, the due regret,
And each banality prescribed of old.
Did he commence "Why let her die for you?"
And rouse the coiled and quiet ugliness
1465 "What is so good to man as man's own life?"
No: but the other did: and, for his pains,
Out, full in face of him, the venom leapt.

"And whom dost thou make bold, son—Ludian slave,
Or Phrugian whether, money made thy ware,
1470 To drive at with revilings? Know'st thou not
I, a Thessalian, from Thessalian sire
Spring and am born legitimately free?

1449| MS:Admetos at <> heart   *1871a*:Admetos, at <> heart,   1454| MS:content the
1871a:content, the   1455| MS:breast   *1871a*:breast,   1456| MS:water serpent half-
surmised—   *1871a*:water-serpent half surmised: 1457| MS:at one §crossed out and
replaced above by§ a bound   *1871a*:bound,   1459| MS:against the invulnerable §crossed
out and replaced above by§ unconquerable   *1872*:against unconquerable
1460| MS:should—   *1871a*:should,   1462| MS:prescribed as man §last two words crossed
out§ of   1464| MS:And §crossed out and replaced above by§ So rouse   *1871a*:And rouse
1465| MS:to one §crossed out and replaced above by§ man as one's §crossed out and replaced
above by§ man's   1466| MS:and for his pains   *1871a*:and, for his pains,
1467| MS:§first word illegibly crossed out and replaced above by§ Out, full in his §crossed out§
face of him, §last two words inserted above§ the venom flung.   *1871a*:venom leapt.
1468| MS:son—Lydian slave   *1871a*:son—Ludian slave,   1469| MS:Or Phrygian
1871a:Or Phrugian   1471| MS:I a Thessalian from   *1871a*:I, a Thessalian, from

Too arrogant art thou; and, youngster words
Casting against me, having had thy fling,
1475 Thou goest not off as all were ended so!
I gave thee birth indeed and mastership
I' the mansion, brought thee up to boot: there ends
My owing, nor extends to die for thee!
Never did I receive it as a law
1480 Hereditary, no, nor Greek at all,
That sires in place of sons were bound to die.
For, to thy sole and single self wast thou
Born, with whatever fortune, good or bad;
Such things as bear bestowment, those thou hast;
1485 Already ruling widely, broad-lands, too,
Doubt not but I shall leave thee in due time:
For why? My father left me them before.
Well then, where wrong I thee?—of what defraud?
Neither do thou die for this man, myself,
1490 Nor let him die for thee!—is all I beg.
Thou joyest seeing daylight: dost suppose
Thy father joys not too? Undoubtedly,
Long I account the time to pass below,
And brief my span of days; yet sweet the same:
1495 Is it otherwise to thee who, impudent,
Didst fight off this same death, and livest now
Through having sneaked past fate apportioned thee,
And slain thy wife so? Cryest cowardice
On me, I wonder, thou—whom, poor poltroon,
1500 A very woman worsted, daring death

1473| MS:thou; and, youngster-words   *1889a*:thou, and, youngster words
1478| MS:owing nor   *1871a*:owing, nor   1480| MS:Hereditary, nor, nor
1871a:Hereditary, no, nor   1481| MS:in place of sons §last four words inserted above§
1482| MS:For to   *1871a*:For, to   1484| MS:Such §added in margin§ All §crossed out§
things that §crossed out and replaced above by§ as < > hast—   *1871a*:hast;
1485| MS:broadlands too   *1871a*:broad-lands, too,   1486| MS:time   *1871a*:time:
1488| MS:wrong I thee? §last two words and punctuation inserted above§
1492| MS:too?   Assuredly §crossed out§ Undoubtedly   *1871a*:too? Undoubtedly,
1494| MS:days, yet   *1871a*:days; yet   1495| MS:who impudent   *1871a*:who, impudent,
1499| MS:thou—the poor poltroon   *1889a*:thou—whom, poor poltroon,

Just for the sake of thee, her handsome spark?
Shrewdly hast thou contrived how not to die
For evermore now: 'tis but still persuade
The wife, for the time being, to take thy place!
1505 What, and thy friends who would not do the like,
These dost thou carp at, craven thus thyself?
Crouch and be silent, craven! Comprehend
That, if thou lovest so that life of thine,
Why, everybody loves his own life too:
1510 So, good words, henceforth! If thou speak us ill,
Many and true an ill thing shalt thou hear!"

There you saw leap the hydra at full length!
Only, the old kept glorying the more,
The more the portent thus uncoiled itself,
1515 Whereas the young man shuddered head to foot,
And shrank from kinship with the creature. Why
Such horror, unless what he hated most,
Vaunting itself outside, might fairly claim
Acquaintance with the counterpart at home?
1520 I would the Chorus here had plucked up heart,
Spoken out boldly and explained the man,
If not to men, to Gods. That way, I think,
Sophokles would have led their dance and song.
Here, they said simply "Too much evil spoke
1525 On both sides!" As the young before, so now
They bade the old man leave abusing thus.

"Let him speak,—I have spoken!" said the youth:
And so died out the wrangle by degrees

1501| MS:thee her *1871a*:thee, her   1502| MS:Cleverly §crossed out and replaced above by§ Shrewdly <> thou found out §last two words crossed out and replaced above by one word§ contrived how not §inserted above§   1504| MS:wife for <> being—die for §last two words crossed out§ take *1889a*:wife, for <> being, to take
1505| MS:like *1889a*:like,   1508| MS:That if *1871a*:That, if   1510| MS:ill *1871a*:ill,   1513| MS:old man kept <> more *1871a*:old kept <> more,
1517| MS:horror unless *1871a*:horror, unless   1518| MS:fairly §inserted above§ claim perchance §crossed out§   1519| MS:home. *1871a*:home: *1889a*:home?
1521| MS:man *1889a*:man,   1524| MS:spoke! *1871a*:spoke   1528| MS:wrangling §altered to§ wrangle by degrees. *1871a*:degrees, *1889a*:degrees

In wretched bickering. "If thou wince at fact,
1530 Behoved thee not prove faulty to myself!"

"Had I died for thee I had faulted more!"

"All's one, then, for youth's bloom and age to die?"

"Our duty is to live one life, not two!"

"Go then, and outlive Zeus, for aught I care!"

1535 "What, curse thy parents with no sort of cause?"

"Curse, truly! All thou lovest is long life!"

"And dost not thou, too, all for love of life,
Carry out now, in place of thine, this corpse?"

"Monument, rather, of thy cowardice,
1540 Thou worst one!"
      "Not for me she died, I hope!
That, thou wilt hardly say!"
        "No, simply this:
Would, some day, thou mayst come to need myself!"

"Meanwhile, woo many wives—the more will die!"

"And so shame thee who never dared the like!"

1529| MS:Some wretched bickering—"if *1871a:*In wretched bickering. "If
1532| MS:then for *1871a:*then, for 1534| MS:Go, then §inserted above§ and out
§inserted above§ live longer than §last two words crossed out§ Zeus self, for me!" §last three
words crossed out and replaced above by four words§ for aught I care!" *1871a:*Go then < >
Zeus, for 1535| MS:parents without §altered to§ with 1537| MS:"Well, and dost
thou not, all *1871a:* "And dost thou not, too, all 1538| MS:now, this corpse? in place of
thine, §last four words and punctuation marked for transposition to follow *now,*§
*1871a:*corpse?" 1540| MS:one!" §¶§ "It was not for my sake she *1871a:*one!" §¶§ "Not
for me she 1541| MS:say!" §¶§ "No—simply *1871a:*say!" §¶§ "No, simply
1542| *1871a:*may'st *1889a:*mayst 1544| MS:so §inserted above§

1545   "Dear is this light o' the sun-god—dear, I say!"

"Proper conclusion for a beast to draw!"

"One thing is certain: there's no laughing now,
As out thou bearest the poor dead old man!"

"Die when thou wilt, thou wilt die infamous!"

1550   "And once dead, whether famed or infamous,
I shall not care!"
            "Alas and yet again!
How full is age of impudency!"
                      "True!
Thou couldst not call thy young wife impudent:
She was found foolish merely."
                     "Get thee gone!
1555   And let me bury this my dead!"
                      "I go.
Thou buriest her whom thou didst murder first;
Whereof there's some account to render yet
Those kinsfolk by the marriage-side! I think,
Brother Akastos may be classed with me,
1560   Among the beasts, not men, if he omit
Avenging upon thee his sister's blood!"

"Go to perdition, with thy housemate too!
Grow old all childlessly, with child alive,
Just as ye merit! for to me, at least,

1547| MS:laughing here §crossed out§ now   *1871a:*now,   1549| MS:thou shalt §crossed out and replaced above by§ wilt   1550| MS:whether famed or §last two words inserted above§ infamous or §crossed out§   *1871a:*infamous,   1551| MS:and welladay! §crossed out and replaced above by two words§ yet again!   1552| MS:impudency!" "True— *1871a:*impudency!" "True!   1556| MS:first,   *1871a:*first;   1558| MS:One's kinsfolk <> think   *1871a:*Those kindfolk <> think,   1559| MS:me   *1871a:*me,   1560| MS:beasts not men if   *1871a:*beasts, not men,   1561| MS:Avenging on thee this his *1871a:*Avenging upon thee his   1562| MS:perdition with   *1871a:*perdition, with   1563| MS:childlessly with <> alive   *1871a:*childlessly, with <> alive,   1564| MS:merit: for never §crossed out and replaced above by two words§ to me   *1871a:*merit! for

¹⁵⁶⁵ Beneath the same roof ne'er do ye return.
And did I need by heralds' help renounce
The ancestral hearth, I had renounced the same!
But we—since this woe, lying at our feet
I' the path, is to be borne—let us proceed
¹⁵⁷⁰ And lay the body on the pyre."
                                    I think,
What, thro' this wretched wrangle, kept the man
From seeing clear—beside the cause I gave—
Was, that the woe, himself described as full
I' the path before him, there did really lie—
¹⁵⁷⁵ Not roll into the abyss of dead and gone.
How, with Alkestis present, calmly crowned,
Was she so irrecoverable yet—
The bird, escaped, that's just on bough above,
The flower, let flutter half-way down the brink?
¹⁵⁸⁰ Not so detached seemed lifelessness from life
But—one dear stretch beyond all straining yet—
And he might have her at his heart once more,
When, in the critical minute, up there comes
The father and the fact, to trifle time!

¹⁵⁸⁵ "To the pyre!" an instinct prompted: pallid face,
And passive arm and pointed foot, when these
No longer shall absorb the sight, O friends,
Admetos will begin to see indeed
Who the true foe was, where the blows should fall!

---

^{1565|} MS:return: *1871a:*return.   ^{1573|} MS:Was that <> as there   *1871a:*Was, that <>
as full   ^{1574|} MS:before his foot, did   *1871a:*before him, there did   ^{1576|} MS:How
with <> present calmless §altered to§ calmly crowned   *1871a:*How, with <> present, calmly
crowned,   ^{1577|} MS:yet?   *1889a:*yet—   ^{1578|} MS:just §inserted above§ on the
§crossed out§ bough   ^{1579|} MS:let fall, that's §last two words crossed out and replaced above
by one word§ flutter half way <> brink,   *1871a:*half-way <> brink!   *1889a:*brink?
^{1580|} MS:Just so was §last three words crossed out and replaced above by four words§ Not so
§above word illegibly crossed out§ detached seemed lifelessness detached §crossed out§ from
life,   *1871a:*life   ^{1582|} MS:more.   *1889a:*more,   ^{1583|} MS:But in <> minute up
*1871a:*But, in <> minute, up   *1889a:*When, in   ^{1584|} MS:fact to   *1871a:*fact, to
^{1584-85|} MS:§no ¶§   *1889a:*§¶§   ^{1586|} MS:foot, O friends,   *1871a:*friends—
*1889a:*foot, when these   ^{1587|} MS:When these no <> sight,
*1889a:*No <> sight, O friends   ^{1589|} MS:fall.   *1871a:*fall!

1590 So, the old selfish Pheres went his way,
Case-hardened as he came; and left the youth,
(Only half-selfish now, since sensitive)
To go on learning by a light the more,
As friends moved off, renewing dirge the while:

1595 "Unhappy in thy daring! Noble dame,
Best of the good, farewell! With favouring face
May Hermes the infernal, Hades too,
Receive thee! And if there,—ay, there,—some touch
Of further dignity await the good,
1600 Sharing with them, mayst thou sit throned by her
The Bride of Hades, in companionship!"

Wherewith, the sad procession wound away,
Made slowly for the suburb sepulchre.
And lo,—while still one's heart, in time and tune,
1605 Paced after that symmetric step of Death
Mute-marching, to the mind's eye, at the head
O' the mourners—one hand pointing out their path
With the long pale terrific sword we saw,
The other leading, with grim tender grace,
1610 Alkestis quieted and consecrate,—
Lo, life again knocked laughing at the door!
The world goes on, goes ever, in and through,
And out again o' the cloud. We faced about,
Fronted the palace where the mid-hall-gate
1615 Opened—not half, nor half of half, perhaps—
Yet wide enough to let out light and life,
And warmth and bounty and hope and joy, at once.

1590| MS:So the *1871a:*So, the   1591| MS:came, and *1871a:*came; and
1592| MS:Only half selfish <> sensitive, *1871a:*(Only <> sensitive) *1889a:*half-selfish
1594| MS:while— *1871a:*while: 1594-95| MS:§no ¶§ *1871a:*§¶§   1595| MS:daring!
Noble Dame, *1871a:*dame,   1600| MS:them mayst *1871a:*them, may'st *1889a:*mayst
1601| MS:of Hades in *1871a:*of Hades, in   1602| MS:away— *1871a:*away,
1604| MS:heart, kept §crossed out and replaced above by§ in   1609| MS:other, leading
with *1871a:*other leading, with   1612| MS:through *1871a:*through,
1614| MS:mid-hall-door *1889a:*mid-hall-gate   1615| MS:perhaps, *1871a:*perhaps—
1617| MS:warmth, and bounty, and hope, and *1889a:*warmth and bounty and hope and

Festivity burst wide, fruit rare and ripe
Crushed in the mouth of Bacchos, pulpy-prime,
¹⁶²⁰ All juice and flavour, save one single seed
Duly ejected from the God's nice lip,
Which lay o' the red edge, blackly visible—
To wit, a certain ancient servitor:
On whom the festal jaws o' the palace shut,
¹⁶²⁵ So, there he stood, a much-bewildered man.
Stupid? Nay, but sagacious in a sort:
Learned, life long, i' the first outside of things,
Though bat for blindness to what lies beneath
And needs a nail-scratch ere 'tis laid you bare.
¹⁶³⁰ This functionary was the trusted one
We saw deputed by Admetos late
To lead in Herakles and help him, soul
And body, to such snatched repose, snapped-up
Sustainment, as might do away the dust
¹⁶³⁵ O' the last encounter, knit each nerve anew
For that next onset sure to come at cry
O' the creature next assailed,—nay, should it prove
Only the creature that came forward now
To play the critic upon Herakles!

¹⁶⁴⁰ "Many the guests"—so he soliloquized
In musings burdensome to breast before,
When it seemed not too prudent tongue should wag—
"Many, and from all quarters of this world,
The guests I now have known frequent our house,

---

^{1618|} MS:burst down §crossed out and replaced above by§ wide, the rare   *1871a:*wide, fruit rare
^{1619|} MS:Fruit i' the < > pulpy-prime   *1871a:*Crushed in the < > pulpy-prime,
^{1620|} MS:and odour, save < > seed,   *1871a:*and flavour, save < > seed   ^{1623|}   MS:To wit,
§last two words added in margin§ A §altered to§ a < > servitor, to wit, §last two words crossed
out§   *1871a:*servitor: ^{1625|}   MS:So there < > man—   *1871a:*So, there < > man.
^{1627|} MS:things   *1871a:*things,   ^{1629|}   MS:And §added in margin§ Needs §altered to§
needs but §crossed out§ a nail-scratch to be §last two words crossed out and replaced above by
two words§ ere 'tis   ^{1632|}   MS:in Herakles refresh §crossed out and replaced above by two
words§ and help   ^{1635|}   MS:last warfare and §last two words crossed out and replaced
above by one word and punctuation§ encounter, knit   ^{1637|}   MS:nay, though it proved
*1871a:*nay, should it prove   ^{1642|}   MS:too wise that tongue   *1871a:*too prudent, tongue
*1889a:*prudent tongue   ^{1643|}   MS:"Many and   *1871a:* "Many, and

1645   For whom I spread the banquet; but than this,
     Never a worse one did I yet receive
     At the hearth here! One who seeing, first of all,
     The master's sorrow, entered gate the same,
     And had the hardihood to house himself.
1650   Did things stop there! But, modest by no means,
     He took what entertainment lay to hand,
     Knowing of our misfortune,—did we fail
     In aught of the fit service, urged us serve
     Just as a guest expects! And in his hands
1655   Taking the ivied goblet, drinks and drinks
     The unmixed product of black mother-earth,
     Until the blaze o' the wine went round about
     And warmed him: then he crowns with myrtle sprigs
     His head, and howls discordance—twofold lay
1660   Was thereupon for us to listen to—
     This fellow singing, namely, nor restrained
     A jot by sympathy with sorrows here—
     While we o' the household mourned our mistress—mourned,
     That is to say, in silence—never showed
1665   The eyes, which we kept wetting, to the guest—
     For there Admetos was imperative.
     And so, here am I helping make at home
     A guest, some fellow ripe for wickedness,
     Robber or pirate, while she goes her way
1670   Out of our house: and neither was it mine
     To follow in procession, nor stretch forth
     Hand, wave my lady dear a last farewell,
     Lamenting who to me and all of us
     Domestics was a mother: myriad harms

1645| MS:this   *1871a*:this,   1650| MS:Had all §crossed out and replaced above by§ things
stopped   *1871a*:Did things stop   1654| MS:With §crossed out and replaced above by§
Just   1656| MS:unmixed juice §crossed out and replaced above by§ product < > mother-
earth   *1871a*:mother-earth,   1659| MS:head and < > two-fold   *1871a*:head, and
1881:twofold   1660| MS:upon §inserted above§   1663| MS:mistress—mourned
1871a:mistress—mourned,   1669| MS:or thief §crossed out and replaced by§
pirate < > she has gone §last two words crossed out and replaced above by one word§ goes
1672| MS:my queen §crossed out and replaced above by two words§ lady dear

1675 She used to ward away from everyone,
And mollify her husband's ireful mood.
I ask then, do I justly hate or no
This guest, this interloper on our grief?"

"Hate him and justly!" Here's the proper judge
1680 Of what is due to the house from Herakles!
This man of much experience saw the first
O' the feeble duckings-down at destiny,
When King Admetos went his rounds, poor soul,
A-begging somebody to be so brave
1685 As die for one afraid to die himself—
"Thou, friend? Thou, love? Father or mother, then!
None of you? What, Alkestis must Death catch?
O best of wives, one woman in the world!
But nowise droop: our prayers may still assist:
1690 Let us try sacrifice; if those avail
Nothing and Gods avert their countenance,
Why, deep and durable our grief will be!"
Whereat the house, this worthy at its head,
Re-echoed "deep and durable our grief!"
1695 This sage, who justly hated Herakles,
Did he suggest once "Rather I than she!"

1676| MS:husband's angry §crossed out and replaced above by§ ireful   1678| MS:guest,
and §crossed out and replaced above by§ this   1686| MS:friend?" "Thou, lover?
Father, mother   *1871a:*friend? Thou, love? Father or mother   1687| MS:of ye < >
must Death catch? §last two words and punctuation crossed out and replaced above by one
word and punctuation§ depart? §partially erased, with original reading marked for retention§
*1871a:*of you   1689| MS:Nay, but it shall not be if I can help— §entire line crossed out
and replaced above by new line§ But nourish have cheer §last two words crossed out§ hope: it
may be §last three words crossed out§ our §inserted above§ prayers may still §last two words
inserted above§ assist: *1871a:*But nowise droop: our   1690| MS:sacrifice: if that
§crossed out and replaced by§ those   *1871a:*sacrifice; if   1691| MS:and not a §last
two words crossed out§ God §altered to§ Gods extend thy term, §last three words crossed out
and replaced above by three words§ avert their countenance,   1692| MS:durable the
blow, believe! §last two words crossed out and replaced above by three words§ grief will be!
*1871a:*be!"   *1889a:*durable our grief   1693| MS:worthy §above word illegibly crossed
out§   1694| Echoed §altered to§ Re-echoed < > durable the blow"! §crossed out and
replaced above by§ grief   *1871a:*durable our grief!"   1695| MS:This man §altered to§
sage who < > Herakles   *1871a:*sage, who < > Herakles,   1696| MS:he put in with §last
three words crossed out and replaced above by two words§ suggest once

Admonish the Turannos—"Be a man!
Bear thine own burden, never think to thrust
Thy fate upon another and thy wife!
1700 It were a dubious gain could death be doomed
That other, and no passionatest plea
Of thine, to die instead, have force with fate;
Seeing thou lov'st Alkestis: what were life
Unlighted by the loved one? But to live—
1705 Not merely live unsolaced by some thought,
Some word so poor—yet solace all the same—
As 'Thou i' the sepulchre, Alkestis, say!
Would I, or would not I, to save thy life,
Die, and die on, and die for evermore?'
1710 No! but to read red-written up and down
The world 'This is the sunshine, this the shade,
This is some pleasure of earth, sky or sea,
Due to that other, dead that thou mayst live!'
Such were a covetable gain to thee?
1715 Go die, fool, and be happy while 'tis time!"
One word of counsel in this kind, methinks,
Had fallen to better purpose than Ai, ai,
Pheu, pheu, e, papai, and a pother of praise
O' the best, best, best one! Nothing was to hate
1720 In King Admetos, Pheres, and the rest
O' the household down to his heroic self!

1697| MS:Or turn to §last three words crossed out and replaced above by one word§ Admonish
the Turannos—"I advise §last two words crossed out§ Be   1700| MS:gain had §crossed
out and replaced above by§ could death been §altered to§ be   1701| *1871a*:other, yet no
1872:other, and no   1702| MS:thine to die instead had §crossed out and replaced above
by§ have   *1871a*:thine, to die instead, have   1703| MS:what's mere life   *1871a*:what
were life   1706| MS:Or §crossed out and replaced above by§ Some   1707| MS:say—
1871a:say!   1708| MS:Would I or   *1871a*:Would I, or   1710| MS:But live and §last
three words crossed out and replaced above by three words§ No! but to
1711| MS:world—'This   *1871a*:world 'This   1713| MS:to Alkestis §crossed out and
replaced above by two words§ that other <> mightst §crossed out and replaced above by§
may'st *1889a*:mayst   1716| MS:Methinks §crossed out§ some §altered to§ Some
§crossed out and replaced above by§ One   1717| MS:than Ai, Ai,   *1872*:than Ai, ai,
1718| MS:e §above word illegibly crossed out§   1719| MS:one! Nothing here to
1871a:one! Nothing was to   1720| MS:§line added§   *1871a*:king   *1872*:In King
1721| MS:to §inserted below§ his own §crossed out§ heroic

This was the one thing hateful: Herakles
Had flung into the presence, frank and free,
Out from the labour into the repose,
1725　Ere out again and over head and ears
I' the heart of labour, all for love of men:
Making the most o' the minute, that the soul
And body, strained to height a minute since,
Might lie relaxed in joy, this breathing-space,
1730　For man's sake more than ever; till the bow,
Restrung o' the sudden, at first cry for help,
Should send some unimaginable shaft
True to the aim and shatteringly through
The plate-mail of a monster, save man so.
1735　He slew the pest o' the marish yesterday:
To-morrow he would bit the flame-breathed stud
That fed on man's-flesh: and this day between—
Because he held it natural to die,
And fruitless to lament a thing past cure,
1740　So, took his fill of food, wine, song and flowers,
Till the new labour claimed him soon enough,—
"Hate him and justly!"
　　　　　　　　True, Charopé mine!
The man surmised not Herakles lay hid
I' the guest; or, knowing it, was ignorant
1745　That still his lady lived—for Herakles;

1722|　MS:hateful—Herakles　*1871a*:hateful: Herakles　1724|　MS:repose　*1871a*:repose,
1726|　MS:heart of §last two words inserted above§　1728|　MS:body strained <> since
1871a:body, strained <> since,　1729|　MS:Might be §altered to§ lie relaxed §above
words illegibly crossed out§　1730|　MS:And §crossed out and replaced above by§ For <>
ever, till the bow　*1871a*:ever; till the bow,　1734|　MS:of the §crossed out and replaced
above by§ a　1736|　MS:flame-breathed steeds　*1871a*:flame-breathed stud
1738|　MS:it no such feat §last three words crossed out and replaced above by one word§
natural　1739|　MS:to complain of §last two words crossed out and replaced above by
three words§ lament a thing　1740|　MS:So took <> flowers　*1871a*:So, took <> flowers,
1742|　MS:Hate <> justly! <> Charope, sweet! §comma and last word crossed out and
replaced above by§ mine　*1871a*:"Hate <> justly!" <> Charopé
1744|　MS:or knowing　*1889a*:or, knowing　1745|　MS:That Herakles §crossed out and
replaced above by two words and letter§ still his w §last two words and letter crossed out§ still
the §crossed out and replaced above by§ his <> lived, for　*1889a*:lived—for

Or else judged lightness needs must indicate
This or the other caitiff quality:
And therefore—had been right if not so wrong!
For who expects the sort of him will scratch
1750   A nail's depth, scrape the surface just to see
What peradventure underlies the same?

So, he stood petting up his puny hate,
Parent-wise, proud of the ill-favoured babe.
Not long! A great hand, careful lest it crush,
1755   Startled him on the shoulder: up he stared,
And over him, who stood but Herakles!
There smiled the mighty presence, all one smile
And no touch more of the world-weary God,
Through the brief respite. Just a garland's grace
1760   About the brow, a song to satisfy
Head, heart and breast, and trumpet-lips at once,
A solemn draught of true religious wine,
And,—how should I know?—half a mountain goat
Torn up and swallowed down,—the feast was fierce
1765   But brief: all cares and pains took wing and flew,
Leaving the hero ready to begin
And help mankind, whatever woe came next,
Even though what came next should be nought more
Than the mean querulous mouth o' the man, remarked
1770   Pursing its grievance up till patience failed

1746| MS:else §inserted above§ judged such §crossed out§ lightness could but §last two words crossed out and replaced above by two words§ needs must   1747| MS:quality. *1871a:*quality: 1750| MS:depth, down i' §last two words crossed out and replaced above by one word§ scrape   1752| MS:So he <> hate   *1871a:*So, he <> hate, 1753| MS:babe—   *1871a:*babe.   1754| MS:long: a   *1871a:*long! A   1756| MS:him who <> Herakles?   *1871a:*him, who   *1889a:*Herakles!   1758| MS:And not a trace §last three words crossed out and replaced above by three words§ no touch more 1759| MS:respite! Just   *1889a:*respite. Just   1760| MS:song twixt lip and lip §last four words crossed out and replaced above by two words§ to satisfy   1761| MS:breast and trumpet-mouth §*mouth* crossed out and replaced above by§ lips   *1871a:*breast, and 1765| MS:all past §crossed out§ cares and pains §last two words inserted above§ took to §crossed out§ wing   1767| MS:next   *1871a:*next,   1768| MS:be nothing more *1871a:*be nought more   1769| MS:man, here §crossed out§ remarked

And the sage needs must rush out, as we saw
To sulk outside and pet his hate in peace.
By no means would the Helper have it so:
He who was just about to handle brutes
1775 In Thrace, and bit the jaws which breathed the flame,—
Well, if a good laugh and a jovial word
Could bridle age which blew bad humours forth,
That were a kind of help, too!
      "Thou, there!" hailed
This grand benevolence the ungracious one—
1780 "Why look'st so solemn and so thought-absorbed?
To guests a servant should not sour-faced be,
But do the honours with a mind urbane.
While thou, contrariwise, beholding here
Arrive thy master's comrade, hast for him
1785 A churlish visage, all one beetle-brow—
Having regard to grief that's out-of-door!
Come hither, and so get to grow more wise!
Things mortal—know'st the nature that they have?
No, I imagine! whence could knowledge spring?
1790 Give ear to me, then! For all flesh to die,
Is nature's due; nor is there any one
Of mortals with assurance he shall last
The coming morrow: for, what's born of chance
Invisibly proceeds the way it will,
1795 Not to be learned, no fortune-teller's prize.
This, therefore, having heard and known through me,
Gladden thyself! Drink! Count the day-by-day
Existence thine, and all the other—chance!
Ay, and pay homage also to by far
1800 The sweetest of divinities for man,

1771| MS:the man needs *1871a*:the sage needs   1775| MS:In Thrace and bit those jaws
<> flame, *1871a*:In Thrace, and bit the jaws <> flame,—   1777| MS:forth
1871a:forth,   1781| MS:guests, a <> be *1871a*:be, *1889a*:guests a
1789| MS:imagine—whence *1871a*:imagine! whence   1793| MS:for what's *1871a*:for,
what's   1799| pay honour §crossed out and replaced above by§ homage
1800| MS:divinities to man, §last two words crossed out§ we have,
§last two words crossed out and replaced above by two words§ for man,

Kupris! Benignant Goddess will she prove!
But as for aught else, leave and let things be!
And trust my counsel, if I seem to speak
To purpose—as I do, apparently.
1805 Wilt not thou, then,—discarding overmuch
Mournfulness, do away with this shut door,
Come drink along with me, be-garlanded
This fashion? Do so, and—I well know what—
From this stern mood, this shrunk-up state of mind,
1810 The pit-pat fall o' the flagon-juice down throat
Soon will dislodge thee from bad harbourage!
Men being mortal should think mortal-like:
Since to your solemn, brow-contracting sort,
All of them,—so I lay down law at least,—
1815 Life is not truly life but misery."

Whereto the man with softened surliness:
"We know as much: but deal with matters, now,
Hardly befitting mirth and revelry."

"No intimate, this woman that is dead:
1820 Mourn not too much! For, those o' the house itself,
Thy masters live, remember!"
                "Live indeed?
Ah, thou know'st nought o' the woe within these walls!"

"I do—unless thy master spoke me false
Somehow!"
        "Ay, ay, too much he loves a guest,
1825 Too much, that master mine!" so muttered he.

1801| MS:Kupris—benignant   *1871a*:Kupris! Benignant   1806| MS:Mournfulness, and
§crossed out§ do   1808| MS:and,—I < > what,—   *1889a*:and—I < > what—
1810| MS:flaggon juice, my §erased and replaced above by§ down throat,   *1871a*:flagon-juice
1889a:throat   1816| MS:surliness   *1871a*:surliness: 1817| MS:matters now
1871a:matters, now,   1820| MS:much! For §inserted above§ Those §altered to§ those of
§altered to§ o' < > itself   *1871a*:much! For, those < > itself,   1822| MS:Ah, you
§crossed out and replaced above by§ thou   1824| MS:Ay, ay—too < > he loves §last two
words inserted above§ a guest loves, §crossed out§   *1871a*:Ay, ay, too

"Was it improper he should treat me well,
Because an alien corpse was in the way?"

"No alien, but most intimate indeed!"

"Can it be, some woe was, he told me not?"

1830   "Farewell and go thy way! Thy cares for thee—
To us, our master's sorrow is a care."

"This word begins no tale of alien woe!"

"Had it been other woe than intimate,
I could have seen thee feast, nor felt amiss."

1835   "What! have I suffered strangely from my host?"

"Thou cam'st not at a fit reception-time:
With sorrow here beforehand: and thou seest
Shorn hair, black robes."
                 "But who is it that's dead?
Some child gone? or the aged sire perhaps?"

1840   "Admetos' wife, then! she has perished, guest!"

"How sayest? And did ye house me, all the same?"

"Ay: for he had thee in that reverence
He dared not turn thee from his door away!"

"O hapless, and bereft of what a mate!"

1826| MS:well   *1871a:*well,   1832| MS:of stranger's woe"!   *1871a:*of alien woe!"
1834| MS:feast nor   *1871a:*feast, nor   1835| MS:"But have < > my friends §crossed out
and replaced above by§ host?"   *1871a:* "What! have   1837| MS:For sorrow's here
*1871a:*With sorrow here   1838| MS:it that's §last two words inserted above§
1839| MS:gone—or   *1871a:*gone? or   1840| MS:then,—she   *1871a:*then! she
1841| MS:me all   *1871a:*me, all   1842| MS:"Ay,—for   *1871a:* "Ay: for
1843| MS:He would §crossed out and replaced above by§ dared

1845   "All of us now are dead, not she alone!"

"But I divined it! seeing, as I did,
His eye that ran with tears, his close-clipt hair,
His countenance! Though he persuaded me,
Saying it was a stranger's funeral
1850   He went with to the grave: against my wish,
He forced on me that I should enter doors,
Drink in the hall o' the hospitable man
Circumstanced so! And do I revel yet
With wreath on head? But—thou to hold thy peace
1855   Nor tell me what a woe oppressed my friend!
Where is he gone to bury her? Where am I
To go and find her?"
                    "By the road that leads
Straight to Larissa, thou wilt see the tomb,
Out of the suburb, a carved sepulchre."

1860   So said he, and therewith dismissed himself
Inside to his lamenting: somewhat soothed,
However, that he had adroitly spoilt
The mirth of the great creature: oh, he marked
The movement of the mouth, how lip pressed lip,
1865   And either eye forgot to shine, as, fast,
He plucked the chaplet from his forehead, dashed
The myrtle-sprays down, trod them underfoot!
And all the joy and wonder of the wine
Withered away, like fire from off a brand

---

^{1846|}   MS:But <> it—seeing as I did   *1871a:* "But <> it! seeing, as I did,
^{1847|}   MS:tears—his close clipt hair—   *1871a:* tears, his close-clipt hair,
^{1848|}   MS:countenance! But he <> me   *1871a:* countenance! Though he <> me,
^{1851|}   MS:doors   *1871a:* doors,   ^{1852|}   MS:in §altered to§ i' <> man,   *1871a:* in <> man
^{1853|}   MS:revel here   *1871a:* revel yet   ^{1854|}   MS:wreath §over illegible word§ <> But
thou to speak no word §last three words crossed out and replaced above by three words§ hold
thy peace   *1871a:* head? But—thou   ^{1861|}   MS:somewhat §inserted above§ soothed no
less §last two words crossed out§   ^{1862|}   MS:Somewhat—for §last two words crossed out
and replaced above by three words§ However, that he had adroitly dashed   *1889a:* adroitly
spoilt   ^{1865|}   MS:eye let drop the §last three words crossed out and replaced above by two
words§ forgot to   ^{1866|}   MS:forehead, flung §crossed out§ dashed
^{1867|}   MS:underfoot,   *1871a:* underfoot!   ^{1869|}   MS:away like   *1871a:* away, like

1870   The wind blows over—beacon though it be,
Whose merry ardour only meant to make
Somebody all the better for its blaze,
And save lost people in the dark: quenched now!

Not long quenched! As the flame, just hurried off
1875   The brand's edge, suddenly renews its bite,
Tasting some richness caked i' the core o' the tree,—
Pine, with a blood that's oil,—and triumphs up
Pillar-wise to the sky and saves the world:
So, in a spasm and splendour of resolve,
1880   All at once did the God surmount the man.

"O much-enduring heart and hand of mine!
Now show what sort of son she bore to Zeus,
That daughter of Elektruon, Tiruns' child,
Alkmené! for that son must needs save now
1885   The just-dead lady: ay, establish here
I' the house again Alkestis, bring about
Comfort and succour to Admetos so!
I will go lie in wait for Death, black-stoled
King of the corpses! I shall find him, sure,
1890   Drinking, beside the tomb, o' the sacrifice:
And if I lie in ambuscade, and leap
Out of my lair, and seize—encircle him
Till one hand join the other round about—
There lives not who shall pull him out from me,
1895   Rib-mauled, before he let the woman go!
But even say I miss the booty,—say,

1871| MS:means   *1871a:*meant   1873| MS:Save poor lost §last two words inserted above§
*1871a:*And save lost   1874| MS:flame just   *1871a:*flame, just   1875| MS:bite—
*1871a:*bite,   1876| MS:the heart §crossed out and replaced above by§ core <> tree,
*1871a:*tree,—   1877| MS:oil, and   *1871a:*oil,—and   1878| MS:world,   *1871a:*world:
1879| MS:resolve   *1871a:*resolve,   1880| MS:the man surmount himself.   *1871a:*the God
surmount the man.   1881| MS:and soul of mine   *1871a:*and hand of mine!
1882| MS:to Zeus   *1871a:*to Zeus,   1884| MS:Alkmene   *1871a:*Alkmené
1885| MS:lady, ay   *1871a:*lady: ay   1889| MS:o'   *1871a:*of   1890| MS:sacrifice
*1871a:*sacrifice: 1893| MS:about,   *1871a:*about—   1894| MS:me   *1871a:*me,
1896| MS:even if §crossed out and replaced above by§ say

Death comes not to the boltered blood,—why then,
Down go I, to the unsunned dwelling-place
Of Koré and the king there,—make demand,
1900 Confident I shall bring Alkestis back,
So as to put her in the hands of him
My host, that housed me, never drove me off:
Though stricken with sore sorrow, hid the stroke,
Being a noble heart and honouring me!
1905 Who of Thessalians, more than this man, loves
The stranger? Who, that now inhabits Greece?
Wherefore he shall not say the man was vile
Whom he befriended,—native noble heart!"

So, one look upward, as if Zeus might laugh
1910 Approval of his human progeny,—
One summons of the whole magnific frame,
Each sinew to its service,—up he caught,
And over shoulder cast, the lion-shag,
Let the club go,—for had he not those hands?
1915 And so went striding off, on that straight way
Leads to Larissa and the suburb tomb.
Gladness be with thee, Helper of our world!
I think this is the authentic sign and seal
Of Godship, that it ever waxes glad,
1920 And more glad, until gladness blossoms, bursts
Into a rage to suffer for mankind,
And recommence at sorrow: drops like seed
After the blossom, ultimate of all.
Say, does the seed scorn earth and seek the sun?

1897| MS:come <> boultered <> then   *1871a*:comes <> then,   *1889a*:boltered
1899| MS:and her §altered to§ the King, and ask for her—   *1871a*:king there,—make demand,
1902| MS:host, who housed, never <> off.   *1871a*:host, that housed me, never <> off:
1905| MS:of Thessalians loves the stranger more?   *1871a*:of Thessalians, more than this man,
loves   1906| MS:Than this man? Who that   *1871a*:The stranger? Who,
1908| MS:heart!   *1871a*:heart!"   1912| MS:caught   *1871a*:caught,   1913| MS:cast the
1871a:cast, the   1915| MS:off on   *1871a*:off, on   1917| MS:helper   *1871a*:thee,
Helper   1919| MS:Of Godship that <> glad   *1871a*:Of Godship, that <> glad,
1920| MS:glad until   *1871a*:glad, until   1922| MS:sorrow: as the seed   *1871a*:sorrow:
drops like seed   1923| MS:all, *1871a*:all.   1924| MS:Say does   *1871a*:Say, does

1925 Surely it has no other end and aim
Than to drop, once more die into the ground,
Taste cold and darkness and oblivion there:
And thence rise, tree-like grow through pain to joy,
More joy and most joy,—do man good again.

1930 So, to the struggle off strode Herakles.
When silence closed behind the lion-garb,
Back came our dull fact settling in its place,
Though heartiness and passion half-dispersed
The inevitable fate. And presently
1935 In came the mourners from the funeral,
One after one, until we hoped the last
Would be Alkestis and so end our dream.
Could they have really left Alkestis lone
I' the wayside sepulchre! Home, all save she!
1940 And when Admetos felt that it was so,
By the stand-still: when he lifted head and face
From the two hiding hands and peplos' fold,
And looked forth, knew the palace, knew the hills,
Knew the plains, knew the friendly frequence there,
1945 And no Alkestis any more again,
Why, the whole woe billow-like broke on him.

"O hateful entry, hateful countenance
O' the widowed halls!"—he moaned. "What was to be?
Go there? Stay here? Speak, not speak? All was now
1950 Mad and impossible alike; one way
And only one was sane and safe—to die:

1927| MS:there, *1871a*:there: 1930| MS:So, off strode to the struggle Herakles:
1871a:struggle Herakles.   *1872*:So, to the struggle off strode Herakles.
1932| MS:came the §crossed out and replaced above by§ our   1934| MS:fate. And
soon enough   *1871a*:fate. And presently   1936| MS:until you hoped   *1871a*:until we
hoped   1937| MS:end a dream.   *1871a*:end our dream.   1940| MS:when Admetos
saw §altered to§ felt   1941| MS:stand-still, and he   *1871a*:stand-still: when he
1942| MS:fold   *1889a*:fold,   1944| MS:And the sea, and the   *1871a*:Knew the plains,
knew the   1946| MS:billow-like §inserted above§   1946-47| MS:§no ¶§   *1871a*:§¶§
1948| MS:moaned: what   *1871a*:moaned. "What   1949| MS:not speak!
All   *1871a*:not speak? All   1951| MS:die,   *1871a*:die:

Now he was made aware how dear is death,
How loveable the dead are, how the heart
Yearns in us to go hide where they repose,
1955 When we find sunbeams do no good to see,
Nor earth rests rightly where our footsteps fall.
His wife had been to him the very pledge,
Sun should be sun, earth—earth; the pledge was robbed,
Pact broken, and the world was left no world."
1960 He stared at the impossible mad life:
Stood, while they urged "Advance—advance! Go deep
Into the utter dark, thy palace-core!"
They tried what they called comfort, "touched the quick
Of the ulceration in his soul," he said,
1965 With memories,—"once thy joy was thus and thus!"
True comfort were to let him fling himself
Into the hollow grave o' the tomb, and so
Let him lie dead along with all he loved.

One bade him note that his own family
1970 Boasted a certain father whose sole son,
Worthy bewailment, died: and yet the sire
Bore stoutly up against the blow and lived;
For all that he was childless now, and prone
Already to grey hairs, far on in life.
1975 Could such a good example miss effect?
Why fix foot, stand so, staring at the house,
Why not go in, as that wise kinsman would?

1954| MS:hide it where they dwell, *1871a*:hide where they repose, 1957| MS:to him
§inserted above§ the pledge, he said, *1871a*:the very pledge, 1959| MS:The §crossed
out§ pact §altered to§ Pact was §crossed out§ broken <> no world. *1871a*:no world."
1960| MS:life *1871a*:impossible, mad life: *1889a*:impossible mad 1961| MS:Stood,
while they bade "advance *1871a*:Stood, while <> "Advance *1889a*:they urged
"Advance 1962| MS:dark, the palace' core!" *1871a*:dark, thy palace-core!"
1963| MS:comfort, touched *1871a*:comfort, "touched 1964| MS:soul, he *1871a*:soul,"
he 1965| MS:and thus"! *1871a*:and thus!" 1966| MS:was *1871a*:were
1967| MS:and there *1871a*:and so 1968-69| MS:§no ¶§ *1871a*:§¶§
1969| MS:One's comfort was that *1871a*:One bade him note that 1972| *1871a*:lived
1871a:lived; 1973| MS:now and *1871a*:now, and 1976| MS:foot—stand <> house
1871a:foot, stand <> house, 1977| MS:kinsman did? *1871a*:kinsman would?

"O that arrangement of the house I know!
How can I enter, how inhabit thee
1980 Now that one cast of fortune changes all?
Oh me, for much divides the then from now!
Then—with those pine-tree torches, Pelian pomp
And marriage-hymns, I entered, holding high
The hand of my dear wife; while many-voiced
1985 The revelry that followed me and her
That's dead now,—friends felicitating both,
As who were lofty-lineaged, each of us
Born of the best, two wedded and made one;
Now—wail is wedding-chant's antagonist,
1990 And, for white peplos, stoles in sable state
Herald my way to the deserted couch!"

The one word more they ventured was "This grief
Befell thee witless of what sorrow means,
Close after prosperous fortune: but, reflect!
1995 Thou hast saved soul and body. Dead, thy wife—
Living, the love she left. What's novel here?
Many the man, from whom Death long ago
Loosed the life-partner!"
                              Then Admetos spoke:
Turned on the comfort, with no tears, this time.
2000 He was beginning to be like his wife.
I told you of that pressure to the point,
Word slow pursuing word in monotone,
Alkestis spoke with; so Admetos, now,
Solemnly bore the burden of the truth.

1980| MS:one fling of   *1871a*:one cast of   1982| MS:pomp,   *1871a*:pomp
1983| MS:marriage-hymns I *1871a*:marriage-hymns, I   1984| MS:wife, and §crossed out§
while   *1871a*:wife; while   1985| MS:me—and   *1871a*:me and   1986| MS:now,—
then, felicitating both   *1871a*:now,—friends felicitating both,   1988| MS:one:
1871a:one;   1989| MS:Now, wail   *1871a*:Now—wail   1990| MS:And for §crossed out
and replaced above by§ to white peplos, sable §crossed out§ stoles succeed §crossed out§ in
sable   *1871a*:And, for   1991| MS:couch!   *1871a*:couch!"   1991-92| MS:§leaf ends§
1871a:§¶§   1992| MS:The last word <> "The grief   *1871a*:The one word <> "This grief
1998| MS:spoke—   *1871a*:spoke: 1999| MS:time;   *1871a*:time.   2000| MS:wife:
1871a:wife.   2003| MS:with: so Admetos now,   *1871a*:with; so Admetos, now,

²⁰⁰⁵ And as the voice of him grew, gathered strength,
And groaned on, and persisted to the end,
We felt how deep had been descent in grief,
And with what change he came up now to light,
And left behind such littleness as tears.

²⁰¹⁰ "Friends, I account the fortune of my wife
Happier than mine, though it seem otherwise:
For, her indeed no grief will ever touch,
And she from many a labour pauses now,
Renowned one! Whereas I, who ought not live,
²⁰¹⁵ But do live, by evading destiny,
Sad life am I to lead, I learn at last!
For how shall I bear going in-doors here?
Accosting whom? By whom saluted back,
Shall I have joyous entry? Whither turn?
²⁰²⁰ Inside, the solitude will drive me forth,
When I behold the empty bed—my wife's—
The seat she used to sit upon, the floor
Unsprinkled as when dwellers loved the cool,
The children that will clasp my knees about,
²⁰²⁵ Cry for their mother back: these servants too
Moaning for what a guardian they have lost!
Inside my house such circumstance awaits.
Outside,—Thessalian people's marriage-feasts
And gatherings for talk will harass me,

---

²⁰⁰⁶| MS:on and   *1871a:*on, and   ²⁰⁰⁷| MS:deep the man's descent   *1871a:*deep had
been descent   ²⁰⁰⁸| MS:light   *1871a:*light,   ²⁰⁰⁹| MS:Again, and left such
*1871a:*And left behind such   ²⁰⁰⁹⁻¹⁰| *1871a:*§¶ lost in paging§   *1889a:*§¶ restored§
²⁰¹¹| Better §crossed out and replaced above by§ Happier   ²⁰¹⁴| MS:who should not
*1871a:*who ought not   ²⁰¹⁵| MS:live by   *1871a:*live, by   ²⁰¹⁶| MS:life shall I lead
now, I   *1871a:*Sad life am I to lead, I   ²⁰¹⁸| MS:Addressing §crossed out and replaced
above by§ Accosting <> whom there answered §last two words crossed out and replaced
above by one word§ saluted   ²⁰²³| MS:when people used to §last three words crossed out
and replaced above by two words§ dwellers were alive,   *1871a:*dwellers loved the cool,
²⁰²⁴| MS:my about §inserted above§ knees, ab §last two letters crossed out§   *1871a:*my knees
about,   ²⁰²⁸| MS:Outside,—Thessalian folk, whose §last two words crossed out and
replaced above by one word§ people's   ²⁰²⁹| MS:gatherings with women everywhere,
§last three words crossed out and replaced above by five words§ for talk will harrass me,

²⁰³⁰ With overflow of women everywhere;
It is impossible I look on them—
Familiars of my wife and just her age!
And then, whoever is a foe of mine,
And lights on me—why, this will be his word—
²⁰³⁵ 'See there! alive ignobly, there he skulks
That played the dastard when it came to die,
And, giving her he wedded, in exchange,
Kept himself out of Hades safe and sound,
The coward! Do you call that creature—man?
²⁰⁴⁰ He hates his parents for declining death,
Just as if he himself would gladly die!'
This sort of reputation shall I have,
Beside the other ills enough in store.
Ill-famed, ill-faring,—what advantage, friends,
²⁰⁴⁵ Do you perceive I gain by life for death?"

That was the truth. Vexed waters sank to smooth:
'Twas only when the last of bubbles broke,
The latest circlet widened all away
And left a placid level, that up swam
²⁰⁵⁰ To the surface the drowned truth, in dreadful change.
So, through the quiet and submission,—ay,
Spite of some strong words—(for you miss the tone)

---

²⁰³⁰| MS:overflow of §inserted above§   ²⁰³¹| MS:§line added§   ²⁰³²| MS:Women §crossed out§ familiars §altered to§ Familiars   ²⁰³⁵| MS:See him §altered to§ there alive—ignobly—see the man §last three words crossed out§ there   *1871a:*'See there! alive ignobly, there   ²⁰³⁶| MS:That proved §crossed out and replaced above by§ played ²⁰³⁷| MS:And, yielding §crossed out and replaced above by§ giving <> wedded in *1871a:*wedded, in   ²⁰⁴⁰| MS:parents who §altered to§ for refused §altered to§ refusing §crossed out and replaced above by§ declining   ²⁰⁴¹| MS:himself had §crossed out and replaced above by§ would <> died! §altered to§ die!   *1871a:*die!'   ²⁰⁴⁴| MS:ill-faring, thus,— §crossed out and replaced above by§ —what   ²⁰⁴⁵| MS:perceive to me in life *1871a:*perceive I gain by life   ²⁰⁴⁵⁻⁴⁶| *1871a:*§¶ lost in paging§ *1889a:*§¶ restored§ ²⁰⁴⁶| MS:smooth, *1871a:*smooth;   ²⁰⁴⁷| MS:And only <> broke *1871a:*'Twas only <> broke,   ²⁰⁴⁸| MS:And latest <> away, *1871a:*The latest *1889a:*away ²⁰⁴⁹| MS:placid §inserted above§ level quiet, §crossed out§ <> swam §over illegible word§ ²⁰⁵⁰| MS:drowned thing, the dreadful *1871a:*drowned truth, in dreadful ²⁰⁵²| MS:For all §last two words crossed out and replaced above by two words§ Spite of

The grief was getting to be infinite—
Grief, friends fell back before. Their office shrank
2055 To that old solace of humanity—
"Being born mortal, bear grief! Why born else?"
And they could only meditate anew.

"They, too, upborne by airy help of song,
And haply science, which can find the stars,
2060 Had searched the heights: had sounded depths as well
By catching much at books where logic lurked,
Yet nowhere found they aught could overcome
Necessity: not any medicine served,
Which Thrakian tablets treasure, Orphic voice
2065 Wrote itself down upon: nor remedy
Which Phoibos gave to the Asklepiadai;
Cutting the roots of many a virtuous herb
To solace overburdened mortals. None!
Of this sole goddess, never may we go
2070 To altar nor to image: sacrifice
She hears not. All to pray for is—'Approach!
But, oh, no harder on me, awful one,
Than heretofore! Let life endure thee still!
For, whatsoe'er Zeus' nod decree, that same
2075 In concert with thee hath accomplishment.
Iron, the very stuff o' the Chaluboi,
Thou, by sheer strength, dost conquer and subdue;

2053| MS:getting §inserted above§   2055| MS:that poor §crossed out and replaced above
by§ old   2057| MS:meditate once more. *1871a:*meditate anew.   2057-58| MS:§no ¶§
1871a:§¶§   2058| MS:They <> song *1871a:* "They <> song,   2059| MS:can reach
§crossed out and replaced above by§ find   2060| MS:hights; and sounded
*1871a:*heights: had sounded   2061| MS:at logic, where it §last three words crossed out
and replaced above by three words§ books where logic   2062| MS:And nowhere
*1871a:*Yet nowhere   2063| MS:serves *1871a:*served,   2064| MS:Treasured in
Thrakian tablets, Orphic *1871a:*Which Thrakian tablets treasure, Orphic
2065| MS:upon, nor *1871a:*upon: nor   2066| MS:gave the *1871a:*gave to the
2068| MS:To comfort overburdened *1871a:*To solace overburdened   2071| MS:is—
Approach! *1871a:*is—'Approach!   2073| MS:life sustain thee *1871a:*life endure thee
2074| MS:For Zeus, whate'er his nod *1871a:*For, whatsoe'er Zeus' nod   2076| MS:Iron,
itself, §crossed out and replaced above by two words§ the very <> Thaluboi, *1871a:*the
Chaluboi,   2077| MS:Thou by <> strength dost *1871a:*Thou, by <> strength, dost

Nor, of that harsh abrupt resolve of thine,
Any relenting is there!'

                   "O my king!

2080   Thee also, in the shackles of those hands,
Not to be shunned, the Goddess grasped! Yet, bear!
Since never wilt thou lead from underground
The dead ones, wail thy worst! If mortals die,—
The very children of immortals, too,

2085   Dropped mid our darkness, these decay as sure!
Dear indeed was she while among us: dear,
Now she is dead, must she for ever be:
Thy portion was to clasp, within thy couch,
The noblest of all women as a wife.

2090   Nor be the tomb of her supposed some heap
That hides mortality: but like the Gods
Honoured, a veneration to a world
Of wanderers! Oft the wanderer, struck thereby,
Who else had sailed past in his merchant-ship,

2095   Ay, he shall leave ship, land, long wind his way
Up to the mountain-summit, till there break
Speech forth 'So, this was she, then, died of old
To save her husband! now, a deity
She bends above us. Hail, benignant one!

2078| MS:Nor of < > thine   *1871a*:Nor, of < > thine,   2079| MS:there! O my King,
1871a:there!" §¶§ O my king!   *1881*:there!' §¶§ O   *1889a*:there!' §¶§ "O
2081| MS:Unshunnable, the < > Yet bear!   *1871a*:grasped! Yet, bear!   *1872*:Not to be
shunned, the   2083| MS:die,   *1871a*:die,—   2084| MS: of the g §last word and
letter crossed out and replaced above by two words§ immortals too,   *1871a*:immortals, too,
2085| MS:as well.   *1871a*:as sure!   2086| MS:indeed §inserted above§ < > us; dear,
1871a:us: dear,   2087| MS:be.   *1871a*:be: 2088| MS:clasp within thy couch
1871a:clasp, within thy couch,   2089| MS:women for thy wi §last two words and two
letters crossed out§ as a wife: *1871a*:wife.   2091| MS:mortality,— but   *1871a*:mortality:
but   2092| MS:Honored   *1889a*:Honoured   2093| MS:wanderers. Oft
1871a:wanderers! Oft   2094| MS:Else would have sailed   *1871a*:Who else had sailed
2095| MS:leave it §crossed out and replaced above by§ ship, land, and §comma and last word
crossed out and replaced above by§ there, wind   *1871a*:land, long wind   2097| MS:This
speech forth "This was she then   *1871a*:Speech forth "So, this was she, then   *1872*:forth 'So
2098| MS:husband: now   *1871a*:husband! now   2099| MS:us: hail   *1871a*:us. Hail

2100   Give good!' Such voices so will supplicate.

"But—can it be? Alkmené's offspring comes,
Admetos!—to thy house advances here!"

I doubt not, they supposed him decently
Dead somewhere in that winter world of Thrace—
2105   Vanquished by one o' the Bistones, or else
Victim to some mad steed's voracity—
For did not friends prognosticate as much?
It were a new example to the point,
That "children of immortals, dropped by stealth
2110   Into our darkness, die as sure as we!"
A case to quote and comfort people with:
But, as for lamentation, ai and pheu,
Right-minded subjects kept them for their lord.

Ay, he it was advancing! In he strode,
2115   And took his stand before Admetos,—turned
Now by despair to such a quietude,
He neither raised his face nor spoke, this time,
The while his friend surveyed him steadily.
That friend looked rough with fighting: had he strained
2120   Worst brute to breast was ever strangled yet?
Somehow, a victory—for there stood the strength,
Happy, as always; something grave, perhaps;
The great vein-cordage on the fret-worked front,

2100| MS:good!" Such <> supplicate."   *1871a*:supplicate.   *1872*:good!'   Such
2100-1| MS:§¶ called for§   *1872*:§no ¶§   *1889a*:§¶§   2101| MS:But   *1889a:* "But
2102-3| MS:§no¶§   *1872*:§¶§   2105| MS:by him §crossed out and replaced above by§ one
<> Bistones or   *1871a*:Bistones, or   2110| MS:we:"   *1871a*:we!"   2111| MS:with,
1871a:with: 2112| MS:But as <> *ai* s and *pheu* s,   *1871a*:But, as <> ai and pheu,
2113| MS:subjects saved them for their king §crossed out§ lord   *1871a*:subjects kept them <>
lord.   2113-14| *1871a*:§¶ lost in paging§   *1889a*:§¶ restored§   2114| MS:advanced
§altered to§ advancing now §crossed out§ <> strode   *1871a*:strode,
2121| MS:Somehow a victory, for <> strength!   *1871a*:Somehow, a victory—for <> strength,
2123| MS:fretworked brow   *1871a*:fret-worked brow,   *1872*:fret-worked front,

Black-swollen, beaded yet with battle-dew
2125 The yellow hair o' the hero!—his big frame
A-quiver with each muscle sinking back
Into the sleepy smooth it leaped from late.
Under the great guard of one arm, there leant
A shrouded something, live and woman-like,
2130 Propped by the heart-beats 'neath the lion-coat.
When he had finished his survey, it seemed,
The heavings of the heart began subside,
The helpful breath returned, and last the smile
Shone out, all Herakles was back again,
2135 As the words followed the saluting hand.

"To friendly man, behoves we freely speak,
Admetos!—nor keep buried, deep in breast,
Blame we leave silent. I assuredly
Judged myself proper, if I should approach
2140 By accident calamities of thine,
To be demonstrably thy friend: but thou
Told'st me not of the corpse then claiming care,
That was thy wife's, but didst instal me guest
I' the house here, as though busied with a grief
2145 Indeed, but then, mere grief beyond thy gate:
And so, I crowned my head, and to the Gods
Poured my libations in thy dwelling-place,
With such misfortune round me. And I blame—
Certainly blame thee, having suffered thus!
2150 But still I would not pain thee, pained enough:

2124| MS:Black-swollen: and how those battle drops bead yet   *1871a:*Black-swollen, beaded
yet with battle-drops   *1872:*with battle-dew   2125| MS:hero! His   *1871a:*hero!—his
2127| MS:smooth the §crossed out§ it   2129| *1881:*shrowded   *1889a:*shrouded
2133| MS:The helping   *1872:*The helpful   2136| MS:To   *1871a:* "To
2137| MS:buried deep in breast   *1871a:*buried, deep in breast,   2140| MS:thine
*1871a:*thine,   2142| MS:care   *1871a:*care,   2143| MS:did install   *1871a:*didst instal
2144| MS: the dwelling, §crossed out and replaced above by§ house here, as if busied
*1889a:*as though busied   2145| MS:but still §crossed out and replaced above by§ then, a
grief <> gates: *1871a:*then, mere grief <> gate: 2146| MS:so I <> head and
*1871a:*so, I <> head, and   2150| MS:enough,   *1871a:*enough:

So let it pass! Wherefore I seek thee now,
Having turned back again though onward bound,
That I will tell thee. Take and keep for me
This woman, till I come thy way again,
2155   Driving before me, having killed the king
O' the Bistones, that drove of Thrakian steeds:
In such case, give the woman back to me!
But should I fare,—as fare I fain would not,
Seeing I hope to prosper and return,—
2160   Then, I bequeath her as thy household slave.
She came into my hands with good hard toil!
For, what find I, when started on my course,
But certain people, a whole country-side,
Holding a wrestling-bout? as good to me
2165   As a new labour: whence I took, and here
Come keeping with me, this, the victor's prize.
For, such as conquered in the easy work,
Gained horses which they drove away: and such
As conquered in the harder,—those who boxed
2170   And wrestled,—cattle; and, to crown the prize,
A woman followed. Chancing as I did,
Base were it to forego this fame and gain!
Well, as I said, I trust her to thy care:
No woman I have kidnapped, understand!
2175   But good hard toil has done it: here I come!
Some day, who knows? even thou wilt praise the feat!"

Admetos raised his face and eyed the pair:
Then, hollowly and with submission, spoke,
And spoke again, and spoke time after time,

2154| MS:come this way again   *1871a:*come thy way again,   2155| MS:killed §over *slain*§
2156| MS:Of < > Thracian horse: *1871a:*O' < > Thracian steeds: *1889a:*of Thrakian
2157| MS:In that case   *1872:*In such case   2162| MS:For what   *1871a:*For, what
2164| MS:wrestling-bout, as   *1871a:*wrestling-bout? as   2167| MS:For such < > work
*1871a:*For, such < > work,   2169| MS:harder, those   *1871a:*harder,—those
2170| MS:cattle, and   *1871a:*cattle; and   2173| MS:Well §over illegible word§
2176| MS:knows but even < > feat?   *1871a:*knows? even   *1889a:*feat!"   2177| MS:eyed
his friend. §last two words crossed out and replaced above by two words§ the pair:
2178| MS:Then hollowly   *1871a:*Then, hollowly   2179| MS:after time   *1871a:*after time,

95

²¹⁸⁰ When he perceived the silence of his friend
Would not be broken by consenting word.
As a tired slave goes adding stone to stone
Until he stop some current that molests,
So poor Admetos piled up argument
²¹⁸⁵ Vainly against the purpose all too plain
In that great brow acquainted with command.

"Nowise dishonouring, nor amid my foes
Ranking thee, did I hide my wife's ill fate;
But it were grief superimposed on grief,
²¹⁹⁰ Shouldst thou have hastened to another home.
My own woe was enough for me to weep!
But, for this woman,—if it so may be,—
Bid some Thessalian,—I entreat thee, king!—
Keep her,—who has not suffered like myself!
²¹⁹⁵ Many of the Pheraioi welcome thee.
Be no reminder to me of my ills!
I could not, if I saw her come to live,
Restrain the tear! Inflict on me diseased
No new disease: woe bends me down enough!
²²⁰⁰ Then, where could she be sheltered in my house,
Female and young too? For that she is young,
The vesture and adornment prove. Reflect!
Should such an one inhabit the same roof
With men? And how, mixed up, a girl, with youths,
²²⁰⁵ Shall she keep pure, in that case? No light task

^{2180|} MS:Still as he saw the   *1871a:*When he perceived the   ^{2184|} MS:So did Admetos
pile   *1871a:*So poor Admetos piled   ^{2185|} MS:purpose, all   *1889a:*purpose all
^{2187|} MS:Nowise dishonouring—nor mid   *1871a:* "Nowise dishonouring, nor   *1889a:*amid
^{2188|} MS:fate: *1871a:*fate.   *1889a:*fate;   ^{2189|} MS:But were   *1871a:*But it were
^{2190|} MS:That thou should'st hastened to another's   *1871a:*Should'st thou have hastened to
another   *1889a:*Shouldst   ^{2191|} MS:Enough for me to weep, my woe before!   *1871a:*My
own woe was enough for me to weep!   ^{2192|} MS:But for the woman   *1871a:*But, for this
woman   ^{2193|} MS:thee, King!   *1871a:*king!—   ^{2195|} MS:thee!   *1889a:*thee.
^{2197|} MS:her in the house, §last three words crossed out and replaced above by three words§
come to live,   ^{2198|} MS:me, diseased,   *1889a:*me diseased   ^{2199|} MS:woe hardens
§crossed out and replaced above by§ bends me down §inserted above§
^{2202|} MS:Is proved §crossed out§ The §over *by*§ < > adornment pure §crossed out§ prove

To curb the May-day youngster, Herakles!
I only speak because of care for thee.
Or must I, in avoidance of such harm,
Make her to enter, lead her life within
²²¹⁰ The chamber of the dead one, all apart?
How shall I introduce this other, couch
This where Alkestis lay? A double blame
I apprehend: first, from the citizens—
Lest some tongue of them taunt that I betray
²²¹⁵ My benefactress, fall into the snare
Of a new fresh face: then, the dead one's self,—
Will she not blame me likewise? Worthy, sure,
Of worship from me! circumspect my ways,
And jealous of a fault, are bound to be.
²²²⁰ But thou,—O woman, whosoe'er thou art,—
Know, thou hast all the form, art like as like
Alkestis, in the bodily shape! Ah me!
Take,—by the Gods,—this woman from my sight,
Lest thou undo me, the undone before!
²²²⁵ Since I seem—seeing her—as if I saw
My own wife! And confusions cloud my heart,
And from my eyes the springs break forth! Ah me
Unhappy—how I taste for the first time
My misery in all its bitterness!"

²²³⁰ Whereat the friends conferred: "The chance, in truth,
Was an untoward one—none said otherwise.
Still, what a God comes giving, good or bad,
That, one should take and bear with. Take her, then!"

---

^{2206|} MS:youngster Herakles! *1871a:*youngster, Herakles! ^{2207|} MS:thee!
*1889a:*thee. ^{2213|} MS:apprehend,—first from *1871a:*apprehend: first, from
^{2216|} MS:then the <> self, *1871a:*then, the <> self,— ^{2218|} MS:me,—circumspect
*1871a:*me! circumspect ^{2219|} MS:And §added in margin§ Jealous §altered to§ jealous of
the least §last two words crossed out and replaced above by one word a§ ^{2227|} MS:forth!
Ah, me *1889a:*forth! Ah me ^{2231|} MS:otherwise: *1871a:*otherwise.
^{2232|} MS:Still what <> bad *1871a:*Still, what <> bad, ^{2233|} *1881:*then!' *1889a:*then!"

Herakles,—not unfastening his hold

2235 On that same misery, beyond mistake
Hoarse in the words, convulsive in the face,—
"I would that I had such a power," said he,
"As to lead up into the light again
Thy very wife, and grant thee such a grace."

2240 "Well do I know thou wouldst: but where the hope?
There is no bringing back the dead to light."

"Be not extravagant in grief, no less!
Bear it, by augury of better things!"

"'Tis easier to advise 'bear up,' than bear!"

2245 "But how carve way i' the life that lies before,
If bent on groaning ever for the past?"

"I myself know that: but a certain love
Allures me to the choice I shall not change."

"Ay, but, still loving dead ones, still makes weep."

2250 "And let it be so! She has ruined me,
And still more than I say: that answers all."

"Oh, thou hast lost a brave wife: who disputes?"

"So brave a one—that he whom thou behold'st

2234| MS:his gaze §crossed out§ hold   2235| MS:From §crossed out and replaced above by§ On <> misery beyond   1871a:misery, beyond   2239| MS:grace!" 1889a:grace." 2243-44| MS:§¶§   1889a:§¶ lost in paging. Emended to restore ¶; see Editorial Notes§ 2244| MS:'Tis <> "bear up," than   1871a: "Tis <> 'bear up,' than   2245| MS:how make way   1871a:how carve way   2248| MS:Leads §crossed out and replaced above by§ Allures me to choose the lot §last three words crossed out and replaced above by two words§ the choice I "would §crossed out and replaced above by§ shall   2249| MS:Ay, but still <> ones still brings §crossed out and replaced above by§ makes weep!   1871a: "Ay, but, still <> ones, still <> weep!"   1889a:weep."   2251| MS:all.   1871a:all."   2252| MS:who gainsays?   1871a:who disputes?"   2253| MS:whom you behold   1871a:whom thou behold'st

Will never more enjoy his life again!"

2255 "Time will assuage! The evil yet is young!"

"Time, thou mayst say, will; if time mean—to die."

"A wife—the longing for new marriage-joys
Will stop thy sorrow!"
            "Hush, friend,—hold thy peace!
What hast thou said! I could not credit ear!"

2260 "How then? Thou wilt not marry, then, but keep
A widowed couch?"
          "There is not anyone
Of womankind shall couch with whom thou seest!"

"Dost think to profit thus in any way
The dead one?"
          "Her, wherever she abide,
2265 My duty is to honour."
            "And I praise—
Indeed I praise thee! Still, thou hast to pay
The price of it, in being held a fool!"

"Fool call me—only one name call me not!
Bridegroom!"
         "No: it was praise, I portioned thee,
2270 Of being good true husband to thy wife!"

"When I betray her, though she is no more,

2256| MS:"Time, you may   *1871a:*"Time, thou may'st   *1889a:*mayst
2257| MS:marriage—these §crossed out and replaced above by§ joys   *1871a:*marriage-joys
2258| MS:sorrow! §¶§ "Hush, friend, §inserted above§   *1871a:*sorrow!" §¶§
2259| MS:ear!   *1871a:*ear!"   2259-60| MS:§¶§   *1889a:*§¶ lost in paging.
Emended to restore ¶; see Editorial Notes§   2260| MS:then, wilt §crossed out and
replaced above by§ but   2263| MS:profit so in   *1871a:*profit thus in
2265| MS:honor." §¶§   *1881:*honor.' §¶§   *1889a:*honour." §¶§
2266| MS:thee. Still thou   *1871a:*thee! Still, thou   2269| MS:§¶§ "No: praise my
§crossed out and replaced above by§ I <> thee   *1871a:*§¶§ "No: it was praise, I <> thee,

May I die!"
                And the thing he said was true:
For out of Herakles a great glow broke.
There stood a victor worthy of a prize:

2275 The violet-crown that withers on the brow
Of the half-hearted claimant. Oh, he knew
The signs of battle hard fought and well won,
This queller of the monsters!—knew his friend
Planted firm foot, now, on the loathly thing

2280 That was Admetos late! "would die," he knew,
Ere let the reptile raise its crest again.
If that was truth, why try the true friend more?

"Then, since thou canst be faithful to the death,
Take, deep into thy house, my dame!" smiled he.

2285 "Not so!—I pray, by thy Progenitor!"

"Thou wilt mistake in disobeying me!"

"Obeying thee, I have to break my heart!"

"Obey me! Who knows but the favour done
May fall into its place as duty too?"

2290 So, he was humble, would decline no more
Bearing a burden: he just sighed "Alas!
Wouldst thou hadst never brought this prize from game!"

"Yet, when I conquered there, thou conqueredst!"

---

²²⁷²| MS:§¶§ And he said the thing was   *1871a:*§¶§ And the thing he said, was   *1889a:*said
was   ²²⁷³| MS:broke— *1871a:*broke.   ²²⁷⁴| MS:of the §crossed out and replaced
above by§ a prize— *1871a:*prize: ²²⁷⁸| MS:This man that §last two words crossed out§
quelled §altered to§ queller of §inserted above§   ²²⁷⁹| MS:foot now on   *1871a:*foot,
now, on   ²²⁸⁰| MS:was himself §crossed out and replaced above by§ Admetos late:
"would *1871a:*late! "would   ²²⁸³| MS: 'Then   *1871a:*"Then   ²²⁸⁴| MS:Take, to
§crossed out and replaced above by two words§ deep into thy noblest §crossed out§ house, the
noble §last two words crossed out and replaced above by one word§ my dame!" said §crossed
out and replaced below by§ smiled   ²²⁸⁸| MS:favor *1889a:*favour
²²⁹²| *1871a:*Would'st *1889a:*Wouldst   ²²⁹³| MS:conqueredst too!" *1871a:*conqueredst!"

"All excellently urged! Yet—spite of all,
2295   Bear with me! let the woman go away!"

"She shall go, if needs must: but ere she go,
See if there *is* need!"
                    "Need there is! At least,
Except I make thee angry with me, so!"

"But I persist, because I have my spice
2300   Of intuition likewise: take the dame!"

"Be thou the victor, then! But certainly
Thou dost thy friend no pleasure in the act!"

"Oh, time will come when thou shalt praise me! Now—
Only obey!"
                    "Then, servants, since my house
2305   Must needs receive this woman, take her there!"

"I shall not trust this woman to the care
Of servants."
                    "Why, conduct her in, thyself,
If that seem preferable!"
                                "I prefer,
With thy good leave, to place her in thy hands!"

2310   "I would not touch her! Entry to the house—
That, I concede thee."
                    "To thy sole right hand,
I mean to trust her!"
                            "King! Thou wrenchest this

2295| MS:me—let   *1871a:*me! let   2298| MS:Except §added in margin§ Unless
§crossed out§ I   2299| MS:"But I persist because   *1871a:*persist, because   *1889a:*'But
§emended to§ "But §see Editorial Notes§   2300| MS:intuition also §crossed out and
replaced above by§ likewise: take   2301| MS:victor then   *1871a:*victor, then
2303| MS:"O   *1871a:*"Oh   2304| MS:§¶§ "Then, since, it seems, §last three words crossed
out and replaced above by two words§ servants, since   2307| MS:§¶§ "Why §over illegible
word§   2311| MS:right-hand,   *1889a:*right hand,

101

Out of me by main force, if I submit!"

"Courage, friend! Come, stretch hand forth! Good! Now touch
2315   The stranger-woman!"
                              "There! A hand I stretch—
As though it meant to cut off Gorgon's head!"

"Hast hold of her?"
                      "Fast hold."
                                    "Why, then, hold fast
And have her! and, one day, asseverate
Thou wilt, I think, thy friend, the son of Zeus,
2320   He was the gentle guest to entertain!
Look at her! See if she, in any way,
Present thee with resemblance of thy wife!"

Ah, but the tears come, find the words at fault!
There is no telling how the hero twitched
2325   The veil off: and there stood, with such fixed eyes
And such slow smile, Alkestis' silent self!
It was the crowning grace of that great heart,
To keep back joy: procrastinate the truth
Until the wife, who had made proof and found
2330   The husband wanting, might essay once more,
Hear, see, and feel him renovated now—
Able to do, now, all herself had done,
Risen to the height of her: so, hand in hand,
The two might go together, live and die.

2315| MS:stranger!" §punctuation partially erased§ -woman!" §¶§ "There! The hand
1871a:§¶§ "There! A hand   2316| MS:head!   *1871a*:head!"
2318| MS:her, friend! and so affirm, one day,   *1871a*:her! and, one day, asseverate
2320| MS:the sort of guest   *1871a*:the gentle guest   2321| MS:her! If §crossed out§ See
2325| MS:off, and <> stood with   *1871a*:off: and <> stood, with
2327| MS:heart   *1871a*:heart,   2328| MS:That he §crossed out and replaced above by§
To keep <> joy, procrastinate so long, §last two words and comma crossed out§ the
1871a:joy: procrastinate   2329| MS:wife who   *1871a*:wife, who
2321| MS:feel §over *touch*§   2333| MS:her,—so   *1871a*:her: so

2335 Beside, when he found speech, you guess the speech.
He could not think he saw his wife again:
It was some mocking God that used the bliss
To make him mad! Till Herakles must help:
Assure him that no spectre mocked at all;
2340 He was embracing whom he buried once.
Still,—did he touch, might he address the true,—
True eye, true body of the true live wife?

And Herakles said, smiling, "All was truth.
Spectre? Admetos had not made his guest
2345 One who played ghost-invoker, or such cheat!
Oh, he might speak and have response, in time!
All heart could wish was gained now—life for death:
Only, the rapture must not grow immense:
Take care, nor wake the envy of the Gods!"

2350 "Oh thou, of greatest Zeus true son,"—so spoke
Admetos when the closing word must come,
"Go ever in a glory of success,
And save, that sire, his offspring to the end!
For thou hast—only thou—raised me and mine
2355 Up again to this light and life!" Then asked
Tremblingly, how was trod the perilous path
Out of the dark into the light and life:
How it had happened with Alkestis there.

And Herakles said little, but enough—

2340| MS:once; *1871a*:once.   2341| MS:touch, did §crossed out and replaced above by§ might he speak to §last two words crossed out and replaced above by one word§ address   2343| MS:smiling, §comma crossed out§ "All   *1889a*:smiling "All   2344| MS:not turned his   *1871a*:not made his   2346| MS:speak to §altered to§ and <> response in *1871a*:response, in   2347| MS:now: death for §crossed out§ proved life: *1871a*:now— life for death: 2348| MS:immense—   *1871a*:immense: 2350| MS:Then he said §last three words crossed out§ "O   *1889a*:"Oh   2351| MS:Admetos at the end §last three words crossed out§ when   2353| MS:save that sire his   *1871a*:save, that sire, his   2355| MS:Into this <> life!" And then he asked   *1871a*:Up again to this <> life!" Then asked   2356| MS:Tremblingly how was §over *it*§   *1871a*:Tremblingly, how   2358-59| MS:§no ¶§   *1871a*:§¶§   2359| MS:little but   *1871a*:little, but

2360 How he engaged in combat with that king
O' the dæmons: how the field of contest lay
By the tomb's self: how he sprang from ambuscade,
Captured Death, caught him in that pair of hands.

But all the time, Alkestis moved not once
2365 Out of the set gaze and the silent smile;
And a cold fear ran through Admetos' frame:
"Why does she stand and front me, silent thus?"

Herakles solemnly replied "Not yet
Is it allowable thou hear the things
2370 She has to tell thee; let evanish quite
That consecration to the lower Gods,
And on our upper world the third day rise!
Lead her in, meanwhile; good and true thou art,
Good, true, remain thou! Practise piety
2375 To stranger-guests the old way! So, farewell!
Since forth I fare, fulfil my urgent task
Set by the king, the son of Sthenelos."

Fain would Admetos keep that splendid smile
Ever to light him. "Stay with us, thou heart!
2380 Remain our house-friend!"

"At some other day!

2360| MS:in fight with that fell king *1871a*:in combat with that king   2361| MS:dæmons,
where the *1871a*:dæmons: how the   2362| MS:tomb's side, §crossed out and replaced
above by§ self, how *1871a*:self: how   2363| MS:Caught §crossed out and replaced above
by§ Captured   2364| MS:the while, Alkestis <> once, §comma partially erased§
1871a:the time, Alkestis <> once   2365| MS:smile, *1871a*:smile;   2367| MS:me
silent *1871a*:me, silent   2369| MS:allowable to hear *1871a*:allowable thou hear
2370| MS:thee; are §crossed out and replaced above by§ let §word illegibly crossed out§
evanished §alterd to§ evanish   2372| MS:upper §inserted above§   2374| MS:And so
remain still! Practise *1871a*:Good, true, remain thou! Practice   2375| MS:As for me,
forth <> my task *1871a*:Since forth <> my urgent task   2377| MS:by my lord, the
1871a:by the king, the   2377-78| *1871a*:§¶ lost in paging§ *1889a*:§¶ restored§
2378| MS:would Admetos feast on §last two words crossed out and replaced above by one
word§ have that frien §crossed out§ splendid *1871a*:would Admetos keep that

104

Now, of necessity, I haste!" smiled he.

"But mayst thou prosper, go forth on a foot
Sure to return! Through all the tetrarchy
Command my subjects that they institute
2385   Thanksgiving-dances for the glad event,
And bid each altar smoke with sacrifice!
For we are minded to begin a fresh
Existence, better than the life before;
Seeing I own myself supremely blest."

2390   Whereupon all the friendly moralists
Drew this conclusion: chirped, each beard to each:
"Manifold are thy shapings, Providence!
Many a hopeless matter Gods arrange.
What we expected never came to pass:
2395   What we did not expect, Gods brought to bear;
So have things gone, this whole experience through!"

Ah, but if you had seen the play itself!
They say, my poet failed to get the prize:
Sophokles got the prize,—great name! They say,

---

^{2382|} MS:But may'st <> prosper, faring §crossed out and replaced above by§ go <> on the
§inserted above§ foot   *1871a:*"But <> on a foot   ^{2383|} MS:Ensuring §crossed out§
Sure to return! In §crossed out and replaced above by§ Through all my §crossed out and
replaced above by§ the   ^{2384|} MS:Command the citizens §last two words crossed out and
replaced above by three words§ my subjects that   ^{2386|} MS:And make each   *1871a:*And
bid each   ^{2387|} MS:begin a new life §crossed out§   *1871a:*begin a fresh
^{2388|} MS:And §crossed out and replaced above by§ Existence, <> the old §crossed out§ life
^{2389|} MS:Such as man should, supremely blest as I.   *1871a:*Seeing, I own myself supremely
blest."   *1872:*Seeing I   ^{2391|} MS:conclusion; and §crossed out§ chirped, each §over
illegible word§ beard §inserted above§ to each—   *1871a:*conclusion: chirped <> each:
^{2392|} MS:Manifold   *1871a:*"Manifold   ^{2393|} MS:matter comes to p §last two words and
letter crossed out and replaced above by two words§ Gods effect §crossed out§ arrange:
*1871a:*arrange.   ^{2394|} MS:expected, never <> pass,   *1871a:*pass:
*1889a:*expected never   ^{2395|} MS:did not §last two words inserted above§ expected
§altered to§ expect, not, §crossed out§   ^{2396|} MS:through!   *1871a:*through!"
^{2396-97|} MS:§rule and paging instruction; see Editorial Notes§
^{2398|} MS:say my   *1871a:*say, my   ^{2399|} MS:say   *1871a:*say,

2400 Sophokles also means to make a piece,
Model a new Admetos, a new wife:
Success to him! One thing has many sides.
The great name! But no good supplants a good,
Nor beauty undoes beauty. Sophokles
2405 Will carve and carry a fresh cup, brimful
Of beauty and good, firm to the altar-foot,
And glorify the Dionusiac shrine:
Not clash against this crater in the place
Where the God put it when his mouth had drained,
2410 To the last dregs, libation life-blood-like,
And praised Euripides for evermore—
The Human with his droppings of warm tears.

Still, since one thing may have so many sides,
I think I see how,—far from Sophokles,—
2415 You, I, or anyone might mould a new
Admetos, new Alkestis. Ah, that brave
Bounty of poets, the one royal race
That ever was, or will be, in this world!
They give no gift that bounds itself and ends
2420 I' the giving and the taking: theirs so breeds
I' the heart and soul o' the taker, so transmutes
The man who only was a man before,
That he grows godlike in his turn, can give—
He also: share the poets' privilege,
2425 Bring forth new good, new beauty, from the old.

2401| MS:Model afresh §crossed out and replaced above by two words§ a new Admetos, and the §last two words crossed out and replaced above by two words§ a new   2402| MS:sides: 1871a:sides.   2404| MS:beauty fights with beauty   1871a:beauty undoes beauty 2405| MS:brim-full   1871a:brimful   2407| MS:the Dionusian shrine,   1871a:the Dionusiac shrine: 2408| MS:Nor clash   1871a:Not crash <> crater, in   1889a:crater in 2409| MS:drained   1871a:drained,   2410| MS:last drop §crossed out and replaced above by§ dregs libation   1871a:dregs, libation   2411| MS:forever-more—   1871a:for evermore— 2412-13| MS:§no ¶§   1871a:§¶§   2414| MS:how, far <> Sophokles,   1871a:how,—far <> Sophokles,—   2415| MS:mould again §crossed out§ a   1871a:any one   1889a:anyone 2416| Admetos, and §crossed out and replaced above by§ new   2418| MS:was or <> be in 1871a:was, or <> be, in   2422| MS:man that only   1871a:man who only 2423| MS:god-like   1881:godlike   2424| MS:also, share   1871a:also: share

As though the cup that gave the wine, gave, too,
The God's prolific giver of the grape,
That vine, was wont to find out, fawn around
His footstep, springing still to bless the dearth,
2430   At bidding of a Mainad. So with me:
For I have drunk this poem, quenched my thirst,
Satisfied heart and soul—yet more remains!
Could we too make a poem? Try at least,
Inside the head, what shape the rose-mists take!

2435   When God Apollon took, for punishment,
A mortal form and sold himself a slave
To King Admetos till a term should end,—
Not only did he make, in servitude,
Such music, while he fed the flocks and herds,
2440   As saved the pasturage from wrong or fright,
Curing rough creatures of ungentleness:
Much more did that melodious wisdom work
Within the heart o' the master: there, ran wild
Many a lust and greed that grow to strength
2445   By preying on the native pity and care,
Would else, all undisturbed, possess the land.

And these, the God so tamed, with golden tongue,
That, in the plenitude of youth and power,
Admetos vowed himself to rule thenceforth

2428| MS:The vine <> to wander and embrace §last three words crossed out and replaced
above by two words§ find out, fawn   *1871a:*That vine   2429| MS:springing up §crossed
out and replaced above by§ still <> the land §crossed out§ dearth,   2430| MS:§line
added§ a Mainad: so <> me—   *1871a:*a Mainad. So <> me: 2431| MS:So we
§crossed out§ I <> drunk Alk §last three letters crossed out§ this poem, cured §crossed
out and replaced below by§ quenched our §altered to§ my   *1871a:*For I
2432| MS:Comforted heart   *1871a:*Satisfied heart   2433| MS:least   *1871a:*least,
2434| MS:head what   *1871a:*head, what   2435| MS:took for punishment   *1871a:*took,
for punishment,   2443| MS:there ran   *1871a:*there, ran   2444| MS:grows
*1871a:*grow   2445| MS:native §inserted above§ <> and the love §last two words crossed
out and replaced above by one word§ cares   *1871a:*care,   2446| MS:land: *1871a:*land.
2446-47| MS:§no ¶§   *1871a:*§¶§   2447| MS:these, with golden tongue,
§last three words marked for transposition to follow *tamed,*§

²⁴⁵⁰ In Pherai solely for his people's sake,
Subduing to such end each lust and greed
That dominates the natural charity.

And so the struggle ended. Right ruled might:
And soft yet brave, and good yet wise, the man
²⁴⁵⁵ Stood up to be a monarch; having learned
The worth of life, life's worth would he bestow
On all whose lot was cast, to live or die,
As he determined for the multitude.
So stands a statue: pedestalled sublime,
²⁴⁶⁰ Only that it may wave the thunder off,
And ward, from winds that vex, a world below.

And then,—as if a whisper found its way
E'en to the sense o' the marble,—"Vain thy vow!
The royalty of its resolve, that head
²⁴⁶⁵ Shall hide within the dust ere day be done:
That arm, its outstretch of beneficence,
Shall have a speedy ending on the earth:
Lie patient, prone, while light some cricket leaps
And takes possession of the masterpiece,
²⁴⁷⁰ To sit, sing louder as more near the sun.
For why? A flaw was in the pedestal;
Who knows? A worm's work! Sapped, the certain fate
O' the statue is to fall, and thine to die!"

Whereat the monarch, calm, addressed himself

---

²⁴⁵²| MS:charity: *1871a*:charity.   ²⁴⁵²⁻⁵³| MS:§no ¶§ *1871a*:§¶§   ²⁴⁵⁷| MS:cast,
his feet be §last two words and two letters crossed out and replaced above by three words§ to
live or   ²⁴⁵⁸| MS:multitude: *1871a*:multitude.   ²⁴⁵⁹| MS:statue pedestalled
sublime   *1871a*:statue: pedestalled sublime,   ²⁴⁶⁰| MS:off *1871a*:off,
²⁴⁶¹⁻⁶²| MS:§no ¶§ *1871a*:§¶§   ²⁴⁶²| MS:Whereat §crossed out and replaced above by
two words§ And then, as <> whisper made its   *1871a*:then,—as <> whisper found its
²⁴⁶⁵| MS:done, *1871a*:done: ²⁴⁶⁶| MS:arm, and §crossed out and replaced above by§
one outstretch *1871a*:arm, its outstretch   ²⁴⁶⁷| MS:earth, *1871a*:earth:
²⁴⁶⁸| MS:patient there while *1871a*:patient, prone, while   ²⁴⁷⁰| MS:sit, there used §last
two words crossed out§ sing   ²⁴⁷¹| MS:pedestal, *1871a*:pedestal;   ²⁴⁷³⁻⁷⁴| MS:§no
¶§ *1889a*:§¶§   ²⁴⁷⁴| MS:monarch calm addressed *1871a*:monarch, calm, addressed

²⁴⁷⁵ To die, but bitterly the soul outbroke—
"O prodigality of life, blind waste
I' the world, of power profuse without the will
To make life do its work, deserve its day!
My ancestors pursued their pleasure, poured
²⁴⁸⁰ The blood o' the people out in idle war,
Or took occasion of some weary peace
To bid men dig down deep or build up high,
Spend bone and marrow that the king might feast
Entrenched and buttressed from the vulgar gaze.
²⁴⁸⁵ Yet they all lived, nay, lingered to old age:
As though Zeus loved that they should laugh to scorn
The vanity of seeking other ends
In rule than just the ruler's pastime. They
Lived; I must die."

           And, as some long last moan
²⁴⁹⁰ Of a minor suddenly is propped beneath
By note which, new-struck, turns the wail, that was,
Into a wonder and a triumph, so
Began Alkestis: "Nay, thou art to live!
The glory that, in the disguise of flesh,
²⁴⁹⁵ Was helpful to our house,—he prophesied
The coming fate: whereon, I pleaded sore
That he,—I guessed a God, who to his couch
Amid the clouds must go and come again,
While we were darkling,—since he loved us both,
²⁵⁰⁰ He should permit thee, at whatever price,
To live and carry out to heart's content

---

²⁴⁷⁵| MS:the word outbroke— *1871a*:the soul outbroke—   ²⁴⁷⁷| world of
1871a:world, of   ²⁴⁸²| MS:bid them dig   *1871a*:bid men dig   ²⁴⁸⁴| MS:vulgar eye.
1871a:vulgar gaze.   ²⁴⁸⁵| MS:age   *1871a*:age: ²⁴⁸⁷| *1871a*:ends,   *1889a*:ends
²⁴⁸⁸| *1871a*:rule, than   *1889a*:rule than   ²⁴⁸⁹| MS:die." And as   *1871a*:die." §¶§ And,
as   ²⁴⁹¹| MS:wail that was   *1871a*:wail, that was,   ²⁴⁹³| MS:Began §crossed out
and replaced above by two words§ Grew from Alkestis: "Friend, thou   *1871a*:Began
Alkestis: "Nay, thou   ²⁴⁹⁴| MS:The glory §crossed out and replaced above by§ splend
our that   *1871a*:The glory that   ²⁴⁹⁵| MS:helpful in our   *1871a*:helpful to our
²⁴⁹⁶| MS:fate: and when I   *1871a*:fate: whereon, I   ²⁴⁹⁷| MS:god who   *1871a*:a God, who
²⁴⁹⁸| MS:again   *1871a*:again,   ²⁴⁹⁹| MS:both   *1871a*:both,   *1889a*:both," §emended
to§ both, §see Editorial Notes§   ²⁵⁰⁰| MS:thee at < > price   *1871a*:thee, at < > price,

Soul's purpose, turn each thought to very deed,
Nor let Zeus lose the monarch meant in thee.

"To which Apollon, with a sunset smile,
2505 Sadly—'And so should mortals arbitrate!
It were unseemly if they aped us Gods,
And, mindful of our chain of consequence,
Lost care of the immediate earthly link:
Forwent the comfort of life's little hour,
2510 In prospect of some cold abysmal blank
Alien eternity,—unlike the time
They know, and understand to practise with,—
No,—our eternity—no heart's blood, bright
And warm outpoured in its behoof, would tinge
2515 Never so palely, warm a whit the more:
Whereas retained and treasured—left to beat
Joyously on, a life's length, in the breast
O' the loved and loving—it would throb itself
Through, and suffuse the earthly tenement,
2520 Transform it, even as your mansion here
Is love-transformed into a temple-home
Where I, a God, forget the Olumpian glow,
I' the feel of human richness like the rose:
Your hopes and fears, so blind and yet so sweet
2525 With death about them. Therefore, well in thee

2502| MS:turn thy thought *1871a*:turn each thought   2503| MS:thee. *1889a*:thee.
2503-4| MS:§no ¶§ *1871a*:§¶§   2504| MS:To *1889a*:To §emended to§ "To §see
Editorial Notes§   2505| MS:Sadly—'And <> mortals deem' he said: *1871a*:mortals
arbitrate! *1889a*:Sadly—"And §emended to§ Sadly—'And §see Editorial Notes§
2506| MS:'It <> aped the gods *1871a*:aped us Gods, *1889a*:It   2507| MS:of the chain
1871a:of our chain   2508| MS:link, *1871a*:link: 2509| MS:hour *1871a*:hour,
2511| MS:eternity, unlike *1871a*:eternity,—unlike   2512| MS:with; *1871a*:with,—
2513| MS:Therefore, eternity <> blood, whole §crossed out§ bright *1871a*:No,—our eternity
2514| MS:behoof will tinge *1871a*:behoof, would tinge   2516| MS:retained, the treasure
1871a:retained and treasured   2518| MS:loving, it *1871a*:loving,—it
2519| Through and *1871a*:Through, and   2520| MS:With §illegible word§ §last two words
crossed out and replaced above by one word§ Transform   2520-22| MS:here / Where
1871a:here / Is <> temple-home / Where   2523| MS:rose, *1871a*:rose:
2524| MS:Of hopes and fears so <> sweet. *1871a*:Your hopes and fears, so <> sweet,
1881:sweet   2524-25| MS:§line added and illegibly erased§   2525| MS:With
love about them. Wherefore *1871a*:With death about them. Therefore

110

To look, not on eternity, but time:
To apprehend that, should Admetos die,
All, we Gods purposed in him, dies as sure:
That, life's link snapping, all our chain is lost.
2530 And yet a mortal glance might pierce, methinks,
Deeper into the seeming dark of things,
And learn, no fruit, man's life can bear, will fade:
Learn, if Admetos die now, so much more
Will pity for the frailness found in flesh,
2535 Will terror at the earthly chance and change
Frustrating wisest scheme of noblest soul,
Will these go wake the seeds of good asleep
Throughout the world: as oft a rough wind sheds
The unripe promise of some field-flower,—true!
2540 But loosens too the level, and lets breathe
A thousand captives for the year to come.
Nevertheless, obtain thy prayer, stay fate!
Admetos lives—if thou wilt die for him!'

"So was the pact concluded that I die,
2545 And thou live on, live for thyself, for me,
For all the world. Embrace and bid me hail,
Husband, because I have the victory—
Am, heart, soul, head to foot, one happiness!"

Whereto Admetos, in a passionate cry,
2550 "Never, by that true word Apollon spoke!

2526| MS:§line added§ time— *1871a*:time: 2528| MS:All the Gods <> him dies as sure— *1871a*:All, we Gods <> him, dies as sure: 2529| MS:And, life's <> all the chain is lost *1871a*:That, life's <> all our chain is lost. 2531| MS:things *1871a*:things, 2532| MS:And show no fruit, a life <> fade— *1871a*:And learn, no fruit, man's life <> fade: 2533| MS:Show, if <> now, more by much *1871a*:Learn, if <> now, so much more 2538| MS:as when a *1871a*:as oft a 2540| level and *1871a*:level, and 2542| MS:fate, *1871a*:fate! 2543| MS:if §over so§ <> him!' *1889a*:him!" §emended to§ him!' §see Editorial Notes§ 2543-44| MS:§no ¶§ *1871a*:§¶§ 2544| MS:So *1889a*:"So 2546| MS:world: embrace *1871a*:world. Embrace 2547| MS:victory, *1871a*:victory: *1889a*:victory— 2548| MS:Heart and soul *1871a*:Am, heart, soul 2548-49| MS:§no ¶§ *1871a*:§¶§ 2549| MS:Whereto Ademetos in *1871a*:Whereto Ademetos, in 2550| MS: 'Never *1871a*:"Never

All the unwise wish is unwished, oh wife!
Let purposes of Zeus fulfil themselves,
If not through me, then through some other man!
Still, in myself he had a purpose too,
2555   Inalienably mine, to end with me:
This purpose—that, throughout my earthly life,
Mine should be mingled and made up with thine,—
And we two prove one force and play one part
And do one thing. Since death divides the pair,
2560   'Tis well that I depart and thou remain
Who wast to me as spirit is to flesh:
Let the flesh perish, be perceived no more,
So thou, the spirit that informed the flesh,
Bend yet awhile, a very flame above
2565   The rift I drop into the darkness by,—
And bid remember, flesh and spirit once
Worked in the world, one body, for man's sake.
Never be that abominable show
Of passive death without a quickening life—
2570   Admetos only, no Alkestis now!"

Then she: "O thou Admetos, must the pile
Of truth on truth, which needs but one truth more
To tower up in completeness, trophy-like,
Emprize of man, and triumph of the world,
2575   Must it go ever to the ground again

---

^{2552|} MS:The purposes <> themselves   *1871a:*Let purposes <> themselves,
^{2553|} MS:me then <> man: *1871a:*me, then <> man!   ^{2554|} MS:too   *1871a:*too,
^{2555|} MS:§line added§ me—   *1871a:*me: ^{2556|} that throughout <> life   *1871a:*that,
throughout <> life,   ^{2557|} MS:I should <> with thee,   *1871a:*Mine should <> with
thine,—   ^{2559|} MS:thing: since   *1871a:*thing. Since   ^{2562|} MS:flesh go then and
be felt §over *seen*§ no   *1871a:*flesh perish, be perceived no   ^{2563|} MS:While thou the
*1871a:*So thou, the   ^{2564|} MS:Bendest, a very flame, awhile §marked for transposition
to follow *Bendest*§ above   *1871a:*Bend yet awhile   ^{2565|} MS:by   *1871a:*by,—
^{2566|} MS:Bidding remember how both §last two words crossed out§ flesh   *1871a:*And bid
remember, flesh   ^{2568|} MS:For be there no §last four words crossed out and replaced
above by four words§ Shut eyes to that abominable   *1871a:*Never be that   ^{2569|} MS:O'
the passive <> without the quickening   *1871a:*Of passive <> without a quickening
^{2570-71|} MS:§no ¶§   *1871a:*§¶§   ^{2571|} MS:she "O   *1889a:*she: "O   ^{2574|} MS:The
emprize of man, the triumph <> world—   *1871a:*Emprize of man, and triumph <> world,

Because of some faint heart or faltering hand,
Which we, that breathless world about the base,
Trusted should carry safe to altitude,
Superimpose o' the summit, our supreme
2580 Achievement, our victorious coping-stone?
Shall thine, Beloved, prove the hand and heart
That fail again, flinch backward at the truth
Would cap and crown the structure this last time,—
Precipitate our monumental hope
2585 And strew the earth ignobly yet once more?
See how, truth piled on truth, the structure wants,
Waits just the crowning truth I claim of thee!
Wouldst thou, for any joy to be enjoyed,
For any sorrow that thou mightst escape,
2590 Unwill thy will to reign a righteous king?
Nowise! And were there two lots, death and life,—
Life, wherein good resolve should go to air,
Death, whereby finest fancy grew plain fact
I' the reign of thy survivor,—life or death?
2595 Certainly death, thou choosest. Here stand I
The wedded, the beloved one: hadst thou loved
Her who less worthily could estimate
Both life and death than thou? Not so should say
Admetos, whom Apollon made come court
2600 Alkestis in a car, submissive brutes
Of blood were yoked to, symbolizing soul
Must dominate unruly sense in man.

2576| MS:faultering *1889a*:faltering   2577| MS:We, all that *1871a*:Which we, that
2580| MS:Achievement, the victorious coping-stone,— *1871a*:Achievement, our victorious
coping-stone?   2582| MS:fail once more §last two words crossed out and replaced above
by one word§ again   2583| MS:time, *1871a*:time,—   2585| MS:To strew
1889a:And strew   2588| *1871a*:Would'st *1889a*:Wouldst
2589| MS:*1871a*:might'st *1889a*:mightst   2590| MS:the *1871a*:thy
2592| MS:Life wherein *1871a*:Life, wherein   2593| MS:Death whereby *1871a*:Death,
whereby   2596| MS:wedded wife, the loved one: hadst *1871a*:wedded, the beloved:
hadst *1889a*:beloved one §punctuation decayed§ hadst §emended to§ one: hadst §see
Editorial Notes§   2597| MS:One who <> worthily made estimate *1871a*:worthily could
estimate *1889a*:Her who   2598| MS:Of life *1871a*:Both life   2599| MS:Admetos
whom *1871a*:Admetos, whom   2600| MS:car submissive *1871a*:car, submissive
2602| MS:That §over *Shal*§ dominates *1871a*:Must dominate

Then, shall Admetos and Alkestis see
Good alike, and alike choose, each for each,
2605 Good,—and yet, each for other, at the last,
Choose evil? What? thou soundest in my soul
To depths below the deepest, reachest good
In evil, that makes evil good again,
And so allottest to me that I live
2610 And not die—letting die, not thee alone,
But all true life that lived in both of us?
Look at me once ere thou decree the lot!"

Therewith her whole soul entered into his,
He looked the look back, and Alkestis died.

2615 And even while it lay, i' the look of him,
Dead, the dimmed body, bright Alkestis' soul
Had penetrated through the populace
Of ghosts, was got to Koré,—throned and crowned
The pensive queen o' the twilight, where she dwells
2620 Forever in a muse, but half away
From flowery earth she lost and hankers for,—
And there demanded to become a ghost
Before the time.

                          Whereat the softened eyes
Of the lost maidenhood that lingered still
2625 Straying among the flowers in Sicily,
Sudden was startled back to Hades' throne

---

²⁶⁰³| What? Shall *1871a*:Then, shall ²⁶⁰⁵| MS:Good, and <> last *1871a*:Good,—and
<> last, ²⁶⁰⁷| MS:deepest, then—some good *1871a*:deepest, reachest good
²⁶⁰⁸| MS:Of evil that <> again— *1871a*:In evil, that <> again, ²⁶¹⁰| MS:die—but
§crossed out§ let §altered to§ letting die not <> alone *1871a*:letting die, not <> alone,
²⁶¹¹| MS:us! *1871a*:us? ²⁶¹²⁻¹³| MS:§no ¶§ *1871a*:§¶§ ²⁶¹⁴⁻¹⁵| MS:§no ¶§
1871a:§¶§ ²⁶¹⁵| MS:while she lay i' <> him *1871a*:while it lay, i' <> him,
²⁶¹⁷| MS:penetrated all §crossed out and replaced above by§ through ²⁶¹⁹| MS:twilight
where *1871a*:twilight, where ²⁶²³| MS:time. Whereat *1871a*:time. §¶§
Whereat ²⁶²⁴| MS:the much maidenhood that still remained *1871a*:the lost
maidenhood that lingered still ²⁶²⁵| MS:among far §crossed out and replaced
above by§ the ²⁶²⁶| MS:Plucked of a sudden back to Hades now
1871a:Sudden was startled back to Hades' throne, *1889a*:throne

114

By that demand: broke through humanity
Into the orbed omniscience of a God,
Searched at a glance Alkestis to the soul,
2630 And said—while a long slow sigh lost itself
I' the hard and hollow passage of a laugh:

"Hence, thou deceiver! This is not to die,
If, by the very death which mocks me now,
The life, that's left behind and past my power,
2635 Is formidably doubled. Say, there fight
Two athletes, side by side, each athlete armed
With only half the weapons, and no more,
Adequate to a contest with their foe:
If one of these should fling helm, sword and shield
2640 To fellow—shieldless, swordless, helmless late—
And so leap naked o'er the barrier, leave
A combatant equipped from head to heel,
Yet cry to the other side 'Receive a friend
Who fights no longer!' 'Back, friend, to the fray!'
2645 Would be the prompt rebuff; I echo it.
Two souls in one were formidable odds:
Admetos must not be himself and thou!"

And so, before the embrace relaxed a whit,
The lost eyes opened, still beneath the look;
2650 And lo, Alkestis was alive again,
And of Admetos' rapture who shall speak?

So, the two lived together long and well.
But never could I learn, by word of scribe

2627| MS:demand, broke *1871a*:demand: broke   2629| MS:soul *1871a*:soul,
2631| MS:laugh, *1871a*:laugh: 2631-32| MS:§no ¶§ *1871a*:§¶§   2632| MS:"Back,
thou <> die *1871a*:"Hence, thou <> die,   2633| MS:When, by *1871a*:If, by
2634| MS:life that's <> power *1871a*:life, that's <> power,   2635| MS:fought
1871a:fight   2638| MS:with the foe: *1871a*:with their foe: 2644| MS:longer!'
Back <> fray! *1871a*:longer!' 'Back <> fray!'   2645| MS:§line added§
2646| MS:one is formidable odds— *1871a*:one were formidable odds: 2647-48| MS:§no
¶§ *1871a*:§¶§   2648| MS:the long §crossed out§ embrace   2649| MS:look,
1871a:look;   2651-52| MS:§no ¶§ *1871a*:§¶§   2652| MS:So the *1871a*:So, the

Or voice of poet, rumour wafts our way,
2655 That—of the scheme of rule in righteousness,
The bringing back again the Golden Age,
Which, rather than renounce, our pair would die—
That ever one faint particle came true,
With both alive to bring it to effect:
2660 Such is the envy Gods still bear mankind!

So might our version of the story prove,
And no Euripidean pathos plague
Too much my critic-friend of Syracuse.

"Besides your poem failed to get the prize:
2665 (That is, the first prize: second prize is none).
Sophokles got it!" Honour the great name!
All cannot love two great names; yet some do:
I know the poetess who graved in gold,
Among her glories that shall never fade,
2670 This style and title for Euripides,
The Human with his droppings of warm tears.

I know, too, a great Kaunian painter, strong
As Herakles, though rosy with a robe
Of grace that softens down the sinewy strength:
2675 And he has made a picture of it all.
There lies Alkestis dead, beneath the sun,
She longed to look her last upon, beside

2855| MS:That of their §altered to§ the   *1871a:*That,—of   *1889a:*That—of
2655-58| MS:righteousness, / The couple fain had died before renounce, / Ever one first faint
<> true   *1871a:*righteousness, / The bringing back again the Golden Age, / Our couple,
rather than renounce, would die— / Ever <> true,   *1889a:*righteousness, /,/ Which, rather
than renounce, our pair would die— / That ever one faint   2659| MS:effect—
*1871a:*effect: 2663-64| MS:§leaf ends§   *1871a:*§¶§   2664-66| MS:prize: / Sophokles
<> Honor   *1871a:*prize: / (That is, the first prize: second prize is none). / Sophokles
*1889a:*it!" Honour   2667| MS:All do §crossed out§ cannot   2668| MS:the woman
that has named the w §last five words and letter crossed out and replaced above by five words§
poetess who graved in gold   *1871a:*gold,   2669| MS:fade   *1871a:*fade,   2672| MS:Also
there is a Kaunian   *1871a:*I know, too, a great Kaunian   2674| MS:strength,   *1871a:*strength:
2675| MS:of the scene. §last two words crossed out and replaced above by two words§ it all.
2676| MS:dead, while §crossed out§ beneath the sun   *1871a:*sun,

The sea, which somehow tempts the life in us
To come trip over its white waste of waves,
2680 And try escape from earth, and fleet as free.
Behind the body, I suppose there bends
Old Pheres in his hoary impotence;
And women-wailers, in a corner crouch
—Four, beautiful as you four—yes, indeed!—
2685 Close, each to other, agonizing all,
As fastened, in fear's rhythmic sympathy,
To two contending opposite. There strains
The might o' the hero 'gainst his more than match,
—Death, dreadful not in thew and bone, but like
2690 The envenomed substance that exudes some dew
Whereby the merely honest flesh and blood
Will fester up and run to ruin straight,
Ere they can close with, clasp and overcome
The poisonous impalpability
2695 That simulates a form beneath the flow
Of those grey garments; I pronounce that piece
Worthy to set up in our Poikilé!

And all came,—glory of the golden verse,
And passion of the picture, and that fine
2700 Frank outgush of the human gratitude
Which saved our ship and me, in Syracuse,—
Ay, and the tear or two which slipt perhaps
Away from you, friends, while I told my tale,
—It all came of this play that gained no prize!
2705 Why crown whom Zeus has crowned in soul before?

2678| MS:sea which   *1871a:*sea, which   2679| MS:§line added§ waves   *1871a:*waves,
2680| MS:earth and   *1871a:*earth, and   2682| MS:his impotence of grief,   *1871a:*his
hoary impotence;   2684| MS:§line added§ —Four beautiful   *1871a:*—Four, beautiful
2685| MS:all   *1871a:*all,   2692| MS:straight   *1871a:*straight,   2693| MS:and
conquer so   *1871a:*and overcome   2696| MS:garments: I have seen §last two words
crossed out and replaced above by one word§ pronounce   *1871a:*garments; I
2697| MS:in the §crossed out and replaced above by§ our   2697-98| MS:§no ¶§
1871a:§¶§   2699| MS:that good   *1871a:*that fine   2701| MS:That saved my life, I
say, in Syracuse,   *1871a:*Which saved our ship and me, in Syracuse,—
2703| MS:you the while   *1871a:*you, friends, while   2705| MS:§following last line of
poem§ L. D. I. E. / Begun and ended in May, 1872. / RB §see Editorial Notes§

PRINCE HOHENSTIEL-SCHWANGAU, Saviour of Society

Edited by Allan C. Dooley and Susan E. Dooley

PRINCE HOHENSTIEL-SCHWANGAU, SAVIOUR OF SOCIETY

῾Ύδραν φονεύσας, μυρίων τ᾽ ἄλλων πόνων
διῆλθον ἀγέλας . . .
τὸ λοίσθιον δὲ τονδ᾽ ἔτλην τάλας πόνον,
. . . δῶμα θριγκῶσαι κακοῖς.

I slew the Hydra, and from labour pass'd
To labour—tribes of labours! Till, at last,
Attempting one more labour, in a trice,
Alack, with ills *I crowned the edifice.*

---

⁴| MS:§Greek words illegibly crossed out§ δομα   ⁵| MS:past   *1871b*:pass'd
⁶| MS:labours §last letter crossed out§   ⁸| MS:Alack, §added in margin§ With
§altered to§ with ills, I, luckless, §crossed out§ *crowned   1871b*:ills I *crowned*

PRINCE HOHENSTIEL-SCHWANGAU, SAVIOUR OF SOCIETY

1871

You have seen better days, dear? So have I—
And worse too, for they brought no such bud-mouth
As yours to lisp "You wish you knew me!" Well,
Wise men, 'tis said, have sometimes wished the same,
5   And wished and had their trouble for their pains.
Suppose my Œdipus should lurk at last
Under a pork-pie hat and crinoline,
And, lateish, pounce on Sphynx in Leicester Square?
Or likelier, what if Sphynx in wise old age,
10   Grown sick of snapping foolish people's heads,
And jealous for her riddle's proper rede,—
Jealous that the good trick which served the turn
Have justice rendered it, nor class one day
With friend Home's stilts and tongs and medium-ware,—
15   What if the once redoubted Sphynx, I say,
(Because night draws on, and the sands increase,
And desert-whispers grow a prophecy)
Tell all to Corinth of her own accord,
Bright Corinth, not dull Thebes, for Laïs' sake
20   Who finds me hardly grey, and likes my nose,
And thinks a man of sixty at the prime?
Good! It shall be! Revealment of myself!
But listen, for we must co-operate;
I don't drink tea: permit me the cigar!

25   First, how to make the matter plain, of course—
What was the law by which I lived. Let's see:
Ay, we must take one instant of my life
Spent sitting by your side in this neat room:
Watch well the way I use it, and don't laugh!
30   Here's paper on the table, pen and ink:

---

§MS in Balliol College Library, Oxford. Ed. 1871b, 1889a§   ⁸| MS:latish
1889a:lateish   ¹³| MS:it nor *1871b*:it, nor   ¹⁵| MS:redoubtable
1871b:redoubted   ²³| MS:co-operate: *1871b*:co-operate;
²⁷| MS:Ay, let §crossed out and replaced above by§ we   ³⁰| MS:ink *1871b*:ink:

Give me the soiled bit—not the pretty rose!
See! having sat an hour, I'm rested now,
Therefore want work: and spy no better work
For eye and hand and mind that guides them both,
35   During this instant, than to draw my pen
From blot One—thus—up, up to blot Two—thus—
Which I at last reach, thus, and here's my line
Five inches long and tolerably straight:
Better to draw than leave undrawn, I think,
40   Fitter to do than let alone, I hold,
Though better, fitter, by but one degree.
Therefore it was that, rather than sit still
Simply, my right-hand drew it while my left
Pulled smooth and pinched the moustache to a point.

45   Now I permit your plump lips to unpurse:
"So far, one possibly may understand
Without recourse to witchcraft!" True, my dear.
Thus folks begin with Euclid,—finish, how?
Trying to square the circle!—at any rate,
50   Solving abstruser problems than this first
"How find the nearest way 'twixt point and point."
Deal but with moral mathematics so—
Master one merest moment's work of mine,
Even this practising with pen and ink,—
55   Demonstrate why I rather plied the quill
Than left the space a blank,—you gain a fact,
And God knows what a fact's worth! So proceed
By inference from just this moral fact
—I don't say, to that plaguy quadrature
60   "What the whole man meant, whom you wish you knew,"
But, what meant certain things he did of old,
Which puzzled Europe,—why, you'll find them plain,
This way, not otherwise: I guarantee,
Understand one, you comprehend the rest.
65   Rays from all round converge to any point:
Study the point then ere you track the rays!

31| MS:rose—   *1871b*:rose!   34| MS:both   *1871b*:both,   37| MS:and leave
§crossed out and replaced above by§ here's   47| MS:Without   *1871b*:"Without
1889a:"Without §emended to§ Without §see Editorial Notes§
64| MS:One understand §last two words marked for transposition to§ Understand one

The size o' the circle's nothing; subdivide
Earth, and earth's smallest grain of mustard-seed,
You count as many parts, small matching large,
70   If you can use the mind's eye: otherwise,
Material optics, being gross at best,
Prefer the large and leave our mind the small—
And pray how many folk have minds can see?
Certainly you—and somebody in Thrace
75   Whose name escapes me at the moment. You—
Lend me your mind then! Analyse with me
This instance of the line 'twixt blot and blot
I rather chose to draw than leave a blank,
Things else being equal. You are taught thereby
80   That 'tis my nature, when I am at ease,
Rather than idle out my life too long,
To want to do a thing—to put a thought,
Whether a great thought or a little one,
Into an act, as nearly as may be.
85   Make what is absolutely new—I can't,
Mar what is made already well enough—
I won't: but turn to best account the thing
That's half-made—that I can. Two blots, you saw
I knew how to extend into a line
90   Symmetric on the sheet they blurred before—
Such little act suffficed, this time, such thought.

Now, we'll extend rays, widen out the verge,
Describe a larger circle; leave this first
Clod of an instance we began with, rise
95   To the complete world many clods effect.
Only continue patient while I throw,
Delver-like, spadeful after spadeful up,
Just as truths come, the subsoil of me, mould
Whence spring my moods: your object,—just to find,

---

⁷²| MS:small, *1871b*:small—   ⁷³| MS:many have the mind and §altered to§ can
1871b:many folks have minds can   ⁸⁴| MS:be: *1871b*:be.   ⁸⁸| MS:saw,
1871b:saw   ⁹¹| MS:sufficed, such thought. this time, §last two words marked for
transposition to follow *sufficed*,§   ⁹⁵| MS:effect— *1871b*:effect.
⁹⁸⁻⁹⁹| MS:The §altered to§ the subsoil of me, mould §new line break inserted§
of all §last two words crossed out and replaced above by two words§ Whence spring my moods
§marked for continuation with *: your*§ / Just as truths come, §last four words marked for
transposition to beginning of 98§ :your object,—just to find,

¹⁰⁰ Alike from handlift and from barrow-load,
What salts and silts may constitute the earth—
If it be proper stuff to blow man glass,
Or bake him pottery, bear him oaks or wheat—
What's born of me, in brief; which found, all's known.
¹⁰⁵ If it were genius did the digging-job,
Logic would speedily sift its product smooth
And leave the crude truths bare for poetry;
But I'm no poet, and am stiff i' the back
What one spread fails to bring, another may.
¹¹⁰ In goes the shovel and out comes scoop—as here!

I live to please myself. I recognize
Power passing mine, immeasurable, God—
Above me, whom He made, as heaven beyond
Earth—to use figures which assist our sense.
¹¹⁵ I know that He is there as I am here,
By the same proof, which seems no proof at all,
It so exceeds familiar forms of proof.
Why "there," not "here"? Because, when I say "there,"
I treat the feeling with distincter shape
¹²⁰ That space exists between us: I,—not He,—
Live, think, do human work here—no machine,
His will moves, but a being by myself,
His, and not He who made me for a work,
Watches my working, judges its effect,
¹²⁵ But does not interpose. He did so once,
And probably will again some time—not now,
Life being the minute of mankind, not God's,
In a certain sense, like time before and time
After man's earthly life, so far as man
¹³⁰ Needs apprehend the matter. Am I clear?

---

^{102|} MS:glass   *1871b*:glass,   ^{104|} MS:brief: which   ^{105|} MS:If 'twere but genius
1871b:If it were genius   ^{107|} MS:poetry.   *1871b*:poetry;
^{113|} MS:me whom   *1871b*:me, whom   ^{114|} MS:figures and §crossed out and replaced
above by§ which <> sense   *1871b*:sense.   ^{116|} MS:all   *1871b*:all,
^{118|} MS:here"? Because when <> there"   *1871b*:here"? Because, when <> there,"
^{121|} MS:machine   *1871b*:machine,   ^{125|} MS:interpose: He   *1871b*:interpose. He
^{127|} MS:the §inserted above§ mankind's §last letter altered to§ of minute §marked for
transposition with *mankind*§ and §crossed out and replaced above by§ not God's, gift §crossed
out§   *1871b*:mankind, not   ^{128-30|} MS:§lines added vertically in margin§

Suppose I bid a courier take to-night
(. . . Once for all, let me talk as if I smoked
Yet in the Residenz, a personage:
I must still represent the thing I was,
135   Galvanically make dead muscle play,
Or how shall I illustrate muscle's use?)
I could then, last July, bid courier take
Message for me, post-haste, a thousand miles.
I bid him, since I have the right to bid,
140   And, my part done so far, his part begins;
He starts with due equipment, will and power,
Means he may use, misuse, not use at all,
At his discretion, at his peril too.
I leave him to himself: but, journey done,
145   I count the minutes, call for the result
In quickness and the courier quality,
Weigh its worth, and then punish or reward
According to proved service; not before.
Meantime, he sleeps through noontide, rides till dawn,
150   Sticks to the straight road, tries the crooked path,
Measures and manages resource, trusts, doubts
Advisers by the wayside, does his best
At his discretion, lags or launches forth,
(He knows and I know) at his peril too.
155   You see? Exactly thus men stand to God:
I with my courier, God with me. Just so
I have His bidding to perform; but mind
And body, all of me, though made and meant
For that sole service, must consult, concert
160   With my own self and nobody beside,
How to effect the same: God helps not else.
'Tis I who, with my stock of craft and strength,
Choose the directer cut across the hedge,
Or keep the foot-track that respects a crop.
165   Lie down and rest, rise up and run,—live spare,

---

^{133|}   MS:personage—   *1871b*:personage: ^{138|}   MS:Letter §crossed out and replaced
above by§ Message <> miles: *1871b*:miles.   ^{140|}   MS:begins,   *1871b*:begins;
^{146|}   MS:§line added§   ^{148|}   MS:before: *1871b*:before.   ^{150|}   MS:straight path
§crossed out and replaced above by§ road <> crooked way, §crossed out and replaced above
by§ path,   ^{155|}   MS:thus I §crossed out and replaced above by§ men   ^{156|}   MS:§line
added§ me: just   *1871b*:me. Just   ^{157|}   MS:perform: but   *1871b*:perform; but
^{163|}   MS:hedge   *1871b*:hedge,   ^{164|}   MS:crop,—   *1871b*:crop.

Feed free,—all that's my business: but, arrive,
Deliver message, bring the answer back,
And make my bow, I must: then God will speak,
Praise me or haply blame as service proves.
170 To other men, to each and everyone,
Another law! what likelier? God, perchance,
Grants each new man, by some as new a mode,
Intercommunication with Himself,
Wreaking on finiteness infinitude;
175 By such a series of effects, gives each
Last His own imprint: old yet ever new
The process: 'tis the way of Deity.
How it succeeds, He knows: I only know
That varied modes of creatureship abound,
180 Implying just as varied intercourse
For each with the creator of them all.
Each has his own mind and no other's mode.
What mode may yours be? I shall sympathize!
No doubt, you, good young lady that you are,
185 Despite a natural naughtiness or two,
Turn eyes up like a Pradier Magdalen
And see an outspread providential hand
Above the owl's-wing aigrette—guard and guide—
Visibly o'er your path, about your bed,
190 Through all your practisings with London-town.
It points, you go; it stays fixed, and you stop;
You quicken its procedure by a word
Spoken, a thought in silence, prayer and praise.
Well, I believe that such a hand may stoop,
195 And such appeals to it may stave off harm,
Pacify the grim guardian of this Square,
And stand you in good stead on quarter-day:
Quite possible in your case; not in mine.
"Ah, but I choose to make the difference,

175| MS:of results, gives   *1871b*:of effects, gives   176| MS:Last, His own imprint; old
1871b:Last His own imprint: old   186| MS:a Pradier Magdalen,   *1871b*:a Pradier
Magdalen   190| MS:with London-town: *1871b*:with London-town.
191| MS:points—you go: it < > stop: *1871b*:points, you go; it < > stop;   194| MS:a
Hand   *1871b*:hand   198| MS:case: not   *1871b*:case; not   199| MS:Ah   *1871b*:"Ah

200 Find the emancipation?" No, I hope!
    If I deceive myself, take noon for night,
    Please to become determinedly blind
    To the true ordinance of human life,
    Through mere presumption—that is my affair,
205 And truly a grave one; but as grave I think
    Your affair, yours, the specially observed,—
    Each favoured person that perceives his path
    Pointed him, inch by inch, and looks above
    For guidance, through the mazes of this world,
210 In what we call its meanest life-career
    —Not how to manage Europe properly,
    But how keep open shop, and yet pay rent,
    Rear household, and make both ends meet, the same.
    I say, such man is no less tasked than I
215 To duly take the path appointed him
    By whatsoever sign he recognize.
    Our insincerity on both our heads!
    No matter what the object of a life,
    Small work or large,—the making thrive a shop,
220 Or seeing that an empire take no harm,—
    There are known fruits to judge obedience by.
    You've read a ton's weight, now, of newspaper—
    Lives of me, gabble about the kind of prince—
    You know my work i' the rough; I ask you, then,
225 Do I appear subordinated less
    To hand-impulsion, one prime push for all,
    Than little lives of men, the multitude
    That cried out, every quarter of an hour,
    For fresh instructions, did or did not work,
230 And praised in the odd minutes?

                        Eh, my dear?

200| MS:emancipation? No   *1871b*:emancipation?" No   203| MS:life   *1871b*:life,
205| MS:one: but   *1871b*:one; but   206| MS:specially-observed,—   *1871b*:specially
observed,—   207| MS:favored   *1889a*:favoured   212| MS:shop and   *1871b*:shop,
and   213| MS:household, yet make   *1871b*:household, and make
215| MS:appointed each   *1871b*:appointed him   216| MS:sign we recognize:
1871b:sign he recognize.   220| MS:The §crossed out and replaced above by§ Or
222| MS:ton's-weight   *1871b*:ton's weight   224| MS:rough: I   *1871b*:rough; I
228| MS:out every < > hour   *1871b*:out, every < > hour,

Such is the reason why I acquiesced
In doing what seemed best for me to do,
So as to please myself on the great scale,
Having regard to immortality
235   No less than life—did that which head and heart
Prescribed my hand, in measure with its means
Of doing—used my special stock of power—
Not from the aforesaid head and heart alone,
But every sort of helpful circumstance,
240   Some problematic and some nondescript:
All regulated by the single care
I' the last resort—that I made thoroughly serve
The when and how, toiled where was need, reposed
As resolutely at the proper point,
245   Braved sorrow, courted joy, to just one end:
Namely, that just the creature I was bound
To be, I should become, nor thwart at all
God's purpose in creation. I conceive
No other duty possible to man,—
250   Highest mind, lowest mind, no other law
By which to judge life failure or success:
What folk call being saved or cast away.

Such was my rule of life: I worked my best
Subject to ultimate judgment, God's not man's.

255   Well then, this settled,—take your tea, I beg,
And meditate the fact, 'twixt sip and sip,—

235| MS:than this §crossed out§ life—just as §last two words crossed out and replaced
above by three words§ did that which   237| MS:used §inserted above§ my particular
§crossed out and replaced above by§ special   240| MS:§line added§ nondescript;
1871b:nondescript: 244| MS:resolutely to the   *1889a*:resolutely at the
245| MS:Braved pain or §last two words crossed out and replaced above by one word§
sorrow, courted pleasure §crossed out and replaced above by§ joy, <> end   *1871b*:end:
247| MS:become—nor   *1871b*:become, nor   249| MS:man,   *1871b*:man,—
250| MS:Highest and §crossed out and replaced above by§ mind, lowest mind,—no
1889a:lowest mind, no   251| MS:success   *1871b*:success: 252| MS:—What folks
1871b:What   *1889a*:folk   253| MS:life, I   *1871b*:life; I   *1889a*:life: I
254| MS:man's.   *1889a*:man's §emended to§ man's. §see Editorial Notes§
254-55| MS:§¶§   *1889a*:§no ¶; emended to restore ¶; see Editorial Notes§
256| MS:fact 'twixt   *1871b*:fact, 'twixt

This settled—why I pleased myself, you saw,
By turning blot and blot into a line,
O' the little scale,—we'll try now (as your tongue
260   Tries the concluding sugar-drop) what's meant
To please me most o' the great scale. Why, just now,
With nothing else to do within my reach,
Did I prefer making two blots one line
To making yet another separate
265   Third blot, and leaving those I found unlinked?
It meant, I like to use the thing I find,
Rather than strive at unfound novelty:
I make the best of the old, nor try for new.
Such will to act, such choice of action's way,
270   Constitute—when at work on the great scale,
Driven to their farthest natural consequence
By all the help from all the means—my own
Particular faculty of serving God,
Instinct for putting power to exercise
275   Upon some wish and want o' the time, I prove
Possible to mankind as best I may.
This constitutes my mission,—grant the phrase,—
Namely, to rule men—men within my reach,
To order, influence and dispose them so
280   As render solid and stabilify
Mankind in particles, the light and loose,
For their good and my pleasure in the act.
Such good accomplished proves twice good to me—
Good for its own sake, as the just and right,

257| MS:myself, to wit, §last two words crossed out and replaced above by two words§ you saw,
258| MS:a bar, §crossed out and replaced above by§ line,   259| MS:we'll ask §crossed out
and replaced above by§ try now—as   *1871b:*now (as   260| MS:sugar-drop—what's
265| MS:blot and < > found in peace? §last two words crossed out and replaced above by one
word§ unlinked? *1871b:*blot, and   266| MS:means *1871b:*meant
267| MS:at the §crossed out§ unfound and new §last two words crossed out and replaced
above by one word§ novelty: 268| MS:old, by preference. §last two words crossed out
and replaced above by four words§ nor try for new.   270| MS:Constitute, when
*1871b:*Constitute—when   273| MS:§line added§   276| MS:to the world §last two
words crossed out and replaced above by one word§ mankind < > may— *1871b:*may.
278| MS:men—those within *1871b:*men—men within   279| MS:To §added in margin§
Order §altered to§ order, and §crossed out§ influence   281| MS:the loose and light,
§last word marked for transposition with *loose*§   282| MS:act: *1871b:*act.
283| MS:accomplished, proves *1871b:*accomplished proves

131

285 And, in the effecting also, good again
To me its agent, tasked as suits my taste.

Is this much easy to be understood
At first glance? Now begin the steady gaze!

My rank—(if I must tell you simple truth—
290 Telling were else not worth the whiff o' the weed
I lose for the tale's sake)—dear, my rank i' the world
Is hard to know and name precisely: err
I may, but scarcely over-estimate
My style and title. Do I class with men
295 Most useful to their fellows? Possibly,—
Therefore, in some sort, best; but, greatest mind
And rarest nature? Evidently no.
A conservator, call me, if you please,
Not a creator nor destroyer: one
300 Who keeps the world safe. I profess to trace
The broken circle of society,
Dim actual order, I can redescribe
Not only where some segment silver-true
Stays clear, but where the breaks of black commence
305 Baffling you all who want the eye to probe—
As I make out yon problematic thin
White paring of your thumb-nail outside there,
Above the plaster-monarch on his steed—
See an inch, name an ell, and prophecy
310 O' the rest that ought to follow, the round moon
Now hiding in the night of things: that round,
I labour to demonstrate moon enough

286| MS:task §altered to§ tasked that §crossed out and replaced above by§ as
287| MS:thus   *1871b*:this   293| MS:overestimate   *1871b*:over-estimate
295| MS:to my fellows   *1871b*:to their fellows   296| MS:best: but   *1871b*:best; but
299| MS:one who works §last two words crossed out§   300| MS:To §crossed out and
replaced above by§ Who keep §altered to§ keeps < > safe. There I clearly §last three words
crossed out and replaced above by three words§ I profess to
304| MS:Comes §crossed out and replaced above by§ Stays   306| MS:problematic orb
§crossed out and replaced above by§ thin   308| MS:That dots §last two
words crossed out and replaced above by one word§ Above the plaster monarch
1871b:plaster-monarch   310| MS:follow,—the   *1871b*:follow, the
311| MS:That's §crossed out and replaced above by§ Now < > round   *1871b*:round,

For the month's purpose,—that society,
Render efficient for the age's need:
³¹⁵ Preserving you in either case the old,
Nor aiming at a new and greater thing,
A sun for moon, a future to be made
By first abolishing the present law:
No such proud task for me by any means!
³²⁰ History shows you men whose master-touch
Not so much modifies as makes anew:
Minds that transmute nor need restore at all.
A breath of God made manifest in flesh
Subjects the world to change, from time to time,
³²⁵ Alters the whole conditions of our race
Abruptly, not by unperceived degrees
Nor play of elements already there,
But quite new leaven, leavening the lump,
And liker, so, the natural process. See!
³³⁰ Where winter reigned for ages—by a turn
I' the time, some star-change, (ask geologists)
The ice-tracts split, clash, splinter and disperse,
And there's an end of immobility,
Silence, and all that tinted pageant, base
³³⁵ To pinnacle, one flush from fairyland
Dead-asleep and deserted somewhere,—see!—
As a fresh sun, wave, spring and joy outburst.
Or else the earth it is, time starts from trance,
Her mountains tremble into fire, her plains
³⁴⁰ Heave blinded by confusion: what result?

---

^{313|} MS:the night's §crossed out and replaced above by§ night's <> society— *1871b*:society,
^{314|} To prove §last two words crossed out and replaced above by one word§ Render <>
need— *1871b*:need: ^{315|} MS:old *1871b*:old, ^{316|} MS:And not another newer
§altered to§ new and *1871b*:Nor aiming at a new ^{319|} MS:Not such a task *1871b*:No
such proud task ^{320|} MS:you §inserted above§ men with the §last two words crossed out
and replaced above by one word§ whose ^{321|} §line added§ anew, *1871b*:anew:
^{322|} MS:all; *1871b*:all. ^{327|} MS:of the elements *1871b*:of elements
^{331|} MS:the world §crossed out and replaced above by§ time ^{333|} MS:of the stability,
1871b:of immobility, ^{334|} MS:that ghastly §crossed out and replaced above by§ tinted
^{335|} MS:one §inserted above§ out- §crossed out and replaced above by§ faint §crossed out§
flushed §altered to§ flush ^{336|} MS:deserted far away §last two words crossed out and
replaced above by one word§ somewhere, see, *1871b*:somewhere,—see!—
^{337|} MS:sun, sea, spring <> outbreak: §altered to§ outburst: *1871b*:sun, wave, spring <>
outburst. ^{338|} MS:§line added§ ^{339|} MS:mountain §altered to§ mountains
trembles §altered to§ tremble ^{340|} MS:Heaves §altered to§ Heave

New teeming growth, surprises of strange life
Impossible before, a world broke up
And re-made, order gained by law destroyed.
Not otherwise, in our society
345 Follow like portents, all as absolute
Regenerations: they have birth at rare
Uncertain unexpected intervals
O' the world, by ministry impossible
Before and after fulness of the days:
350 Some dervish desert-spectre, swordsman, saint,
Law-giver, lyrist,—oh, we know the names!
Quite other these than I. Our time requires
No such strange potentate,—who else would dawn,—
No fresh force till the old have spent itself.
355 Such seems the natural œconomy.
To shoot a beam into the dark, assists:
To make that beam do fuller service, spread
And utilize such bounty to the height,
That assists also,—and that work is mine.
360 I recognize, contemplate, and approve
The general compact of society,
Not simply as I see effected good,
But good i' the germ, each chance that's possible
I' the plan traced so far: all results, in short,
365 For better or worse of the operation due
To those exceptional natures, unlike mine,
Who, helping, thwarting, conscious, unaware,
Did somehow manage to so far describe

---

³⁴²| MS:world unmade §crossed out and replaced above by§ broke-up   *1871b*:broke up
³⁴⁵| MS:portents, change §crossed out and replaced above by§ all   ³⁴⁶| MS:they befall
our race §last two words crossed out and replaced above by two words§ at rare   *1871b*:they
have birth at   ³⁴⁷| MS:At rare, §last two words crossed out§ uncertain §altered to§
Uncertain, unexpected dates §crossed out§ intervals,   *1871b*:Uncertain unexpected intervals
³⁴⁸| MS:by ministrations §altered to§ ministry all as new: §last three words crossed out and
replaced above by one word§ impossible   ³⁴⁹| MS:§line added§   ³⁵⁰| MS:desert-
spectre, savage §crossed out and replaced above by§ swordsman,   ³⁵¹| MS:Law-giving
§altered to§ Law-giver <> men §crossed out and replaced above by§ we <> names!—
1871b:names!   ³⁵⁵| MS:That §crossed out and replaced above by§ Such <> economy.
1889a:œconomy.   ³⁵⁷| MS:fullest service—spread   *1871b*:fuller service, spread
³⁵⁸| MS:utilize its bounty   *1871b*:utilize such bounty   ³⁵⁹| MS:and such §crossed out
and replaced above by§ that   ³⁶⁰| MS:recognize, §inserted above§ contemplate and
1871b:contemplate, and   ³⁶¹| MS:society   *1871b*:society,   ³⁶³| MS:germ,—each
§inserted above§ chance that's §inserted above§ possibility §altered to§ possible

This diagram left ready to my hand,
370   Waiting my turn of trial. I see success,
See failure, see what makes or mars throughout.
How shall I else but help complete this plan
Of which I know the purpose and approve,
By letting stay therein what seems to stand,
375   And adding good thereto of easier reach
To-day than yesterday?

                So much, no more!
Whereon, "No more than that?"—inquire aggrieved
Half of my critics: "nothing new at all?
The old plan saved, instead of a sponged slate
380   And fresh-drawn figure?"—while, "So much as that?"
Object their fellows of the other faith:
"Leave uneffaced the crazy labyrinth
Of alteration and amendment, lines
Which every dabster felt in duty bound
385   To signalize his power of pen and ink
By adding to a plan once plain enough?
Why keep each fool's bequeathment, scratch and blur

---

³⁷⁰| MS:Waiting §added in margin§ <> trial; since §crossed out and replaced above by word illegibly erased§ I see the good,— §last two words crossed out§ success,   *1871b*:trial. I
³⁷¹| MS:The §crossed out and replaced above by§ And failure, and §crossed out and replaced above by§ guess what   *1871b*:See failure, see what   ³⁷²| MS:What §crossed out and replaced above by§ How <> I do §crossed out and replaced above by§ else <> complete §inserted above§   ³⁷³| MS:which I see §crossed out and replaced above by§ know the intention §crossed out and replaced above by§ purpose   ³⁷⁴| MS:stay what <> stand, therein §last word marked for transposition to follow *stay*§   ³⁷⁵| MS:adding what may pro §last two words and syllable crossed out and replaced above by two words§ good thereto   ³⁷⁷| MS:And thereupon,— §last two words crossed out and replaced above by one word§ Whereon,   ³⁷⁸| MS:critics: "Nothing   *1871b*:"nothing   ³⁷⁹| MS:saved—instead *1871b*:saved, instead   ³⁸¹⁻⁸²| MS:Object as many—§last two words crossed out and replaced above by two words§ their fellows— "Leave that labyrinth §line marked for division, with resulting two lines expanded by additional words inserted above§ of the other faith: / "Leave that §crossed out and replaced above by three words§ uneffaced the foolish labyrinth   *1871b*:the crazy labyrinth   ³⁸³| MS:and improvement §crossed out and replaced above by§ amendment   ³⁸⁵| MS:To make §crossed out and replaced above by§ signalize his mark with, leave as legacy— §last five words crossed out and replaced above by five words§ power of pen and ink   ³⁸⁶| MS:to what §crossed out and replaced above by two words§ a plan once was §crossed out§ plain   ³⁸⁷| MS:You keep their blot §last two words crossed out and replaced above by five words§ this §crossed out and replaced at L by§ each fool's bequeathment, scratch and blurr—bequeathments, these, §last two words crossed out§   *1871b*:Why keep <> blurr   *1889a*:blur

Which overscrawl and underscore the piece—
Nay, strengthen them by touches of your own?"

390 Well, that's my mission, so I serve the world,
Figure as man o' the moment,—in default
Of somebody inspired to strike such change
Into society—from round to square,
The ellipsis to the rhomboid, how you please,
395 As suits the size and shape o' the world he finds.
But this I can,—and nobody my peer,—
Do the best with the least change possible:
Carry the incompleteness on, a stage,
Make what was crooked straight, and roughness smooth,
400 And weakness strong: wherein if I succeed,
It will not prove the worst achievement, sure,
In the eyes at least of one man, one I look
Nowise to catch in critic company:
To-wit, the man inspired, the genius' self
405 Destined to come and change things thoroughly.
He, at least, finds his business simplified,
Distinguishes the done from undone, reads
Plainly what meant and did not mean this time
We live in, and I work on, and transmit
410 To such successor: he will operate
On good hard substance, not mere shade and shine.
Let all my critics, born to idleness

391| MS:And prove §crossed out and replaced above by§ Figure as the man   *1871b*:as man
395| MS:world to-day. §crossed out and replaced above by two words§ he finds.
396| MS:can,—and §crossed out and replaced above by§ with §crossed out; *and* marked for retention§ nobody so §altered to§ for well,— §last two words crossed out and replaced above by one word§ my peer,   *1871b*:peer,—   398| MS:on a   *1871b*:on, a
399| MS:roughness, smooth,   *1871b*:roughness smooth,   400| MS:strong: If having §last two words crossed out and replaced above by two words§ wherein if I succeed, so far, §last two words crossed out§   401| MS:not be §crossed out and replaced above by§ prove
402-3| MS:§lines added§ I' < > / < > to find §crossed out and replaced above by§ catch in critic-company: *1871b*:In < > / < > critic company: 404| MS:To one man, §last two words crossed out and replaced above by hyphen and syllable§ -wit, the man §inserted above§
405| MS:Who is §last two words crossed out and replaced above by one word§ Destined < > thoroughly: *1871b*:thoroughly.   406| MS:simplified—   *1871b*:simplified,
407| MS:undone—reads   *1871b*:undone, reads   409| MS:You live
1871b:We live   411| MS:mere shadow §altered to§ shade now. §crossed out and replaced above by two words§ and shine.   412| MS:all the others §last two words crossed out and replaced above by two words§ my critics

136

And impotency, get their good, and have
Their hooting at the giver: I am deaf—
415 Who find great good in this society,
Great gain, the purchase of great labour. Touch
The work I may and must, but—reverent
In every fall o' the finger-tip, no doubt.
Perhaps I find all good there's warrant for
420 I' the world as yet: nay, to the end of time,—
Since evil never means part company
With mankind, only shift side and change shape.
I find advance i' the main, and notably
The Present an improvement on the Past,
425 And promise for the Future—which shall prove
Only the Present with its rough made smooth,
Its indistinctness emphasized; I hope
No better, nothing newer for mankind,
But something equably smoothed everywhere,
430 Good, reconciled with hardly-quite-as-good,
Instead of good and bad each jostling each.
"And that's all?" Ay, and quite enough for me!
We have toiled so long to gain what gain I find
I' the Present,—let us keep it! We shall toil
435 So long before we gain—if gain God grant—
A Future with one touch of difference
I' the heart of things, and not their outside face,—

413| MS:good and   1871b:good, and   414| MS:giver: for his pains! §last three words
crossed out§ I agree! §last two words crossed out and replaced above by three words§ I am
deaf—   415| MS:Who see §erased and replaced above by§ find much §crossed out and
replaced above by§ great   416| MS:Much §crossed out and replaced above by§ Great
gain, was §crossed out and replaced above by§ the purchased §altered to§ purchase by a world
of pains §last five words crossed out and replaced above by four words§ of much §crossed out
and replaced above by§ great labour; touch   1871b:labour. Touch   418| MS:of the
finger-tip, be sure! §last two words crossed out and replaced above by two words§ no doubt.
1871b:o'   420| MS:yet, nay—to <> time,   1871b:yet: nay, to <> time,—
422| MS:mankind, §kind, inserted above§   423| MS:main, nay §crossed out and replaced
above by§ and   429-31| MS:equably good everywhere / Instead <> bad at in §last two
words crossed out and replaced above by one word§ each jostling   1871b:equably smoothed
everywhere, / Good <> hardly-quite-as-good, / Instead   431-32| MS:§¶ called for in
margin§ And <> all? Ay   1871b:"And <> all?" Ay   1871b:§no ¶§   433| MS:long
gaining what gain §inserted above§   1871b:long to gain   434| MS:This §crossed out and
replaced above by two words§ I' the Present—let   1871b:the Present,—let   437| MS:and
§inserted above§ not on the §last two words crossed out and replaced above by one word§ their

Let us not risk the whiff of my cigar
For Fourier, Comte, and all that ends in smoke!

440 This I see clearest probably of men
With power to act and influence, now alive:
Juster than they to the true state of things;
In consequence, more tolerant that, side
By side, shall co-exist and thrive alike
445 In the age, the various sorts of happiness
Moral, mark!—not material—moods o' the mind
Suited to man and man his opposite:
Say, minor modes of movement—hence to there,
Or thence to here, or simply round about—
450 So long as each toe spares its neighbour's kibe,
Nor spoils the major march and main advance.
The love of peace, care for the family,
Contentment with what's bad but might be worse—
Good movements these! and good, too, discontent,
455 So long as that spurs good, which might be best,
Into becoming better, anyhow:
Good—pride of country, putting hearth and home
I' the back-ground, out of undue prominence:
Good—yearning after change, strife, victory,
460 And triumph. Each shall have its orbit marked,

438| MS:not §inserted above§ risk—well,— §crossed out§ the   439| MS:For Fourier,
Comte and   *1871b*:For Fourier, Comte, and   440| MS:men,   *1871b*:men
441| MS:alive—   *1871b*:alive: 442| MS:things: *1871b*:things;   443| MS:By
§crossed out and replaced above by§ In   444| MS:side shall <> co-exist, and
1871b:side, shall <> co-exist and   446| MS:§line added§ Moral and not   *1871b*:Moral,
mark!—not   447| MS:man §altered to§ men and man §altered to§ men his §altered to§
their opposite—   *1871b*:man and man his opposite: 448| MS:What I call §last three
words crossed out and replaced above by one word§ Say,—minor   *1871b*:Say, minor
449| MS:Or §over As§ <> here or   *1871b*:here, or   450| each foot spares   *1871b*:each
toe spares   453| MS:with all §crossed out and replaced above by§ what's bad that
§crossed out and replaced above by§ which §crossed out and replaced by§ and might
1871b:bad but might   455| MS:that stays §crossed out and replaced above by§ spurs
457| MS:And pride §erasure§ the land—killing §last three words crossed out and replaced
above by three words§ of country, putting   *1871b*:Good—pride   458| MS:§line added§
prominence,   *1871b*:prominence: 459| MS:And yearning <> strife, overthrow,
§crossed out§ victory,   *1871b*:Good—yearning   460| MS:triumph; each <> orbit free,
§crossed out and replaced above by§ marked,   *1871b*:triumph. Each

But no more,—none impede the other's path
In this wide world,—though each and all alike
Save for me, fain would spread itself through space
And leave its fellow not an inch of way.
465   I rule and regulate the course, excite,
Restrain: because the whole machine should march
Impelled by those diversely-moving parts,
Each blind to aught beside its little bent.
Out of the turnings round and round inside,
470   Comes that straightforward world-advance, I want,
And none of them supposes God wants too
And gets through just their hindrance and my help.
I think that to have held the balance straight
For twenty years, say, weighing claim and claim,
475   And giving each its due, no less no more,
This was good service to humanity,
Right usage of my power in head and heart,
And reasonable piety beside.
Keep those three points in mind while judging me!
480   You stand, perhaps, for some one man, not men,—
Represent this or the other interest,
Nor mind the general welfare,—so, impugn
My practice and dispute my value: why?
You man of faith, I did not tread the world
485   Into a paste, and thereof make a smooth
Uniform mound whereon to plant your flag,

461| MS:And no   *1871b*:But no   462| MS:world,—who, each <> alike,   *1871b*:world,—
though each   *1889a*:alike   463| MS:But for me, wants to §last two words crossed out and
replaced above by two words§ fain would   *1871b*:Save for   464| MS:way: *1871b*:way.
465| course,—excite,   *1871b*:course, excite,   466| MS:Restrain,—because
1871b:Restrain: because   468| MS:bent: *1871b*:bent.   469| MS:turnings-round
1871b:turnings round   470| MS:straight-forward world's-advance §altered to§ world-
advance   *1889a*:straightforwrd   471| MS:them thinks §crossed out and replaced above
by§ supposes <> too—   *1871b*:too   472| MS:Ay, §crossed out§ and §altered to§ And
<> just §inserted above§   474| MS:and claim   *1871b*:and claim,   475| MS:due no
1871b:due, no   478| MS:piety to God: §last two words crossed out and replaced above by
one word§ beside: 480| MS:Who §crossed out and replaced above by§ You
482| MS:And not §last two words crossed out and replaced above by two words§ Nor mind <>
welfare,—you §crossed out and replaced above by§ so impugn   *1871b*:so, impugn
483| MS:my worth: for §last two words crossed out and replaced above by one word§ value:
why?   484| MS:faith, I would §crossed out and replaced above by§ did not pound
§crossed out and replaced above by§ tread   485| MS:paste and   *1871b*:paste, and

The lily-white, above the blood and brains!
Nor yet did I, you man of faithlessness,
So roll things to the level which you love,
490 That you could stand at ease there and survey
The universal Nothing undisgraced
By pert obtrusion of some old church-spire
I' the distance! Neither friend would I content,
Nor, as the world were simply meant for him,
495 Thrust out his fellow and mend God's mistake.
Why, you two fools,—my dear friends all the same,—
Is it some change o' the world and nothing else
Contents you? Should whatever was, not be?
How thanklessly you view things! There's the root
500 Of the evil, source of the entire mistake:
You see no worth i' the world, nature and life,
Unless we change what is to what may be,
Which means, may be, i' the brain of one of you!
"Reject what is?"—all capabilities—
505 Nay, you may style them chances if you choose—
All chances, then, of happiness that lie
Open to anybody that is born,
Tumbles into this life and out again,—
All that may happen, good and evil too,
510 I' the space between, to each adventurer
Upon this 'sixty, Anno Domini:
A life to live—and such a life! a world
To learn, one's lifetime in,—and such a world!
How did the foolish ever pass for wise

489| MS:level that §crossed out and replaced above by§ which you love   *1871b:*love,
490| MS:and enjoy §crossed out and replaced above by§ survey   492| MS:some abbey
§crossed out and replaced above by§ old   494| MS:And, if §crossed out and replaced
above by§ since the world was simply made §crossed out and replaced above by§ meant
*1871b:*Nor, as the world were simply   497| MS:You §crossed out and replaced above by§
Contents you   500| MS:O'   *1871b:*Of   502| MS:be   *1871b:*be,   503| MS:That
is §last two words crossed out and replaced above by two words§ Which means,—may be in
§altered to§ i'   *1871b:*be, i'   504| MS:What is!—all capabilities for good—
1871b:"Reject what is?"—all capabilities—   505| MS:may call §crossed out and replaced
above by§ style   510| MS:In §altered to§ I'   511| MS:this 'Sixty   *1871b:*'sixty
513| MS:world!—   *1871b:*world!   514| MS:Who §crossed out and replaced above by§
How ever were §crossed out and replaced above by§ did the fools §altered to§ foolish that
§crossed out§ passed §altered to§ pass   *1871b:*However   *1889a:*How did the foolish ever pass

515 By calling life a burden, man a fly
Or worm or what's most insignificant?
"O littleness of man!" deplores the bard;
And then, for fear the Powers should punish him,
"O grandeur of the visible universe
520 Our human littleness contrasts withal!
O sun, O moon, ye mountains and thou sea,
Thou emblem of immensity, thou this,
That, and the other,—what impertinence
In man to eat and drink and walk about
525 And have his little notions of his own,
The while some wave sheds foam upon the shore!"
First of all, 'tis a lie some three-times thick:
The bard,—this sort of speech being poetry,—
The bard puts mankind well outside himself
530 And then begins instructing them: "This way
I and my friend the sea conceive of you!
What would you give to think such thoughts as ours
Of you and the sea together?" Down they go
On the humbled knees of them: at once they draw
535 Distinction, recognize no mate of theirs
In one, despite his mock humility,
So plain a match for what he plays with.   Next,
The turn of the great ocean-playfellow,

515| MS:fly,   *1871b*:fly   516| MS:worm, or   517| MS:man!" and then, for fear
1871b:man!" deplores the bard;   518| MS:The < > punish his egregious lie,   *1871b*:And
then, for fear the < > punish him,   520| MS:Man's §crossed out and replaced above by§
That §crossed out and replaced by§ Our human §inserted above§ littleness of man §last two
words crossed out§ contrasts   521| MS:moon, Ye < > sea   *1871b*:ye < > sea,
523| MS:That and   *1889a*:That, and   526| MS:while thy §crossed out and replaced
above by§ some < > shore!   *1871b*:shore!"   528| MS:§line added§ of thing being
1871b:of speech being   530| MS:instructing it §crossed out and replaced above by§ us—
"This   *1871b*:instructing them: "This   531| MS:you—§crossed out and replaced above
by§ men §erased; *you* marked for retention§   *1871b*:you!   532| MS:would you §crossed
out and replaced above by word, possibly *men*, crossed out; *you* marked for retention§ < > as I
think §last two words crossed out and replaced above by one word§ ours
533| MS:Of you §crossed out and replaced above by§ men §erased; *you* marked for retention§
together? Down   *1871b*:together?" Down   534| MS:them,—no fear §last two words
crossed out and replaced above by two words§ at once   *1871b*:them: at   535| MS:distinctions,—recognize   *1871b*:distinction, recognize   538| MS:ocean-play-
fellow;   *1871b*:ocean-play-fellow,   *1889a*:ocean-playfellow,

When the bard, leaving Bond Street very far
540   From ear-shot, cares not to ventriloquize,
But tells the sea its home-truths: "You, my match?
You, all this terror and immensity
And what not? Shall I tell you what you are?
Just fit to hitch into a stanza, so
545   Wake up and set in motion who's asleep
O' the other side of you, in England, else
Unaware, as folk pace their Bond Street now,
Somebody here despises them so much!
Between us,—they are the ultimate! to them
550   And their perception go these lordly thoughts:
Since what were ocean—mane and tail, to boot—
Mused I not here, how make thoughts thinkable?
Start forth my stanza and astound the world!
Back, billows, to your insignificance!
555   Deep, you are done with!"

                    Learn, my gifted friend,
There are two things i' the world, still wiser folk
Accept—intelligence and sympathy.
You pant about unutterable power

539-41| MS:§lines added between 538 and 542 and in margin§   542| MS:all these §altered to§ this terrors §altered to§ terror and immensities §altered to§ immensity   545| Perturb §crossed out and replaced above by two words§ Wake up and make §crossed out and replaced above by§ set   546| MS:On §altered to§ O' <> you,—in England, §last two words inserted above§ else unaware §crossed out§ *1871b:*you, in *1889a:*you in §emended to§ you, in §see Editorial Notes§   547| MS:§line added§ Unaware as they pace *1871b:*Unaware, as folk pace   549| MS:ultimate—to *1871b:*ultimate! to   550| MS:lordly §inserted above§ thoughts: if you §last two words crossed out§   551| MS:For §crossed out and replaced above by§ Since what your waves, foam and main and all, §last seven words crossed out and replaced above by six words§ were ocean—mane and tail beside—§crossed out and replaced above by two words§ to boot— *1871b:*tail, to   552| MS:Were §crossed out and replaced above by§ Mused <> here to make them fit for §last two words crossed out§ thought §altered to§ thoughts thinkable? *1871b:*here, how make   553-54| MS:§lines added§ and impress §crossed out and replaced above by§ astound <> / <> insignificance,— *1871b:*insignficance!   555| MS:§¶§ Now §crossed out and replaced above by§ Learn, my learned §crossed out and replaced above by§ gifted friends, *1871b:*friend,
556| MS:There's §altered to§ There but one §last two words crossed out and replaced above by two words§ are two <> world the simply §crossed out and replaced above by word illegibly crossed out; *simply* marked for retention§ wise *1871b:*world, still wiser folk
557| MS:Admire §crossed out and replaced above by§ Accept <> sympathy: *1871b:*sympathy.
558| MS:You tell me of §last three words crossed out and replaced above by two words illegibly crossed out; replaced below by two words§ pant about

I' the ocean, all you feel but cannot speak?
560 Why, that's the plainest speech about it all.
You did not feel what was not to be felt.
Well, then, all else but what man feels is nought—
The wash o' the liquor that o'erbrims the cup
Called man, and runs to waste adown his side,
565 Perhaps to feed a cataract,—who cares?
I'll tell you: all the more I know mankind,
The more I thank God, like my grandmother,
For making me a little lower than
The angels, honour-clothed and glory-crowned:
570 This is the honour,—that no thing I know,
Feel or conceive, but I can make my own
Somehow, by use of hand or head or heart:
This is the glory,—that in all conceived,
Or felt or known, I recognize a mind
575 Not mine but like mine,—for the double joy,—
Making all things for me and me for Him.
There's folly for you at this time of day!
So think it! and enjoy your ignorance
Of what—no matter for the worthy's name—
580 Wisdom set working in a noble heart,
When he, who was earth's best geometer
Up to that time of day, consigned his life
With its results into one matchless book,
The triumph of the human mind so far,

---

⁵⁸⁵ All in geometry man yet could do:
And then wrote on the dedication-page
In place of name the universe applauds,
"But, God, what a geometer art Thou!"
I suppose Heaven is, through Eternity,
⁵⁹⁰ The equalizing, ever and anon,
In momentary rapture, great with small,
Omniscience with intelligency, God
With man,—the thunder-glow from pole to pole
Abolishing, a blissful moment-space,
⁵⁹⁵ Great cloud alike and small cloud, in one fire—
As sure to ebb as sure again to flow
When the new receptivity deserves
The new completion. There's the Heaven for me.
And I say, therefore, to live out one's life
⁶⁰⁰ I' the world here, with the chance,—whether by pain
Or pleasure be the process, long or short
The time, august or mean the circumstance
To human eye,—of learning how set foot
Decidedly on some one path to Heaven,
⁶⁰⁵ Touch segment in the circle whence all lines
Lead to the centre equally, red lines
Or black lines, so they but produce themselves—
This, I do say,—and here my sermon ends,—
This makes it worth our while to tenderly
⁶¹⁰ Handle a state of things which mend we might,
Mar we may, but which meanwhile helps so far.
Therefore my end is—save society!

---

^{585|} MS:geometry that man could do— *1871b*:geometry man yet could do:
^{586|} MS:dedication-page, *1871b*:dedication-page   ^{588|}   *1871b*:'But   *1889a*:"But
^{589|} MS:eternity, *1871b*:through Eternity,   ^{593|}   MS:from cloud §crossed out and replaced above by§ pole to   ^{594|}   MS:Abolishing, for one bright §last three words crossed out and replaced above by two words§ a blissful   ^{595|}   MS:alike §inserted above§
^{596|} MS:sure to flow again, §*again* marked for transposition to follow *sure*§
^{597|} MS:As the *1871b*:When the   ^{598|}   me— *1871b*:mc.
^{599|} MS:And I do §crossed out§ say, that §crossed out and replaced above by§ therefore,—to *1871b*:therefore, to   ^{605|}   MS:Some segment *1871b*:Touch segment   ^{608|}   MS:and here §crossed out and replaced above by§ so my *1871b*:and here my
^{609|} MS:our §inserted above§   ^{610|}   MS:might *1871b*:might,   ^{611|}   MS:And §over *But*§ mar <> but meanwhile works so far— *1871b*:Mar <> but which meanwhile helps so far.   ^{612|}   MS:my word §crossed out and replaced above by§ end

"And that's all?" twangs the never-failing taunt
O' the foe—"No novelty, creativeness,
615 Mark of the master that renews the age?"
"Nay, all that?" rather will demur my judge
I look to hear some day, nor friend nor foe—
"Did you attain, then, to perceive that God
Knew what He undertook when He made things?"
620 Ay: that my task was to co-operate
Rather than play the rival, chop and change
The order whence comes all the good we know,
With this,—good's last expression to our sense,—
That there's a further good conceivable
625 Beyond the utmost earth can realize:
And, therefore, that to change the agency,
The evil whereby good is brought about—
Try to make good do good as evil does—
Were just as if a chemist, wanting white,
630 And knowing black ingredients bred the dye,
Insisted these too should be white forsooth!
Correct the evil, mitigate your best,
Blend mild with harsh, and soften black to gray

613| MS:all?" cry my §last two words crossed out and replaced above by two words§ is the
never-failing friends §crossed out§ foes §crossed out§ cry   *1871b*:all?" twangs the never-failing
taunt   614| MS:O' §added in margin§ The fools §altered to§ foe   615| MS:Touch
of the great mind §last two words crossed out and replaced above by one word§ master
1871b:Mark of   616| MS:Nay, §added in margin§ "And §crossed out§ all   *1871b*:"Nay
617| MS:That is to speak some   *1871b*:I look to hear some   619| MS:what He was about
§last two words crossed out and replaced above by one word§ undertook <> he   *1871b*:when
He   620| MS:And §crossed out and replaced above by§ Ay: that your §crossed out and
replaced above by§ my   623| MS:And this,—its §crossed out and replaced above by§
good's   *1871b*:With this   625| MS:realize—   *1871b*:realize: 626| MS:And to try an
§last three words crossed out and replaced above by one word and punctuation§ ,therefore,
<> agency   *1871b*:agency,   628| MS:good breed §crossed out and replaced above by§
work good   *1871b*:good do good   629| MS:if the §crossed out and replaced above by§ a
<> wanting §crossed out and replaced above by§ liking §crossed out; *wanting* marked for
retention§   630| MS:And seeing §crossed out and replaced above by§ knowing
631| MS:Wanted that §last two words crossed out and replaced above by one word§ Insisted
these, too, should   *1871b*:these too should   632| MS:§line added in margin§ Correct
and §crossed out and replaced above by two words§ the evil   633| MS:Blend
§added in margin§ Soften the black §last three words partially crossed out and replaced above
by three words§ mild with harsh and blend it §last two words crossed out and replaced above
by two words§ soften black into §altered to§ to   *1871b*:harsh, and

If gray may follow with no detriment
635   To the eventual perfect purity!
But as for hazarding the main result
By hoping to anticipate one half
In the intermediate process,—no, my friends!
This bad world, I experience and approve;
640   Your good world,—with no pity, courage, hope,
Fear, sorrow, joy,—devotedness, in short,
Which I account the ultimate of man,
Of which there's not one day nor hour but brings,
In flower or fruit, some sample of success,
645   Out of this same society I save—
None of it for me! That I might have none,
I rapped your tampering knuckles twenty years.
Such was the task imposed me, such my end.

Now for the means thereto.   Ah, confidence—
650   Keep we together or part company?
This is the critical minute! "Such my end?"
Certainly; how could it be otherwise?
Can there be question which was the right task—
To save or to destroy society?
655   Why, even prove that, by some miracle,
Destruction were the proper work to choose,
And that a torch best remedies what's wrong
I' the temple, whence the long procession wound
Of powers and beauties, earth's achievements all,
660   The human strength that strove and overthrew,—
The human love that, weak itself, crowned strength,—

634| MS:If that may be yet bring §last three words crossed out and replaced above by two
words§ follow with   *1871b:*If gray may   638| MS:my judge: §crossed out and replaced
above by§ fools!   *1871b:*my friends!   639| MS:§line added§   640| MS:Your §added
in margin§ A §crossed out§ good   641| MS:sorrow, and §crossed out§ joy <> short
*1871b:*short,   643| MS:And which §inserted above§ <> brings   *1871b:*Of which <>
brings,   644| MS:fruit, a sample   *1871b:*fruit, some sample   646| MS:§line added
in margin§ of that §crossed out and replaced above by§ it   647| MS:§line added between
645 and 648§ tampering fingers §crossed out and replaced above by§ knuckles
648-49| MS:§¶ called for in margin§   *1871b:*§¶§   *1889a:*§¶ lost in paging. Emended to restore ¶;
see Editorial Notes§   658| MS:winds   *1871b:*wound   659| MS:Of honours §crossed
out and replaced above by§ powers and glories §crossed out and replaced above by§ beauties
660| MS:human §inserted above§ <> and overcame,—   *1871b:*and overthrew,—

The instinct crying "God is whence I came!"—
The reason laying down the law "And such
His will i' the world must be!"—the leap and shout
665 Of genius "For I hold His very thoughts,
The meaning of the mind of Him!"—nay, more,
The ingenuities, each active force
That turning in a circle on itself
Looks neither up nor down but keeps the spot,
670 Mere creature-like, and, for religion, works,
Works only and works ever, makes and shapes
And changes, still wrings more of good from less,
Still stamps some bad out, where was worst before,
So leaves the handiwork, the act and deed,
675 Were it but house and land and wealth, to show
Here was a creature perfect in the kind—
Whether as bee, beaver, or behemoth,
What's the importance? he has done his work
For work's sake, worked well, earned a creature's praise;—
680 I say, concede that same fane, whence deploys
Age after age, all this humanity,
Diverse but ever dear, out of the dark
Behind the altar into the broad day
By the portal—enter, and, concede there mocks
685 Each lover of free motion and much space

662| MS:crying 'God is whence we §crossed out and replaced above by§ I came'—
1871b:crying "God <> came!"— 663| MS:law 'And *1871b*:law "And
664| MS:be,'—the *1871b*:be!"—the 665| MS:genius "For I have his *1871b*:genius "For
I hold His 666| MS:mind of him §altered to§ Him!",—nay, more *1871b*:mind of
Him!"—nay *1889a*:more, 669| MS:the path, §crossed out and replaced above by§ spot,
672| MS:changes, and §crossed out and replaced above by§ still 673| MS:And less of evil
from the more, so before, §first eight words crossed out and replaced above by eight words§
Still stamps some bad out, where was worst 674| MS:And §crossed out and replaced
above by§ So leaves his best of creatureship, behind his house, §last seven words crossed out
and replaced above by six words§ the handiwork, the act and deed *1871b*:deed,
675| MS:And lands §last two words crossed out and replaced above by six words§ Were it but
house and lands *1871b*:land 676| MS:in his §altered to§ the kind *1871b*:kind—
677| MS:Whether §crossed out and then marked for retention§ as the §crossed out§ bee, or
the §last two words crossed out§ beaver, or the §crossed out§ behemoth, 679| MS:praise:
1871b:praise;— 680| MS:say, the fane from whence we see defile *1871b*:say, concede
that same fane, whence deploys 681-82| MS:§one line expanded to two lines§ Age after
age, §last three words added in margin§ All this humanity, §solidus added§ / Diverse but ever
dear, §last four words inserted above§ out 684| MS:portal—why, suppose, inside, there
1871b:portal—enter, and, concede there 685| MS:free movement §crossed out and
replaced above by§ motion and wide §crossed out and replaced above by§ much

A perplexed length of apse and aisle and nave,—
Pillared roof and carved screen, and what care I?—
Which irk the movement and impede the march,—
Nay, possibly, bring flat upon his nose
690   At some odd break-neck angle, by some freak
Of old-world artistry, that personage
Who, could he but have kept his skirts from grief
And catching at the hooks and crooks about,
Had stepped out on the daylight of our time
695   Plainly the man of the age,—still, still, I bar
Excessive conflagration in the case.
"Shake the flame freely!" shout the multitude:
The architect approves I stuck my torch
Inside a good stout lantern, hung its light
700   Above the hooks and crooks, and ended so.
To save society was well: the means
Whereby to save it,—there begins the doubt
Permitted you, imperative on me;
Were mine the best means? Did I work aright
705   With powers appointed me?—since powers denied
Concern me nothing.

            Well, my work reviewed
Fairly, leaves more hope than discouragement.
First, there's the deed done: what I found, I leave,—
What tottered, I kept stable: if it stand

686| MS:A labyrinth §crossed out and replaced above by two words§ perplexed length < >
ailse §corrected to§ aisle   687| MS:Pillared length §crossed out and replaced above by§
roof   688| MS:That mar §crossed out and replaced above by§ irk   *1889a:*Which irk
689| MS:And §crossed out and replaced above by§ Nay, possibly bring < > his face
*1871b:*possibly, bring < > his nose   695| MS:Confessed the man   *1871b:*Plainly the man
696| MS:The remedy o' the torch to cure what's wrong—   *1871b:*Excessive conflagration in
the case.   697| MS:§line added§ "Show a light freely!" cry the   *1871b:*"Shake the flame
freely!" shout the   698| MS:The Architect < > stuck the torch   *1871b:*architect < > stuck
my torch   699| MS:lanthorn, hung the same   *1871b:*lantern, hung its light
702| MS:Whereby I §altered to§ to saved §altered to§ save   703| MS:you, and pressing
hard §last three words crossed out and replaced above by one word§ imperative on me:
*1871b:*me;   704| MS:Were §over illegible erasure§ they §crossed out and replaced above
by§ mine   705| MS:me?—for §crossed out and replaced above by§ since
706| MS:§¶§ Well, I did so §last three words crossed out and replaced above by two words§ my
work   707| MS:Fairly, §added in margin§ Leaves me with §last two words crossed out§ more

710　One month, without sustainment, still thank me
　　　The twenty years' sustainer! Now, observe,
　　　Sustaining is no brilliant self-display
　　　Like knocking down or even setting up:
　　　Much bustle these necessitate; and still
715　To vulgar eye, the mightier of the myth
　　　Is Hercules, who substitutes his own
　　　For Atlas' shoulder and supports the globe
　　　A whole day,—not the passive and obscure
　　　Atlas who bore, ere Hercules was born,
720　And is to go on bearing that same load
　　　When Hercules turns ash on Œta's top.
　　　'Tis the transition-stage, the tug and strain,
　　　That strike men: standing still is stupid-like.
　　　My pressure was too constant on the whole
725　For any part's eruption into space
　　　Mid sparkles, crackling, and much praise of me.
　　　I saw that, in the ordinary life,
　　　Many of the little make a mass of men
　　　Important beyond greatness here and there;
730　As certainly as, in life exceptional,
　　　When old things terminate and new commence,
　　　A solitary great man's worth the world.
　　　God takes the business into His own hands
　　　At such time: who creates the novel flower
735　Contrives to guard and give it breathing-room:

710| MS:month, my hand removed §last three words crossed out and replaced above by two words§ without sustainment, thank me still　*1871b:*sustainment, still thank me
711| MS:twenty-years sustainer. Now　*1871b:*twenty years' sustainer! Now
714| MS:necessitate: and　*1871b:*necessitate; and　　715| MS:To the vulgar eye, the strength is the §last three words crossed out and replaced above by two words§ strong man §crossed out and replaced by one word§ mightier of　*1871b:*To vulgar
716| MS:Is Hercules that §crossed out and replaced above by§ who　*1871b:*I Hercules, who
721| MS:When Hercules is §crossed out and replaced above by§ turns <> top:　*1871b:*top.
723| MS:standing-still　*1871b:*standing still　　725| MS:eruption out of bounds §last three words crossed out and replaced above by two words§ into space
726| MS:With §crossed out and replaced above by§ Mid <> crackles §altered to§ crackling
727| MS:that in <> life　*1871b:*that, in <> life,　　729| MS:Worth more than single §last four words crossed out and replaced above by two words§ Important beyond
730| MS:Just §crossed out and replaced above by§ As　　731| MS:§line added§
733| MS:his　*1871b:*into His　　735| MS:to save §crossed out and replaced above by three words§ guard and give it, §comma crossed out§

I merely tend the corn-field, care for crop,
And weed no acre thin to let emerge
What prodigy may stifle there perchance,
—No, though my eye have noted where he lurks.
⁷⁴⁰ Oh those mute myriads that spoke loud to me—
The eyes that craved to see the light, the mouths
That sought the daily bread and nothing more,
The hands that supplicated exercise,
Men that had wives, and women that had babes,
⁷⁴⁵ And all these making suit to only live!
Was I to turn aside from husbandry,
Leave hope of harvest for the corn, my care,
To play at horticulture, rear some rose
Or poppy into perfect leaf and bloom
⁷⁵⁰ When, mid the furrows, up was pleased to sprout
Some man, cause, system, special interest
I ought to study, stop the world meanwhile?
"But I am Liberty, Philanthropy,
Enlightenment, or Patriotism, the power
⁷⁵⁵ Whereby you are to stand or fall!" cries each:
"Mine and mine only be the flag you flaunt!"
And, when I venture to object "Meantime,
What of yon myriads with no flag at all—

---

⁷³⁶| MS:merely §inserted above§ <> for the wide §last two words crossed out§ crop
⁷³⁷| MS:And slash §crossed out and replaced above by§ weed   ⁷³⁸| MS:perchance
1871b:perchance,   ⁷³⁹| MS:where it lurks: *1871b*:where he lurks.   ⁷⁴⁰| MS:speak
1871b:spoke   ⁷⁴³| MS:exercise— *1871b*:exercise,   ⁷⁴⁴| MS:wives and
1871b:wives, and   ⁷⁴⁵| MS:live— *1871b*:live!   ⁷⁴⁸| MS:rear that §crossed out and
replaced above by§ some   ⁷⁴⁹| MS:Called Liberty §last two words crossed out and
replaced above by two words§ Or poppy into full §crossed out and replaced above by§ perfect
blood-red bloom *1871b*:perfect leaf and bloom   ⁷⁵⁰| MS:When mid the furrows, §last
three words inserted above§ somebody §second syllable crossed out and replaced above by§
where, §crossed out and replaced by§ up <> to write a book §last three words crossed out and
replaced above by one word§ sprout *1871b*:When, mid   ⁷⁵¹| MS:§line added§ Some
man §last two words added in margin§ A §crossed out§ cause, a §crossed out§ system
⁷⁵²| MS:study, stopping §last four letters crossed out and replaced above by§ the
⁷⁵³| MS:am Liberty, Enlightenment, §crossed out and replaced above by§ Philanthropy,
⁷⁵⁴| MS:Philanthropy, nay §last two words crossed out and replaced above by three words§
Enlightenment, or Patriotism, the   ⁷⁵⁵| MS:you solely §inserted above, crossed out and
replaced by two words§ are to   ⁷⁵⁶| MS:only is your §last two words crossed out and
replaced above by two words§ be the flag to §crossed out and replaced above by§ you
⁷⁵⁸| MS:of the §crossed out and replaced above by§ yon

My crop which, who flaunts flag must tread across?"
760 "Now, this it is to have a puny mind!"
Admire my mental prodigies: "down—down—
Ever at home o' the level and the low,
There bides he brooding! Could he look above,
With less of the owl and more of the eagle eye,
765 He'd see there's no way helps the little cause
Like the attainment of the great. Dare first
The chief emprize; dispel yon cloud between
The sun and us; nor fear that, though our heads
Find earlier warmth and comfort from his ray,
770 What lies about our feet, the multitude,
Will fail of benefaction presently.
Come now, let each of us awhile cry truce
To special interests, make common cause
Against the adversary—or perchance
775 Mere dullard to his own plain interest!
Which of us will you choose?—since needs must be
Some one o' the warring causes you incline
To hold, i' the main, has right and should prevail:
Why not adopt and give it prevalence?
780 Choose strict Faith or lax Incredulity,—

759| MS:The §crossed out and replaced above by§ My crop, in §comma and *in* crossed out
and replaced above by two words§ which, who flaunting §altered to§ flaunts yours I §last two
words crossed out and replaced above by two words§ flag, must   *1871b:*flag must
760| MS:a little §crossed out and replaced above by§ puny mind!"—   *1871b:*mind!"
761| MS:mental §inserted above§ men of §last two words crossed out and replaced above by
two words§ prodigies of genius: §crossed out§   *1871b:*prodigies: "down
762| MS:Down, §crossed out§ ever §altered to§ Ever on §crossed out and replaced above by
three words§ at home o'   763| MS:There is §crossed out and replaced above by§ bides
he brooding! did §crossed out and replaced above by§ could   *1871b:*brooding! Could
764| MS:o' the mole §crossed out and replaced above by§ owl <> o'   *1871b:*of <> of
766| MS:the success §crossed out and replaced above by§ attainment <> great: gain §crossed
out and replaced above by§ dare   *1871b:*great. Dare   767| MS:The main §crossed out
and replaced above by§ chief <> cloud athwart §crossed out and replaced above by§ between
*1871b:*emprise *1889a:*emprize   768| MS:us, nor   *1871b:*us; nor
769| MS:earliest benefit §crossed out and replaced above by§ satisfaction from   *1871b:*earlier
warmth and comfort from   772| MS:awhile make §crossed out and replaced above by§
cry   773| MS:We special interests, cry §crossed out and replaced above by§ make
*1871b:*To special   775| MS:The dullard <> interest.   *1871b:*Mere dullard
<> interest!   777| MS:warring §inserted above§   778| MS:To judge §crossed out
and replaced above by§ hold <> main, what's §crossed out and replaced above by§ has <>
prevail,   *1871b:*prevail: 780| MS:strict §inserted above§

King, Caste and Cultus—or the Rights of Man,
Sovereignty of each Proudhon o'er himself,
And all that follows in just consequence!
Go free the stranger from a foreign yoke;
785 Or stay, concentrate energy at home;
Succeed!—when he deserves, the stranger will.
Comply with the Great Nation's impulse, print
By force of arms,—since reason pleads in vain,
And, mid the sweet compulsion, pity weeps,—
790 Hohenstiel-Schwangau on the universe!
Snub the Great Nation, cure the impulsive itch
With smartest fillip on a restless nose
Was ever launched by thumb and finger! Bid
Hohenstiel-Schwangau first repeal the tax
795 On pig-tails and pomatum, and then mind
Abstruser matters for next century!
Is your choice made? Why then, act up to choice!
Leave the illogical touch now here now there
I' the way of work, the tantalizing help
800 First to this, then the other opposite:
The blowing hot and cold, sham policy,
Sure ague of the mind and nothing more,
Disease of the perception or the will,
That fain would hide in a fine name! Your choice,
805 Speak it out and condemn yourself thereby!"

782| MS:The §crossed out§ Sovereignty of each man §crossed out and replaced above by§
Proudhon   783| MS:in plain §crossed out and replaced above by§ just
785| MS:Stay, and §inserted above§ concentrate your §crossed out§ energies §altered to§ energy
at home,   1871b:Or stay, concentrate <> home;   786| MS:Succeed!—if §crossed out
and replaced above by§ when   787| MS:great 1871b:the Great   788-89| MS:§lines
added§   788| MS:reason in §inserted above§ vainly §altered to§ vain pleads, §last word
marked for transposition to precede in§   789| MS:And mid a §crossed out and replaced
above by§ the <> weep,   1871b:And, mid <> weeps,—   791| MS:great   1871b:the
Great   792| MS:on the §crossed out and replaced above by§ a   794| MS:first reduce
§crossed out and replaced above by§ compound   1871b:first repeal   795| MS:pomatum
and   1889a:pomatum, and   796| MS:matters the §crossed out and replaced above by§
for   797| MS:to it! §crossed out and replaced above by§ choice!
798| MS:Leave this §crossed out and replaced above by§ the <> touch now
§inserted above§ here and §crossed out and replaced above by§ now   799| MS:of help
§crossed out and replaced above by§ work, this §crossed out and replaced above by§ the
800| MS:Now §crossed out and replaced above by§ First to that §altered to§ this then §over
now§   1889a:this, then   801| MS:cold—sham policy—   1871b:cold, sham policy,
804| MS:That tries to §last two words crossed out and replaced above by two words§ fain would

Well, Leicester-square is not the Residenz:
Instead of shrugging shoulder, turning friend
The deaf ear, with a wink to the police—
I'll answer—by a question, wisdom's mode.
810   How many years, o' the average, do men
Live in this world? Some score, say computists.
Quintuple me that term and give mankind
The likely hundred, and with all my heart
I'll take your task upon me, work your way,
815   Concentrate energy on some one cause:
Since, counsellor, I also have my cause,
My flag, my faith in its effect, my hope
In its eventual triumph for the good
O' the world. And once upon a time, when I
820   Was like all you, mere voice and nothing more,
Myself took wings, soared sunward, and thence sang
"Look where I live i' the loft, come up to me,
Groundlings, nor grovel longer! gain this height,
And prove you breathe here better than below!
825   Why, what emancipation far and wide
Will follow in a trice! They too can soar,
Each tenant of the earth's circumference
Claiming to elevate humanity,
They also must attain such altitude,
830   Live in the luminous circle that surrounds
The planet, not the leaden orb itself.
Press out, each point, from surface to yon verge
Which one has gained and guaranteed your realm!' "

806| MS:Well, friend, since this §last three words crossed out and replaced above by one
word§ Leicester-square   808| MS:with §crossed out and then marked for retention§
809| MS:answer—with §crossed out and replaced above by§ by   811| MS:score,
computists say. §last two words marked for transposition§   815| MS:§line added in
margin§   816| MS:Yes, depend on it §last four words crossed out and replaced above by
three words§ Since, friend §crossed out§ counsellor, I also §inserted above§
819| MS:world: and when I §last two words marked for transposition to follow *time*,§ once
1871b:world. And   820| MS:like yourselves §crossed out and replaced above by two
words§ all you—a §crossed out and replaced above by§ mere   *1871b*:you, mere
821| MS:sun-ward   *1889a*:sunward   822| MS:'Look   *1871b*:"Look
823| MS:longer! Gain <> height: *1871b*:gain <> height,   824| MS:And, prove <>
below,   *1871b*:And prove <> below!   826| MS:trice! "We too can soar,   *1871b*:trice!
They too can soar,   827-28| MS:§lines added§   829| MS:We also   *1871b*:They also
831| MS:The leaden §crossed out§ planet <> itself—   *1871b*:itself.   833| MS:has
touched §crossed out and replaced above by§ gained <> our   *1871b*:your

Ay, still my fragments wander, music-fraught,
835   Sighs of the soul, mine once, mine now, and mine
For ever! Crumbled arch, crushed aqueduct,
Alive with tremors in the shaggy growth
Of wild-wood, crevice-sown, that triumphs there
Imparting exultation to the hills!
840   Sweep of the swathe when only the winds walk
And waft my words above the grassy sea
Under the blinding blue that basks o'er Rome,—
Hear ye not still—"Be Italy again"?
And ye, what strikes the panic to your heart?
845   Decrepit council-chambers,—where some lamp
Drives the unbroken black three paces off
From where the greybeards huddle in debate,
Dim cowls and capes, and midmost glimmers one
Like tarnished gold, and what they say is doubt,
850   And what they think is fear, and what suspends
The breath in them is not the plaster-patch
Time disengages from the painted wall
Where Rafael moulderingly bids adieu,
Nor tick of the insect turning tapestry
855   Which a queen's finger traced of old, to dust;
But some word, resonant, redoubtable,
Of who once felt upon his head a hand
Whereof the head now apprehends his foot.
"Light in Rome, Law in Rome, and Liberty

834| MS:still there §crossed out and replaced above by§ my wander fragments §last two words marked for transposition§   836| MS:ever; broken §crossed out and replaced above by§ crumbled arch, grey §crossed out and replaced above by§ crushed   *1871b:*ever! Crumbled 837-39| MS:§lines added§   839| MS:Tossing its exultation <> hills—   *1871b:*Imparting exultation <> hills!   841| MS:Bearing §crossed out and replaced above by two words§ And waft   842| MS:that beats §crossed out and replaced above by§ basks 843| MS:again!"   *1871b:*again?"   *1889a:*again"?   844| MS:§line added§ heart *1871b:*heart?   845| MS:council chambers? §question mark altered to§,—where the §crossed out and replaced below by§ some   846| MS:Leaves §crossed out and replaced above by§ Drives   847| MS:greybeards cluster §crossed out and replaced above by§ huddle   848| MS:Dim §over *Their*§ <> capes, with §crossed out§ and one is §last two words crossed out and replaced above by one word§ midmost   850| MS:they feel §replaced above by§ think   853| MS:§line added§ adieu—   *1871b:*adieu,   854| MS:o' *1871b:*of   855| MS:To dust which some §crossed out and replaced above by§ a <> old, *1871b:*old;   *1889a:*Which <> old, to dust;   856| MS:redoubtable   *1871b:*redoubtable, 857| MS:felt your §crossed out and replaced above by§ upon his head that hand   *1871b:*head a hand   858| MS:apprehends this foot—   *1871b:*apprehends his foot.

860   O' the soul in Rome—the free Church, the free State!
Stamp out the nature that's best typified
By its embodiment in Peter's Dome,
The scorpion-body with the greedy pair
Of outstretched nippers, either colonnade
865   Agape for the advance of heads and hearts!"
There's one cause for you! one and only one,
For I am vocal through the universe,
I' the workshop, manufactory, exchange
And market-place, sea-port and custom-house
870   O' the frontier: listen if the echoes die—
"Unfettered commerce! Power to speak and hear,
And print and read! The universal vote!
Its rights for labour!" This, with much beside,
I spoke when I was voice and nothing more,
875   But altogether such an one as you
My censors. "Voice, and nothing more, indeed!"
Re-echoes round me: "that's the censure, there's
Involved the ruin of you soon or late!
Voice,—when its promise beat the empty air:
880   And nothing more,—when solid earth's your stage,
And we desiderate performance, deed
For word, the realizing all you dreamed
In the old days: now, for deed, we find at door

860| MS:Of §altered to§ O' the §inserted above§ soul   861-65| MS:§lines added vertically
in margin§   861| MS:Stamp §above two words illegibly crossed out§ <> nature that's
best §last three words above words illegibly crossed out§   862| MS:embodiment in §last
two words above words illegibly crossed out§   863| MS:scorpion-body <> pair—
1871b:pair   *1889a*:scorpion body   864| MS:Those outstretched nippers of its
collonade—   *1871b*:Of outstretched nippers, either collonade   866| MS:§line added
above 867§ you!—one <> one—   *1871b*:you! one <> one,   867| MS:For am I §last two
words crossed out and replaced above by two words§ I am <> thro the universe
1871b:through the universe,   868| MS:work-shop   *1889a*:workshop
870| MS:frontier,—doubt not soon my worlds will die— §last seven words crossed out and
replaced above by five words§ listen if the echoes die—   *1871b*:frontier: listen
871| MS:hear!   *1871b*:hear,   872| MS:Every man vote his §last four words crossed out
and replaced above by seven words§ And print & read! The universal suffrage §crossed out§
vote!   *1871b*:print and read   873| MS:§line added to R of 872§ / Labour §crossed out
and replaced above by§ Its <> labour!"—this, & much   *1871b*:labour!" This, with much
875| MS:And §crossed out and replaced above by§ But   876| MS:censors.
"Voice—and <> more indeed!"   *1871b*:censors. "Voice, and <> more,
indeed!"   879| MS:beats <> air,—   *1871b*:beat <> air: 883| MS:I' <> days.
Then, indeed, we   *1871b*:In <> days: now, for deed, we

O' the council-chamber posted, mute as mouse,
885 Hohenstiel-Schwangau, sentry and safeguard
O' the greybeards all a-chuckle, cowl to cape,
Who challenge Judas,—that's endearment's style,—
To stop their mouths or let escape grimace,
While they keep cursing Italy and him.
890 The power to speak, hear, print and read is ours?
Ay, we learn where and how, when clapped inside
A convict-transport bound for cool Cayenne!
The universal vote we have: its urn,
We also have where votes drop, fingered-o'er
895 By the universal Prefect. Say, Trade's free
And Toil turned master out o' the slave it was:
What then? These feed man's stomach, but his soul
Craves finer fare, nor lives by bread alone,
As somebody says somewhere. Hence you stand
900 Proved and recorded either false or weak,
Faulty in promise or performance: which?"
Neither, I hope. Once pedestalled on earth,
To act not speak, I found earth was not air.
I saw that multitude of mine, and not
905 The nakedness and nullity of air
Fit only for a voice to float in free.
Such eyes I saw that craved the light alone,

885| MS:Hohenstiel-Schwangau, sentinel §altered to§ sentry and safe §inserted above§
886| MS:greybeards while they §last two words crossed out and replaced above by word and syllable§ all a- 887| MS:And §crossed out and replaced above by§ Who
888| MS:mouths, or make §crossed out and replaced above by§ let grimace himself, §crossed out and replaced above by§ escape, 1871b:mouths or let escape grimace,
890| MS:speak, and §crossed out§ hear, and §crossed out§ print 891| MS:we learn §crossed out and replaced above by§ see where 1871b:we learn where
893| MS:have—its 1871b:have: its 894| MS:All §crossed out and replaced above by six words§ We also have where votes drop 895| MS:free, 1871b:free 896| MS:And Toil's <> master for §crossed out and replaced above by two words§ out o' <> was, 1871b:And Toil <> was: 897| MS:then? These are but daily bread §last four words crossed out and replaced above by three words§ feed man's mouth at best: his 1871b:man's stomach, but his 899| MS:As the Old book §last three words crossed out and replaced above by one word§ somebody <> somewhere. Hence you 1871b:somewhere. So you
900| MS:Proved by the record either 1871b:Proved and recorded either 901-2| MS:§¶ called for in margin§ 1871b:§no ¶§ 903| MS:With §crossed out and replaced above by§ To <> air— 1871b:air. 906| MS:only §inserted above§ for the §crossed out and replaced above by§ my voice <> free— 1871b:for a voice <> free. 907| MS:I saw §marked for transposition to follow *eyes*§ such §altered to§ Such eyes

Such mouths that wanted bread and nothing else,
Such hands that supplicated handiwork,
910 Men with the wives, and women with the babes,
Yet all these pleading just to live, not die!
Did I believe one whit less in belief,
Take truth for falsehood, wish the voice revoked
That told the truth to heaven for earth to hear?
915 No, this should be, and shall; but when and how?
At what expense to these who average
Your twenty years of life, my computists?
"Not bread alone" but bread before all else
For these: the bodily want serve first, said I;
920 If earth-space and the life-time help not here,
Where is the good of body having been?
But, helping body, if we somewhat baulk
The soul of finer fare, such food's to find
Elsewhere and afterward—all indicates,
925 Even this self-same fact that soul can starve
Yet body still exist its twenty years:
While, stint the body, there's an end at once
O' the revel in the fancy that Rome's free,
And superstition's fettered, and one prints
930 Whate'er one pleases and who pleases reads .

908| MS:Their §crossed out and replaced above by§ Such <> nothing else §crossed out and replaced above by§ more §crossed out§ else,   909| MS:The §crossed out and replaced above by§ Such <> supplicated §word illegibly crossed out and replaced above by§ handiwork,   910| MS:Hands that had §last three words crossed out and replaced above by three words§ Men with the wives and women that had §last three words crossed out and replaced above by three words§ families §crossed out and replaced by§ women with the babes 1871b:wives, and <> babes,   911| MS:And §crossed out and replaced above by§ Yet all these working hard §last two words crossed out and replaced above by two words§ pleading just to simply §crossed out§ live, not die. 1871b:die!   914| MS:heaven that §crossed out and replaced above by§ for earth might §crossed out and replaced above by§ to   917| MS:Some §crossed out and replaced above by§ Your <> life, say §replaced above by§ my   919| MS:these,—material §crossed out and replaced above by two words§ the bodily <> say I! 1871b:these: the <> said I;   920| MS:If the §crossed out§ earth-space   921| MS:of the body 1871b:of body   922| MS:Say §crossed out and replaced above by§ But   923| MS:fare, that food's 1871b:fare, such food's   925| MS:self-same §inserted above§ fact in question §last two words crossed out and replaced above by one word§ that   926| MS:And §crossed out and replaced above by§ Yet body yet §crossed out and replaced above by§ still <> years, 1871b:years: 927| MS:body,— there's 1871b:body, there's   928| MS:in the thought §crossed out and replaced above by§ fancy <> Rome §altered to§ Rome's is §crossed out§ free 1871b:free,

The same, and speaks out and is spoken to,
And divers hundred thousand fools may vote
A vote untampered with by one wise man,
And so elect Barabbas deputy
935 In lieu of his concurrent. I who trace
The purpose written on the face of things,
For my behoof and guidance—(whoso needs
No such sustainment, sees beneath my signs,
Proves, what I take for writing, penmanship,
940 Scribble and flourish with no sense for me
O' the sort I solemnly go spelling out,—
Let him! there's certain work of mine to show
Alongside his work: which gives warranty
Of shrewder vision in the workman—judge!)
945 I who trace Providence without a break
I' the plan of things, drop plumb on this plain print
Of an intention with a view to good,
That man is made in sympathy with man
At outset of existence, so to speak;
950 But in dissociation, more and more,
Man from his fellow, as their lives advance
In culture; still humanity, that's born
A mass, keeps flying off, fining away
Ever into a multitude of points,
955 And ends in isolation, each from each:
Peerless above i' the sky, the pinnacle,—

932| MS:And any hundred <> fools §inserted above§   933| MS:man,— 1871b:man,
934| MS:That they §last two words crossed out and replaced above by two words§ And so <>
Barabbas and not Christ. §last three words crossed out and replaced above by one word§
deputy.   935-37| MS:Nor §crossed out and replaced above by§ In <> concurrent. §¶
called for in margin§ I who trace / For <> guidance;—whoso   1871b:§no ¶§ I who trace /
The <> things, / For <> guidance—(whoso   939| MS:penmanship
1871b:penmanship,   941| MS:out,   1871b:out,—   942| MS:him! there's
1871b:him! there's   943| MS:work,—which gives evidence §crossed out and replaced
above by§ warranty   1871b:work: which   944| MS:shrewder eye §crossed out§ vision
945| MS:I, who   1871b:I who   947| MS:good—   1871b:good,
950| MS:And in   1871b:But in   952| MS:culture,— till humanity that §altered to§ that's
sprung, §crossed out and replaced above by§ lay §crossed out and replaced by§ born,
1871b:culture; still, humanity, that's   954| MS:into unnumbered §crossed out and
replaced above by two words§ a multitude   955| MS:from each,—   1871b:from each:
956| MS:the blue §crossed out and replaced above by§ sky

Absolute contact, fusion, all below
At the base of being. How comes this about?
This stamp of God characterizing man
960   And nothing else but man in the universe—
That, while he feels with man (to use man's speech)
I' the little things of life, its fleshly wants
Of food and rest and health and happiness,
Its simplest spirit-motions, loves and hates,
965   Hopes, fears, soul-cravings on the ignoblest scale,
O' the fellow-creature,—owns the bond at base,—
He tends to freedom and divergency
In the upward progress, plays the pinnacle
When life's at greatest (grant again the phrase!
970   Because there's neither great nor small in life).
"Consult thou for thy kind that have the eyes
To see, the mouths to eat, the hands to work,
Men with the wives, and women with the babes!"
Prompts Nature. "Care thou for thyself alone
975   I' the conduct of the mind God made thee with!
Think, as if man had never thought before!
Act, as if all creation hung attent
On the acting of such faculty as thine,
To take prime pattern from thy masterpiece!"

957| MS:Nothing but §last two words crossed out and replaced above by one word§ Absolute <> fusion, down §crossed out and replaced above by§ all   958| MS:about— *1871b:*about?   959| MS:of God and §crossed out§ character of §crossed out and replaced above by four letters§ izin man   *1871b:*characterizing   960| MS:nothing but man in this universe—   *1871b:*nothing else but man in the universe—   961| MS:That while <> man, (to   *1871b:*That, while <> man (to   962| MS:life,— the §crossed out and replaced above by§ its <> wants,   *1871b:*life, its <> wants   963| MS:§line added§ happiness,— *1871b:*happiness,   964| MS:Its §added in margin§ And §crossed out§   965| MS:And §crossed out§ Hopes, and §crossed out§ fears, soul-cravings §inserted above§   966| MS:Of §altered to§ O' <> owns a common §last two words crossed out and replaced above by four words§ the bond o' the base,—   *1871b:*bond at base,—   968| MS:I' <> progress,—plays   *1871b:*In <> progress, plays   969| MS:phrase—   *1871b:*phrase!   970| MS:life)   *1871b:*life.)   *1889a:*life).   971| MS:for the kind   *1871b:*for thy kind   972| MS:That see, the mouths that eat, the hands that work,   *1871b:*To see, the mouths to eat, the hands to work,   973| MS:Men that have §last two words crossed out and replaced above by two words§ with the wives and women that have §last two words crossed out and replaced above by two words§ with the   *1871b:*wives, and   975| MS:with—   *1871b:*with!   976| MS:Think—as <> before—   *1871b:*Think, as <> before!   977| MS:Act—as *1871b:*Act, as   979| MS:take first §crossed out and replaced above by§ prime

980 Nature prompts also: neither law obeyed
To the uttermost by any heart and soul
We know or have in record: both of them
Acknowledged blindly by whatever man
We ever knew or heard of in this world.
985 "Will you have why and wherefore, and the fact
Made plain as pikestaff?" modern Science asks.
"That mass man sprung from was a jelly-lump
Once on a time; he kept an after course
Through fish and insect, reptile, bird and beast,
990 Till he attained to be an ape at last
Or last but one. And if this doctrine shock
In aught the natural pride" . . . Friend, banish fear,
The natural humility replies!
Do you suppose, even I, poor potentate,
995 Hohenstiel-Schwangau, who once ruled the roast,—
I was born able at all points to ply
My tools? or did I have to learn my trade,
Practise as exile ere perform as prince?
The world knows something of my ups and downs:
1000 But grant me time, give me the management
And manufacture of a model me,
Me fifty-fold, a prince without a flaw,—
Why, there's no social grade, the sordidest,
My embryo potentate should blink and scape.

980| MS:That's §crossed out and replaced above by two words§ Nature prompts also—neither
1871b:also: neither   982| MS:Whereof I read the §last four words crossed out and
replaced above by five words§ I know or have in   *1871b*:We know   984| MS:I ever
1871b:We ever   985| MS:you know §crossed out and replaced above by§ have <>
wherefore—and   *1871b*:wherefore, and   986| MS:pikestaff?" Modern <> asks—
1871b:modern <> asks.   988| MS:time; whence he §last two words crossed out and
replaced above by two words§ he kept <> course,   *1871b*:course   989| MS:reptile bird
<> beast   *1871b*:reptile, bird <> beast,   990| MS:attained and was §last two words
crossed out and replaced above by two words§ to be   993| MS:Let natural <> reply.
1871b:The natural <> replies!   994| MS:suppose, the §crossed out and replaced above
by§ poor potentate, §last two words marked for transposition to follow *I*,§ even I,
995| MS:Hohenstiel-Schwangau who <> the §word illegibly crossed out§ world, §crossed out
and replaced above by§ roast,   *1871b*:roast,—   997| MS:tools,—or   *1871b*:tools? or
999| MS:down—   *1871b*:downs: 1000| MS:grant the §crossed out and replaced above by§
me time, and give the §crossed out and replaced above by§ me management   *1871b*:time, give
me the management   1001| MS:Of §crossed out and replaced above by§ And
manufacturing §altered to§ manufacture of §inserted above§   1004| MS:scape: *1871b*:scape.

1005 King, all the better he was cobbler once,
He should know, sitting on the throne, how tastes
Life to who sweeps the doorway. But life's hard,
Occasion rare; you cut probation short,
And, being half-instructed, on the stage
1010 You shuffle through your part as best you can,
And bless your stars, as I do. God takes time.
I like the thought He should have lodged me once
I' the hole, the cave, the hut, the tenement,
The mansion and the palace; made me learn
1015 The feel o' the first, before I found myself
Loftier i' the last, not more emancipate;
From first to last of lodging, I was I,
And not at all the place that harboured me.
Do I refuse to follow farther yet
1020 I' the backwardness, repine if tree and flower,
Mountain or streamlet were my dwelling-place
Before I gained enlargement, grew mollusc?
As well account that way for many a thrill
Of kinship, I confess to, with the powers
1025 Called Nature: animate, inanimate,
In parts or in the whole, there's something there
Man-like that somehow meets the man in me.
My pulse goes altogether with the heart
O' the Persian, that old Xerxes, when he stayed

1005| MS:cobbler first §crossed out§ once,   1007| MS:doorway. But time's §crossed out
and replaced above by§ life's brief §crossed out and replaced above by§ short, §crossed out
and replaced by§ hard,   1008| MS:Occasion's §altered to§ Occasion   1009| MS:And
being half-instructed on   1871b:And, being half-instructed, on   1010| MS:And §crossed
out and replaced above by§ To shuffle < > you may,   1871b:You shuffle   1889a:best you can,
1011| MS:time—   1871b:time.   1012| MS:lodged my soul §last two words crossed out and
replaced above by two words§ me once   1014| MS:palace; let §crossed out and replaced
above by§ made   1015| MS:of §altered to§ o'   1016| MS:Loftier §added in margin§
I' the second, lofty and §last three words crossed out and replaced above by three words§ last,
not more   1017| MS:And so §last two words crossed out and replaced above by two
words§ From first to the end §lst two words crossed out and replaced above by one word§ last
1019| MS:Nor do §last two words crossed out§ I §altered to§ Do I §inserted above§ hinder you
go §last three words crossed out and replaced above by three words§ refuse to follow
1020| MS:backwardness, and prove that §last three words crossed out and replaced above by
two words§ content that tree and flower   1871b:backwardness, repine if tree and flower,
1021| MS:or clod §crossed out and replaced above by§ streamlet were once
§crossed out§ my dwelling-place, §comma over partially erased question mark§
1871b:dwelling-place   1022| MS:§line added§   1027| MS:me—   1871b:me.

1030 His march to conquest of the world, a day
I' the desert, for the sake of one superb
Plane-tree which queened it there in solitude:
Giving her neck its necklace, and each arm
Its armlet, suiting soft waist, snowy side,
1035 With cincture and apparel. Yes, I lodged
In those successive tenements; perchance
Taste yet the straitness of them while I stretch
Limb and enjoy new liberty the more.
And some abodes are lost or ruinous;
1040 Some, patched-up and pieced-out, and so transformed
They still accommodate the traveller
His day of lifetime. O you count the links,
Descry no bar of the unbroken man?
Yes,—and who welds a lump of ore, suppose
1045 He likes to make a chain and not a bar,
And reach by link on link, link small, link large,
Out to the due length—why, there's forethought still
Outside o' the series, forging at one end,
While at the other there's—no matter what,
1050 The kind of critical intelligence
Believing that last link had last but one

1032| MS:Plane-tree that §crossed out and replaced above by§ which < > it in the §last two words crossed out and replaced above by two words§ there in solitude, *1871b*:solitude:
1033| MS:Hanging §crossed out and replaced above by§ Giving her arms with armlets §last three words crossed out and replaced above by three words§ neck its necklace
1034| MS:With §crossed out and replaced above by§ Its < > soft §inserted above§ waist, silver §crossed out and replaced above by§ snowy 1036| MS:tenements; my sage §last two words crossed out and replaced above by one word§ perchance 1038| MS:enjoy the more. §last two words marked for transposition to follow *liberty*§ new liberty
1039| MS:some of them §last two words crossed out and replaced above by one word§ abodes < > ruinous, *1871b*:ruinous; 1040| MS:Or patched-up and pieced out, and so §last four words inserted above§ transformed and serving t §last two words and letter crossed out§
1042| MS:life-time. O you hold the links! *1871b*:you count the links. *1889a*:lifetime
1043| MS:§line added§ There was no < > man! *1871b*:Descry no < > man?
1044| MS:who §over illegible word§ takes §crossed out and replaced above by§ welds
1045| MS:He chooses §crossed out and replaced above by§ likes 1046| MS:by link and §crossed out and replaced above by§ on 1047| MS:there's wisdom §crossed out and replaced above by§ fore-thought *1871b*:forethought 1049| MS:what, *1871b*:what *1889a*:what §emended to§ what, §see Editorial Notes§ 1050| MS:§line added in margin§ 1051| MS:Explaining how §last two words crossed out and replaced above by two words§ Believing that < > last-but-one *1871b*:last but one

For parent, and no link was, first of all,
Fitted to anvil, hammered into shape.
Else, I accept the doctrine, and deduce
1055 This duty, that I recognize mankind,
In all its height and depth and length and breadth.
Mankind i' the main have little wants, not large:
I, being of will and power to help, i' the main,
Mankind, must help the least wants first. My friend,
1060 That is, my foe, without such power and will,
May plausibly concentrate all he wields,
And do his best at helping some large want,
Exceptionally noble cause, that's seen
Subordinate enough from where I stand.
1065 As he helps, I helped once, when like himself,
Unable to help better, work more wide;
And so would work with heart and hand to-day,
Did only computists confess a fault,
And multiply the single score by five,
1070 Five only, give man's life its hundred years.
Change life, in me shall follow change to match!
Time were then, to work here, there, everywhere,

1052| MS:parent and no first §marked for transposition to follow *was*§ link was at
1871b:parent, and <> was, first   1053| MS:§line added§ Nor put on the §crossed out§
forge and §crossed out and replaced above by§ nor hammered   1871b:Fitted to anvil,
hammered   1054| MS:Well, I   1871b:Else, I   1055| MS:This §altered to§ The
consequence: §crossed out and replaced above by two words§ duty that I feel with all §last
three words crossed out and replaced above by one word§ recognize   1871b:This duty
1056| MS:§line added§ its length and breadth §last three words marked for transposition with
height and depth§ and height and depth.   1058| MS:I, trusted with a §last three words
crossed out and replaced above by four words§ being of will and   1059| MS:first: my
1871b:first. My   1060| MS:is, each §crossed out and replaced above by§ my foe, of mine
§last two words crossed out§   1061| MS:all they §crossed out and replaced above by§ he
have §crossed out§ wields,   1062| MS:do their §crossed out and replaced above by§ his
<> helping the §crossed out and replaced above by§ some <> wants, §altered to§ want,
1065| MS:I did as he §last four words crossed out and replaced above by three words§ As he
helps, I did §crossed out and replaced above by§ helped   1066| MS:better, as §crossed
out and replaced above by§ work   1067| MS:with all §crossed out and replaced above by§
heart <> to-day   1871b:to-day,   1068| MS:Would §crossed out and replaced above by§
Did <> confess mistake §crossed out§ a fault,   1069| MS:single §inserted above§ score of
years §last two words crossed out§ by ten,   1871b:by five,   1070| MS:Ten only
1871b:Five only   1071| MS:Concede them, you §crossed out and replaced above by§
friends shall see me set to work! §last four words crossed out and replaced above by four
words§ a change to match!   1871b:Change llife, in me shall follow change
1072| MS:were §inserted above§ <> there, and §crossed out§

By turns and try experiment at ease!
Full time to mend as well as mar: why wait
1075 The slow and sober uprise all around
O' the building? Let us run up, right to roof,
Some sudden marvel, piece of perfectness,
And testify what we intend the whole!
Is the world losing patience? "Wait!" say we:
1080 "There's time: no generation needs to die
Unsolaced; you've a century in store!"
But, no: I sadly let the voices wing
Their way i' the upper vacancy, nor test
Truth on this solid as I promised once.
1085 Well, and what is there to be sad about?
The world's the world, life's life, and nothing else.
'Tis part of life, a property to prize,
That those o' the higher sort engaged i' the world,
Should fancy they can change its ill to good,
1090 Wrong to right, ugliness to beauty: find
Enough success in fancy turning fact,
To keep the sanguine kind in countenance
And justify the hope that busies them:
Failure enough,—to who can follow change
1095 Beyond their vision, see new good prove ill
I' the consequence, see blacks and whites of life

1074| MS:There's §crossed out and replaced above by§ Full   1077| MS:Some outwork,
pillared §last two words crossed out and replaced above by two words§ sudden marvel, piece
1078| MS:whole.   *1871b*:whole!   1079| MS:the whole losing <> Wait," say   *1871b*:the
world losing <> Wait!" say   1081| MS:Unsolaced; we've a   *1871b*:Unsolaced; you've a
1082| MS:No, no   *1871b*:But, no   1083| MS:nor move   *1871b*:nor test
1084| MS:Hand on <> as they promised   *1871b*:Truth on <> as I promised
1085| MS:what seems §crossed out and replaced above by§ is <> to grow §crossed out and
replaced above by§ be   1087| MS:property for good, §last two words crossed out and
replaced above by two words§ to prize,   1088| MS:o' the higher sort §last four words
inserted above§ engaged thereon, §crossed out and replaced above by three words§ i' the
world,   1089| MS:ill to §last two words inserted above§   1090| MS:beauty: nay—
1871b:beauty: find   1091| MS:fact   *1871b*:fact,   1092| MS:the hopeful §crossed out
and replaced above by§ sanguine   1093| MS:the work §crossed out and replaced above
by§ hope <> them,—   *1871b*:them: 1094| MS:enough to who can see the §last two
words crossed out and replaced above by one word§ follow what §crossed out§
1871b:enough,—to   1095| MS:§Word, perhaps *Constricts*, crossed out and replaced above
by§ Beyond   1096| MS:consequence,—the blacks   *1871b*:consequence, see blacks

Shift square indeed, but leave the chequered face
Unchanged i' the main,—failure enough for such,
To bid ambition keep the whole from change,
1100 As their best service. I hope nought beside.
No, my brave thinkers, whom I recognize,
Gladly, myself the first, as, in a sense,
All that our world's worth, flower and fruit of man!
Such minds myself award supremacy
1105 Over the common insignificance,
When only Mind's in question,—Body bows
To quite another government, you know.
Be Kant crowned king o' the castle in the air!
Hans Slouch,—his own, and children's mouths to feed
1110 I' the hovel on the ground,—wants meat, nor chews
"The Critique of Pure Reason" in exchange.
But, now,—suppose I could allow your claims
And quite change life to please you,—would it please?
Would life comport with change and still be life?
1115 Ask, now, a doctor for a remedy:
There's his prescription. Bid him point you out

1097| MS:Shift place §crossed out and replaced above by§ squares < > chequer-work §last
syllable crossed out§ face *1871b*:square < > the chequered 1098| MS:Unchanged, §last
syllable crossed out and replaced above by three words§ altered in the main,—enough for me
1871b:Unchanged i' the main,—failure enough for such 1099| MS:from harm §crossed
out§ change *1871b*:change, 1100| MS:As its best service. and §crossed out and
replaced above by§ I < > beside— *1871b*:As their best < > beside. 1101| MS:thinkers!
whom *1871b*:thinkers, whom 1102| MS:Gladly, §added in margin§ Myself < > in a
certain §last two words crossed out§ sense *1871b*:in a sense, 1103| MS:fruit thereof,
§crossed out and replaced above by two words§ of man, *1871b*:man! 1104| MS:Fit to
§last two words crossed out and replaced above by two words§ The §crossed out and replaced
in margin by§ Prime minds that may claim a clear §last five words crossed out and replaced
above by four words§ I allow §last two words crossed out§ myself award supremacy
1871b:Such minds 1105| MS:insignificance,— *1871b*:insignificance,
1106| MS:Well, §crossed out and replaced above by§ When 1107| MS:another sort of
rule §last three words crossed out and replaced above by one word§ government, you know—
1871b:know. 1108| MS:Herr Heine's §last two words crossed out and replaced above by
three words§ Be Kant crowned < > air— *1871b*:air! 1109| MS:Hans, with §comma and
last word crossed out and replaced above by§ Slouch,—his own and
1111| MS:'The Pure Critique of Reason' in exchange,— *1871b*:"The < > Reason" in
exchange. *1889a*:"The Critique of Pure Reason" 1111-12| MS:§¶ called for in margin§
1871b:§no¶§ 1112| MS:Well §crossed out and replaced above by§
But, now—suppose *1871b*:now,—suppose 1115| MS:Ask, §first letter over *I*§ a
physician §last two words crossed out and replaced above by three words§ now, a doctor
1116| MS:prescription. Ask §crossed out and replaced above by§ Bid

Which of the five or six ingredients saves
The sick man. "Such the efficacity?
Then why not dare and do things in one dose
1120   Simple and pure, all virtue, no alloy
Of the idle drop and powder?" What's his word?
The efficacity, neat, were neutralized:
It wants dispersing and retarding,—nay
Is put upon its mettle, plays its part
1125   Precisely through such hindrance everywhere,
Finds some mysterious give and take i' the case,
Some gain by opposition, he foregoes
Should he unfetter the medicament.
So with this thought of yours that fain would work
1130   Free in the world: it wants just what it finds—
The ignorance, stupidity, the hate,
Envy and malice and uncharitableness
That bar your passage, break the flow of you
Down from those happy heights where many a cloud
1135   Combined to give you birth and bid you be
The royalest of rivers: on you glide
Silverly till you reach the summit-edge,
Then over, on to all that ignorance,
Stupidity, hate, envy, bluffs and blocks,
1140   Posted to fret you into foam and noise.
What of it? Up you mount in minute mist,

1118| MS:man. That's the   *1871b*:man. "Such the   1121| MS:drops §altered to§ drop and powders §altered to§ powder? "Nay," he laughs, §last three words and punctuation crossed out§ what's   *1871b*:powder?" What's   1122| MS:neat, §inserted above§ < > neutralized—   *1871b*:neutralized: 1123| MS:retarding too,— §crossed out§ nay 1125| MS:through this §crossed out and replaced above by§ such < > everywhere— *1871b*:everywhere,   1126| MS:There's §crossed out and replaced above by§ Finds 1127| MS:opposition, we forego   *1871b*:opposition, he foregoes   1128| MS:Should we unfetter   *1871b*:Should he unfetter   1131| MS:stupidity,—the hate   *1871b*:stupidity, the hate,   1132| MS:malice §crossed out and then marked for retention§ and uncharitableness,   *1871b*:uncharitableness   1133| That prove §crossed out§ bar < > the flow of §last three words inserted above§   1134| MS:from your §crossed out and replaced above by§ those   1136| MS:rivers—on   *1871b*:rivers: on   1138| MS:on the §crossed out and replaced above by§ to   1139| MS:Stupidity, and malice §last two words crossed out and replaced above by two words§ hate, envy   1140| MS:Set there §last two words crossed out and replaced above by one word§ Posted to spoil §crossed out and replaced above by§ fret your §altered to§ you forcefullness §crossed out and replaced above by§ in to < > noise: *1871b*:into < > noise.   1141| MS:it? There §crossed out and replaced above by§ Don't §crossed out and replaced by§ Up < > minute §inserted above§ mist again, §crossed out§

And bridge the chasm that crushed your quietude,
A spirit-rainbow, earthborn jewelry
Outsparkling the insipid firmament
1145 Blue above Terni and its orange-trees.
Do not mistake me! You, too, have your rights!
Hans must not burn Kant's house above his head
Because he cannot understand Kant's book:
And still less must Hans' pastor burn Kant's self
1150 Because Kant understands some books too well.
But, justice seen to on this little point,
Answer me, is it manly, is it sage
To stop and struggle with arrangements here
It took so many lives, so much of toil,
1155 To tinker up into efficiency?
Can't you contrive to operate at once,—
Since time is short and art is long,—to show
Your quality i' the world, whate'er you boast,
Without this fractious call on folks to crush
1160 The world together just to set you free,
Admire the capers you will cut perchance,
Nor mind the mischief to your neighbours?

                                                      "Age!

Age and experience bring discouragement,"
You taunt me: I maintain the opposite.

1144| MS:Outsparkling heaven's §crossed out and replaced above by§ the   1145| MS:§line added§   1146| MS:Oh, I remember! §last three words crossed out and replaced below by four words§ Do not mistake me!   1147| MS:not go §crossed out§ burn <> head, *1889a*:head   1148| MS:book— *1871b*:book: 1150| MS:Because he understands the §crossed out and replaced above by§ all book §altered to§ books too well— *1871b*:Because Kant understands some books too well.   1152| MS:Answer now §crossed out and replaced above by§ me   1153| MS:To find such fault §last three words crossed out and replaced above by three words§ stop and struggle with the §crossed out§ arrangements   1154| MS:It took took §crossed out§ so many centuries §crossed out and replaced above by three words§ lives, so much of toil *1871b*:toil,   1155| MS:efficiency?— *1871b*:efficiency?   1157| MS:long,—and §crossed out and replaced above by§ to 1159| MS:fractious cry that §last two words crossed out and replaced above by three words§ call on folks   1161| MS:And see §crossed out and replaced above by§ watch §crossed out; *And* crossed out and replaced above by§ Observe the marvel that will come of that, *1871b*:Admire the capers you will cut perchance,   1162| MS:neighbours? §¶ called for in margin§ No! *1871b*:neighbours? §¶§ "Age!   1163| MS:"Age *1871b*:Age

1165   Am I discouraged who,—perceiving health,
     Strength, beauty, as they tempt the eye of soul,
     Are uncombinable with flesh and blood,—
     Resolve to let my body live its best,
     And leave my soul what better yet may be
1170   Or not be, in this life or afterward?
     —In either fortune, wiser than who waits
     Till magic art procure a miracle.
     In virtue of my very confidence
     Mankind ought to outgrow its babyhood,
1175   I prescribe rocking, deprecate rough hands,
     While thus the cradle holds it past mistake.
     Indeed, my task's the harder—equable
     Sustainment everywhere, all strain, no push—
     Whereby friends credit me with indolence,
1180   Apathy, hesitation. "Stand stock-still
     If able to move briskly? 'All a-strain'—
     So must we compliment your passiveness?

1165| MS:Is one §last two words crossed out and replaced above by two words§ Am I < > who, perceiving §crossed out and replaced above by two words§ aware that §crossed out; *perceiving* marked for retention§ *1871b:*who,—perceiving   1166| MS:Strength, and §crossed out§ beauty, §syllable above, perhaps *euph*, crossed out§ each in its, §last three words crossed out and replaced above by three words§ in its §inserted above§ perfection §last three words crossed out§ each and all, §last three words crossed out§ as one §altered to§ they sees them with the mind, §last four words inserted below and then crossed out§ §*sees* crossed out and replaced above by§ tempt §next five words added above§ the eye o' the mind §crossed out and replaced above by§ soul   *1871b:*of soul,   1167| MS:Are not to §last two worfds crossed out§ un §inserted above§ combinable   1168| MS:let his §crossed out and replaced above by§ my   1169| MS:leave the mind §last two words crossed out and replaced above by two words§ my soul what miracles shall §last two words crossed out and replaced above by three words§ better yet may   1170| MS:life §crossed out and replaced above by word illegibly crossed out; *life* marked for retention§ or afterward?— *1871b:*afterward?   1171| MS:In either case, far §last two words crossed out and replaced above by one word§ fortune   *1871b:*—In   1172| MS:art have wrought the §last three words crossed out and replaced above by two words§ procure a   1173| MS:of your §crossed out and replaced above by§ my   1175| MS:I shall keep §last two words crossed out and replaced above by one word§ prescribe rocking, and rather than §last three words crossed out and replaced above by one word§ deprecate   1176| MS:§line added§
1177| MS:Indeed that §crossed out and replaced below by§ my   1179| MS:Whereby you credit   *1871b:*Whereby friends credit   1180| MS:hesitation: who §crossed out§ "Stands §altered to§ "Stand stock- §inserted above§   1181| MS:briskly? All a-strain *1871b:*briskly? 'All a-strain'—   1182| MS:§line added§ You please to compliment, mere passiveness?   *1871b:*So must we compliment your passiveness?

Sound asleep, rather!"

                 Just the judgment passed
Upon a statue, luckless like myself,
1185   I saw at Rome once! 'Twas some artist's whim
To cover all the accessories close
I' the group, and leave you only Laocoön
With neither sons nor serpents to denote
The purpose of his gesture. Then a crowd
1190   Was called to try the question, criticize
Wherefore such energy of legs and arms,
Nay, eyeballs, starting from the socket. One—
I give him leave to write my history—
Only one said "I think the gesture strives
1195   Against some obstacle we cannot see."
All the rest made their minds up. "'Tis a yawn
Of sheer fatigue subsiding to repose:
The statue's 'Somnolency' clear enough!"

There, my arch stranger-friend, my audience both
1200   And arbitress, you have one half your wish,
At least: you know the thing I tried to do!
All, so far, to my praise and glory—all
Told as befits the self-apologist,—
Who ever promises a candid sweep

1184| MS:a certain §crossed out and replaced above by§ statue   1185| MS:once: 'twas
*1871b:*once! 'Twas   1186| MS:cover up the §last two words crossed out and replaced
above by four words§ all the accesories up §crossed out§ close   1191| MS:Why that §last
two words crossed out and replaced above by two words§ Wherefore the outstretch of those
legs and arms   *1871b:*Wherefore such energy of legs and arms,   1192| MS:eyeballs,
even, §last towrd and both commas crossed out and replaced above by§ starting
1193| MS:I wish I had that man would §last two words crossed out and replaced above by two
words§ he may §last two words crossed out; all but first word of line crossed out and replaced
above by four words§ give him leave to   1194| MS:said, "I < > gesture's §altered to§
gesture strife §altered to§ strives   1196| MS:up. "'Tis the §crossed
out and replaced above by§ a   1197| MS:Of mere fatigue   *1871b:*Of sheer fatigue
1198| MS:statue's name §crossed out§ 'Somnolency   1199| MS:my sweet stranger-friend,
my §crossed out and replaced above by§ fit §crossed out; *my* marked for retention§   *1871b:*my
arch stranger-friend   1201| MS:At least: §last two words inserted above§ You < > do—
*1871b:*you < > do!   1202| MS:so far, §last two words inserted above§
1203| MS:as becomes §altered to§ befits the self-apologist—   *1871b:*self-apologist,—

¹²⁰⁵ And clearance of those errors miscalled crimes
None knows more, none laments so much as he,
And ever rises from confession, proved
A god whose fault was—trying to be man.
Just so, fair judge,—if I read smile aright—
¹²¹⁰ I condescend to figure in your eyes
As biggest heart and best of Europe's friends,
And hence my failure. God will estimate
Success one day; and, in the mean time—you!

I dare say there's some fancy of the sort
¹²¹⁵ Frolicking round this final puff I send
To die up yonder in the ceiling-rose,—
Some consolation-stakes, we losers win!
A plague of the return to "I—I—I
Did this, meant that, hoped, feared the other thing!"
¹²²⁰ Autobiography, adieu! The rest
Shall make amends, be pure blame, history
And falsehood: not the ineffective truth,
But Thiers-and-Victor-Hugo exercise.

---

^{1206|} MS:he— *1871b:*he,   ^{1207|} MS:confession proved   *1871b:*confession, proved
^{1209|} MS:Not otherwise §last two words crossed out and replaced above by four words§ Just so, sweet judge,—if I read §crossed out and then marked for retention§   *1871b:*so, fair judge
^{1210|} MS:I condescend to §last three words crossed out and replaced above by three words§ Contritely do I §last three words crossed out; original reading marked for retention§
^{1211|} MS:of friends to man   *1871b:*of Europe's friends,   ^{1212|} MS:failure—God
*1871b:*failure. God   ^{1213|} MS:day—and   *1871b:*day; and   ^{1215|} MS:round that
§crossed out§ yon final <> sent *1871b:*round this final <> send   ^{1216|} MS:the plaster-
rose,—   *1871b:*the ceiling-rose,—   ^{1217|} MS:consolation-stakes which §crossed out and
replaced above by§ we   *1871b:*consolation-stakes, we   ^{1218|} MS:It all §crossed
out and replaced above by§ just comes of §last four words crossed out and replaced above by
four words§ The fault is in §last four words crossed out and replaced by six words§ A plague of
the return to the tempting §crossed out and replaced above by§ incessant
§crossed out§ "I—I—I   *1871b:*to "I—I—I   ^{1219|} MS:hoped—feared—the <> thing"!
*1871b:*hoped, feared the <> thing!"   ^{1220|} MS:The rest shall be §last four words crossed
out and replaced above by two words§ Autobiography—adieu! The   *1871b:*Autobiography,
adieu   ^{1221|} MS:make amends: §last two words inserted above§ be <> blame—all
§crossed out and replaced above by§ mere §crossed out§ history   *1871b:*amends, be <>
blame, history   ^{1222|} MS:falsehood, not a particle of §last three words crossed out and
replaced above by two words§ the ineffective   *1871b:*falsehood: not   ^{1223|} MS:But
Thiers-and-Victor Hugo-exercise.   *1871b:*But Thiers-and-Victor-Hugo exercise

Hear what I never was, but might have been
1225 I' the better world where goes tobacco-smoke!
Here lie the dozen volumes of my life:
(Did I say "lie"? the pregnant word will serve).
Cut on to the concluding chapter, though!
Because the little hours begin to strike.
1230 Hurry Thiers-Hugo to the labour's end!

Something like this the unwritten chapter reads.

Exemplify the situation thus!
Hohenstiel-Schwangau, being, no dispute,
Absolute mistress, chose the Assembly, first,
1235 To serve her: chose this man, its President
Afterward, to serve also,—specially
To see that folk did service one and all.
And now the proper term of years was out
When the Head-servant must vacate his place,
1240 And nothing lay so patent to the world
As that his fellow-servants one and all
Were—mildly to make mention—knaves or fools,
Each of them with his promise flourished full

1224| MS:Listen to §last two words crossed out and replaced above by one word§ Hear <>
never §inserted above§ was, not §crossed out§ and §crossed out and replaced above by§ but
§crossed out; *and* marked for retention§ will §crossed out and replaced above by two words§
might have be §altered to§ been   *1871b:*was, but might   1225| MS:the other §crossed
out and replaced above by§ better <> tobacco-smoke.   *1871b:*tobacco-smoke!
1226-27| MS:§lines added§ Here, lie <> / <> lie?—" the <> serve.)   *1871b:*Here lie <> /
<> lie?" the   *1889a:*say "lie"? the <> serve).   1228| MS:Lie §crossed out§ Cut on
§inserted above§ <> though,   *1871b:*though!   1229| MS:strike,—   *1871b:*strike.
1230| MS:Take the §last two words crossed out and replaced above by one word§ Hurry
historian at §crossed out and replaced above by§ to his volume- §crossed out and replaced
above by§ labour's end.   *1871b:*Hurry Thiers-Hugo to the labour's end!
1231| MS:reads—   *1871b:*reads.   1232| MS:thus: *1871b:*thus!   1233| MS:being,
past §crossed out and replaced above by§ no   1235| MS:her, and §crossed out and
replaced above by§ chose this Prince, its President,   *1871b:*her: chose this man, its President
1236| MS:Afterward, §inserted above§   1237| MS:By §crossed out and replaced above by§
To seeing §altered to§ see that §inserted above§ they did   *1889a:*that folk did
1238| MS:out,   *1889a:*out   1239| MS:place: *1889a:*place,   1240| MS:nothing was
so   *1871b:*nothing lay so   1242| MS:mildly be the §last two words crossed out and
replaced above by two words§ make the mention   *1871b:*make we mention   *1889a:*mildly to
make mention   1243| MS:his project §crossed out and replaced above by§ purpose—
flourished   *1871b:*purpose flourished   *1889a:*his promise flourished

I' the face of you by word and impudence,
1245 Or filtered slyly out by nod and wink
And nudge upon your sympathetic rib—
That not one minute more did knave or fool
Mean to keep faith and serve as he had sworn
Hohenstiel-Schwangau, once her Head away.
1250 Why should such swear except to get the chance,
When time should ripen and confusion bloom,
Of putting Hohenstielers-Schwangauese
To the true use of human property—
Restoring souls and bodies, this to Pope,
1255 And that to King, that other to his planned
Perfection of a Share-and-share-alike,
That other still, to Empire absolute
In shape of the Head-servant's very self
Transformed to Master whole and sole? each scheme
1260 Discussible, concede one circumstance—
That each scheme's parent were, beside himself,
Hohenstiel-Schwangau, not her serving-man
Sworn to do service in the way she chose
Rather than his way: way superlative,
1265 Only,—by some infatuation,—his
And his and his and everyone's but hers

1245| MS:slyly §inserted above§   1249| MS:once that Head away: *1871b:*away.
*1889a:*once her Head   1250| MS:What §altered to§ Why had §crossed out and replaced
above by§ did he sworn §altered to§ swear for but §last two words crossed out and replaced
above by one word§ except   *1871b:*did such swear   *1889a:*Why should such
1251| MS:should §over *was*§ ripe §altered to§ ripen and fit §crossed out§ confusion come,
§crossed out and replaced above by§ bloom,   1253| MS:To their §altered to§ the < >
use—restore such §dash and last two words crossed out and replaced above by three words§ of
all such §last two words crossed out§ human §inserted above§   *1871b:*property?
*1889a:*property—   1254| MS:Restore them, souls and §last two words inserted above§ < >
this—to   *1871b:*Restoring souls < > this to   1256| MS:a social §crossed out and replaced
above by§ share and share-alike,   *1871b:*a Share-and-share-alike,   1257| MS:still to
Empire in §altered to§ i' the shape §last three words crossed out and replaced above by one
word§ absolute   *1871b:*still, to   1258| MS:I' the shape §last three words added in
margin§ Of §altered to§ of < > very §inserted above§ self §solidus added§ transformed
§altered to§ Transformed §crossed out§   *1871b:*In shape   1259| MS:Transformed
§added in margin§ To §altered to§ to master < > sole: each   *1889a:*to Master < > sole? each
1262| MS:Hohenstiel-Schwangau—not §altered to§ no her §crossed out and replaced above
by§ mere serving-man   *1871b:*Hohenstiel-Schwangau, not her serving-man
1264| MS:And not §last two words crossed out and replaced above by two words§
Rather than this way, way §inserted above§ superlatively §altered to§ superlative, best,
§crossed out§   *1871b:*than his way: way   1266| MS:hers—   *1871b:*hers

Who stuck to just the Assembly and the Head.
I make no doubt the Head, too, had his dream
Of doing sudden duty swift and sure
1270 On all that heap of untrustworthiness—
Catching each vaunter of the villany
He meant to perpetrate when time was ripe,
Once the Head-servant fairly out of doors,—
And, caging here a knave and there a fool,
1275 Cry "Mistress of your servants, these and me,
Hohenstiel-Schwangau! I, their trusty Head,
Pounce on a pretty scheme concocting here
That's stopped, extinguished by my vigilance.
Your property is safe again: but mark!
1280 Safe in these hands, not yours, who lavish trust
Too lightly. Leave my hands their charge awhile!
I know your business better than yourself:
Let me alone about it! Some fine day,
Once we are rid of the embarrassment,
1285 You shall look up and see your longings crowned!"
Such fancy might have tempted him be false,
But this man chose truth and was wiser so.
He recognized that for great minds i' the world
There is no trial like the appropriate one
1290 Of leaving little minds their liberty
Of littleness to blunder on through life,

1267| MS:Who §over *Which*§ was §crossed out and replaced above by three words§ stuck
to just <> Head. nought else. §last two words crossed out§   1268| MS:doubt that
Head <> had its §crossed out and replaced above by§ his   *1871b*:doubt the Head
1269| MS:sudden service §crossed out and replaced above by§ duty   1271| MS:Laying
§crossed out and replaced above by§ Catching   1273| MS:And §crossed out and replaced
above by§ Once   1275| MS:of all §crossed out§ the servants   *1889a*:of your servants
1276| MS:Hohenstiel-Schwangau, I, the trusty one, §crossed out and replaced above by§ Head,
1871b:Hohenstiel-Schwangau! I, their trusty   1277| MS:pretty §inserted above§ scheme in
mid- §last word and syllable crossed out§ concotion §altered to§ concocting here!
1871b:here   1279| MS:again—but   *1871b*:again: but   1280| MS:yours who
1871b:yours, who   1281| MS:hands alone §crossed out and replaced above by§ their
1283| MS:it; some   *1871b*:it! Some   1284| MS:§line added§ Now we   *1871b*:Once we
1286| MS:§line added§ fancy might <> tempted to be   *1889a*:fancy may <> tempted him be
1287| MS:man feared God and   *1871b*:man chose truth and   1288| MS:He saw §crossed
out and replaced above by§ recognized <> for the §crossed out§ great <> in §altered to§ i'
the §over *this*§   1291| MS:to §crossed out and replaced above by§ which §crossed out; *to*
marked for retention§ blunder §altered to§ blunders §last letter crossed out§

Now, aiming at right ends by foolish means,
Now, at absurd achievement through the aid
Of good and wise endeavour—to acquiesce
¹²⁹⁵ In folly's life-long privilege, though with power
To do the little minds the good they need,
Despite themselves, by just abolishing
Their right to play the part and fill the place
I' the scheme of things He schemed who made alike
¹³⁰⁰ Great minds and little minds, saw use for each.
Could the orb sweep those puny particles
It just half-lights at distance, hardly leads
I' the leash—sweep out each speck of them from space
They anticize in with their days and nights
¹³⁰⁵ And whirlings round and dancings off, forsooth,
And all that fruitless individual life
One cannot lend a beam to but they spoil—
Sweep them into itself and so, one star,
Preponderate henceforth i' the heritage
¹³¹⁰ Of heaven! No! in less senatorial phrase,
The man endured to help, not save outright
The multitude by substituting him
For them, his knowledge, will and way, for God's:

---

¹²⁹²| MS:Now, §added in margin§ Willing the §last two words crossed out and replaced above
by two words§ arriving at < > end by the §crossed out§ foolish   *1871b*:Now, aiming at
1889a:ends   ¹²⁹³| MS:Or else §last two words crossed out and replaced above by one
word§ Now, the §crossed out and replaced above by§ some absurd   *1871b*:Now, at absurd
¹²⁹⁴| MS:Of §altered to§ O' the good and wise: the trial to endure §crossed out§ acquiesce
1871b:Of good and wise means: trial   *1889a*:wise endeavour—to   ¹²⁹⁵| MS:I' the §last
two words added in margin§ That §crossed out§ life-long blunder §crossed out and replaced
above by§ privilege,—having will and power   *1871b*:In folly's life-long privilege—though with
power   *1889a*:privilege, though   ¹²⁹⁶| MS:they want,   *1871b*:they need,
¹²⁹⁷| MS:by just §crossed out and replaced above by§ mere §crossed out; *just* marked for
retention§ abolishment §altered to§ abolishing   ¹²⁹⁹| MS:things by Him who
1871b:things He schemed who   ¹³⁰⁰| MS:little minds, their use
1871b:little minds, saw use   ¹³⁰²| MS:Of satellites §last two words crossed
out§ it §altered to§ It just §inserted above§ half-lights in the §last two words crossed out and
replaced above by one word§ at   ¹³⁰³| MS:leash, through Heaven §last two words
crossed out§ —sweep out each speck of §last four words nserted above§ < > from the §crossed
out§ space   *1871b*:leash—sweep   ¹³⁰⁴| MS:They turn about §last two words crossed out
and replaced above by one word§ anticize   ¹³⁰⁵| MS:And turnings round and keepings
off   *1871b*:And whirlings round and dancings off   ¹³¹⁰| MS:heaven:—or, in
1871b:heaven! No! in   ¹³¹¹| MS:help—not   *1871b*:help, not   ¹³¹³| MS:way for
theirs: §crossed out and replaced above by§ God's: *1871b*:way, for

Nor change the world, such as it is, and was
1315 And will be, for some other, suiting all
Except the purpose of the maker. No!
He saw that weakness, wickedness will be,
And therefore should be: that the perfect man
As we account perfection—at most pure
1320 O' the special gold, whate'er the form it take,
Head-work or heart-work, fined and thrice-refined
I' the crucible of life, whereto the powers
Of the refiner, one and all, are flung
To feed the flame, he saw that e'en the block
1325 Such perfect man holds out triumphant, breaks
Into some poisonous ore, gold's opposite,
At the very purest, so compensating
Man's Adversary—what if we believe?—
For earlier stern exclusion of his stuff.
1330 See the sage, with the hunger for the truth,
And see his system that's all true, except
The one weak place that's stanchioned by a lie!
The moralist who walks with head erect
I' the crystal clarity of air so long,
1335 Until a stumble, and the man's one mire!
Philanthropy undoes the social knot
With axe edge, makes love room 'twixt head and trunk:

---

¹³¹⁴| MS:Changing the world such *1871b*:Not change the world, such *1889a*:Nor change
¹³¹⁵| MS:suiting answering §crossed out§ all ¹³¹⁶| MS:But §crossed out and replaced
above by§ Except <> Maker *1871b*:maker ¹³²¹| MS:thrice refined *1871b*:thrice-
refined ¹³²²| MS:life whereto *1871b*:life, whereto ¹³²³| MS:were *1889a*:are
¹³²⁴| MS:the flame §last two words inserted above§ their utmost,—e'en that block,—
1871b:block, *1889a*:flame, he saw that e'en the block ¹³²⁵| MS:He holds out,
breathlessly triumphant,—breaks *1871b*:out breathlessly *1889a*:Such perfect man holds out
triumphant, breaks ¹³²⁶| MS:ore its opposite *1871b*:ore, its opposite, *1889a*:ore,
gold's opposite, ¹³²⁷| MS:purest, com §crossed out§ so ¹³²⁸| MS:The Adversary
1871b:believe? *1889a*:Man's Adversary <> believe?— ¹³²⁹| MS:For all that stern
1871b:For earlier stern ¹³³⁰| MS:with the passion §crossed out and replaced above by§
hunger §crossed out, marked for retention, then reiterated above§ for the §last two words
crossed out§ *1871b*:hunger for the truth, ¹³³²| MS:I' the *1871b*:The one
¹³³³| MS:moralist, that walks *1889a*:moralist who walks ¹³³⁴| MS:chrystal <> long
1871b:crystal <> long, ¹³³⁵| MS:Until—one §crossed out and replaced above by§ a
stumble and <> mire: *1871b*:Until a stumble, and <> mire! ¹³³⁶| MS:Philanthropy,
that cuts §last two words crossed out and replaced above by one word§ undoes
1871b:Philanthropy undoes ¹³³⁷| MS:trunk. *1871b*:trunk! *1889a*:trunk:

Religion—but, enough, the thing's too clear!
Well, if these sparks break out i' the greenest tree,
1340 Our topmost of performance, yours and mine,
What will be done i' the dry ineptitude
Of ordinary mankind, bark and bole,
All seems ashamed of but their mother-earth?
Therefore throughout Head's term of servitude
1345 He did the appointed service, and forbore
Extraneous action that were duty else,
Done by some other servant, idle now
Or mischievous: no matter, each his own—
Own task, and, in the end, own praise or blame!
1350 He suffered them strut, prate and brag their best,
Squabble at odds on every point save one,
And there shake hands,—agree to trifle time,
Obstruct advance with, each, his cricket-cry
"Wait till the Head be off the shoulders here!
1355 Then comes my King, my Pope, my Autocrat,
My Socialist Republic to her own—

---

¹³³⁸| MS:Religion—oh, enough *1871b*:Religion—but, enough ¹³³⁹| MS:green
1871b:greenest ¹³⁴⁰| MS:The §crossed out and replaced in margin by§ Earth's §crossed
out and replaced above by three words§ So, to make §crossed out§ Our §inserted above§ top-
most §last syllable inserted above§ of earth's §last two words crossed out and replaced above
by one word, illegibly crossed out§ of §inserted above§ performances §altered to§
performance, conceive §crossed out§ yours ¹³⁴¹| MS:What shall be < > dry, the
multitude §last two words crossed out and replaced above by one word§ ineptitude
1871b:What will be ¹³⁴²| MS:mankind, §last syllable inserted above§ that makes the
mass §last four words crossed out and replaced above by three words§ coarse §crossed out§
bark and ¹³⁴³| MS:For which §last two words crossed out and replaced above by two
words§ All seems < > of save §crossed out and replaced above by§ but its mother-earth?
1871b:but their mother-earth? ¹³⁴⁴| MS:throughout his term *1889a*:throughout
Head's term ¹³⁴⁸| MS:mischievous—no *1871b*:mischievous: no ¹³⁴⁹| MS:task
and < > blame. *1871b*:task, and < > blame! ¹³⁵⁰| MS:He §crossed out and replaced
above by§ —Suffered let §crossed out and replaced above by§ bade §crossed out§ them
speechify §crossed out and replaced above by three words§ strut and prate and < > best—
1871b:He suffered < > strut, prate < > best, ¹³⁵¹| MS:Squabble, at odds §last two words
inserted above§ *1871b*:Squabble at ¹³⁵²| MS:MS:there strike §crossed out and
replaced above by§ shake hands, in friendship §last two words crossed out and replaced above
by two words§ agree to wasting §altered to waste the §inserted above§ time, *1871b*:hands,—
agree to trifle time, ¹³⁵³| MS:Obstructing §last syllable crossed out and replaced above
by one word§ the work with each his *1871b*:Obstruct advance with, each, his
¹³⁵⁴| MS:is *1871b*:be ¹³⁵⁵| MS:my < > Pope, my Emp §last three
letters crossed out and replaced above by§ Autocrat, ¹³⁵⁶| MS:socialist republic to his
right §crossed out§ own— *1871b*:My Socialist Republic to her own—

To-wit, that property of only me,
Hohenstiel-Schwangau who conceits herself
Free, forsooth, and expects I keep her so!"
1360 —Nay, suffered when, perceiving with dismay
Head's silence paid no tribute to their noise,
They turned on him. "Dumb menace in that mouth,
Malice in that unstridulosity!
He cannot but intend some stroke of state
1365 Shall signalize his passage into peace
Out of the creaking,—hinder transference
O' the Hohenstielers-Schwangauese to king,
Pope, autocrat, or socialist republic! That's
Exact the cause his lips unlocked would cry!
1370 Therefore be stirring: brave, beard, bully him!
Dock, by the million, of its friendly joints,
The electoral body short at once! who did,
May do again, and undo us beside.
Wrest from his hands the sword for self-defence,
1375 The right to parry any thrust in play
We peradventure please to meditate!"
And so forth; creak, creak, creak: and ne'er a line
His locked mouth oped the wider, till at last
O' the long degraded and insulting day,

---

^{1357|} MS:§line added§ of everyone, *1871b:*of only me, ^{1358|} MS:Hohenstiel-Schwangau that conceits *1871b:*Hohenstiel-Schwangau who conceits ^{1359|} MS:expects we keep *1871b:*expects I keep ^{1361|} MS:His silence *1889a:*Head's silence ^{1362|} MS:him. "What §crossed out and replaced above by§ Much §crossed out§ menace §altered to§ Menace in that man §crossed out and replaced above by§ dumb mouth *1871b:*him. "Dumb menace in that mouth, ^{1363|} MS:in this §crossed out and replaced above by§ such unstridulosity! *1871b:*in that unstridulosity! ^{1367|} MS:to King, *1871b:*king, ^{1368|} MS:Pope, Autocrat, or Socialist Republic *1871b:*autocrat, or socialist republic ^{1369|} MS:cry: *1871b:*cry! ^{1370|} MS:Therefore begin, do §last two words crossed out and replaced above by two words§ be wary §crossed out and replaced above by§ stirring <> him, *1871b:*him! ^{1372|} MS:once—who did— *1871b:*once! who did, ^{1373|} MS:beside: *1871b:*beside. ^{1375|} MS:thrust he please *1871b:*thrust in play ^{1376|} MS:We haply may appear §last three words crossed out and replaced above by two words§ peradventure please ^{1377|} MS:creak, creak, creak,—and *1871b:*creak, creak, creak: and ^{1378|} MS:His shut §inserted above§ mouth §crossed out and replaced above by§ lips §crossed out; *mouth* marked for retention§ unlocked the §last two words crossed out and replaced above by two words§ was §crossed out; *the* marked for retention§ oped the wider till the §crossed out and replaced above by§ at *1871b:*His locked mouth oped the wider, till ^{1379|} MS:degraded and insulting §last three words inserted above§ day, when §crossed out§

1380   Sudden the clock told it was judgment-time.
    Then he addressed himself to speak indeed
    To the fools, not knaves: they saw him walk straight down
    Each step of the eminence, as he first engaged,
    And stand at last o' the level,—all he swore.
1385   "People, and not the people's varletry,
    This is the task you set myself and these!
    Thus I performed my part of it, and thus
    They thwarted me throughout, here, here, and here:
    Study each instance! yours the loss, not mine.
1390   What they intend now is demonstrable
    As plainly: here's such man, and here's such mode
    Of making you some other than the thing
    You, wisely or unwisely, choose to be,
    And only set him up to keep you so.
1395   Do you approve this? Yours the loss, not mine.
    Do you condemn it? There's a remedy.
    Take me—who know your mind, and mean your good,
    With clearer brain and stouter arm than they,
    Or you, or haply anybody else—
1400   And make me master for the moment! Choose
    What time, what power you trust me with: I too
    Will choose as frankly ere I trust myself
    With time and power: they must be adequate
    To the end and aim, since mine the loss, with yours,

1380| MS:When §crossed out§ Sudden   1381| MS:himself §second syllable crossed out and restored§ to a §inserted above§ speak §altered to§ speach §altered back to§ speak   1382| MS:§line added between 1381 and 1385§ the crowd, aghast to see him   *1871b*:the fools, not knaves: they saw him   1383-84| MS:§lines added in margin§ step o'   *1871b*:step of   1386| MS:myself and §last two words inserted above§ <> these: *1871b*:these!   1388| MS:me i' the rest §last three words crossed out and replaced above by§ throughout   1389| MS:instance: yours   *1871b*:instance! yours   1391| MS:plainly: here's the §crossed out and replaced above by§ such <> here's his §crossed out and replaced above by§ such   1393| MS:chose *1871b*:choose   1396| MS:remedy *1871b*:remedy.   1397| MS:me you §crossed out and replaced above by§ who know <> mind and <> good *1871b*:me—who <> mind, and <> good,   1398| MS:With better §crossed out and replaced above by§ clearer head and stronger hand §last two words crossed out and replaced above by two words§ stouter arm <> they *1871b*:they, *1889a*:clearer brain and   1399| MS:you or haply §inserted above§ *1871b*:you, or   1400| MS:moment—choose *1871b*:moment! Choose   1403| MS:With the §crossed out§ time and power as they seem adequate *1871b*:power: they must be adequate   1404| MS:end we §crossed out and replaced above by§ and aim: at §crossed out and replaced above by§ since <> loss with yours *1871b*:aim, since <> loss, with yours,

1405 If means be wanting; once their worth approved,
Grant them, and I shall forthwith operate—
Ponder it well!—to the extremest stretch
O' the power you trust me: if with unsuccess,
God wills it, and there's nobody to blame."

1410 Whereon the people answered with a shout
"The trusty one! no tricksters any more!"
How could they other? He was in his place.

What followed? Just what he foresaw, what proved
The soundness of both judgments,—his, o' the knaves
1415 And fools, each trickster with his dupe,—and theirs,
The people's, in what head and arm could help.
There was uprising, masks dropped, flags unfurled,
Weapons outflourished in the wind, my faith!
Heavily did he let his fist fall plumb
1420 On each perturber of the public peace,
No matter whose the wagging head it broke—
From bald-pate craft and greed and impudence
Of night-hawk at first chance to prowl and prey
For glory and a little gain beside,
1425 Passing for eagle in the dusk of the age,—
To florid head-top, foamy patriotism

1405| MS:be absent §crossed out and replaced above by§ wanting: once   1871b:wanting; once
1407| MS:well—to   1871b:well!—to   1408| MS:O' the power §last three words inserted
above§ You   1871b:you   1409| MS:it, nobody will §crossed out and replaced above by§
can be to   1871b:it, and there's nobody to   1411| MS:one, no   1871b:one! no
1412| MS:other? I was in my place.   1871b:other? He was in his place.   1412-13| MS:§¶
called for in margin§   1871b:§¶§   1889a:§¶ lost in paging. Emended to restore ¶; see
Editorial Notes§   1413| MS:what I foresaw,—what   1871b:what he foresaw, what
1414| MS:judgments,—mine, o'   1871b:judgments,—his, o'   1416| MS:The People, in
the §crossed out and replaced above by§ what <> arm should help.   1871b:people
1889a:people's <> arm could help.   1417| MS:uprising, the §crossed out§ masks
1418| MS:Weapons at brandish §crossed out and replaced above by§ flourish in
1871b:Weapons outflourished in   1419| MS:did I let my fist descend §crossed out§ fall
1871b:did he let his fist   1422| MS:bald pate spectacles and §crossed out§ all a-stare
§crossed out and replaced above by three words§ greed and impudence   1871b:bald-pate
craft and greed   1423| MS:As the §crossed out§ night-hawk   1871b:Of night-hawk
1424| MS:§line added§   1425| MS:dusk, to §crossed out§ o' the age,   1871b:dusk o' the
age,—   1426| MS:foamy eloquence, §crossed out and replaced above by§ patriotism

And tribunitial daring, breast laid bare
Thro' confidence in rectitude, with hand
On private pistol in the pocket: these
1430 And all the dupes of these, who lent themselves
As dust and feather do, to help offence
O' the wind that whirls them at you, then subsides
In safety somewhere, leaving filth afloat,
Annoyance you may brush from eyes and beard,—
1435 These he stopped: bade the wind's spite howl or whine
Its worst outside the building, wind conceives
Meant to be pulled together and become
Its natural playground so. What foolishness
Of dust or feather proved importunate
1440 And fell 'twixt thumb and finger, found them gripe
To detriment of bulk and buoyancy.
Then followed silence and submission. Next,
The inevitable comment came on work
And work's cost: he was censured as profuse
1445 Of human life and liberty: too swift
And thorough his procedure, who had lagged
At the outset, lost the opportunity
Through timid scruples as to right and wrong.
"There's no such certain mark of a small mind"
1450 (So did Sagacity explain the fault)
"As when it needs must square away and sink
To its own small dimensions, private scale
Of right and wrong,—humanity i' the large,

1427| MS:bare, *1871b*:bare   1428| MS:§line added in margin§ rectitude—one hand
1871b:rectitude, with hand   1429| MS:And §crossed out and replaced above by§ On
private §inserted above§   1431| MS:to §inserted above§   1433| MS:Safely §altered
to§ Safe §crossed out§ Out of reach §last three words crossed out and replaced above by two
words§ In safety, somewhere, safe as §last two words crossed out§ leaving   *1871b*:In safety
somewhere   1434| MS:beard. *1871b*:beard,—   1435| MS:I stopped the wind
§altered to§ wind's out §crossed out and replaced above by§ spite, bade it §crossed out and
replaced above by§ wind howl   *1871b*:These he stopped: bade the wind's spite howl
1438| MS:so: the §crossed out§ what   *1871b*:so. What   1439| MS:feather was
importunate, *1871b*:feather proved importunate   1441| MS:And §crossed out and
replaced above by§ To   1443| MS:comment, judging work, *1871b*:comment came on
work   1444| MS:cost: they §crossed out§ I was   *1871b*:cost: he was
1446| MS:thorough my procedure, which had   *1871b*:thorough his procedure, who had
1450| MS:So did Sagacity enforce §crossed out and replaced above by§ explain my fault
1871b:(So <> explain the fault)   1451| MS:it §inserted above§

The right and wrong of the universe, forsooth!
1455 This man addressed himself to guard and guide
Hohenstiel-Schwangau. When the case demands
He frustrate villany in the egg, unhatched,
With easy stamp and minimum of pang
E'en to the punished reptile, 'There's my oath
1460 Restrains my foot,' objects our guide and guard,
'I must leave guardianship and guidance now:
Rather than stretch one handbreadth of the law,
I am bound to see it break from end to end.
First show me death i' the body politic:
1465 Then prescribe pill and potion, what may please
Hohenstiel-Schwangau! all is for her sake:
'Twas she ordained my service should be so.
What if the event demonstrate her unwise,
If she unwill the thing she willed before?
1470 I hold to the letter and obey the bond
And leave her to perdition loyally.'
Whence followed thrice the expenditure we blame
Of human life and liberty: for want
O' the by-blow, came deliberate butcher's-work!"
1475 "Elsewhere go carry your complaint!" bade he.
"Least, largest, there's one law for all the minds,

1454| MS:o' *1871b:*of   1455| MS:man professed §crossed out and replaced above by§
addressed   1456| MS:Hohenstiel-Schwangau: does the <> demand   *1871b:*Hohenstiel-
Schwangau. When the <> demands   1457| MS:i' *1871b:*in   1459| MS:Even <>
reptile? 'There's   *1871b:*E'en <> reptile, 'There's   1460| MS:§two words *guide* and
guard marked for transposition, then reinstated§   1461| MS:guardianship now time is
come: *1871b:*guardianship and guidance now: 1462| MS:I must not stretch <> law
*1871b:*Rather then stretch <> law,   1463| MS:Before I see <> to end   *1871b:*I am
bound to see <> to end.   1464| MS:I must have §last three words crossed out and
replaced above by three words§ First of all, death in §altered to§ i'   *1871b:*First show me
death   1465| MS:Afterward, try what medicine §last three words crossed out and
replaced above by four words§ pill and potion, what you §crossed out and replaced above by§
may   *1871b:*Then prescribe pill   1466| MS:Hohenstiel-Schwangau—all <> sake—
*1871b:*Hohenstiel-Schwangau! all <> sake: 1468| MS:her a fool, §last two words crossed
out and replaced above by one word§ unwise,   1469| MS:And she un §inserted above§
wills   *1871b:*If she unwill   1471| MS:And give §crossed out and replaced above by§ hand
her   *1871b:*And leave her   1472| MS:So follows   *1871b:*Whence followed
1474| MS:by-blow, this §crossed out and replaced above by§ comes   *1871b:*came
1474-75| MS:§¶ called for in margin§   *1871b:*no ¶§   1475| MS:complaint!," my friends
§last two words crossed out and replaced above by two words§ I say §last
two words crossed out§ said he: *1871b:*complaint!" bade he.

181

Here or above: be true at any price!
'Tis just o' the great scale, that such happy stroke
Of falsehood would be found a failure. Truth
1480 Still stands unshaken at her base by me,
Reigns paramount i' the world, for the large good
O' the long late generations,—I and you
Forgotten like this buried foolishness!
Not so the good I rooted in its grave."

1485 This is why he refused to break his oath,
Rather appealed to the people, gained the power
To act as he thought best, then used it, once
For all, no matter what the consequence
To knaves and fools. As thus began his sway,
1490 So, through its twenty years, one rule of right
Sufficed him: govern for the many first,
The poor mean multitude, all mouths and eyes:
Bid the few, better favoured in the brain,
Be patient nor presume on privilege,
1495 Help him or else be quiet,—never crave
That he help them,—increase, forsooth, the gulf
Yawning so terribly 'twixt mind and mind
I' the world here, which his purpose was to block
At bottom, were it by an inch, and bridge,
1500 If by a filament, no more, at top.
Equalize things a little! And the way
He took to work that purpose out, was plain

---

¹⁴⁷⁸| MS:on §altered to§ o' <> scale, my §crossed out and replaced above by two words§ that
such   ¹⁴⁷⁹| MS:falsehood were pronounced a   *1871b:*falsehood would be found a
¹⁴⁸²| MS:Of <> late §inserted above§   *1871b:*O'   ¹⁴⁸³| MS:this buried §crossed out
and replaced above by§ slaughtered foolishness—   *1871b:*this buried foolishness!
¹⁴⁸⁷| MS:best, and used   *1871b:*best, then used   ¹⁴⁸⁹| MS:fools. And thus <> his rule.
*1871b:*fools. As thus <>'his sway,   ¹⁴⁹⁰| MS:through the twenty <> of reign §crossed
out§ right   *1871b:*through its twenty   ¹⁴⁹²| MS:multitude, of §crossed out and replaced
above by§ all   ¹⁴⁹⁴| MS:privilege   *1871b:*patient, nor <> privilege,   *1889a:*patient nor
¹⁴⁹⁵| MS:him, §over *me*§ or   *1889a:*him or   ¹⁴⁹⁶| MS:he §over *I*§ helped <> increased
<> the gulf §crossed out, then marked for retention§ chasm §crossed out§   *1871b:*help <>
increase   ¹⁴⁹⁷| MS:Which yawns so <> 'twixt man and man   *1871b:*Yawning so <>
'twixt mind and mind   ¹⁴⁹⁸| MS:here, and my §crossed out and replaced above by§ his
*1871b:*here, which his   ¹⁵⁰⁰| MS:top—   *1871b:*top.   ¹⁵⁰¹| MS:Some §crossed out§
equalized §altered to§ Equalize things §inserted above§ a little. And   *1871b:*little! And
¹⁵⁰²| MS:work his purpose—what so plain   *1871b:*work that purpose out, was plain

Enough to intellect and honesty
And—superstition, style it if you please,
1505 So long as you allow there was no lack
O' the quality imperative in man—
Reverence. You see deeper? thus saw he,
And by the light he saw, must walk: how else
Was he to do his part? a man's, with might
1510 And main, and not a faintest touch of fear,
Sure he was in the hand of God who comes
Before and after, with a work to do
Which no man helps nor hinders. Thus the man,—
So timid when the business was to touch
1515 The uncertain order of humanity,
Imperil, for a problematic cure
Of grievance on the surface, any good
I' the deep of things, dim yet discernible—
This same man, so irresolute before,
1520 Show him a true excrescence to cut sheer,
A devil's-graft on God's foundation-stock,
Then—no complaint of indecision more!
He wrenched out the whole canker, root and branch,
Deaf to who cried that earth would tumble in
1525 At its four corners if he touched a twig.
Witness that lie of lies, arch-infamy,

1503| MS:As that, to   *1871b*:Enough to   1504| MS:superstition, call §crossed out and
replaced above by§ style < > you choose §crossed out§ please,   1505| MS:there lived in
him   *1871b*:there was no lack   1506| MS:A quality imperative as §crossed out and
replaced above by§ in each—   *1871b*:O' the quality < > in man—   1507| MS:Reverence:
you see deeply §altered to§ deeper, thus   *1871b*:Reverence. You see deeper? thus
1508| MS:walk, how else?   *1871b*:walk: how else   1509| MS:Therefore he did his part, the
man's, §last two words crossed out, then marked for retention§ with might and main §last two
words crossed out§   *1871b*:Was he to do his part? the   *1889a*:part? a man's
1510| MS:And main, §inserted above§ < > faintest §inserted above§   1513| MS:helps or
hinders. Thus our Prince,—   *1871b*:helps nor hinders. Thus the man,—
1516| MS:problematic good §crossed out§ cure   1519| MS:same hand, so   *1871b*:same
man, so   1520| MS:Give him §last two words crossed out and replaced above by two
words§ Show but a clear §crossed out and replaced above by§ plain §crossed out§ excrescence
1871b:Show him a true excrescence   1521| MS:Some devil's-graft < > foundation-stone,
1871b:A devil's-graft   *1889a*:foundation-stock,   1524| MS:Careless
§crossed out and replaced above by two words§ Deaf to who cried the world would
1889a:cried that earth would   1525| MS:he tugged that way. §last three words crossed out
and replaced above by three words§ plucked a twig.   *1871b*:he touched a

When the Republic, with her life involved
In just this law—"Each people rules itself
Its own way, not as any stranger please"—
1530 Turned, and for first proof she was living, bade
Hohenstiel-Schwangau fasten on the throat
Of the first neighbour that claimed benefit
O' the law herself established: "Hohenstiel
For Hohenstielers! Rome, by parity
1535 Of reasoning, for Romans? That's a jest
Wants proper treatment,—lancet-puncture suits
The proud flesh: Rome ape Hohenstiel forsooth!"
And so the siege and slaughter and success
Whereof we nothing doubt that Hohenstiel
1540 Will have to pay the price, in God's good time
Which does not always fall on Saturday
When the world looks for wages. Anyhow,
He found this infamy triumphant. Well:
Sagacity suggested, make this speech!
1545 "The work was none of mine: suppose wrong wait,
Stand over for redressing? Mine for me,
My predecessors' work on their own head!
Meantime there's plain advantage, should we leave
Things as we find them. Keep Rome manacled
1550 Hand and foot: no fear of unruliness!
Her foes consent to even seem our friends

1527| MS:the Republic, all tis §last two words crossed out and replaced above by two words§ with all life   *1889a:*with her life   1528| MS:just §inserted above§ this one §crossed out§ law—each People   *1871b:*law—"Each people   1529| MS:way, and §crossed out§ not as any §last two words inserted above§ <> please—   *1871b:*please"—   1530| MS:living now, *1871b:*living, bade   1531| MS:Hohenstiel-Schwangau, fastened   *1871b:*Hohenstiel-Schwangau fasten   1533| MS:established: Hohenstiel   *1871b:*established: "Hohenstiel   1534| MS:For the §crossed out§ Hohenstielers   1535| MS:for the §crossed out§ Romans   1537| MS:forsooth!   *1871b:*forsooth!"   1539| MS:Whereof I nothing   *1871b:*Whereof we nothing   1540| MS:pay for, all §last two words crossed out and replaced above by two words§ the price, <> time,   *1889a:*time   1542| MS:any how,   *1889a:*anyhow,   1543-45| MS:I found <> Well,— / The work §crossed out; *work* marked for retention§ <> suppose it §crossed out and replaced above by§ wrong   *1871b:*He found <> / Sagacity suggested, make this speech! / "The   *1889a:*triumphant. Well: 1547| MS:head.   *1871b:*head!   1548| MS:Meantime, there's some §crossed out and replaced above by§ plain   *1889a:*Meantime there's   1549| MS:them: here's a people tied §last four words crossed out and replaced above by three words§ keep Rome manacled   *1871b:*them. Keep   1551| MS:Her enemies §crossed out and replaced above by§ foes <> to be §crossed out and replaced above by two words§ even seem

So long, no longer. Then, there's glory got
By boldness and bravado to the world:
The disconcerted world must grin and bear
1555   The old saucy writing, 'Grunt thereat who may,
So shall things be, for such my pleasure is—
Hohenstiel-Schwangau's.' How that reads in Rome
I' the Capitol where Brennus broke his pate,
And lends a flourish to our journalists!"
1560   Only, it was nor read nor flourished of,
Since, not a moment did such glory stay
Excision of the canker! Out it came,
Root and branch, with much roaring, and some blood,
And plentiful abuse of him from friend
1565   And foe. Who cared? Not Nature who assuaged
The pain and set the patient on his legs
Promptly: the better! had it been the worse,
'Tis Nature you must try conclusions with,
Not he, since nursing canker kills the sick
1570   For certain, while to cut may cure, at least.
"Ah," groaned a second time Sagacity,
"Again the little mind, precipitate,
Rash, rude, when even in the right, as here!

1552| MS:longer. Then there's   *1871b*:longer. Then, there's   1553| MS:I' the little §crossed out and replaced above by§ boldness <> world,   *1871b*:world.   *1889a*:By boldness <> world: 1554| MS:The startled §crossed out and replaced above by§ disconcerted <> bear—   *1871b*:bear   1555| MS:writing,—"Grunt who will §crossed out and replaced above by§ may §last two words marked for transposition to follow *thereat*§ thereat, *1871b*:writing,—'Grunt   *1889a*:writing, 'Grunt   1557| MS:Hohenstiel-Schwangau"—how <> reads in Rome §last two words crossed out and replaced above by one word§ abroad §crossed out; *in Rome* marked for retention§   *1871b*:Hohenstiel-Schwangau.' How *1889a*:Hohenstiel-Schwangau's.' How   1558| MS:his head §crossed out and replaced above by§ pate!   *1889a*:pate,   1559-61| MS:And what a <> journalists!"— / Not for a moment one mean motive stayed   *1871b*:journalists!" / Only, it was nor read nor flourished of, / Since, not a moment did such glory stay   *1889a*:And lends a   1563| MS:Roots §altered to§ Root and all §crossed out and replaced above by§ branch <> roaring and <> blood   *1871b*:roaring, and <> blood,   1565| MS:foe: who <> Nature, that assuaged *1871b*:foe. Who   *1889a*:cared? Not Nature who assuaged   1567| MS:Promptly—the better! Had   *1871b*:Promptly: the better! had   1568| MS:'Tis Nature he must *1871b*:'Tis Nature you must   1569-71| MS:Not me §altered to§ him, if §crossed out and replaced above by§ since <> cankers kill a man. / "Ah," groaned the comment of Sagacity *1871b*:Not he <> canker kills the sick / For certain, while to cut may cure, at least. / "Ah," groaned a second time Sagacity,   1572| MS:mind,—precipitate   *1871b*:mind, precipitate,   1573| MS:And §crossed out§ rash §altered to§ Rash, rude §inserted above§

The great mind knows the power of gentleness,
¹⁵⁷⁵ Only tries force because persuasion fails.
Had this man, by prelusive trumpet-blast,
Signified 'Truth and Justice mean to come,
Nay, fast approach your threshold! Ere they knock,
See that the house be set in order, swept
¹⁵⁸⁰ And garnished, windows shut, and doors thrown wide!
The free State comes to visit the free Church:
Receive her! or . . . or . . . never mind what else!'
Thus moral suasion heralding brute force,
How had he seen the old abuses die,
¹⁵⁸⁵ And new life kindle here, there, everywhere,
Roused simply by that mild yet potent spell—
Beyond or beat of drum or stroke of sword—
Public opinion!"

"How, indeed?" he asked,
"When all to see, after some twenty years,
¹⁵⁹⁰ Were your own fool-face waiting for the sight,
Faced by as wide a grin from ear to ear
O' the knaves who, while the fools were waiting, worked—

---

¹⁵⁷⁴| MS:mind does its work with §last four words crossed out and replaced above by four words§ knows the power of   ¹⁵⁷⁵| MS:Never §crossed out and replaced above by§ Only <> force before §crossed out and replaced above by§ because   ¹⁵⁷⁷| MS:justice come at §last two words crossed out and replaced above by two words§ mean to   *1871b*:and Justice
¹⁵⁷⁸| MS:Set §crossed out and replaced above by§ Have §crossed out§ Nay, §added in margin§ <> your §inserted above§ threshold; ere <> knock, at door, §last two words crossed out§ *1871b*:threshold! Ere   ¹⁵⁷⁹| MS:that you set §last two words crossed out§ the <> be set §last two words inserted above§   ¹⁵⁸⁰| MS:shut and <> wide. *1871b*:shut, and <> wide!   ¹⁵⁸¹| MS:Quick, §crossed out and replaced above by§ The §crossed out§ the §altered to§ The free church in §last two words crossed out and replaced above by four words§ state comes to visit the free state §crossed out§ church   *1871b*:free State <> Church:
¹⁵⁸²⁻⁸⁴| MS:her—or . . or . . never <> else!" / How <> die,   *1871b*:her! or <> else!' / Thus moral suasion heralding brute force, / How   *1889a*:her! or . . . or . . . never
¹⁵⁸⁷| MS:§line added§ Beyond all beat of drum and stroke   *1871b*:Beyond or beat of drum or stroke   ¹⁵⁸⁸| MS:opinion!" How indeed, sage sirs, §last two words crossed out§ he   *1871b*:opinion!" §¶§ "How, indeed?" he   ¹⁵⁸⁹| MS:Whcn   *1871b*:"When
¹⁵⁹⁰| MS:Where §altered to§ Were just one §last two words crossed out and replaced above by two words§ your own   ¹⁵⁹¹| MS:And one §last two words crossed out and replaced above by§ wide a   *1871b*:Faced by   ¹⁵⁹²| MS:knaves that, while you §inserted above; crossed out and replaced above by§ the fools so §inserted above§ waited, worked— *1871b*:fools were waiting, worked—   *1889a*:knaves who, while

Broke yet another generation's heart—
Twenty years' respite helping! Teach your nurse
1595 'Compliance with, before you suck, the teat!'
Find what that means, and meanwhile hold your tongue!"

Whereof the war came which he knew must be.

Now, this had proved the dry-rot of the race
He ruled o'er, that, i' the old day, when was need
1600 They fought for their own liberty and life,
Well did they fight, none better: whence, such love
Of fighting somehow still for fighting's sake
Against no matter whose the liberty
And life, so long as self-conceit should crow
1605 And clap the wing, while justice sheathed her claw,—
That what had been the glory of the world
When thereby came the world's good, grew its plague
Now that the champion-armour, donned to dare
The dragon once, was clattered up and down
1610 Highway and by-path of the world at peace,
Merely to mask marauding, or for sake
O' the shine and rattle that apprized the fields
Hohenstiel-Schwangau was a fighter yet,

---

¹⁵⁹⁴| MS:your gran §crossed out§ nurse   ¹⁵⁹⁵| MS:with—before you suck the teat—'
1871b:with, before you suck, the teat!'   ¹⁵⁹⁶| MS:Whatever §crossed out and replaced
above by two words§ Find what <> means! and meanwhile §last two words inserted above§
Hold §altered to§ hold <> tongue! with me! §last two words crossed out§   *1871b*:means, and
<> tongue!"   ¹⁵⁹⁷⁻⁹⁸| MS:§no ¶§   *1871b*:§¶§   ¹⁵⁹⁸| MS:had been §crossed out and
replaced above by§ proved   ¹⁵⁹⁹| *1871b*:in   *1889a*:i'   ¹⁶⁰⁰| MS:fought well,
§crossed out§ <> own §inserted above§   ¹⁶⁰¹| MS:better: thence, such   *1871b*:better:
whence, such   ¹⁶⁰²| MS:Of the §crossed out§ fighting farther §crossed out and replaced
above by two words§ somehow on, for new §crossed out§ fighting's   *1871b*:somehow still for
¹⁶⁰³| MS:Against no matter whose §last four words crossed out and then marked for
retention§   ¹⁶⁰⁵| MS:wing while justice cried con §last word and syllable crossed out and
replaced above by one word§ sheathed   *1871b*:wing, while   ¹⁶⁰⁷| MS:thereby grew
§crossed out§ came §last three words inserted above§ <> good, §illegible word crossed out
and replaced above by§ grew its shame §crossed out§ plague   ¹⁶⁰⁹| MS:once, did service
up   *1871b*:once, was clattered up   ¹⁶¹⁰| MS:bye-path <> peace   *1871b*:by-path <>
peace,   ¹⁶¹¹| MS:To mask <> for simple sake   *1871b*:Merely to <> for sake
¹⁶¹³| MS:Hohenstiel-Schwangau was §crossed out and replaced above by§ is the §crossed out
and replaced above by§ a <> yet:—   *1871b*:Hohenstiel-Schwangau was a <> yet,

187

And would be, till the weary world suppressed
1615   Her peccant humours out of fashion now.
Accordingly the world spoke plain at last,
Promised to punish who next played with fire.

So, at his advent, such discomfiture
Taking its true shape of beneficence,
1620   Hohenstiel-Schwangau, half-sad and part-wise,
Sat: if with wistful eye reverting oft
To each pet weapon, rusty on its peg,
Yet, with a sigh of satisfaction too
That, peacefulness become the law, herself
1625   Got the due share of godsends in its train,
Cried shame and took advantage quietly.
Still, so the dry-rot had been nursed into
Blood, bones and marrow, that, from worst to best,
All,—clearest brains and soundest hearts save here,—
1630   All had this lie acceptable for law
Plain as the sun at noonday—"War is best,
Peace is worst; peace we only tolerate
As needful preparation for new war:
War may be for whatever end we will—
1635   Peace only as the proper help thereto.
Such is the law of right and wrong for us
Hohenstiel-Schwangau: for the other world,

1614-18| MS:Till the world rise and put a nuisance down. / So <> advent, time had wrought a change— §last five words crossed out and replaced above by two words§ such discomfiture *1871b:*And would be, till the weary world suppressed / A peccant humour out of fashion now. / Accordingly the world spoke plain at last, / Promised to punish who next played with arms. §¶§ So   *1889a:*suppressed / Her peccant humours <> / / <> with fire. §¶§   1619| MS:§line added§   1621| MS:Sat, if   *1871b:*Sat: if   1622| MS:To the §crossed out and replaced above by§ each old weapons §altered to§ weapon rusty on the §crossed out and replaced above by§ its   *1871b:*each pet weapon   *1889a:*weapon, rusty   1623| MS:Still, not §inserted above and crossed out§ without §altered to§ with a sigh of §last two words inserted above§ <> too,   *1871b:*Yet, with <> too   1624| MS:peacefulness had been compelled all round §last five words crossed out and replaced above by three words§ proclaimed the law, herself   *1871b:*peacefulness become the   1625| MS:of the §crossed out§ Godsends   *1871b:*godsends   1627| MS:Well, so that dry rot   *1871b:*Still, so the dry-rot   1628| MS:marrow, all from   *1871b:*marrow, that from   1629| MS:Ay, clearest <> here—   *1871b:*All,—clearest <> here,—   1630| MS:That this lie was accepted for a law   *1871b:*All had this lie acceptable for law   1631| MS:noonday: war   *1871b:*noonday—"War   1633| MS:war;   *1871b:*war: 1634| MS:we please—   *1871b:*we will—   1637| MS:—Hohenstiel-Schwangau,—for the world outside

As naturally, quite another law.
Are we content? The world is satisfied.
1640 Discontent? Then the world must give us leave
To strike right, left, and exercise our arm
Torpid of late through overmuch repose,
And show its strength is still superlative
At somebody's expense in life or limb:
1645 Which done,—let peace succeed and last a year!"
Such devil's-doctrine so was judged God's law,
We say, when this man stepped upon the stage,
That it had seemed a venial fault at most
Had he once more obeyed Sagacity.
1650 "You come i' the happy interval of peace,
The favourable weariness from war:
Prolong it! artfully, as if intent
On ending peace as soon as possible.
Quietly so increase the sweets of ease
1655 And safety, so employ the multitude,
Put hod and trowel so in idle hands,
So stuff and stop up wagging jaws with bread,
That selfishness shall surreptitiously
Do wisdom's office, whisper in the ear
1660 Of Hohenstiel-Schwangau, there's a pleasant feel
In being gently forced down, pinioned fast
To the easy arm-chair by the pleading arms

---

*1871b:*Hohenstiel-Schwangau: for the other world,   1638| MS:naturally quite <> law—
*1871b:*naturally, wuite <> law.   1639| MS:satisfied: *1871b:*satisfied.
1641| MS:Strike right and left to exercise   *1889a:*To strike right, left, and exercise
1642| MS:§line added§ Turned torpid §last two words added in margin§ Inactive §crossed
out§ thro' the overmuch   *1871b:*Torpid of late through overmuch   1645| MS:done,—
content shall reign a certain space.   *1871b:*done,—let peace succeed and last a year!"
1646| MS:This §crossed out and replaced above by§ Such   1647| MS:I say <> this prince
stepped   *1871b:*We say <> this man stepped   1649| MS:he—once more—obeyed
*1871b:*he once more obeyed   1652| MS:it,—artfully as   *1871b:*it!—artfully, as   *1889a:*it!
artfully   1655-56| MS:§one line expanded to two lines§ employ the multitude, / §last two
words and solidus inserted above§ Put hod and trowel in §last five words inserted above§ the
idle hands,   *1871b:*trowel so in idle   1657| MS:stop the wagging jaws §last three words
inserted above§   *1889a:*stop up wagging   1659| MS:Take §crossed out and replaced
above by§ Do wisdom's place and do its §last four words crossed out§ office, teach §crossed
out and replaced above by§ whisper   1660| MS:O' §added in margin§
Hohenstiel-Schwangau there's   *1871b:*Of Hohenstiel-Schwangau, there's

O' the world beseeching her to there abide
Content with all the harm done hitherto,
1665 And let herself be petted in return,
Free to re-wage, in speech and prose and verse,
The old unjust wars, nay—in verse and prose
And speech,—to vaunt new victories shall prove
A plague o' the future,—so that words suffice
1670 For present comfort, and no deeds denote
That—tired of illimitable line on line
Of boulevard-building, tired o' the theatre
With the tuneful thousand in their thrones above,
For glory of the male intelligence,
1675 And Nakedness in her due niche below,
For illustration of the female use—
That she, 'twixt yawn and sigh, prepares to slip
Out of the arm-chair, wants fresh blood again
From over the boundary, to colour-up
1680 The sheeny sameness, keep the world aware
Hohenstiel-Schwangau's arm needs exercise
Despite the petting of the universe!
Come, you're a city-builder: what's the way
Wisdom takes when time needs that she entice
1685 Some fierce tribe, castled on the mountain-peak,
Into the quiet and amenity

1663| MS:to there §crossed out and replaced above by§ sit abide   *1871b:*to there abide
1666| MS:to re-fight §second syllable crossed out and replaced above by§ wage in speech, and
<> verse   *1871b:*speech and <> verse,   1667| MS:unjust fights §crossed out and
replaced above by§ wars   1668| MS:victories as vile   *1871b:*victories, as   *1889a:*victories
shall prove   1669| MS:To plague i' the <> so the words expire in §last two words crossed
out and replaced above by two words§ but §crossed out§ suffice   *1871b:*A plague o' the <>
so that   1671| MS:That,—tired of that §crossed out§ illimitable   *1889a:*That—tired
1673| MS:tuneful §inserted above§   1674| MS:§line added§ the intellect of man,
*1871b:*the male intelligence,   1675| MS:her §over the§ <> below,—   *1871b:*below,
1676| MS:§line added§ the woman's use—   *1871b:*the female use—   1677| MS:She,—
'twixt a yawn <> prepare   *1871b:*She, 'twixt <> prepares   *1889a:*That she, 'twixt yawn
1678| MS:o' the arm chair, want some blood   *1871b:*of the arm-chair, wants   *1889a:*wants
fresh blood   1681| MS:Hohenstiel-Schwangau must content herself   *1871b:*must have
exercise   *1889a:*Hohenstiel-Schwangau's arm needs exercise   1683| MS:city-builder,—
what's   *1871b:*city-builder: what's   1684| MS:Nature takes   *1871b:*Wisdom takes
1685| MS:tribe, castled §crossed out and replaced above by word illegibly crossed out; *castled*
marked for retention§ <> mountain-peak   *1871b:*mountain-peak,   1686| MS:the valley
§crossed out and replaced above by§ pastures §crossed out§ quiet

O' the meadow-land below? By crying 'Done
With fight now, down with fortress?' Rather—'Dare
On, dare ever, not a stone displace!'
1690 Cries Wisdom: 'Cradle of our ancestors,
Be bulwark, give our children safety still!
Who of our children please may stoop and taste
O' the valley-fatness, unafraid,—for why?
At first alarm they have thy mother-ribs
1695 To run upon for refuge: foes forget
Scarcely that Terror on her vantage-coign,
Couchant supreme among the powers of air,
Watches—prepared to pounce—the country wide!'
Meanwhile the encouraged valley holds its own,
1700 From the first hut's adventure in descent,
Half home, half hiding place,—to dome and spire
Befitting the assured metropolis:
Nor means offence to the fort which caps the crag,
All undismantled of a turret-stone,

1687| MS:Of <> crying §last syllable crossed out and replaced above by one word§ of "Done
1871b:O' <> crying 'Done   1688| MS:With fighting,—down <> fortress?" Rather—
"Dare   *1871b*:With fight now <> fortress?' Rather—'Dare   1689| MS:On, forever,
§first syllable crossed out and replaced above by one word§ dare ever, thus invincible, §last
two words crossed out§ not <> displaced,   *1871b*:displaced!'   *1889a*:displace!'
1690| MS:§line added§ She cries, Thou cradle   *1871b*:Cries Wisdom, 'Cradle   *1889a*:wisdom:
'Cradle   1691| MS:Be §added in margin§ Thou §crossed out§ bulwark of our children's
§inserted below§ safety,—thanks to thee §punctuation and last three words crossed out§ still!
1871b:bulwark, give our children safety   1692| MS:of thy §crossed out and replaced
above by§ our children will §crossed out and replaced below by§ please, may   *1889a*:please
may   1694| MS:alarm, he hath thy mother-sides §last syllable crossed out§ ribs
1871b:alarm, they have thy   *1889a*:alarm they   1695| MS:run into §crossed out and
replaced above by§ upon   1696| MS:Scarcely the §crossed out and replaced above by§
what Terror on her pinnacle,   *1871b*:her vantage-coigne,   *1889a*:Scarcely that <> vantage-
coign,   1697| MS:supreme §inserted above§ o' the air, §word above illegibly crossed out§
1871b:of air,   1698| MS:Watches the country wide §last three words marked for
transposition to end of line§ —prepared to pounce—"   *1871b*:wide!'   1699| MS:So the
encouraged valley §last three words inserted above§ grows §crossed out and replaced above by
two words§ creeps apace the sparse tent pitching, §crossed out and replaced above by§ house
§crossed out§ and hidin §last six words crossed out§   *1871b*:Meanwhile the encouraged valley
holds its own,   1700-1| MS:§one line expanded to two lines§ the sparse §crossed out and
replaced above by§ first <> adventure in descent §last three words inserted above; solidus
added§ / half §altered to§ Half <> to brick and stone   *1871b*:descent, / <> to dome and spire
1702| MS:Into §crossed out and replaced above by§ Befitting   1703| MS:Meanwhile, the
famous old §crossed out§ fort still caps the crag   *1871b*:Nor means offence to the fort which
caps the crag,   1704| MS:a single §crossed out and replaced above by§ turret-

¹⁷⁰⁵ And bears the banner-pole that creaks at times
Embarrassed by the old emblazonment,
When festal days are to commemorate:
Otherwise left untenanted, no doubt,
Since, never fear, our myriads from below
¹⁷¹⁰ Would rush, if needs were, man the walls again,
Renew the exploits of the earlier time
At moment's notice! But till notice sound,
Inhabit we in ease and opulence!'
And so, till one day thus a notice sounds,
¹⁷¹⁵ Not trumpeted, but in a whisper-gust
Fitfully playing through mute city streets
At midnight weary of day's feast and game—
'Friends, your famed fort's a ruin past repair!
Its use is—to proclaim it had a use
¹⁷²⁰ Obsolete long since. Climb and study there
How to paint barbican and battlement
I' the scenes of our new theatre! We fight
Now—by forbidding neighbours to sell steel
Or buy wine, not by blowing out their brains!
¹⁷²⁵ Moreover, while we let time sap the strength
O' the walls omnipotent in menace once,
Neighbours would seem to have prepared surprise—
Run up defences in a mushroom-growth,

---

¹⁷⁰⁵| MS:Bears the main banner-pole a-blaze §crossed out and replaced above by two words§
that creaks   *1871b*:And bears the banner-pole   ¹⁷⁰⁶| MS:With the §last two words
crossed out and replaced above by three words§ Embarrassed by the old emblazonment—
1871b:emblazonment,   ¹⁷⁰⁷⁻⁸| MS:§lines added§ commemorate— / But otherwise
untenanted, no doubt.   *1871b*:commemorate. / Otherwise left untenanted, no doubt,
1889a:commemorate: ¹⁷⁰⁹| MS:Empty,—now soon §last three words crossed out and
replaced below by three words§ But, never fear,   *1871b*:Since, never   ¹⁷¹⁰| MS:walls
once more   *1871b*:more,   *1889a*:walls again,   ¹⁷¹¹| MS:§line added§ the glories of
1871b:the exploits of   ¹⁷¹²| MS:At a moment's   *1871b*:At moment's
¹⁷¹³| MS:opulence.   *1871b*:opulence!'   ¹⁷¹⁴| MS:so till   *1871b*:so, till
¹⁷¹⁶| MS:playing in the city §inserted above§   *1871b*:playing through mute city
¹⁷¹⁷| MS:of much §crossed out and replaced above by§ day's   ¹⁷¹⁸| MS:Friends, the
§crossed out and replaced above by§ your <> repair—   *1871b*:'Friends <> repair!
¹⁷²⁰| MS:Gone away long ago §crossed out and replaced above by§ since; go §crossed out and
replaced above by two words§ climb to study   *1871b*:Stolen away <> since. Climb
1889a:Obsolete long <> Climb and study   ¹⁷²²| MS:theatre; we   *1871b*:theatre! We
¹⁷²⁴| MS:brains: *1871b*:brains!   ¹⁷²⁷| MS:have §inserted above§
¹⁷²⁸| MS:mushroom-growth   *1871b*:mushroom-growth,

For all the world like what we boasted: brief—
1730   Hohenstiel-Schwangau's policy is peace!' "

Ay, so Sagacity advised him filch
Folly from fools: handsomely substitute
The dagger o' lath, while gay they sang and danced,
For that long dangerous sword they liked to feel,
1735   Even at feast-time, clink and make friends start.
No! he said "Hear the truth, and bear the truth,
And bring the truth to bear on all you are
And do, assured that only good comes thence
Whate'er the shape good take! While I have rule,
1740   Understand!—war for war's sake, war for sake
O' the good war gets you as war's sole excuse,
Is damnable and damned shall be. You want
Glory? Why so do I, and so does God.
Where is it found,—in this paraded shame,—
1745   One particle of glory? Once you warred
For liberty against the world, and won:
There was the glory. Now, you fain would war
Because the neighbour prospers overmuch,—
Because there has been silence half-an-hour,
1750   Like Heaven on earth, without a cannon-shot
Announcing Hohenstielers-Schwangauese
Are minded to disturb the jubilee,—
Because the loud tradition echoes faint,
And who knows but posterity may doubt

1730| MS:peace!" *1871b:*peace!' "   1732| MS:My people's §last two words crossed out§
folly §altered to§ Folly from them, §crossed out and replaced above by two words§ fools:
handsomely   1733| MS:lath, the §crossed out§ while they §crossed out and replaced
above by§ people §crossed out§ gay they §last two words inserted above§ drank §crossed out
and replaced above by§ sang *1871b:*danced *1889a:*danced,   1734| MS:feel *1871b:*feel,
1735| MS:clink for §crossed out and replaced above by two words§ and make friends to hear
§last two words crossed out§ start.   1736| MS:said,—Hear *1871b:*said "Hear
1739| MS:Whatever the shape it §crossed out and replaced above by§ good take. While I rule
here, *1871b:*Whate'er < > take! While I have rule,   1740| MS:Understand,—war for
< > for the sake *1871b:*Understand!—war *1889a:*sake, war for sake   1741| MS:as its
sole §last two words crossed out and replaced above by two words§ war's one excuse *1871b:*war's
sole excuse   1742| MS:damned §inserted above§ shall not §crossed out§ be
1747| MS:glory: now *1871b:*glory. Now   1749| MS:half-an-hour *1871b:*half-an-hour,
1750| MS:heaven's, on *1871b:*Like Heaven on   1752| MS:the public §crossed out§ jubilee,—
1753| MS:the old §crossed out and replaced above by§ loud < > faint— *1871b:*faint,

1755   If the great deeds were ever done at all,
Much less believe, were such to do again,
So the event would follow: therefore, prove
The old power, at the expense of somebody!
Oh Glory,—gilded bubble, bard and sage
1760   So nickname rightly,—would thy dance endure
One moment, would thy vaunting make believe
Only one eye thy ball was solid gold,
Hadst thou less breath to buoy thy vacancy
Than a whole multitude expends in praise,
1765   Less range for roaming than from head to head
Of a whole people? Flit, fall, fly again,
Only, fix never where the resolute hand
May prick thee, prove the glassy lie thou art!
Give me real intellect to reason with,
1770   No multitude, no entity that apes
One wise man, being but a million fools!
How and whence wishest glory, thou wise one?
Wouldst get it,—didst thyself guide Providence,—
By stinting of his due each neighbour round
1775   In strength and knowledge and dexterity
So as to have thy littleness grow large
By all those somethings once, turned nothings now,

---

¹⁷⁵⁵| MS:were really §crossed out and replaced above by§ ever <> all,—   *1871b*:all,
¹⁷⁵⁷| MS:follow—therefore   *1871b*:follow: therefore   ¹⁷⁵⁹| MS:Oh, Glory <> bubble,—
keep thy style,— §last three words crossed out and replaced above by three words§ said and
sung §crossed out§ bard   *1871b*:bubble, bard   *1889a*:Oh Glory   ¹⁷⁶⁰| MS:Have
§crossed out and replaced above by§ So nicknamed §altered to§ nickname
¹⁷⁶¹| MS:One moment, could §last three words inserted above§ Thy mocking make
1871b:moment, would thy   *1889a*:thy vaunting make   ¹⁷⁶²| MS:one §inserted above§
upturned foolish §crossed out§ eye <> was gold,   *1889a*:one eye <> was solid gold,
¹⁷⁶³| MS:Had'st   *1889a*:Hadst   ¹⁷⁶⁴| MS:expends at once,   *1871b*:expends in praise,
¹⁷⁶⁶| MS:people! fall, flit §last two words marked for transposition§   *1871b*:people? Flit
¹⁷⁶⁸| MS:May find §crossed out and replaced above by§ prick thee, and §crossed out and
replaced above by§ prove the lie <> art, at once!   *1889a*:the glassy lie thou art!
¹⁷⁶⁹| MS:me a man that §last three words crossed out and replaced above by two words§ real
intellect I may reason   *1871b*:intellect to reason   ¹⁷⁷⁰| MS:multitude, that §crossed out§
no   ¹⁷⁷²| MS:How gettest thou the §last three words crossed out and replaced above by
three words§ and whence wishest   ¹⁷⁷³| MS:Would'st <> did'st thyself play §crossed out
and replaced above by§ guide   *1889a*:Wouldst <> didst   ¹⁷⁷⁴| MS:of their §crossed out
and replaced above by§ his due all §crossed out and replaced above by§ each neighbours
§altered to§ neighbour   ¹⁷⁷⁶| MS:grown   *1871b*:grow   ¹⁷⁷⁷| MS:somethings, once
1871b:nothings, now,   *1889a*:somethings once <> nothings now,

As children make a molehill mountainous
By scooping out a trench around their pile,
1780 And saving so the mudwork from approach?
Quite otherwise the cheery game of life,
True yet mimetic warfare, whereby man
Does his best with his utmost, and so ends
A victor most of all in fair defeat.
1785 Who thinks,—would he have no one think beside?
Who knows, who does,—save his must learning die
And action cease? Why, so our giant proves
No better than a dwarf, once rivalry
Prostrate around him. Let the whole race stand
1790 For him to try conclusions fairly with!
Show me the great man would engage his peer
Rather by grinning 'Cheat, thy gold is brass!'
Than granting 'Perfect piece of purest ore!
Still, is it less good mintage, this of mine?'
1795 Well, and these right and sound results of soul
I' the strong and healthy one wise man,—shall such
Be vainly sought for, scornfully renounced
I' the multitude that make the entity—
The people?—to what purpose, if no less,

---

¹⁷⁷⁸| MS:As if one made a   *1871b:*As children make a   ¹⁷⁷⁹| MS:out the plain into a
trench   *1889a:*out a trench around their pile,   ¹⁷⁸⁰| MS:so one's favourite from offence
*1871b:*so their favourite from approach?   *1889a:*so the mudwork from   ¹⁷⁸²| MS:warfare
whereby   *1871b:*warfare, whereby   ¹⁷⁸⁴| MS:The victor   *1889a:*A victor
¹⁷⁸⁵| MS:Who Thinks   *1871b:*thinks   ¹⁷⁸⁶| MS:Who Knows, who Acts §crossed out and
replaced above by§ Does,—must all the learning die,   *1871b:*knows, who does,—must other
learning die   *1889a:*does,—save his must learning   ¹⁷⁸⁷| MS:The action perish? Why,
the §crossed out and replaced above by§ our giant stands §crossed out§ proves   *1871b:*And
action   *1889a:*action cease? Why, so our   ¹⁷⁸⁸| MS:dwarf, with all §crossed out§
*1889a:*dwarf, once rivalry   ¹⁷⁸⁹| MS:him: 'let   *1871b:*him. 'Let   *1889a:*him. Let
¹⁷⁹⁰| MS:And try <> fairly,' he cries first.   *1871b:*fairly!' he   *1889a:*For him to try <> fairly
with!   ¹⁷⁹¹| MS:the Poet §crossed out and replaced above by two words§ great man
would o'ertop §crossed out and replaced above by§ excel §crossed out§ engage §inserted
above§   ¹⁷⁹³| MS:Rather §crossed out§ than §altered to§ Than granting 'Never gold was
§last three words crossed out and replaced above by three words§ Perfect piece of purer
§altered to§ purest yet §crossed out and replaced above by§ ore!   ¹⁷⁹⁴| MS:it not less
§inserted above as alternate§ good   *1871b:*it less good   ¹⁷⁹⁶| MS:healthy single §crossed
out and replaced above by two words§ one wise <> shall these §crossed out and replaced
above by§ such   ¹⁷⁹⁷| MS:vainly §inserted above§ sought in vain §last two words crossed
out§   ¹⁷⁹⁹| MS:The §crossed out and replaced above by§ A people,—to <> purpose if
no more §crossed out and replaced above by§ less   *1871b:*people?—to <> purpose, if no less,

1800   In power and purity of soul, below
       The reach of the unit than, by multiplied
       Might of the body, vulgarized the more,
       Above, in thick and threefold brutishness?
       See! you accept such one wise man, myself:
1805   Wiser or less wise, still I operate
       From my own stock of wisdom, nor exact
       Of other sort of natures you admire,
       That whoso rhymes a sonnet pays a tax,
       Who paints a landscape dips brush at his cost,
1810   Who scores a septett true for strings and wind
       Mulcted must be—else how should I impose
       Properly, attitudinize aright,
       Did such conflicting claims as these divert
       Hohenstiel-Schwangau from observing me?
1815   Therefore, what I find facile, you be sure,
       With effort or without it, you shall dare—
       You, I aspire to make my better self
       And truly the Great Nation. No more war
       For war's sake, then! and,—seeing, wickedness
1820   Springs out of folly,—no more foolish dread
       O' the neighbour waxing too inordinate
       A rival, through his gain of wealth and ease!

1800| MS:Above, §added in margin; crossed out and replaced above by§ Below, I' §altered to§ i' the power <> soul,   *1871b:*In power <> soul, below   1801| MS:unit, than in multiplied   *1871b:*unit than, in   *1889a:*than, by multiplied   1803| MS:Above him; Do men band for §last four words crossed out and replaced above by three words§ thick and threefold   *1871b:*Above, in thick   1804| MS:Friends, you   *1871b:*See! you 1805| MS:still §inserted above§   1806| MS:Just from my stock of wisdom—nor *1871b:*From my own stock of wisdom, nor   1807| MS:O' the other <> of sages §crossed out and replaced above by§ natures you admire   *1871b:*Of other <> admire, 1808| MS:whoso pens §crossed out and replaced above by§ rhymes a poem §crossed out and replaced above by§ sonnet   1809| MS:Who tints a Venus does so §last two words crossed out and replaced above by two words§ dips brush   *1871b:*Who paints a landscape dips 1811| MS:how shall I   *1871b:*how should I   1813| MS:While these §crossed out and replaced above by five words§ such conflicting claims as these   *1871b:*Did such 1815| MS:what I do easily, §last two words crossed out and replaced above by three words§ find facile, you   1816| MS:§line added§   1818| MS:With §crossed out and replaced above by§ And <> Nation—no   *1871b:*the Great Nation. No   1819| MS:then,—and *1871b:*then! and   1821| MS:waxing so inordinate   *1871b:*waxing too inordinate 1822| MS:rival through his greater §crossed out and replaced above by two words§ gains of <> ease   *1871b:*rival, through his gain <> ease!

What?—keep me patient, Powers!—the people here,
Earth presses to her heart, nor owns a pride
1825 Above her pride i' the race all flame and air
And aspiration to the boundless Great,
The incommensurably Beautiful—
Whose very falterings groundward come of flight
Urged by a pinion all too passionate
1830 For heaven and what it holds of gloom and glow:
Bravest of thinkers, bravest of the brave
Doers, exalt in Science, rapturous
In Art, the—more than all—magnetic race
To fascinate their fellows, mould mankind
1835 Hohenstiel-Schwangau-fashion,—these, what?—these
Will have to abdicate their primacy
Should such a nation sell them steel untaxed,
And such another take itself, on hire
For the natural sen'night, somebody for lord
1840 Unpatronized by me whose back was turned?
Or such another yet would fain build bridge,
Lay rail, drive tunnel, busy its poor self
With its appropriate fancy: so there's—flash—
Hohenstiel-Schwangau up in arms at once!
1845 Genius has somewhat of the infantine:
But of the childish, not a touch nor taint

---

¹⁸²³| MS:That—keep <> People here   *1871b:*What?—keep <> people here,
¹⁸²⁴| MS:Than whom earth <> heart no pride   *1871b:*Earth <> heart, nor owns a pride
¹⁸²⁵| MS:the Race <> and air, §crossed out and replaced above by§ shine §crossed out; *air*
marked for retention§   *1871b:*race <> air   ¹⁸²⁶| MS:boundless §inserted above§ Great,
and Fair §last two words crossed out§   ¹⁸²⁸| MS:faulterings   *1889a:*falterings
¹⁸²⁹| MS:pinion §word inserted above and illegibly crossed out§   ¹⁸³⁰| MS:For Heaven
<> holds §word inserted above and illegibly crossed out§ <> glow!   *1871b:*heaven <> glow:
¹⁸³³| MS:the, more <> all, magnetic Race   *1871b:*the—more <> all—magnetic race
¹⁸³⁴| MS:fascinate thy fellows   *1871b:*fascinate their fellows   ¹⁸³⁵| MS:Hohenstiel-
Schwangau-fashion,—thou, yea—thou—   *1871b:*Hohenstiel-Schwangau-fashion,—these,
what?—these   ¹⁸³⁶| MS:abdicate thy primacy   *1871b:*abdicate their primacy
¹⁸³⁷| MS:sell thee steel   *1871b:*sell them steel   ¹⁸⁴⁰| MS:by thee whose back is turned—
*1871b:*by me whose back was turned?   ¹⁸⁴¹| MS:And such an other still §crossed out and
replaced above by§ yet   *1871b:*Or such   ¹⁸⁴²| MS:its small §crossed out and replaced
above by§ poor   ¹⁸⁴³| MS:fancy: but §crossed out and replaced above by§ so
¹⁸⁴⁵| MS:infantine,   *1871b:*onfantine: ¹⁸⁴⁶| MS:childish not a particle §crossed out
and replaced above by three words§ touch or taint   *1871b:*childish, not

Except through self-will, which, being foolishness,
Is certain, soon or late, of punishment.
Which Providence avert!—and that it may
¹⁸⁵⁰ Avert what both of us would so deserve,
No foolish dread o' the neighbour, I enjoin!
By consequence, no wicked war with him,
While I rule!

Does that mean—no war at all
When just the wickedness I here proscribe
¹⁸⁵⁵ Comes, haply, from the neighbour? Does my speech
Precede the praying that you beat the sword
To ploughshare, and the spear to pruning-hook,
And sit down henceforth under your own vine
And fig-tree through the sleepy summer month,
¹⁸⁶⁰ Letting what hurly-burly please explode
On the other side the mountain-frontier? No,
Beloved! I foresee and I announce
Necessity of warfare in one case,
For one cause: one way, I bid broach the blood

---

¹⁸⁴⁷| MS:Except by §crossed out and replaced above by§ through self-will which is foolishness
1871b:self-will, which, being foolishness,   ¹⁸⁴⁸| MS:And certain < > punishment—
1871b:Is certain < > punishment.   *1889a*:punishment §emended to§ punishment. §see
Editorial Notes§   ¹⁸⁴⁹| MS:may—   *1871b*:may   ¹⁸⁵⁰| MS:§line added§
¹⁸⁵¹| MS:neighbour, I assent §crossed out§ enjoin,   *1871b*:enjoin!   ¹⁸⁵²| MS:By
consequence, §last two words inserted above§ No   *1871b*:no   ¹⁸⁵³| MS:While I reign
§crossed out and replaced above by§ rule! §¶§ And §crossed out and replaced above by§ Does
< > means §altered to§ mean,—no   *1871b*:mean—no   ¹⁸⁵⁴| MS:Though §crossed out
and replaced above by§ When   ¹⁸⁵⁵| MS:Comes, this time, §last two words crossed out
and replaced above by one word§ haply < > neighbour's self? §inserted above§   All §crossed
out§ my §altered to§ My   *1871b*:neighbour? Does my   ¹⁸⁵⁶| MS:Preludes the < > that
§inserted above§ you to §crossed out§ beat   *1871b*:Precede the   ¹⁸⁵⁷| MS:ploughshare
and < > pruning-hook   *1871b*:plough-share, and < > pruning-hook,   *1889a*:ploughshare
¹⁸⁵⁸| MS:sitting §altered to§ sit down §inserted above§   ¹⁸⁵⁹| MS:fig-tree in §crossed out
and replaced above by§ through < > summer-time mood §last word and preceding syllable
crossed out and replaced above by syllable§ -month   *1871b*:summer month,
¹⁸⁶⁰| MS:hurly-burly will expend §second syllable crossed out and replaced above by syllable§
lode itself §crossed out§   *1871b*:hurly-burly please explode   ¹⁸⁶²⁻⁶³| MS:§one line
expanded to two lines§ Beloved,—I forsee and I §last three words inserted above§ announce
§solidus added§ necessity §altered to§ Necessity   *1871b*:Beloved! I forsee
¹⁸⁶⁴| MS:Of war—the §last three words crossed out and replaced above by three words§ For
one cause: < > I dare speak §last two words crossed out and replaced above by two words§ bid
broach the word §crossed out and replaced above by§ blood

¹⁸⁶⁵ O' the world. For truth and right, and only right
And truth,—right, truth, on the absolute scale of God,
No pettiness of man's admeasurement,—
In such case only, and for such one cause,
Fight your hearts out, whatever fate betide
¹⁸⁷⁰ Hands energetic to the uttermost!
Lie not! Endure no lie which needs your heart
And hand to push it out of mankind's path—
No lie that lets the natural forces work
Too long ere lay it plain and pulverized—
¹⁸⁷⁵ Seeing man's life lasts only twenty years!
And such a lie, before both man and God,
Proving, at this time present, Austria's rule
O'er Italy,—for Austria's sake the first,
Italy's next, and our sake last of all,
¹⁸⁸⁰ Come with me and deliver Italy!
Smite hip and thigh until the oppressor leave
Free from the Adriatic to the Alps
The oppressed one! We were they who laid her low
In the old bad day when Villany braved Truth
¹⁸⁸⁵ And Right, and laughed 'Henceforward, God deposed,
Satan we set to rule for evermore
I' the world!'—whereof to stop the consequence,
And for atonement of false glory there
Gaped at and gabbled over by the world,
¹⁸⁹⁰ I purpose to get God enthroned again
For what the world will gird at as sheer shame

---

^{1866|} MS:truth,—right, truth §dash and last two words inserted above§ ^{1867|} MS:No
petty §altered to§ pettiness piece §crossed out§ of Man's admeasurement, *1871b:*man's
admeasurement,— ^{1868|} MS:§line added§ In this case <> for this one cause *1871b:*In
such case <> for such one cause, ^{1869|} MS:whatever consequence §crossed out and
replaced above by two words§ end befall *1871b:*whatever fate betide ^{1870|} MS:Follow
§crossed out and replaced above by§ Hands ^{1871|} MS:endure <> needs man's heart
*1871b:*not! Endure <> needs your heart ^{1873|} MS:Such lie as lets *1871b:*No lie that
lets ^{1875|} MS:§line added§ years. *1871b:*years! ^{1877|} MS:Being, at
*1889a:*Proving, at ^{1879|} MS:and your §altered to§ our ^{1880|} MS:deliver Italy,
*1871b:*deliver Italy! ^{1885|} MS:and said §crossed out and replaced above by§ laughed
"Henceforward *1871b:*laughed 'Henceforward ^{1886|} MS:The Devil is to *1889a:*Satan
we set to ^{1887|} MS:world!"—whereof you §crossed out and replaced above by§ we see
the *1871b:*world!'—whereof to stop the ^{1888|} MS:And, for <> of the glory *1871b:*And
for <> of false glory ^{1890|} MS:Now purpose *1871b:*We purpose *1889a:*I purpose
^{1891|} MS:will grin §*gird* inserted above as alternate§ at as §inserted above§ *1871b:*will gird at

I' the cost of blood and treasure. 'All for nought—
Not even, say, some patch of province, splice
O' the frontier?—some snug honorarium-fee
1895   Shut into glove and pocketed apace?'
(Questions Sagacity) 'in deference
To the natural susceptibility
Of folks at home, unwitting of that pitch
You soar to, and misdoubting if Truth, Right
1900   And the other such augustnesses repay
Expenditure in coin o' the realm,—but prompt
To recognize the cession of Savoy
And Nice as marketable value!' No,
Sagacity, go preach to Metternich,
1905   And, sermon ended, stay where he resides!
Hohenstiel-Schwangau, you and I must march
The other road! war for the hate of war,
Not love, this once!" So Italy was free.

What else noteworthy and commendable
1910   I' the man's career?—that he was resolute
No trepidation, much less treachery
On his part, should imperil from its poise
The ball o' the world, heaved up at such expense
Of pains so far, and ready to rebound,

1892| MS:treasure, all   *1871b:*treasure. 'All   1893| MS:"Not   *1871b:*Not
1894| MS:the weak §inserted above§ frontier §crossed out§ the §inserted above and crossed out§ boundary §crossed out§ snug §inserted above§   *1871b:*the frontier?—some snug
1895| MS:into hand §crossed out and replaced above by§ glove <> apace"   *1871b:*apace?'
1896| MS:(Suggests Sagacity) "in   *1871b:*(Questions Sagacity) 'in   1898| MS:of those heig §last two words crossed out and replaced above by two words§ that pitch
1900| MS:the rest of the §last three words crossed out and replaced above by three words§ other such augustnesses   1903| MS:value!" No,   *1871b:*value!' No,
1904| MS:to Metternich   *1871b:*to Metternich,   1905| MS:And sermon ended §last two words inserted above§ stay <> resides; when sermon's done §crossed out§ o'er §last three words crossed out§   *1871b:*And, sermon ended, stay <> resides!   1906| MS:Hohenstiel-Schwangau come along with me §last four words crossed out and replaced above by five words§ you and I will §crossed out and replaced above by§ must march   *1871b:*Hohenstiel-Schwangau, you   1907-9| MS:I' the <> road!' §¶ called for in margin§ And §crossed out and replaced above by§ So <> free. / What   *1871b:*The <> road! war for the hate of war, / Not love, this once!" So <> free. §¶§ What   1910| MS:career?—That   *1871b:*that   1911| MS:Not §altered to§ No   1913| MS:ball o' the §last three words inserted above§   1914| MS:Of labour, and §last two words crossed out and replaced above by one word§ toil §crossed out and replaced by§ pains <> and §inserted above§

1915 Let but a finger maladroitly fall,
Under pretence of making fast and sure
The inch gained by late volubility,
And run itself back to the ancient rest
At foot o' the mountain. Thus he ruled, gave proof
1920 The world had gained a point, progressive so,
By choice, this time, as will and power concurred,
O' the fittest man to rule; not chance of birth,
Or such-like dice-throw. Oft Sagacity
Was at his ear: "Confirm this clear advance,
1925 Support this wise procedure! You, elect
O' the people, mean to justify their choice
And out-king all the kingly imbeciles;
But that's just half the enterprise: remains
You find them a successor like yourself,
1930 In head and heart and eye and hand and aim,
Or all done 's undone; and whom hope to mould
So like you as the pupil Nature sends,
The son and heir's completeness which you lack?
Lack it no longer! Wed the pick o' the world,
1935 Where'er you think you find it. Should she be
A queen,—tell Hohenstielers-Schwangauese
'So do the old enthroned decrepitudes
Acknowledge, in the rotten hearts of them,
Their knell is knolled, they hasten to make peace
1940 With the new order, recognize in me
Your right to constitute what king you will,
Cringe therefore crown in hand and bride on arm,
To both of us: we triumph, I suppose!'

1916-17| MS:§lines added§ inch of gain o' the volubility,   *1871b:*inch gained by late volubility,
1918| MS:And find §crossed out and replaced above by§ run   1919| MS:mountain.
There he reigned §crossed out and replaced above by§ ruled   *1871b:*mountain. Thus he
1920| MS:had made §crossed out and replaced above by§ gained advance so far, by choice
§last five words crossed out and replaced above by four words§ a point, progressive so,
1921| MS:§line added§ By choice §added in margin§ So far, §last two words crossed out§
1922| MS:birth   *1871b:*birth,   1923| MS:suchlike dice-throw. Soon §crossed out and
replaced above by§ Oft   *1871b:*such-like   1927| MS:imbeciles: *1871b:*imbeciles;
1928| MS:But §added in margin§ That's §altered to§ that's   1930| MS:§line added§
1931| MS:undone: and   *1871b:*undone; and   1934| MS:world—   *1871b:*world,
1935| MS:§line added§ it: shall she   *1871b:*it. Should she   1936| MS:A Queen? Tell
*1871b:*queen,—tell   1938| MS:Acknowledge in < > them   *1871b:*Acknowledge, in < >
them,   1941| MS:what King   *1871b:*king   1942| MS:And so cringe, crown
*1871b:*Cringe therefore crown   1943| MS:us—we   *1871b:*us: we

Is it the other sort of rank?—bright eye,
1945 Soft smile, and so forth, all her queenly boast?
Undaunted the exordium— 'I, the man
O' the people, with the people mate myself:
So stand, so fall. Kings, keep your crowns and brides!
Our progeny (if Providence agree)
1950 Shall live to tread the baubles underfoot
And bid the scarecrows consort with their kin.
For son, as for his sire, be the free wife
In the free state!' "

That is, Sagacity
Would prop up one more lie, the most of all
1955 Pernicious fancy that the son and heir
Receives the genius from the sire, himself
Transmits as surely,—ask experience else!
Which answers,—never was so plain a truth
As that God drops his seed of heavenly flame
1960 Just where He wills on earth: sometimes where man
Seems to tempt—such the accumulated store
Of faculties—one spark to fire the heap;
Sometimes where, fire-ball-like, it falls upon
The naked unpreparedness of rock,
1965 Burns, beaconing the nations through their night.

1944| MS:of Queen §crossed out and replaced above by§ rank,—bright   *1871b*:rank?—bright
1945| MS:her Queenly   *1871b*:queenly   1946| MS:exordium "I   *1871b*:exordium—'I
1947| MS:myself—   *1871b*:myself: 1948| MS:fall—Kings   *1871b*:fall. Kings
1949| MS:progeny—if Providence so please—   *1871b*:progeny (if Providence agree)
1951| MS:the bugbears consort <> kin—   *1871b*:the scarecrows consort <> kin.
1952| MS:For him §crossed out and replaced above by§ son <> sire,—be   *1871b*:sire, be
1953| MS:state!" That is, they counseled him   *1871b*:state!' §¶§ That is, Sagacity   §emended
to§ state!' " §¶§ That §see Editorial Notes§   1954| MS:To prop <> lie, that most
1871b:Would prop <> lie, the most   1955| MS:Pernicious folly of the   *1871b*:Pernicious
fancy that the   1956| MS:That gets that §last three words crossed out and replaced above
by one word§ Receiving genius   *1871b*:Receives the genius   1958| MS:Who answers
never   *1871b*:Which answers,—never   1959| MS:drops that seed   *1871b*:drops his seed
1960| MS:earth; sometimes   *1871b*:earth: sometimes   1961| MS:Seems ready with §last
two words crossed out and replaced above by four words§ to tempt—such the <> store
§crossed out and then marked for retention§   1962| MS:faculties—that spark would fire
the heap—   *1871b*:faculties—one spark to fire the heap;   1963| MS:where, fireball-like,
§last three words inserted above§ it lights §crossed out and replaced below by§ burns upon
1871b:fire-ball-like, it falls upon   1965| MS:A beacon to the   *1871b*:Burns, beaconing the

Faculties, fuel for the flame? All helps
Come, ought to come, or come not, crossed by chance,
From culture and transmission. What's your want
I' the son and heir? Sympathy, aptitude,
1970 Teachableness, the fuel for the flame?
You'll have them for your pains: but the flame's self,
The novel thought of God shall light the world?
No, poet, though your offspring rhyme and chime
I' the cradle,—painter, no, for all your pet
1975 Draws his first eye, beats Salvatore's boy,—
And thrice no, statesman, should your progeny
Tie bib and tucker with no tape but red,
And make a foolscap-kite of protocols!
Critic and copyist and bureaucrat
1980 To heart's content! The seed o' the apple-tree
Brings forth another tree which hears a crab:
'Tis the great gardener grafts the excellence
On wildings where he will.

         "How plain I view,
Across those misty years 'twixt me and Rome"—
1985 (Such the man's answer to Sagacity)
"The little wayside temple, half-way down
To a mild river that makes oxen white
Miraculously, un-mouse-colours skin,

---

^{1966|} MS:flame? All that   *1871b:*flame? All helps   ^{1967|} MS:Comes <> or comes not, by all §last two words crossed out and replaced above by two words§ crossed by chance *1871b:*Come <> or come not <> chance,   ^{1968|} MS:From §added in margin§ By §crossed out§ <> transmission: what's   *1871b:*transmission. What's   ^{1969|} MS:heir to be? §last two words crossed out§ Sympathy   *1871b:*I'   ^{1972|} MS:The §crossed out and replaced above by§ Next <> God that §crossed out and replaced above by§ shall lights §altered to§ light the world   *1871b:*The <> world?   ^{1974|} MS:cradle,—Painter *1871b:*painter   ^{1975|} MS:eye, as did §last two words crossed out and replaced above by one word§ beats <> boy,   *1871b:*boy,—   ^{1976|} MS:no, Statesman   *1871b:*statesman   ^{1978|} MS:foolscap-kite §hyphen and last syllable inserted above§ of some §crossed out§ protocols!   ^{1981|} MS:another—tree §inserted above dash§ but the fruit's §last two words crossed out and replaced above by one word§ bears a crab—   *1871b:*another tree which bears a crab: ^{1982|} MS:great Gardener   *1871b:*gardener   ^{1983|} MS:where He will. How <> I see—   *1871b:*he will. §¶§ "How <> I view,   ^{1984-86|} MS:§line 1984 added between 1983 and 1986§ and Rome— / The <> temple half way   *1871b:*and Rome"— / (Such the man's answer to Sagacity) / "The <> temple, half   *1889a:*half-way   ^{1987|} MS:To that mild   *1871b:*To a mild   ^{1988|} MS:§line added§ Miraculously, nor mouse-coloured more,   *1871b:*Miraculously, un-mouse-colours hide,   *1889a:*un-mouse-colours skin,

Or so the Roman country people dream!
1990 I view that sweet small shrub-embedded shrine
On the declivity, was sacred once
To a transmuting Genius of the land,
Could touch and turn its dunnest natures bright,
—Since Italy means the Land of the Ox, we know.
1995 Well, how was it the due succession fell
From priest to priest who ministered i' the cool
Calm fane o' the Clitumnian god? The sire
Brought forth a son and sacerdotal sprout,
Endowed instinctively with good and grace
2000 To suit the gliding gentleness below—
Did he? Tradition tells another tale.
Each priest obtained his predecessor's staff,
Robe, fillet and insignia, blamelessly,
By springing out of ambush, soon or late,
2005 And slaying him: the initiative rite
Simply was murder, save that murder took,
I' the case, another and religious name.
So it was once, is now, shall ever be
With genius and its priesthood in this world:
2010 The new power slays the old—but handsomely.
There he lies, not diminished by an inch
Of stature that he graced the altar with,

[1989] MS:Still so <> people say, §crossed out and replaced above by§ dream— §*say* also replaced below by§ boast— *1871b*:Or so <> dream! [1989-90] MS:§cancelled line in margin§ 'Italy' means the Land o' the Ox, they say. §last two words crossed out and replaced above by two words§ 'tis said [1990] MS:And that sweet §*one* inserted above as alternate§ small shrub-embedded §last two words inserted above§ shrine on the declivity §last three words crossed out§ *1871b*:I view that [1991] MS:declivity was *1871b*:declivity, was [1992] MS:To the transmuting <> land *1871b*:To a transmuting <> land, [1993] MS:§line added§ touch and §inserted above§ <> natures into §crossed out§ bright, [1994] MS:know *1871b*:know. [1995] MS:how did §crossed out§ was [1996] MS:Of §crossed out and replaced above by§ From [2000] MS:That §crossed out and replaced above by§ To [2001] MS:he? The learned tell us otherwise §last two words crossed out§ another tale: *1871b*:he? Tradition tells <> tale. [2002] MS:predecessor's post §crossed out§ staff, [2003] MS:fillet, and insignia, priesthood bore, §last two words crossed out and replaced above by one word§ blamelessly, *1871b*:fillet and [2005] MS:him,—the §inserted above§ initiating rule §last two words altered to§ initiative rite *1871b*:him: the [2006] MS:Simply by §crossed out and replaced above by§ was murder,—only, §crossed out and replaced above by two words§ save that *1871b*:murder, save [2009] MS:With Genius *1871b*:genius [2010] MS:new man §crossed out and replaced above by§ power <> old one §crossed out and replaced above by§ —but handsomely— *1871b*:handsomely. [2012] MS:O' the stature *1871b*:Of stature

Though somebody of other bulk and build
Cries 'What a goodly personage lies here
2015 Reddening the water where the bulrush roots!
May I conduct the service in his place,
Decently and in order, as did he,
And, as he did not, keep a wary watch
When meditating 'neath yon willow shade!'
2020 Find out your best man, sure the son of him
Will prove best man again, and, better still
Somehow than best, the grandson-prodigy!
You think the world would last another day
Did we so make us masters of the trick
2025 Whereby the works go, we could pre-arrange
Their play and reach perfection when we please?
Depend on it, the change and the surprise
Are part o' the plan: 'tis we wish steadiness;
Nature prefers a motion by unrest,
2030 Advancement through this force which jostles that.
And so, since much remains i' the world to see,
Here's the world still, affording God the sight."
Thus did the man refute Sagacity
Ever at this old whisper in his ear:

2013| MS:Only a personage §last three words crossed out and replaced above by two words§
Though somebody   2014-15| MS:§lines added§ Cries "What   1871b:Cries 'What
2016| MS:And build §crossed out and replaced below by§ May I conducts §altered to§ conduct
2017-18| MS:§lines added between 2016 and 2023§   2019-22| MS:§lines added vertically in
margin§ 'neath a willow tree §crossed out and replaced below by§ shade!"   1871b:shade!'
1889a:'neath yon willow   2023| MS:Do §crossed out§ you §altered to§ You
2024| MS:Had men §last two words crossed out and replaced above by two words§ Could
§crossed out; *Had* marked for retention§ we so make them §crossed out§ us §last three words
inserted above§ mastered §altered to§ masters   1871b:Did we   2025| MS:go, they could
1871b:go, we could   2026| MS:Its play and have §crossed out and replaced above by§
reach <> when they please.   1871b:Their play <> when we please?   2028| MS:of
§crossed out and replaced above by§ o' the plan—'tis we cry §crossed out and replaced above
by illegible word, replaced above by§ wish steadiness—   1871b:plan: 'tis <> steadiness;
2029| MS:Nature means §crossed out and replaced above by two words§ perfers a
2030| MS:Advancement by §crossed out and replaced above by§ through <> force that jostles
that;   1871b:jostles that.   1889a:force which jostles   2031| MS:And thus it is that,— §last
four words crossed out and replaced above by two words§ so, since much remaining §altered
to§ remains still §crossed out and replaced above by three words§ i' the world
2032| MS:To see i' the world,— §last five words crossed out and replaced above
by four words§ Here is it still affording <> sight.   1871b:still, affording <> sight."
1889a:Here's the world still   2033-34| MS:§lines added; ¶ called for in margin§ So did <>
Sagacity, / Perpetually at whisper <> ear   1871b:§¶ lost in paging§ Thus did <> / Ever at
this one whisper <> ear: 1889a:refute Sagacity / <> this old whisper

2035 "Here are you picked out, by a miracle,
And placed conspicuously enough, folks say
And you believe, by Providence outright
Taking a new way—nor without success—
To put the world upon its mettle: good!
2040 But Fortune alternates with Providence;
Resource is soon exhausted. Never count
On such a happy hit occurring twice!
Try the old method next time!"

"Old enough,"
(At whisper in his ear, the laugh outbroke)
2045 "And mode the most discredited of all,
By just the men and women who make boast
They are kings and queens thereby! Mere self-defence
Should teach them, on one chapter of the law
Must be no sort of trifling—chastity:
2050 They stand or fall, as their progenitors
Were chaste or unchaste. Now, run eye around
My crowned acquaintance, give each life its look
And no more,—why, you'd think each life was led
Purposely for example of what pains
2055 Who leads it took to cure the prejudice,
And prove there's nothing so unproveable
As who is who, what son of what a sire,
And,—inferentially,—how faint the chance
That the next generation needs to fear
2060 Another fool o' the selfsame type as he

2035| MS:"Here am I §last two words crossed out and replaced below by two words§ are you
<> by §crossed out and then marked for retention§   2037| MS:And he §crossed out and
replaced above by§ you believed §altered to§ believe   2038| MS:way—not without
*1871b:*way—nor without   2039| MS:To make §crossed out and replaced above by§ put
2040| MS:What §crossed out and replaced above by§ But <> Providence—   *1871b:*with
Providence;   2041| MS:exhausted! Never   *1871b:*exhausted. Never
?042| MS:twice: *1871b:*twice!   2043-45| MS:§¶§ Old indeed, / And most discredited of
all the modes   *1871b:*§¶§ "Old enough," / (To whisper in his ear, the laugh outbroke) / "And
1889a:<> / (At whisper <> / "And mode the most discredited of all,   2046| MS:just
§inserted above§   2048| MS:them, §inserted above§   2052| MS:life a look
*1871b:*life its look   2055| MS:The liver §last two words crossed out and replaced above by
three words§ Who lead it <> prejudice   *1871b:*leads <> prejudice,   2058| MS:how
small §crossed out and replaced above by§ faint   2059| MS:the succeedin §crossed out and
replaced above by two words§ next generation has §crossed out and replaced above by§ needs

Happily regnant now by right divine
And luck o' the pillow! No: select your lord
By the direct employment of your brains
As best you may,—bad as the blunder prove,
2065 A far worse evil stank beneath the sun
When some legitimate blockhead managed so
Matters that high time was to interfere,
Though interference came from hell itself
And not the blind mad miserable mob
2070 Happily ruled so long by pillow-luck
And divine right,—by lies in short, not truth.
And meanwhile use the allotted minute . . ."

———————

One,—
Two, three, four, five—yes, five the *pendule* warns!
Eh? Why, this wild work wanders past all bound
2075 And bearing! Exile, Leicester-square, the life
I' the old gay miserable time, rehearsed,
Tried on again like cast clothes, still to serve
At a pinch, perhaps? "Who's who?" was aptly asked,
Since certainly I am not I! since when?
2080 Where is the bud-mouthed arbitress? A nod
Out-Homering Homer! Stay—there flits the clue
I fain would find the end of! Yes,—"Meanwhile,
Use the allotted minute!" Well, you see,

2062| MS:pillow! No,—select *1871b*:pillow! No: select   2065| MS:evil was §crossed
out and replaced above by§ stank   2066| MS:When your §crossed out and replaced above
by§ some   2067| MS:interfere *1871b*:interfere,   2068| MS:Had §crossed out and
replaced above by§ Though <> come <> Hell *1871b*:came <> hell   2069| MS:blind,
mad, miserable *1871b*:blind mad miserable   2071| MS:right, and §crossed out and
replaced above by§ —by   2072-74| MS:minute . . §¶§ Ah,— / Eh?—Why <> wild work
§last two words inserted above§ wandering §altered to§ wanders is §crossed out§
1871b:minute . . . §¶§ §rule§ One,— / Two, three, four, five—yes, five the pendule warns! /
Eh? Why   *1889a*:minute . . . §¶§ §emended to§ minute . . ." §¶§ §see Editorial Notes§ <> /
<> *pendule*   2075-78| MS:bearing! 'Who is who' one well may ask— *1871b*:bearing!
Exile, Leicester-square, the life / I' the old gay miserable time, rehearsed, / Tried on again
like cast clothes, still to serve / At a pinch, perhaps? "Who's who?" was aptly asked,
2079| MS:not I! this while: §last two words crossed out and replaced above by two words§ since
when?   2080| MS:bud-mouthed §inserted above§   2081| MS:there floats §crossed
out and replaced above by illegible word, crossed out in turn and replaced above by§ flits

(Veracious and imaginary Thiers,
2085 Who map out thus the life I might have led,
But did not,—all the worse for earth and me—
Doff spectacles, wipe pen, shut book, decamp!)
You see 'tis easy in heroics! Plain
Pedestrian speech shall help me perorate.
2090 Ah, if one had no need to use the tongue!
How obvious and how easy 'tis to talk
Inside the soul, a ghostly dialogue—
Instincts with guesses,—instinct, guess, again
With dubious knowledge, half-experience: each
2095 And all the interlocutors alike
Subordinating,—as decorum bids,
Oh, never fear! but still decisively,—
Claims from without that take too high a tone,
—("God wills this, man wants that, the dignity
2100 Prescribed a prince would wish the other thing")—
Putting them back to insignificance
Beside one intimatest fact—myself
Am first to be considered, since I live
Twenty years longer and then end, perhaps!
2105 But, where one ceases to soliloquize,
Somehow the motives, that did well enough
I' the darkness, when you bring them into light

2084-87| MS:§lines added between 2083 and 2088 and in margin§   2088| MS:It comes so
easy   *1871b:*You see 'tis easy   2091| MS:easy when 'tis §last two words crossed out and
replaced above by two words§ 'tis to   2092| MS:soul, mere §crossed out and replaced
above by§ make ghostly   *1871b:*soul, a ghostly   2093| MS:guesses, both of them §last
three words crossed out and replaced above by two words§ instinct, guess, again
*1871b:*guesses,—instinct   2094| MS:half-experience, all §crossed out§ each   *1871b:*half-
experience: each   2095| MS:§line added§   2097| MS:§line added§ Oh §word
illegibly crossed out and replaced above by§ never   *1871b:*Oh, never   2099| MS:("God
<> that, my §crossed out and replaced above by§ the   *1871b:*—("God
2100| MS:As the world understands §last four words crossed out and replaced above by five
words§ Prescribed myself §crossed out and replaced above by two words§ a prince would wish
the <> thing)"   *1871b:*thing")—   2102| MS:Beside that §crossed out and replaced
above by§ this intimatest   *1871b:*Beside one intimatest   2103| MS:considered, with my
life §last three words crossed out and replaced above by three words§ since I live
2104| MS:then an §crossed out§ end   2105| MS:But when one <> soliloquize
*1871b:*But, where one <> soliloquize,   2106| MS:motives that   *1871b:*motives, that
2107| MS:darkness, brought up to the light of day §last seven words crossed out and replaced
above by six words§ when you bring them into light,   *1871b:*light

208

Are found, like those famed cave-fish, to lack eye
And organ for the upper magnitudes.
2110　The other common creatures, of less fine
Existence, that acknowledge earth and heaven,
Have it their own way in the argument.
Yes, forced to speak, one stoops to say—one's aim
Was—what it peradventure should have been:
2115　To renovate a people, mend or end
That bane come of a blessing meant the world—
Inordinate culture of the sense made quick
By soul,—the lust o' the flesh, lust of the eye,
And pride of life,—and, consequent on these,
2120　The worship of that prince o' the power o' the air
Who paints the cloud and fills the emptiness
And bids his votaries, famishing for truth,
Feed on a lie.

　　　　　Alack, one lies oneself
Even in the stating that one's end was truth,
2125　Truth only, if one states as much in words!
Give me the inner chamber of the soul
For obvious easy argument! 'tis there
One pits the silent truth against a lie—
Truth which breaks shell a careless simple bird,
2130　Nor wants a gorget nor a beak filed fine,
Steel spurs, and the whole armoury o' the tongue,

2108|　MS:famed §inserted above§ <> to want §crossed out and replaced above by§ lack an
§crossed out§ eye §altered to§ eyes §restored to§ eye　　　　2109|　MS:And organ §last two
words inserted above§ For §altered to§ for <> magnitudes: and in §last two words crossed
out§　*1871b*:magnitudes.　　　　2110-11|　MS:§one line expanded to two lines§ The others,
§altered to§ other, §next five words inserted above to complete 2110§ common creatures, of
less fine / Existence §inserted below to begin 2111§ that　　　　2113|　MS:Yes, in loud speech,
one has §crossed out and replaced above by§ stoops to say—my aim　*1871b*:Yes, forced to
speak, one <> say—one's aim　　　　2114|　MS:Was,—what <> been;—　*1871b*:Was—what
1889a:been:　　　　2115|　MS:renovate my people　*1871b*:renovate a people
2116|　MS:of the §crossed out and replaced above by§ a <> meant to be—　*1871b*:meant the
world—　　　　2117|　MS:made fine §crossed out and replaced above by§ quick
2122|　MS:votary §altered to§ votaries　　　　2123|　MS:lie. §¶§ Ay, so §last two words crossed out
and replaced above by one word§ Alack, one　　　　2124|　MS:truth　*1871b*:truth,
2125|　MS:Triumphant, what §crossed out and replaced above by§ if　*1871b*:Truth only, if
2126|　MS:inner-chamber　*1871b*:inner chamber　　　　2127|　MS:argument: 'tis
1871b:argument! 'tis　　　　2131|　MS:Steel-spurs and　*1871b*:Steel spurs　*1889a*:spurs, and

To equalize the odds. But, do your best,
Words have to come: and somehow words deflect
As the best cannon ever rifled will.

2135   "Deflect" indeed! nor merely words from thoughts
But names from facts: "Clitumnus" did I say?
As if it had been his ox-whitening wave
Whereby folk practised that grim cult of old—
The murder of their temple's priest by who
2140   Would qualify for his succession. Sure—
Nemi was the true lake's style. Dream had need
Of the ox-whitening piece of prettiness
And so confused names, well known once awake.

So, i' the Residenz yet, not Leicester-square,
2145   Alone,—no such congenial intercourse!—
My reverie concludes, as dreaming should,
With daybreak: nothing done and over yet,
Except cigars! The adventure thus may be,
Or never needs to be at all: who knows?
2150   My Cousin-Duke, perhaps, at whose hard head
—Is it, now—is this letter to be launched,

2132| MS:the game. §crossed out and replaced above by§ odds. But do   *1871b:*odds. But,
do   2133| MS:somehow §inserted above§ words must needs §last two words crossed out§
deflect   2134-44| MS:cannon e'er was §last two words crossed out and replaced above by
one word§ ever rifled does §crossed out§ will. / §¶ called for in margin§ So < > Residenz still
§crossed out and replaced above by§ yet §2135-43 not in MS§   *1871b:*will. / §¶§ So
1889a:§2135-43 added§ §¶ lost in paging. Emended to restore ¶; see Editorial Notes§
2145| MS:§line added vertically in margin§ nor §altered to§ no with §crossed out and replaced
above by§ such congenial company,— §crossed out and replaced above by§ intercourse
*1871b:*intercourse!—   2146| MS:Concludes my reverie §marked for transposition to§
My reverie concludes, as such §crossed out§ dreams §altered to§ dreaming should,
§crossed out and replaced above by§ must, §crossed out; *should,* marked for retention§
2147-48| MS:§one line expanded to two lines§ With daybreak: §next five words inserted above
to complete 2147§ nothing done and over yet, / Yes §crossed out and replaced below by two
words to begin 2148§ Except cigars. the §altered to§ The < > thus might be   *1871b:*cigars!
The < > thus may be,   2149| MS:at all §last two words crossed out and then marked for
retention§   2150| MS:My §over *The*§   2151| MS:it §inserted above§ now—is
§inserted above§ < > letter really §crossed out§ to be launched   *1871b:*it, now < > launched,

The sight of whose grey oblong, whose grim seal,
Set all these fancies floating for an hour?

Twenty years are good gain, come what come will!
2155 Double or quits! The letter goes! Or stays?

---

²¹⁵²| MS:whose white §crossed out and replaced above by§ grey oblong, and red §crossed out and replaced above by§ grim *1871b:*oblong, whose grim ²¹⁵³| MS:Set all these §last two words crossed out and replaced above by§ many fancies *1871b:*Set all these fancies ²¹⁵³⁻⁵⁴| MS:§no ¶ called for§ *1871b:*§¶§ ²¹⁵⁴| MS:Well, §crossed out and replaced above by§ The §crossed out§ twenty §altered to§ Twenty < > good §inserted above§ ²¹⁵⁵| MS:§following last line of poem§ L. D. I. E.

EDITORIAL NOTES

BALAUSTION'S ADVENTURE

Emendations to the Text

The following emendations have been made to the 1889a copy-text:

l. 541: In all copies of 1889a collated, there is no punctuation at the end of this line, which concludes the sentence beginning at line 535; the period found in MS-1881 is restored.

l. 647: In all copies of 1889a collated, the final *e* is missing from the word *become.* The MS-1881 reading is restored.

l. 852: MS-1881 read *Lybian flute;* 1889a has *Lydian.* Though the ancient Greeks traced some of their musical modes to the country of Lydia in Asia Minor, Euripides calls the flute that Admetus will forgo *Libyan* (*Alcestis,* 346). On the assumption that B meant to follow his source, the MS-1881 reading is restored—though *Libyan* would have been the correct transliteration.

l. 1417: In all copies of 1889a collated, the punctuation at the end of this line has decayed; the MS-1881 reading is restored.

l. 1293: In 1889a, the initial letter of the word *the* is missing, though space for it remains. The MS-1881 reading is restored (interestingly, this error was corrected in the second impression [1889]).

l. 2299: At the beginning of this line in all copies of 1889a collated, one of the required two quotation marks is missing, though space for it remains. The MS-1881 reading is restored.

l. 2499: The long speech of Alcestis to Admetus, which includes her quotation of Apollo, runs from line 2493 through 2548. B's punctuation is essentially correct in his MS, but in 1889a, attempting to remedy several later errors (see following emendations), he mistakenly inserted closing quotation marks at the end of this line. Since Alcestis must continue speaking for another forty-three lines, the MS-1881 reading is restored, removing the quotation marks.

l. 2504: When revising for 1871a, B added a paragraph break after line 2503, which ends the plea to Apollo which Alcestis reports to Admetus. Double quotation marks should have preceded line 2504 to indicate that Alcestis continues speaking; without them it may seem that line 2504 and the first word of the next line are spoken by Balaustion. The MS is clear on this matter, but none of the following editions corrected the error that arose in 1871a; opening quotation marks have been inserted.
l. 2505: MS-1881 have the correct single quotation mark opening Alcestis' quotation of Apollo's response to her plea. But these same texts have an extra quotation mark at the beginning of the following line. B failed to cancel this second mark when he revised line 2505 in the MS. In 1889a he removed the excess punctuation, but simultaneously changed the blameless single quotation mark in line 2505 to an erroneous double one. The MS-1881 reading is restored.
l. 2543: Since this line ends Apollo's speech as quoted by Alcestis, a single quotation mark is required at the end of the line. MS-1881 have the correct punctuation, but 1889a, consonant with the error made back in line 2505, closes the speech with double quotation marks. The MS-1881 reading is restored.
l. 2596: In all copies of 1889a collated, only a fragment of a punctuation mark appears after the word *one*. Since all earlier texts have a colon preceding the word *hadst*, a colon is inserted here.

In addition, the compositors of 1888-89 frequently used B's paragraph breaks to divide one page from another. As a consequence, certain interruptions and shifts in the discourse disappeared in the copy-text. We have restored paragraph breaks lost in this way in *Balaustion's Adventure* at ll. 909-10, 1054-55, 1296-97, 2243-44, and 2259-60.

Composition

Balaustion's Adventure was entirely composed in London during May 1871, according to B's note at the end of his MS (see variant listings, l. 2705; the "1872" he wrote there was a slip of the pen, since the poem was published in August, 1871). B had shared with EBB a lifelong interest in Euripides, but the writing of *Balaustion's Adventure* was prompted by two specific events in the spring of 1871. As B acknowledges in his dedication, one of these was a request by Katrine Cecilia, Countess Cowper that he take up the Alcestis myth as a subject (see B's Dedication and n. below). What the Countess said to B and how she "imposed" the writing of *Balaustion's Adventure* on him appear to have gone unrecorded; perhaps DeVane is right in his conjecture that the poem had some connection with the approaching tenth anniversary of EBB's death (*Hbk.*, 350).

The second event was even more immediate: the completion and exhibition of a painting entitled "Hercules Wrestling with Death for the Body of Alcestis" by the Bs' friend Frederic Leighton. (The painting is now in the Wadsworth Athenaeum in Hartford, Connecticut.) This picture, which B describes in ll. 2672-97, was exhibited at the Royal Academy in May 1871, the very month when B wrote his poem. For over two years Leighton worked on the painting, and B's close friendship with him makes it very likely that B saw the work in progress more than once during that time (see Griffin and Minchin, 245-46). Twice before B had provided verses to accompany pictures by Leighton (DeVane, *Hbk*, 353; see this edition, 6.169 and n.), and *Balaustion's Adventure* might be thought of as another example on the grand scale. But it is worth noting that the one key element of the Alcestis story that neither Euripides nor Browning dramatizes is precisely the one that Leighton portrays: Heracles wrestling with Death. The possible interplay between B's work and Leighton's has been illuminated by C. Maxwell, who suggests C. W. Gluck's opera *Alceste* as a stimulus to both artists ("Robert Browning and Frederic Leighton: 'Che Farò Senza Euridice?'" *RES* 44 [1993], 362-72).

Despite the sunny atmosphere of *Balaustion's Adventure* and B's description of it as a "May-month amusement," the work involved sensitive issues in the poet's recent life. Readers have detected signs of anxiety in B's handling of the Alcestis myth, which perhaps inevitably evoked memories of EBB's death and even of B's involvement with Lady Ashburton in 1869. The poem's autobiographical associations are interestingly explored by Irvine and Honan (ch. 24, especially 457-60; see also B. Miller, *Robert Browning: a Portrait* [N. Y., 1953], 268-69).

Sources

The account of the Athenian campaign in Sicily found in Plutarch's life of Nicias serves as a backdrop to the opening of *Balaustion's Adventure*. Section 29 provided the germ for the experiences of the fictional Balaustion. The following passages from Plutarch are relevant:

> Most of the Athenian prisoners perished in the quarries
> from sickness and from their wretched diet, for they were

given no more than a pint of meal and a half pint of water a day. A number were stolen away and sold as slaves, or contrived to pass themselves off as servants and these men, when they were sold, were branded on the forehead with the figure of a horse. . . .

A few were rescued because of their knowledge of Euripides, for it seems that the Sicilians were more devoted to his poetry than any other Greeks living outside the mother country. Even the smallest fragments of his verses were learned from every stranger who set foot on the island . . . . At any rate there is a tradition that many of the Athenian soldiers who returned home safely visited Euripides to thank him for their deliverance which they owed to his poetry. Some of them told him that they had been given their freedom in return for teaching their masters all they could remember of his works, while others . . . had been given food and water for reciting some of his lyrics. We need not be surprised then at the story of the ship from Caunus, which found itself pursued by pirates and made for the harbour of Syracuse. At first the Syracusans refused to let her enter; then later they asked the crew whether they knew any of Euripides' songs, and on learning that they did, gave them leave to bring in their vessel.

(Plutarch, 240-41)

In constructing a frame-narrative, B also consulted Thucydides' *History of the Peloponnesian War* for information about the Peloponnesian war during which the action of *Balaustion's Adventure* occurs. The disastrous Athenian expedition against Syracuse in Sicily (415-13 B.C.), recounted at length in Book 7 of Thucydides and retold in Plutarch ("Nicias," 12-30), immediately precedes the action of the poem. For an overview of the Persian Wars, in which the Greeks had been more successful, B relied on the *Histories* of Herodotus, Bks. 7 and 8; but Plutarch's *Lives* also contains accounts of the battle of Salamis ("Themistocles," 9-16; "Aristedes," 8-9) referred to at the beginning of the poem. The story of Athenian prisoners gaining their freedom by reciting passages from Euripides appears only in Plutarch, though the suffering and eventual release of the prisoners is described in Thucydides (7.86-87). Plutarch's anecdote is alluded to as an example of the power of poetry in Byron's *Childe Harold's Pilgrimage* (4.16, 136-44), which B admired. As S. N. Deane noted ("Robert Browning and Alciphron," *Classical Journal* 9 [1914], 277-78), B also borrowed details at the beginning of *Balaustion's Adventure* from the letters of Alciphron, a Greek author of the late second century A.D., whose works the Bs owned (*Reconstruction*, A35) and to whom B alludes in *Pippa Passes* (1841) (1.2.93; this edition, 3.38). It is likely that he knew Pausanias, who described 2nd century Athens in the first 30 chapters of his *Description of Greece.*

The major literary source for the rest of *Balaustion's Adventure* is *Alcestis*, Euripides' earliest surviving play. From l. 358 through 2396, B's "transcript" of *Alcestis* stays close to the original, sometimes translating directly, sometimes summarizing, with occasional interpolations and commentaries by Balaustion and others. The Admetus myth, as distilled by the *Oxford Companion to Classical Literature* (ed. M. C. Howatson [Oxford, 1989], 6), is as follows:

> When Zeus killed Asclepius for restoring Hippolytus to life,
> Apollo, the father of Asclepius, furious at this treatment of
> his son, took vengeance on the Cyclopes who had forged Zeus's
> thunderbolt, and slew them. To expiate this crime Zeus made
> him for a year the servant of Admetus, who treated him kindly.
> Apollo in gratitude helped him to win Alcestis as his bride. At
> the bridal feast it was revealed that Admetus was fated to die
> imminently, but Apollo again intervened and by making the Fates
> drunk persuaded them to grant Admetus longer life, provided
> that at the appointed hour of his death he could persuade
> someone else to die for him. Admetus' father and mother having
> refused, his wife Alcestis consented, and accordingly died.
> Just after this, Heracles, on his way to one of his Labours,
> visited the palace of Admetus who, in obedience to the laws
> of hospitality, concealed his wife's death and welcomed the
> hero. Heracles presently discovered the truth, went out to
> intercept Death, set upon him, and took from him Alcestis,
> whom he then restored to her husband.

Exactly which edition of Euripides B worked from is not known, but among the several collections in his library were two authoritative modern editions of the Greek text: the Paley edition of 1857-60 and the Nauck edition of 1866, purchased in May of 1871, the month in which he conducted his "transcription" (*Reconstruction*, A886 and A890). However, he wrote *Balaustion's Adventure* in London, where he had access to a wealth of classical materials, and the text of *Alcestis* was so well-established that any sound edition could have served as B's source.

In the frame-narrative, B has his young Euripides-enthusiast Balaustion recall a performance of *Alcestis*, reporting the movements and behavior of the characters and occasionally commenting on the events and themes of the play. He endowed Balaustion with a perfect memory for dialogue, and except for her occasional summaries of longer choruses, she translates most of the 1163 lines of *Alcestis* into effective, concentrated English. What B meant to suggest by calling this portion of the poem a "transcript" remains moot. He usually follows his source as closely as any literal translation would, yet his speaker's elisions and intrusions produce effects beyond the Euripidean original.

Text and Publication

The Balliol Manuscript   The manuscript of *Balaustion's Adventure* preserved today in the Balliol College Library consists of 105 leaves of lined paper, including a title page, the dedication and epigraph, and 103 pages of verse. Though the binding of the MS has obscured the evidence, B apparently folded sheets of foolscap into folios, composing on the resulting rectos and leaving the versos for additions, revisions, and trial readings. Such a practice would explain the page-numbering system of the Balliol MS, in which alternating leaves (i.e., the first of each folio) bear numbers in B's hand. Inconsistencies in the numbering sequence suggest that B numbered each fresh folio as he began it. For example, though the verses are continuous except for additions and revisions, there is no leaf [8a]; following leaf 8 are two folios numbered 9. Similarly, though the text is uninterrupted, there is no leaf [46a]. B wrote twenty-two lines (1197-1218) on the verso of leaf 24, with instructions to insert them on the recto after line 1196 (see variant listings); this is the largest of many insertions and alterations in the MS.

The number of revisions and additions in the MS testifies that it is the compositional document, not a fair copy. Yet its overall legibility and the absence of sizable insertions or transpositions also confirm what the MS of *The Ring and the Book* suggested: by this time in his career, B wrote his verse swiftly and confidently. Differences in pen-point and ink color indicate at least two stages of composition, as does the substantial number of cases where entire lines have been inserted between pre-existing lines.

At the end of the MS appear the four letters that become a regular feature in the Balliol MSS: "L. D. I. E.," standing for *Laus Deo in excelsis*, "Praise God in the highest," the poet's expression of thanks that his labor is completed. He also added "Begun and ended in May, 1872," making a mistake in the year, which should have been "1871" since *Balaustion's Adventure* was published that August.

The Balliol MS is more sparsely punctuated than the published work. This is especially true regarding end-line punctuation and commas for appositive phrases; both were often added during the proofing of the 1871 first edition. The poem includes long passages of stychomythia as well as many instances in which one speaker quotes another, and B did not always keep meticulous track of his quotation marks. Lines 444-68, for example, require double quotation marks at the beginning and ending of each line to indicate the stychomythia between Herakles and Death. In the MS, B did not enter any of these marks, apparently adding them (along with many other missing quotation marks throughout the poem) in proof for the first edition. Some problems, such as those at ll. 240 and 242, were rectified in 1872, but others were not sorted out until 1889a, and at some places emendation is still required.

In revising, B added paragraph breaks at many places throughout the MS where the verses as composed ran continuously. With a horizontal line and/or a marginal note, B called for paragraphs at ll. 4, 289, 336, 443, 717, 1012, 1052, 1197, 1219, 1640, 1816, 2101, 2136, and 2335. All but one of these (at l. 443) appeared in the printed texts, and since they are thus not truly variants, we do not record them in the variant listings. That B was, as usual, attending to even the slightest details of printing is indicated by his instruction to his printers at ll. 2396-97. To separate two major sections of Balaustion's discourse, he drew a double rule at the bottom of the leaf numbered 46. At the upper left corner of the following leaf, he wrote the words "Half-page" next to a bracket before l. 2397. No edition was set up this way, though 1871a, 1872, and 1881 have double white line spaces above and below the rule.

Throughout the MS, B inserted new lines during revision. The lined paper he used resulted in ample, regular spacing in the first draft, with sufficient room between lines for additional lines to be squeezed in. In the variant listings such revisions are noted with the editorial comment §line added§.

The First Edition (1871a) *Balaustion's Adventure* was published on 8 August 1871, according to an announcement in the *Athenaeum* on 5 August. The poem had been advertised for several weeks before this, and although B tried to dampen the expectations of his friends, the volume was a surprising success. To Isa Blagden he wrote, "don't expect great things of what was only, what I call it, a May-month amusement"; and he deprecated the poem as "next to nothing in the shape of a book" to Edith Story (McAleer, 364; Hudson, 164). But the reviews were positive, and B reported that the 2500 copies of the first impression of the first edition were sold out by the end of January, 1872: "Balaustion,—the second edition is in the press . . . 2500 in five months, is a good sale for the likes of me" (McAleer, 372).

The Second Impression of 1871a (*1872*)   What B and his publisher called the "second edition" of *Balaustion's Adventure* was announced in the *Athenaeum* on 17 February 1872. The volume was paged and bound identically to 1871a, though its title-page bears the words "second edition" and the date 1872. It was, in fact, a reimpression of 1871a, incorporating twenty-five small revisions to punctuation and wording. Four of these have to do with confusion in the quotation marks; two errors were introduced which had to be corrected later. Though stereotyping would have been common for Smith, Elder by this date, the spacing adjustments made when the revisions were inserted show that both 1871a and 1872 were printed from types, not plates. The second impression, or perhaps unaltered further impressions, continued to be advertised (sometimes with the words "second edition" and sometimes not) by Smith, Elder for almost a decade.

The Second Edition (*1881*)   In 1881 Smith, Elder brought out what it termed the "third edition" of *Balaustion's Adventure*. These volumes were printed by Spottiswoode and Company, whereas 1871a and 1872 had been produced by Smith and Elder's own printshop. The volume was designed to replicate the earlier editions as closely as possible in content and typeface, but collation reveals that the text was completely reset. Thus 1881 is the true second edition of the poem, the new typesetting containing just twelve variant readings from 1872 (four of which were new errors). How many copies or impressions of this edition were made is not known; it appeared in advertisements as late as 1885, but it was not among the volumes listed as "still available" at the back of several volumes of 1888-89.

Collected Edition (*1889a*)   *Balaustion's Adventure* filled the first 122 pages of Volume 11 of the 1888-89 *Poetical Works*. The presence in B's final text of most of the corrections made in 1881 suggests that (as usual) the last previous edition was used as copy for the collected edition. The poet edited his text carefully, making over 150 changes in wording, spelling, and punctuation. In attempting to sort out the punctuation of his quotations-within-quotations, he also introduced a number of errors which have required emendation.

The text of *Balaustion's Adventure* is marked by B's idiosyncratic transliterations of classical Greek names. The MS contains numerous instances of B's attempts at exact transliteration, but he imposed his system systematically while proofing the first edition. In a few cases— changing the *c* in *Thracian* to a *k*, for example—he did not complete his task until 1889. Some of the spellings (*Hudra* where we expect *Hydra*, for example) seem quite strange to us now, and they also struck Victorian readers as odd, because the tradition of rendering Greek words in Latinate form was long established. In a preface to *The Agamemnon of Aeschylus* (1877), the poet responded to objections to his practice, asserting that he spelled "Greek names and places precisely as does the Greek author." He sent a copy of his *Agamemnon* to the classicist John Blackie, who responded, "I disagree with you radically with regard to your innovation in English spelling in which domain I am a stout Conservative" (*Intimate Glimpses from Browning's Letter File*, ed. A. J. Armstrong, in *Baylor University's Browning Interests* 8 [1934], 73). But B had claimed in his preface, "I began this practice . . . some six-and-thirty years ago . . . [and] supposed I was doing a simple thing enough" (see *1889a*, 13.264-65). His claim is sound; in "Artemis Prologizes," first published in *Dramatic Lyrics* (*Bells and Pomegrantates* No. III, Nov. 1842; see this edition, 3.224-27), employs such spellings as *Athenai*, *Phiobos,* and *Hippolutos*, establishing the pattern he followed in the 1870s. At the time *Balaustion's Adventure* appeared, he was not alone in attempting non-traditional transliterations. In our century, however, the familiar Latinized spellings have long since prevailed and are used in our Editorial Notes, except when quoting B.

Dedication]   For what is known of the circumstances alluded to in the dedication, see *Composition* above. B had known Katrine Cecilia, wife of Earl Cowper of Wingham, for some years; he socialized with her in London in 1865 (McAleer, 212) and visited one of the family mansions, Wrest Park in Bedfordshire, in 1869 (Hudson, 162). Reiterating his indebtedness to the Countess, B described her to Isa Blagden as "a singularly pretty & kind person" (McAleer, 364). B's gesture of thanks was a last-minute addition to his volume, which had already been advertised (in the *Athenaeum*) as available "in a few days" on 22 July 1871, the day before the date of the dedication.

Epigraph]   Taken from EBB's "The Wine of Cyprus," ll. 89-92. The poem is a celebration of EBB's love of classical Greek literature, as taught to her by H. S. Boyd. "The Wine of Cyprus" appeared in EBB's

1844 *Poems*, which served as B's introduction to EBB and played an important role in their courtship.

2] *Kameiros* Before the creation of the city-state of Rhodes, the island of Rhodes (in the SE Aegean Sea) contained three cities, one of which was Camirus (B's *Kameiros*). Thus we know that Balaustion reports her adventures of the year 412 sometime after 408 B.C., when the city of Rhodes was founded by citizens of the preexisting towns.

4-5] *Petalé, / Phullis, Charopé, Chrusion* The names of Balaustion's friends all appear in Alciphron, the first and last in a catalogue of courtesans (Alciphron, 1.12, 2.13, 4.14).

7-10] *Nikias . . . without a grave* See *Sources* above and ll. 140-45n. below.

11-12] *Rhodes . . . Kameiros* See l. 2n. above.

14-17] *join . . . Sparta . . . Knidos for a fleet* As a member of the Delian league, Rhodes had owed allegiance to Athens since 478 B.C. In the wake of the Athenian defeat at Syracuse, the Rhodians revolted and joined the Peloponnesian League led by Sparta in 412 B.C.; the island soon became the headquarters of the Peloponnesian fleet. Cnidus (B's *Knidos*) was a port city in Asia Minor, a Spartan colony, and an old ally of the Rhodian cities.

21] *Ilissian* I. e., Athenian; the Ilissus is a river in Athens made famous in Plato's *Phaedrus*.

27-39] *die at Athens . . . Euripides* The passage draws on two letters in Alciphron for its passionate evocation of Athens and its glories (Alciphron, 3.15, 4.18), but B may have been recalling Pausanias as well. The *Description of Greece* (1.2-3) finely evokes the approach to Athens from Piraeus and the sights within the walls. B's knowledge of ancient Athens may also have been augmented by news reports of the excavations in 1870 by the Greek Archaeological Society.

28-30] *the gate . . . the tombs* In ancient Athens, burials took place outside the city walls, along the roads that passed through the numerous gates; the important temples to Zeus, Athena, Apollo, and other gods were within the walls. The Diomeian (or Diomeid) Gate was in the E wall of the city, the Hippades Gate in the SE; the largest ancient cemeteries were in the Cerameicus district outside the Dipylon Gate, the main entrance to Athens. There is no connection between the Greek *Diomeidos* and the Diomedes of ancient myth, but B may have been misled by his source (see Alciphron, 3.15, n.16; see also Deane, op. cit.; R. E. Wycherley, *The Stones of Athens* [Princeton, 1978], 253 ff.; J. Travlos, *Pictorial Dictionary of Ancient Athens* [New York, 1971], 159-61).

32] *harsh Lakonia* The Latin name for Sparta, Laconia, derives from the Greek *Lakonike*; Spartan culture was famously *harsh* in the rigid discipline and austerity imposed on all citizens.

33-39]   *Choës and Chutroi . . . Euripides*   A catalogue of events, places, and people associated with ancient Athens, borrowed in part from Alciphron 4.18.11.

33]   *Choës*   Or *khöes*, "wine-jugs": the second day of an important Athenian spring festival of Dionysus called the Anthesteria (mentioned in l. 272), marked by copious drinking of wine.

Chutroi   Or *khytroi*, "pots": the third day of the Anthesteria, when vegetables boiled in pots were offered to placate the spirits of the dead.

sacred grove   The olive groves NW of Athens along the Sacred Way, where Plato's Academy was located. Originally these groves were sacred to the hero Akademos.

34]   *Agora*   The public gathering place and market, NW of the Acropolis in Athens; it was the site of numerous impressive buildings.

Dikasteria   Legal tribunals; also, the courts in which they met.

Poikilé   The *Stoa Poikile* ("painted colonnade") at Athens, a large roofed colonnade whose end-wall was decorated with vast frescoes.

35]   *Pnux*   The hill-side called Pnyx, W of the Acropolis; meetings of the Athenian citizen-assembly were once held there.

Keramikos   That is, the Cerameicus, a district in NW Athens, so-called because potters lived and worked there; it was the site of a vast cemetery which was excavated in the 1870s.

Salamis   An island, visible from the Acropolis, off the coast at the port of Piraeus SW of Athens. At Salamis the Greeks defeated Xerxes and the Persian fleet in 480 B.C.; it was also the birthplace of Euripides (see ll. 133-36nn. below).

36]   *Psuttalia*   A small island near Salamis. In the battles of 480 B.C., the Persians established a garrison on Psyttaleia; after the naval defeat at Salamis, the Persian forces on Psyttaleia were annihilated by the Athenian army (Plutarch, "Aristedes," 9).

Marathon   Marathon, about 20 mi. NE of Athens, was the site in 490 B.C. of another famous Athenian victory over the Persians.

37]   *Dionusiac theatre*   The huge theater of Dionysus, described by Pausanias (1.20.2), was built on the south slope of the Acropolis hill in the time of Pericles; it was extensively excavated in the early 1860s.

39]   *Aischulos*   Aeschylus (525-456 B.C.), the first Classical Greek tragedian whose work survives. Of Aeschylus' eighty or more plays, only seven have come down to modern times, including *Persians*, the *Oresteia* trilogy, and *Prometheus Bound*. Aeschylus was a great favorite with EBB, who translated *Prometheus Bound* twice, the second time with B's assistance.

Sophokles A generation younger than Aeschylus, Sophocles (c. 496-406 B.C.) defeated his predecessor the first time he entered a dramatic competition; only seven of Sophocles' 130 plays have survived, including the tragedies *Antigone, Electra,* and *Oedipus Tyrannus.*

Euripides The third great tragic poet of ancient Greece, Euripides (c. 485-406 B.C.) established himself as a new voice presenting a new perspective on mythic subjects with his *Alcestis* (438 B.C.), the play B has Balaustion recite and summarize. Nineteen of his ninety-two plays survive, and B knew them all well. Euripides' unconventional style and ideas perhaps made him B's favorite among the tragedians, though the Bs owned numerous editions of all three dramatists (*Reconstruction,* A11-24, A884-95, A2168-76).

43] *Kaunos* Plutarch mentions Caunos as the home port of the ship chased by pirates (see *Sources* above). Caunos was a Greek city in SW Asia Minor, on the mainland in the vicinity of Rhodes. Herodotus (5.104-5) reports that Caunos joined other eastern cities in the Ionian Revolt of 499 B.C., siding with Athens against the Persians. Toward the end of the Peloponnesian War, however, Caunos found itself an unwilling host to a large Spartan fleet (Thucydides, 8.39-44).

45] *Psuttalia* See ll. 33-39n. above.

48] *vermilion cheek* A Homeric expression applied to Athenian ships; see *Iliad,* 2.637; *Odyssey,* 9.125.

50] *Point Malea* The Malea promontory is at the southernmost tip of the Peloponnese, in Laconia SE of Sparta. Its *bad fame* stems from the powerful and unpredictable winds in its vicinity. Zeus inflicted a hurricane on Menelaus and the other returning Greeks at Malea, and later the strong winds at Malea drove Odysseus and his men off their homeward course (*Odyssey,* 3.287, 9.80). Herodotus (7.170) reports another instance of Malea's reputation for bad weather: at the battle of Salamis, the Corcyraeans (ancient inhabitants of modern Corfu), having offered support to both Greeks and Persians, held their fleet back, later explaining to the victors that strong winds at Cape Malea had prevented them from joining the battle.

54] *Cos or Crete* From Cape Malea, the island of Cos (in Asia Minor) is back to the E, whence the ship departed; Crete is S of Cape Malea.

58] *pirate-ship* The pirates are mentioned in Plutarch, but B may have known that at the time of Balaustion's sea-journey the ports of Crete (which the Captain thinks lies ahead) had become notorious havens for pirates. Thucydides includes in his Introduction a disquisition on the rise and prevalence of piracy in Greece (1.4-8), and Euripides cites the clearing of the seas of pirates as the seventh labor of Heracles (see ll. 476-77n. below).

62-63] *keles . . . Thessaly* Classical Greek *keles* signifies a small boat. Thucydides uses the word 4.9, 8.38) to describe a fast yacht with one bank of oars, and the term also appears in Homer (*Odyssey*, 5.371).

Two coastal provinces in ancient Greece were called Locris, one on the Gulf of Corinth (Ozolian Locris) and the other on the Euboean Sea (Opuntian Locris); Thucydides refers to pirates operating out of Opuntian Locris (2.32). Herodotus includes these Locrians among the northern peoples who sided with Xerxes during the Persian Wars; he also reports (7.6) that the rulers of *Thessaly*, a northern coastal region of Greece, once went so far as to invite Xerxes to invade them. In the Peloponnesian War, the Ozolian Locrians were allies of Athens and the Opuntian Locrians supported Sparta (Thucydides, 3.95, 2.9); elsewhere he describes how the Thessalians, normally on good terms with Athens by this time, allowed an invading army to move unopposed through their territories toward Athens (4.78-79). Locris and Thessaly stand, in the eyes of the Greek captain who is speaking, as examples of treachery against Athens.

76-80] *That song . . . be lost* For *Salamis*, see l. 35n. above. The Athenian paean was sung both before a battle and as a hymn of victory; this version of it is B's translation of Aeschylus, *Persians*, 402-405.

85] *fifty stadia* The *stade* (Latin *stadium*) was a Greek unit of length ranging between 600 and 740 ft.

86-87] *islet-bar, / Even Ortugia's self* The small island of Ortygia forms the NE enclosure of the great harbor at Syracuse (see following note).

88] *Sicily and Syracuse* A Greek colony was established at Syracuse, on the SE coast of the island of Sicily, in the eighth century B.C. By the fifth century its wealth, power, and cultural preeminence led Athens to seek control over other parts of Sicily. The result was the failed Sicilian Expedition of 415-13 B.C., which ended shortly before Balaustion faced the Syracusans ("last year" according to l. 139).

93] *Kaunians* See l. 43n. above.

95] *the League* See ll. 14-15n. above.

98] *Aischulos* See ll. 39n. and 76-80n. above.

106-7] *that pale . . . corn* From Thucydides 7.87, and Plutarch; see *Sources* above and ll. 140-45n. below.

109-10] *prayed them . . . beards* [Note on Homeric oaths to come—ed.]

130] *veritable Aischulos* See ll. 39n. and 76-80n. above.

132-36] *Euripides . . . at Salamis* Euripides was born at Salamis c. 485 B.C., forty years after Aeschylus and ten years after Sophocles. According to a tradition still accepted in the nineteenth century, however,

Euripides' birth occurred in 480 B.C., on the day that the Greeks defeated the Persians near Salamis. By the time of the events of *Balaustion* Euripides had achieved considerable fame, though some of his greatest plays were yet to come. The *salpinx* was an ancient Greek trumpet (*OED*).

140-45]   *when Gulippos . . . Steed*   Gylippus was a Spartan general who came to Syracuse in 414 B.C. and defeated the Athenian fleet led by Nicias in 413. The Athenian general Demosthenes arrived with reinforcements, but both he and Nicias were captured and executed, along with many others. The surviving prisoners were sent to the stone quarries of Syracuse, where many slowly perished. The branding of Athenians is not mentioned in Thucydides, but is reported by Plutarch (see *Sources* above). The description of Attica as the "region of the steed" appears in Sophocles, *Oedipus at Colonus*, 668; B refers to the same chorus in *Aristophanes' Apology*, 3510-11.

151]   *the Muse*   Presumably the muse of tragic poetry, Melpomene.

154]   *wings to fly . . . world*   Recalling the Homeric formula for powerful speech, "winged words," used dozens of times in the *Odyssey* and the *Iliad*.

158-60]   *new knocking . . . dumb*   From his first efforts to his last, Euripides was continuously attacked (and parodied, as in Aristophanes' *Frogs*) for his stylistic, artistic, and intellectual departures from the conventions of tragic drama established by Aeschylus and Sophocles. Euripides' rationalist skepticism provoked accusations of iconoclasm or even atheism.

161-64]   *God Bacchos . . . mankind*   As the reigning deity of the Athenian theatrical festival called the Great Dionysia, Bacchus (or Dionysus), Greek god of wine and ecstasy, could be deemed the figurative father of playwrights, his *latest child* being Euripides. Son of Zeus and the mortal Semele, Dionysus was born after the other Olympian gods; in *Bacchae* (not written until well after Balaustion had her adventure) Euripides dramatized the refusal of King Pentheus to accept the divinity of Dionysus.

167]   *rhesis*   "A set speech or discourse" (*OED*, where this instance is the earliest citation).

169]   *monostich*   A self-contained single line of poetry

171-80]   *prompt reward . . . thanked him*   Drawn from Plutarch; see *Sources* above.

183]   *Euoi . . . God*   "Euoi" is a joyous exclamation uttered by worshipers of Dionysus; the word appears thus in Aristophanes' *Lysistrata*, 1294, though Euripides rendered the Dionysian cry as "Io" in his *Bacchae.*

184]   *Oöp*   B's transliteration of a Greek sailors' cry, used to pace the oarsmen; it may be translated "In! Out!" See Aristophanes, *The Frogs*, 208; *The Birds*, 1395.

owl-shield   Balaustion is referred to as the captain's "owl-shield" because of her devotion to Athens; warriors sometimes displayed heraldic devices on their shields, and the owl was the emblem of Athens and its goddess, Athena. In this connection, Plutarch tells of the appearance of an owl that was taken as a good omen by the Athenians just before the battle of Salamis ("Themistocles," 12).

185]   *Sacred Anchor*   A name sometimes given by classical Greek authors to a ship's emergency sheet-anchor, and thus figurative for "last hope."

187-88]   *Babai . . . grandsire's song Babai*   is a Greek exclamation of amazement. The *grandsire's song* is the poetry of Homer, where the formula "what a word has escaped the barrier of your teeth!" occurs repeatedly (*Odyssey*, 1.64, 5.22, 19.492, 23.70).

189]   *snow in Thrace*   Snowfalls are common in the mountainous parts of Thrace, the northernmost district of ancient Greece.

207]   *Wild-pomegranate-flower*   The literal meaning of the name "Balaustion," and also (though B seems not have known it at the time) the emblem of Rhodes (Griffin and Minchin, 245).

210]   *the Rosy Isle*   The literal meaning of the name "Rhodes."

211]   *food, drink . . . once*   The pomegranate fruit, because of its compound structure and numerous edible seeds (encased in a moist gel), symbolized fecundity and plenty to the ancient Greeks. B had an enduring fascination with the pomegranate and its meanings; see the notes in this edition on the title he gave to his pamphlet series, "Bells and Pomegranates" (3.343-44, 5.4, 5.334).

214-15]   *strophe . . . proverb-like*   In classical Greek poetry, a *strophe* is a stanza; it is followed by a metrically identical stanza termed the *antistrophe*. In dramatic performances, a "strophe was sung as the chorus proceeded in its dance in one direction, followed by a second stanza, the antistophe . . . sung when the chorus turned and reversed its dance" (*Oxford Companion to Classical Literature* [ed. M. C. Howatson (Oxford, 1989)], 541-42), Since *strophe* means "turn," B employs the literal translation of *antistrophe* in "turn-again." Classical tragedies, especially those of Euripides, usually conclude with a general, *proverb-like* comment by the Chorus on the entire action of the play.

220-222]   *strangest, saddest, sweetest . . . archonship*   Not every lover of Euripides would agree with Balaustion's terms of praise, but *Alcestis*, his earliest surviving play, was performed in 438 B.C., when Glaucinus was chief magistrate (*archon*).

223] *Isle o' the Rose* See ll. 210n. above.

225-26] *the right Lenean feast / In Athens* The Lenaea was a festival honoring Dionysus, during which dramatic competitions were held. The mid-winter celebration of the Lenaea took place in the month called "Lenaion" by the Ionians and "Gamelion" in Athens; the latter would be the "right" name in Balaustion's eyes. The same letter of Alciphron that B drew on for ll. 33-39 mentions the plays performed at the Lenaea (Alciphron, 4.18.10).

229-30] *Herakles . . . talks about* Syracuse is known to have had temples dedicated to Apollo, Athena, and Zeus; B is probably relying on Plutarch for the prominence of Heracles in Syracusan worship. Nicias is said to have had his main camp near a temple of Heracles, who is later described as the national hero of Syracuse ("Nicias," 24, 26; see also Thucydides 7.73).

249-51] *our Kameiros theatre . . . marble row* B describes the generic Greek theater; there are no significant ruins at Kameiros.

255-56] *a whole / Talent* A huge sum, a talent being about 57 lbs. of silver or gold.

258-59] *had not Herakles . . . devoted ones* Balaustion envisions her escape at Syracuse as a recapitulation of the plot of Euripides' *Alcestis.*

271] *Peiraieus* The main port of Athens, Piraeus is about 5 mi. SW of the ancient city.

272] *Anthesterion-month* February; see ll. 33-39n. above. Since each Greek month began at the new moon, Balaustion's wedding, alluded to in the next two lines, will occur in two weeks.

282] *not Aischulos nor Sophokles* See ll. 158-60n. above.

284-85] *Agathon . . . Kephisophon* Poets (or poets manqué) along a declining scale of reputation, all mentioned by Aristophanes in *Frogs.* Agathon (c. 445-400 B.C.) was a respected tragic poet, though only forty lines of his work survive today. Iophon (fl. c. 428 B.C.) was a son of Sophocles and the author of fifty plays, of which only two fragments survive. Cephisophon is alleged to have been a slave of Euripides' who helped write the plays and cuckolded his master.

Both Agathon and Iophon are spoken of favorably in *Frogs* (73, 78, 83-84), but the rumors about Cephisophon figure repeatedly in Aristophanes' ruthless satire on Euripides (944, 1048, 1408-9, 1452-53).

286-87] *A man . . . poet-kind* Though there is little reliable information about his life, Euripides was viewed as solitary to the point of being anti-social.

293-94] *Sokrates . . . him read* Ancient biographies of Euripides report that he was a student and friend of various skeptical philosophers, including Socrates (see W. N. Bates, *Euripides* [N. Y., 1930], 7).

297] *Sit with . . . talk* That is, on Mount Parnassus, sacred to the Muses, where the souls of poets, artists, and philosophers spend eternity.

306-7] *brisk little . . . whippersnapper* The offensive critic is Alfred Austin (1835-1913), who had first attacked B in 1869. Five years after *Balaustion's Adventure* appeared, B launched an onslaught against Austin in "Of Pacchiarotto, and How He Worked in Distemper," and the entire story of B's wrangling with Austin is detailed in the notes to that poem in this edition, 13.321-56. (See also Hood, 358-63.)

310] *mask of the actor move* In classical times, Greek actors wore painted masks made of linen or wood. Though the masks were indicative of the character being presented, the facial expressions of the actors were obscured.

311-14] *fear flitted . . . was gone* The critic of l. 307 is not quoting Balaustion, but ridiculing her with his alliterations.

318] *power that makes* As expressed in *Sordello* 3.928 (1840), in the "Essay on Shelley" (1852), and elsewhere, B agreed with the Greeks in conceiving of poetry as a made thing, and the poet as the maker (see this edition, 2.225, 5.137). The Greek words for "poetry" and "poet" come from the Greek verb ποιέω, "make."

338] *Baccheion* Temple of Bacchus (Dionysus). Since Balaustion is presumably telling her tale in Athens, B may have in mind the small temple of Dionysus on the road to the Academy mentioned by Pausanias (1.29.2).

340] *we five* Balaustion and her friends, named in ll. 4-5.

343] *the poet speaks* That is, Euripides speaks through Balaustion; DeVane misreads the phrase as referring to B himself (*Hbk.*, 354).

360] *Pherai where Admetos ruled* According to legend, the city of Pherae in Thessaly was founded by Pheres, the father of Admetus. By the beginning of Euripides' treatment of the story, Admetus has succeeded to the throne, though Pheres still lives.

361] *there gleamed a God* At this point B commences his "transcript" of Euripides' *Alcestis*. Balaustion follows the events, speeches, and behavior of characters in the play exactly, recapitulating the myth in a different form at the end of the poem. For the basic story, see *Sources* above.

374] *Phoibos' son Asklepios* As sun-god, Apollo was given the epithet *Phoebus*, meaning "the bright"; Asclepius, god of healing, was the offspring of Apollo and a mortal, Coronis.

383] *Moirai* The Greek name of the three Fates. Apollo deceived them by getting them drunk; see *Sources* above, and B's later treatment of this part of the myth in the Prologue to *Parleyings with Certain People of Importance in Their Day* (see this edition, 16.5ff.)

384]   *Pheres*   See l. 360n. above.

412-27]   *Like some dread . . . i' the sky*   This epic simile is not in Euripides' *Alcestis*, but the first two lines of it are suggestive of the figure of Death in Leighton's painting of the confrontation of Heracles and Death (see ll. 2672-75 and nn. below).

438]   *Pelias' daughter*   Alcestis was the daughter of Pelias and Anaxibia, rulers of Iolcus in Thessaly.

455]   *No! Rather . . . mature*   This line of *Alcestis* (50) has provoked much commentary because of its obscurity in the Greek. The Loeb translation by A. S. Way offers a less condensed rendering: "Nay, but to smite with death the ripe for death," and R. Lattimore's version (which incorporates an emendation of the Greek) is "No, only to put their death off. They must die in the end" (*Euripides I* [Chicago, 1955], 9).

476-77]   *Sent by Eurustheus . . . steeds*   As expiation for having killed his wife Megara and their children while he was insane, Heracles was told by the Delphic Oracle to serve Eurystheus, King of Tiryns, for twelve years. Eurystheus imposed many dangerous tasks on Heracles, the most famous of which are known as the Twelve Labors of Heracles. The nature and sequence of the Labors are reported differently by classical authors; for an overview, see R. Graves, *The Greek Myths* (London, 1960), 2.134.6. When Heracles arrives in Pherae in Euripides' play, he is on his way to what Euripides classified (in *Herakles*, 348ff.) as his fourth labor for Eurystheus: he must tame the flesh-eating horses of Diomedes, king of the Bistones in Thrace (for *winter world*, see l. 189n. above).

499-504]   *in came . . . by word*   At several points in *Alcestis*, Euripides breaks his Chorus of Citizens of Pherae into multiple voices, concluding by returning to unison.

505-34]   *What now . . . the first*   These lines, recalled by Balaustion as one speech, are assigned in *Alcestis* (76-111) to alternating halves of a split chorus, which unites into one voice at l. 537.

516]   *Paian*   Literally, "Healer"; an epithet applied to Apollo in his role as a god of healing.

524-26]   *hallowed vase . . . clipt locks*   The pouring of libations and the cutting of hair were ritual signs of mourning in ancient Greece.

539]   *Lukia . . . Ammon's seat*   Figuratively, from "from east to west." Lycia is a district in SW Asia Minor, on the mainland E of Rhodes; in the town of Patara in Lycia there was an oracle of Apollo. The oracle of the Egyptian god Ammon (viewed by Greeks as another manifestation of their Zeus) was in the Lybian desert, ten days' journey W of Thebes, according to Herodotus (1. 182, 2.55, 4.181).

544]   *Phoibos' son*   Asclepius; see *Sources* and l. 374n. above.

547] *Zeus-flung thunder-flame* Zeus killed Asclepius with a thunderbolt; see *Sources* above.

579-80] *before the hearth . . . Mistress* Alcestis prays to Hestia, the Greek goddess of the hearth and the family.

582] *my orphans* The son and daughter of Admetus and Alcestis appear in Euripides' play; the former, Eumelus, has a speaking part, while the unnamed daughter is silent.

590] *myrtle-foliage* In Greek religion the leaves of the myrtle were symbolic of love and marriage, but were also used in burial ceremonies.

622] *they questioned* In *Alcestis*, 199-200, the Chorus asks about Admetus' reaction.

638-54] *What passage . . . comes, too* In *Alcestis* the equivalent lines (213-33) are spoken not by the chorus as a whole but by nine successive individual members, who then chant as one voice through l. 663.

641] *clip the locks* See ll. 524-26n. above.

642-43] *black peplos' fold . . . black robe* The *peplos* was usually a woman's shawl or wrap; the black peplos signified mourning and was worn by both sexes.

645] *king Paian* see l. 516n. above.

655] *Pheraian land* See l. 360n. above.

685] *pharos* Greek for "cloak"; *OED* cites the line as its only example of this meaning in English.

704] *True purple* Cloth dyed with Tyrian purple, a dye extracted from the secretions of shellfish of the genera *Murex* and *Purpura*; the color was associated with nobility.

711] *Charopé* One of Balaustion's friends; see ll. 4-5n. above.

727-28] *nuptial chambers . . . Iolkos* The inconsistency between this remark and the statements in ll. 596-97 and 1982-84, where the marriage seems to have taken place in Pherae, goes unnoticed by Euripides and B, though it is often commented on by classicists (*Alcestis*, 177, 248-49, and 911-17). Iolcus, a city about 10 mi. E of Pherae in Thessaly, was the birthplace of Alcestis.

733] *Charon* As the previous line indicates, Charon is the ferryman who carries the dead across the rivers Styx and Acheron to the realm of Hades; given the earlier references to Aristophanes, it should be mentioned that Charon plays a substantial part in *Frogs* (183ff.)

743] *blue brilliance* Euripides' Alcestis alludes to the glare of Hades' eyes (*Alcestis*, 262), but B has borrowed their color from Leighton's painting. There the figure of Death is given wide-open, piercing blue-gray eyes (see *Composition* above and ll. 2672-75n. below).

797]   *our children*   See l. 582n. above.

852]   *Lybian flute*   Though he employs an unorthodox spelling, B follows his source (*Alcestis*, 346-47) in calling the flute "Libyan." Commentators on Euripides (including Paley, in an edition owned by B) note that he used this expression several times, alluding to the making of flutes from the wood of a species of lotus grown in Libya. See also *Emendations to the Text* above.

865-69]   *tune of Orpheus . . . Charon*   Admetus wishes for the magical power of the mythic poet Orpheus, who by his music nearly recovered his dead wife Eurydice from the Underworld; the region of the dead was ruled over by Hades (euphemistically called *Plouton*, "wealth-giver," in Greek), and Persephone (named *Koré* in Greek myth). The monstrous dog Cerberus guarded the entrance to the Underworld; Heracles captured him as the last of his labors (see ll. 476-77n. above). For Charon, see l. 733n. above.

874]   *cedar*   A wood chosen for coffins because of its resistance to water and to rotting.

890]   *Moirai*   See l. 383n. above.

942-3]   *woe broke . . . Why tell?*   Balaustion passes over two very affecting speeches of lamentation by Ademtus' young son Eumelus (*Alcestis*, 393-403, 406-15).

961]   *To-day . . . end of time*   No equivalent to these words appears in *Alcestis*, but the line does echo the words of Macbeth on hearing of the death of his wife: "Tomorrow, and tomorrow, and tomorrow . . ." (*Macbeth*, 5.5.19-21).

975]   *Drink-sacrifice . . . not*   When Circe instructs Odysseus in the ritual he will use to raise the souls of the dead, she specifies that after pouring libations of milk and honey, wine, and water, he must spill the blood of a ram and a ewe. Once in the realm of Hades, Odysseus finds that only when the spirits have drunk of the blood can they speak with him (Homer, *Odyssey*, 11. 508-30; 12.23-43.

981]   *Clip . . . mane away*   This sign of mourning, parallel to the cutting of locks of hair alluded to in ll. 524-26 and 641, was employed by northern Greeks and by the Persians; it is mentioned by Plutarch ("Alexander," 72) and Herodotus (9.24).

991]   *Pelias*   See l. 438n. above.

995]   *old corpse-conductor*   Charon; see l. 733n. above.

996]   *Acherontian lake*   Acheron is one of the rivers that bounds the kingdom of Hades.

1000]   *seven-stringed mountain-shell*   According to the fourth Homeric Hymn, the god Hermes invented the first lyre by killing a tortoise and fitting its shell with strings; Greek lyres commonly had seven strings.

1002-4]   *At Sparta . . . Karneian month . . . Athenai*   B (following Euripides, in *Alcestis*, 449-52) refers to *Karneia*, the harvest-festival at Sparta, held in the month of Karneios (August-September). The celebrations included a famous musical competition. Admetus apparently claims that the fame of Alcestis will be so great that laments for her will be sung in distant places like Sparta and Athens (*Athenai* in Greek).

1010]   *Kokutos' stream*   Another of the rivers of Hades was Cocytus (B's *Kokutos*); the phrase is appositive to *Hades' hall* and similarly the object of *From.*

1024-26]   *on such . . . allowance*   The diction, which is not anticipated in Euripides, is reminiscent of Antony's declarations of love in *Antony and Cleopatra*, 1.1.15, 36-38.

1041]   *lustral*   Purifying.

1043]   *Bacchos' blood*   Red wine; Bacchus was the god of wine.

1047-51]   *Herakles . . . half man*   The greatest of the Greek heroes, Heracles (Latin *Hercules*) was the son of the god Zeus and the mortal Alcmena. In *Alcestis* he appears as he often did in ancient comedies (including Aristophanes' *Frogs*): boisterous, disruptive, good-hearted, and a friend to humanity.

1058]   *Laboured . . . life long*   See ll. 476-77n. above.

1088-89]   *A certain labour . . . Tirunthian*   As ensuing lines specify, Heracles will soon perform another labor demanded of him by Eurystheus of Tiryns: he must tame the flesh-eating horses of Diomedes, king of the Bistones in Thrace.

1109-10]   *except*   Unless.

1114-16]   *what sire . . . gold throughout*   Diomedes was a son of Ares, Greek god of war, and the nymph Cyrene; Euripides calls the shields of Thrace "golden" (*Alcestis*, 498), alluding to the gold mines in that region.

1122-23]   *Lukaon . . . Kuknos*   B. follows Euripides into confusion. Several characters named Lycaon appear in Greek myth, but nowhere (except in *Alcestis*, 501-2) is he identified as a son of Ares or an opponent of Heracles. Furthermore, Ares apparently named more than one of his sons Cycnus (or Cygnus), and Heracles confronted more than one of them. The Cycnus referred to here is either the son of Ares and Pyrene who challenged Heracles on his search for the golden apples of the Hesperides, or the son of Ares and Pelopia whom Heracles killed during his adventures in Trachis. To add to the difficulties, both of these incidents take place after Heracles rescues Alcestis. In his *Herakles* (389-93) Euripides himself makes the Cycnus episode the fifth labor of Heracles, after his taming of the flesh-eating horses; and the hero's journey through Trachis occurs after his twelve labors are accomplished. See also ll. 476-77n. above. Both B and Euripides feel free to alter the sequence of the adventures of Heracles as poetic circumstance demands—see 1207n. below.

1126]   *Alkmené's son*   Heracles; see ll. 1047-51n. above.

1143]   *sprung from Perseus*   The Greek hero Perseus, himself a child of Zeus, was the great-grandfather of Heracles' mother Alcmena.

1165]   *To be . . . diverse*   As Hamlet thinks they are, in his soliloquy at 3.1.55.

1207]   *which had . . . snake*   In one of his most dangerous labours (traditionally, his second; in Euripides' *Herakles*, his tenth), Heracles had to kill the Hydra, a many-headed poisonous snake.

1209]   *the lion's hide*   Heracles was depicted as clothed in the skin of the Nemean lion, which he had killed as his first labor.

1232-33]   *I went . . . thirsty Argos*   The mortals in Heracles' ancestry are associated with the city of Tiryns, in the southern part of the plain of Argos, where a hot and dry climate prevails.

1260-87]   *Apollon's very self . . . dead but now*   This passage, which recounts Apollo's enforced service to Admetus (see *Sources* above), translates most of a long chorus in *Alcestis* (568-604).

1261]   *lyric Puthian*   Apollo was a god of music, particularly of the lyre; the epithet "Pythian" derives from Apollo's having killed the serpent Python when establishing his temple at Delphi.

1268]   *Othrus' dell*   Othrys is a mountain range at the southern edge of the plain of Thessaly.

1277-83]   *Along by . . . a port*   The burden of this passage, which closely follows Euripides, is "from west to east."

1277]   *Boibian lake*   Lake Boebeis is in NE Thessaly, near Pherae; it is mentioned in Homer as belonging to Admetus' son Eumelus (*Iliad*, 2.711-14).

1279]   *sun's steeds, stabled west*   As god of light, Apollo acquired the epithet "Phoebus" and assimilated the characteristics of an earlier sun-god, Helios. Helios was pictured as driving a fiery chariot from E to W each day.

1281]   *Molossoi*   The people of Molossia, a region of the province of Epirus, due W of Thessaly. The city of Dodona, with its oracle of Zeus, was in Molossia.

1282]   *the Aigaian, up to Pelion's shore*   Mt. Pelion, in eastern Thessaly, overlooks the Aegean Sea.

1394]   *put to the touch*   An allusion to the use of a touchstone, which indicates the purity of gold or silver when rubbed on the metal.

1468-69]   *Ludian slave, / Or Phrugian*   Lydia and Phrygia were regions of Asia Minor, to the E of the Greek cities along the Aegean coast. Herodotus reports that King Croesus subjugated the Lydians, the Phrygians, and many other peoples; after the defeat of Croesus by the Persians in the sixth century B.C., the Lydians were reduced to slave status (Herodotus, 1.29, 155-57). In ensuing centuries, Phrygians and Lydians were regarded as cowards by mainland Greeks.

1500] *worsted* Defeated (cp. *bested*).

1512] *hydra* See l. 1207n. above

1534] *outlive Zeus* Being king of the Olympian gods, Zeus was of course immortal.

1559-61] *Akastos . . . sister's blood* Under Athenian law in Euripides' time, Alcestis' brother Acastus would have been obliged to prosecute the killer of his sister.

1591] *Case-hardened* Attributing this term to Balaustion in the late fifth century B.C. constitutes an extreme anachronism, since both the surface-hardening process and its name date from the seventeenth century A.D.

1597] *Hermes the infernal* Among his other diverse functions, the messenger-god Hermes conducted the souls of the dead to the Underworld.

1601] *Bride of Hades* Persephone (see ll. 865-69n. above).

1634-35] *the dust / O' the last encounter* What the "last encounter" was depends on which record of the labors of Heracles is consulted. In Euripides' own account (*Herakles*, 348-435), the hero would arrive at Pherae after his third labor, capturing the sacred Cerynian hind. Later tradition has the taming of the Diomedean horses (to which Heracles is going in *Alcestis*) as the eighth labor, preceded by his conquest of the Cretan bull.

1656] *unmixed product* Greek wine was sweet and strong, and was customarily diluted with water before it was drunk.

1668-69] *A guest . . . pirate* As does Euripides, B allows for the irritability and bluntness of the servant's comments by suggesting that he is ignorant of the visitor's identity. Balaustion does not grant the servant this latitude (ll. 1679ff.).

1697] *Turannos* Tyrant; in classical usage, an absolute, but not necessarily oppressive, ruler.

1710] *red-written* Written with red ink so as to draw attention.

1717-18] *Ai . . . papai* Greek lamentations, "Woe, woe, alas, alas, oh, strange." *Papai* in particular is associated with extreme pain or distress, as in Aeschylus' *Agamemnon*, 1114; and Sophocles' *Philoctetes*, 754.

1730-34] *the bow . . . a monster* Heracles' first weapon was his club, but after he slew the Hydra, he dipped his arrows in its poisonous blood and used them to kill other enemies, including the bronze-armored Stymphalian birds.

1735] *He slew . . . yesterday* The Hydra lived in the marshes of Lerna, near Argos. Euripides has the killing of the Hydra as Heracles' tenth labor, but Balaustion employs the later traditional sequence.

1742] *Charopé* The name of one of Balaustion's listeners; see ll. 4-5n. above.

1762-64] *A solemn draught . . . fierce* Heracles' appetites were always represented as enormous, especially when he appeared in comedies.

1773] *the Helper* An epithet for Heracles, who takes humanity's part against gods, monsters, and criminals.

1800-1] *sweetest . . . Goddess* The worship of Aphrodite, Greek goddess of love, beauty, and fertility, was said to have originated at Paphos in Cyprus; thus she was often called simply "the Cyprian" (Greek *Kypris*, B's *Kupris*). In the opening of his *Hippolytus*, Euripides has Aphrodite describe herself as benign only to those who humbly worship her.

1858] *Larissa* City in Thessaly about 25 mi. NW of Pherae.

1877] *with a blood that's oil* Balaustion alludes to the flammability of pine-sap or pitch, which burns easily and brightly.

1882-84] *son she bore . . . Alkmené* Heracles' mother Alcmena was a daughter of Electryon; she was born in Mycenae, and married Amphitryon, king of Tiryns (see also ll. 1047-51n., 1143n., and 1232-33n. above).

1890] *Drinking . . . o' the sacrifice* B follows *Alcestis*, 845, but Euripides is indefinite about what Death is supposedly drinking; his hint that it may be a blood-offering made by mourners is echoed in B's l. 1897.

1897] *boltered blood* Clotted blood; B inverts the compound *blood-boltered*, which means "clogged with dried blood" (*OED*).

1898-99] *Down go I . . . king there* In both Euripides' and the traditional list, Heracles visits the Underworld as his twelfth labor. See also ll. 865-69n. above.

1913-14] *lion-shag . . . club* Two of the attributes with which Heracles is usually depicted: the skin of the Nemean lion (see l. 1209n above) and a huge club.

1916] *Larissa* See l. 1858n. above.

1917] *Helper* See l. 1773n. above.

1942] *peplos' fold* See l. 642-43n. above.

1948-59] *"What was . . . no world."* In the MS, this passage is spoken by Balaustion, partly paraphrasing Admetus in *Alcestis* (861-71). When B changed the punctuation to indicate a direct quotation of Admetus, he did not alter the verbs (from *was* to *is*) or the pronouns (from *he* and *his* to *I* and *my*) and thus engendered some confusion.

1961-1977] *they urged . . . would* Balaustion compresses a long exchange between the Chorus and Admetus in *Alcestis* (872-910).

1982-83] *Pelian . . . marriage-hymns* Euripides makes it clear in *Alcestis*, l. 915, that *Pelian* here refers to the pines of Mt. Pelion, which lies near Iolcus, the scene of the wedding of Admetus and Alcestis. See also l. 438n. above.

1990] *white peplos* Worn at the marriage ceremony.

2023] *unsprinkled* Though the Greek in *Alcestis* (947) literally describes the floor as "dusty" or "unswept," B was particularly pleased with his imaginative extension here (Griffin and Minchin, 243-44). He may have recalled Homer's *Odyssey*, 20.149-50, where the nurse Eurycleia orders her maids to sweep out the house and sprinkle the floors.

2059] *science . . . stars* Euripides had studied astronomy with the philosopher Anaxagoras.

2063-68] *not any medicine . . . mortals* The Chorus deprecates the power of even the greatest of healers. Orpheus the poet (see ll. 865-69n above) was credited with discovering medical cures (Pausanias, 9.30.3) preserved on tablets in a temple of Dionysus on Mt. Haemus in Thrace. The *Asklepiadai* were the followers of Asclepius, who gained medical knowledge from his father Apollo (*Phoibos*; see l. 374n. above).

2069] *this sole goddess* That is, Necessity, or Fate.

2076] *Iron . . . Chaluboi* The Chalybes, expert ironworkers on the SE coast of the Black Sea, were ancient Greece's main source of iron.

2104-6] *winter world . . . Bistones . . . steed's voracity* See ll. 189n., 476-77n., 1088-89n. above.

2112] *ai and pheu* See ll. 1717-18 and n. above.

2125] *yellow hair* In Leighton's painting, "Hercules Wrestling with Death for the Body of Alcestis" (see 2672-75n. and *Composition* above), Heracles has golden hair.

2129] *shrouded . . . woman-like* At l. 1006 of *Alcestis*, the Chorus notes the approach of Heracles, who arrives leading the heavily-veiled Alcestis.

2148-49] *And I . . . blame thee* By concealing the death of Alcestis, Admetus has led Heracles into the impropriety of feasting in a house of mourning.

2155-56] *having killed . . . steeds* Heracles visited upon Diomedes the same fate Diomedes had inflicted on his unsuspecting guests: the king was fed to his horses. After this meal, they became tame, and Heracles brought them to Argos.

2195] *Pheraioi* The citizens of Pherae, figured here as "sons of Pheres"; see l. 360n. above.

2206] *May-day youngster* Lusty boy.

2278-81] *his friend . . . again* Balaustion praises Admetus' victory over his previous cowardice by making it analogous to Heracles' killing of the Hydra (see ll. 1730-35 and nn. above).

2285] *thy Progenitor* Zeus.

2316] *cut off Gorgon's head* Admetus likens his gesture to that of Perseus, who beheaded the hideous Gorgon named Medusa with his magic sickle. Since those who looked upon the Gorgon were instantly turned to stone, Perseus averted his face, used his polished shield as a mirror, and struck behind him.

2344-45] *Admetos had not . . . cheat* The Euripidean original (*Alcestis*, 1128) bears the same contempt for necromancers that B expressed in "Mr. Sludge, 'The Medium'" (see this edition, 6.285ff. and nn.).

2361] *dæmons* Spirits. By using this spelling, B passes over a crux in the Greek text (*Alcestis*, 1140).

2370] *evanish* Be dispelled; disappear.

2376-77] *my urgent . . . Sthenelos* Heracles again alludes to the next labor imposed on him by Eurystheus, identified as the son of Sthenelus by Homer (*Iliad*, 19.123).

2383] *tetrarchy* Euripides alludes either to the four regions of Thessaly (one of which Admetus ruled), or to four towns listed by Homer as being in the realm of Admetus (*Iliad*, 2.711).

2392-96] *Manifold are . . . experience through* One of B's favorite passages, the "chorus-ending from Euripides" he admiringly referred to in "Bishop Blougram's Apology" (this edition, 5.299 and n.). Euripides used slightly variant versions of these lines to conclude four of his plays in addition to *Alcestis*. Following this closing, B returns to Balaustion's frame-narrative.

2398-99] *my poet . . . the prize* The surviving records of the competitive drama festivals of Athens report that in 438 B.C. Euripides' tetralogy containing *Alcestis* placed second behind an unknown tetralogy by Sophocles.

2400] *Sophokles . . . a piece* A drama entitled *Admetus* is listed among the lost plays of Sophocles.

2407] *the Dionusiac shrine* All drama was sacred to Dionysus, and the Theatre of Dionysus in Athens was built on the site of the old temple of Dionysus (see also ll. 37n., 161-64n., and 225-26n. above).

2408] *crater* Wine-vessel, specifically one used for mixing wine and water; the Greek is usually rendered as *krater*. Balaustion's critical estimate depends on the distinction between the krater and the drinking cup filled from it.

2412] *The Human . . . warm tears* See *Epigraph* n. above.

2430] *Mainad* A woman inspired to ecstasy by Dionysus; Euripides' play *Bacchae* features a chorus of Mænads.

2489-92] *as some long . . . a triumph* Balaustion alludes to the emotional change that accompanies the transformation of a minor chord into a major. This is accomplished by raising the second note of a chord by a semitone, from the minor third to the major third.

2522]   *Olumpian glow*   Mt. Olympus was the home of the Greek gods, whose palaces sat at the pinnacle of this highest mountain in Greece.

2534-35]   *Will pity . . . terror*   B has Apollo anticipate (as a god may) a central concept in the theory of tragedy propounded in the *Poetics* of Aristotle (384-322 B.C.).

2573]   *trophy-like*   The ancient idea of a trophy was more grandiose and somber than the modern. A Greek trophy was a battlefield memorial set up by the victors; it consisted of large quantities of weapons, standards, and equipment captured from the defeated army, piled around a tree, and consecrated to a god.

2599-2601]   *Admetos . . . yoked to*   Alcestis had many suitors, and to avoid choosing one over another, her father Pelias announced that he would grant her hand only to the man who could yoke a wild boar and a lion to a chariot and drive it around a race-track. Admetus, already one of the suitors, asked the aid of Apollo, who was nearing the end of his year of servitude to Admetus (see *Sources* above). Apollo granted Admetus the favor, enlisting the help of Heracles in taming the wild beasts to the point where they would draw the chariot.

2614]   *He looked . . . died*   Balaustion links the Alcestis story with the myth of Orpheus (see l. 865-69n. above); the poet had gained the release of his wife Eurydice from the Underworld on the condition that he lead her out of the realm of Hades without looking back at her. But as he neared the land of the living, Orpheus turned to assure himself that Eurydice was still behind him, and thus lost her forever. In 1864, B had written an eight-line poem on the subject, to accompany a painting by Frederic Leighton, the artist referred to in ll. 2672-97 (see this edition, 6.167 and nn.).

2618-25]   *Koré . . . in Sicily*   Persephone (*Koré*), daughter of Zeus and Demeter, was seized by Hades to become queen of the Underworld while she was picking flowers in the meadows of Enna in Sicily. Zeus assuaged Demeter's grief at the loss of her child by commanding that Persephone be returned to the living world and her mother for half of each year.

2656]   *Golden Age*   The belief that life in earlier times was idyllic is at least as old as the Greek poet Hesiod (c. 700 B.C.), whose *Theogeny* elevates the first gods of Greece as "the golden race."

2663]   *my critic-friend*   See ll. 306-7 and n. above.

2664-66]   *your poem . . . got it*   See ll. 2398-99 and n. above.

2668-71]   *I know . . . warm tears*   Though the speaker is still Balaustion, not her creator, the reference is to EBB and the quotation from her "The Wine of Cyprus"; see *Epigraph* n. above.

2672-75] *a great Kaunian painter . . . of it all* A renowned painter and sculptor of the late 4th century B.C., Protogenes the Kaunian is mentioned by Pausanias (1.3.5) as one of the noted artists who decorated the bouleuterion (council-house) in Athens. Since Protogenes worked mainly in Rhodes, Balaustion can reasonably know his work, though no authority lists an Alcestis among his paintings. B is performing a time-leap like that of ll. 2668-71 and singing the praises of his friend Frederic Leighton (1830-96). The picture described in the following lines is "Hercules Wrestling with Death for the Body of Alcestis," painted by Leighton between 1869 and 1871 and exhibited at the Royal Academy in the spring of 1871. See *Composition* above.

2684] *you four* Balaustion's listeners; see ll. 4-5 and n. above.

2690-92] *The envenomed substance . . . fester up* A reference to the robe of Nessus, poisoned with the centaur's blood and innocently given to Heracles by his second wife Deianeira. The garment corroded Heracles' flesh and caused him such agony that he laid himself on his funeral pyre and was burned alive.

2697] *Poikilé* See l. 34n. above, but B also means that Leighton's picture deserved its place in the May, 1871 exhibition at the Royal Academy, a venue as prestigious as a classical *stoa* decorated by famous artists.

PRINCE HOHENSTIEL-SCHWANGAU, SAVIOUR OF SOCIETY

Emendations to the Text

The following emendations have been made to the 1889a copy-text:

l. 47: In 1871b and 1889a (but not in MS), this line begins with un-necessary quotation marks. The compositors of 1871b may have mis-takenly imposed the old printers' convention of marking every line of a continuing quotation, a convention also employed in 1888-89 through Volume 10. Elsewhere in the first edition of *Prince Hohenstiel-Schwangau,* and throughout the remaining volumes of 1888-89, modern printing practice is employed. The MS reading is restored.

l. 254: In MS and 1871b, this line ends with a period, as the syntax of the passage requires. There is no punctuation at the end of the line in 1889a; the MS-1871b reading is restored.

ll. 254-55: In MS, these lines are separated by a white line space; the paragraph break falls at the bottom of a page in 1871b. Apparently the compositors of 1888-89 did not see the break, since the lines have been closed up in the copy-text. The MS-1871b spacing is restored.

l. 546: In both MS and 1871b, the word *you* is separated from *in* by punctuation marks; there is no punctuation here in 1889a, though space for it remains. The 1871b reading *you, in* is restored.

l. 569: Both MS and 1871b end this line with a colon whose function is to set up the categories of "honor" and "glory" elaborated in the fol-lowing lines. The line has no end punctuation in 1889a, thus creating a confusing run-on sentence. The MS-1871b reading is restored.

l. 648-49: In MS and 1871b, a paragraph break appears at this point. The break disappeared as a result of a page division in 1889a; the MS-1871b reading is restored.

l. 1049: The comma at the end of this line in MS did not appear in 1871b or 1889a. Without the comma, *no matter what* is forced to modify *the kind of critical intelligence* in l. 1050, rendering the rest of the sen-tence (which ends in l. 1053) grammatically incomplete. With the comma, *no matter what* remains an interjection, allowing the more com-prehensible syntax *at the other there's . . . the kind of critical intelligence.* The MS reading is restored.

l. 1412-13: In MS and 1871b, a paragraph break appears at this point. The break disappeared as a result of a page division in 1889a; the MS-1871b reading is restored.

l. 1848: In MS this line ends with a dash, and in 1871b with a period to conclude the sentence begun in l. 1845; the punctuation disappeared in the copy-text. Though it is possible for the grammar of the sentence to carry over into the next line, rhetorically l. 1849 seems meant to be a sudden interjection. The 1871b reading is restored.

l. 1953: The MS has double quotation marks after *state!* and 1871b replaces these with a single quotation mark, but what is required is the combination of both. This paragraph break marks the end of Sagacity's speech, which began at l. 1924 and has concluded with a suggested explanation offered to the Ideal Prince. To close both this inner quotation and Sagacity's speech, the necessary single and double quotation marks have been inserted.

l. 2072: To mark the end of the Ideal Prince's final speech (which began at l. 2043) B provided ellipses and a rule, but no quotation marks, MS-1889a; the required double quotation marks are inserted.

l. 2144: In MS and 1871b, a paragraph break appears at this point. The break disappeared as a result of a page division in 1889a; the MS-1871b reading is restored.

Composition and Sources

Prince Hohenstiel-Schwangau, Saviour of Society had its origin in the sustained interest B and EBB took in the political career of the French Emperor Louis Napoleon Bonaparte (1808-73). Undoubtedly both poets had read much about Louis Napoleon long before they knew each other. His social activities, particularly his participation in the Eglinton Tournament of 1839, were widely reported during his exile in England in 1838-40. His attempted coup in 1840 and subsequent imprisonment at Ham were followed by English newspapers, and Mary Russell Mitford alluded to him in a letter to EBB of 2 March 1842 (*Correspondence*, 5.251).

Louis Napoleon became President of the French Assembly after the fall of Louis Philippe in 1848, and from that year onwards he was a frequent topic in both B's and EBB's letters. Since they, like other English liberals, hoped the new French Republic would thrive, Louis Napoleon's election as President seemed to be a step back toward empire. From their home in Florence they tried to grasp his motives in sending French troops to Rome in 1849 (*Letters of EBB*, 1.400, 406). In the end, the two poets declared the intervention a mistake, but disagreed on its meaning; EBB wrote:

It seems to me that he [Louis Napoleon] has given proof, as far as the evidence goes, of prudence, integrity, and conscientious patriotism . . . . The Rome business has been miserably managed; this is the great blot on the character of his government. But I, for my own part (my husband is not so minded), do consider that the French motive has been good, the intention pure.

(Letters of EBB, 1.419-20)

Sometimes their observations occurred at close range. On 2 December 1851, facing national elections in the coming year, Louis Napoleon executed a bold coup d'etat. The Bs, sojourning in Paris after a visit to London, witnessed the coup from their apartment on the Champs-Elysées; they could hear gunfire in the streets. EBB now saw Louis Napoleon as a liberal opponent of the monarchists (who had called for a royalist coup in 1850) and believed his promise that he would free Italy from Austrian domination. B's reservations about him deepened because of the violent repression of opponents that occurred before their eyes. Soon they found themselves in firm disagreement; EBB reported that "Robert and I have had some domestic émutes [demonstrations], because he hates some imperial names" (*Letters of EBB* 2.37). Some weeks later B wrote to George Barrett:

Is it not strange that Ba cannot take your view, not to say mine & most people's, of the President's proceedings? I cannot understand it—we differ in our appreciation of facts, too—things that admit of proof. I suppose the split happens in something like this way. We are both found agreeing on the difficulty of the position . . . [but] when Louis Napoleon is found to cut the knot instead of untying it—Ba approves—I demur. . . . [S]he will have it still that "they chose him"—and you return to my answer above, that denies the facts.

(Landis and Freeman, 169)

EBB's point was that shortly after the coup, a national plebiscite had ratified the Second Empire with eight million votes in Louis Napoleon's favor. With that fact established, he assumed the name Napoleon III.

Through the 1850s the Bs followed the Emperor's career with mixed admiration and exasperation. He repeatedly spoke of his wish that Italy might be delivered from Austrian hegemony, but his inability to move decisively turned B more strongly against him. When he finally did act in Italy, the French emperor did not cover himself in glory. In April of 1859 Napoleon III (with the connivance of Cavour; see l. 860n.) sent French troops into N. Italy in an attempt to drive out the Austrians. The initial successes of the French at Magenta and Solferino were ecstatically praised by EBB, rendering the sudden cessation of the war on 11 July all the more incomprehensible to her. She was shocked and affronted: "after all that walking on the clouds for weeks and months, and then the sudden stroke and fall, and the impotent rage against all the nations of the earth . . . who forced the hand of Napoleon, and truncated his great intentions" (*Letters of EBB* 2.320). Italy's ceding of Nice and Savoy to France shortly thereafter gave the appearance of a fee for service (see ll. 893-95, 1892-1903, and nn.), and brought about another argument in the B household. In the midst of a long diatribe against the English, EBB wrote John Forster that "Savoy has given me a pain . . . . I would rather not hear Robert say, for instance: 'It was a great action; but he has taken eighteenpence for it, which is a pity'" (*Letters of EBB* 2.385). EBB's exaltation over the French effort, and her rage at the nations that opposed it, were expressed in "Napoleon III in Italy" and "A Tale of Villafranca," collected in *Poems before Congress* (1860); her despair was recorded in "First News from Villafranca," which B included in EBB's *Last Poems*, published after her death.

It appears that B himself attempted to write something about Louis Napoleon in 1860, with a view toward a joint publication with EBB. Once before, in 1854, they had published jointly on a specific public issue; the pamphlet containing "The Twins" and "A Plea for the Ragged Schools of London" was created for sale at a charity bazaar organized by EBB's sister Arabel (see this edition, 6.117 and nn.). Around March 1860, EBB wrote to Sarianna Browning from Rome:

> Robert and I began to write on the Italian question together, and our plan was (Robert's own suggestion!) to publish jointly. When I showed him my ode on Napoleon he observed that I was gentle to England in comparison to what he had been, but after Villafranca (the Palmerston Ministry having come in) he destroyed his poem and left me alone, and I determined to stand alone. What Robert had written no longer suited the moment . . . .
>
> (*Letters of EBB* 2.368-69)

If B destroyed a poem, he did not discard everything he had thought and written down at the time. Years later, he was able to locate a bit of material that helped to generate *Prince Hohenstiel-Schwangau.* After his return to England following EBB's death in 1861, B kept a critical eye on Napoleon III, but made no direct references to him in print. Shortly after the Emperor's fall from power, however, B asserted that he still planned to write something about the Emperor's career. In January 1871, the minor poet Robert Buchanan asked permission to dedicate his long poem "Napoleon Fallen" to B. Though he refused the honor, B had no objection to Buchanan's harsh attack on Napoleon III: "I think more savagely now of the man, and should say so if needed. I wrote, myself, a monologue in his name twelve years ago, and never could bring the printing to my mind as yet. One day perhaps" (Hood, 145).

This suggests that B had kept a copy of an entire poem, one essentially ready for "the printing," but in other letters around the time of the composition of *Prince Hohenstiel-Schwangau* he was more precise about what he had at hand. Late in the summer of 1871, B and his son Pen took up residence at Milton House, a cottage on the Scottish estate of B's old American friend Ernest Benzon. Having just published *Balaustion's Adventure* in early August, B might have reasonably taken some time off from writing, but the subject of Louis Napoleon's rise and fall thrust itself upon him. He told Isa Blagden on 1 October 1871 about his burst of effort:

> I never at any time in my life turned a holiday into such
> an occasion of work: the quiet and seclusion were too tempting,—
> and, bringing with me a little sketch begun in *Rome in '60,*
> that I have occasionally fancied I should like to finish, or
> rather expand,—I have written about 1800 absolutely new lines
> or more, and shall have the whole thing out of hand by the
> early winter,—what *I* can't help thinking a sample of my very
> best work . . . .
>
> (McAleer, 367)

The above was written a day after he had noted on his MS at l. 1908: "Milton House, Glen Fincastle, Perths. / Sept.30 '71." This has the form of his typical commemorative end-notes, but it is unlikely that he thought the poem finished just then. The frame-story of the exiled Prince and "bud-mouthed arbitress" is incomplete, and the last voice heard in l. 1908 is the dreaming Prince's idealized projection of himself. Probably B broke off work in September and recorded his accomplishment so far, anticipating the sense of pride in his letter to Isa Blagden. The note is canceled in the MS, replaced a week later by one on the last leaf. What may be the poet's comment on his compositional method was noted by a guest of B's friend Benjamin Jowett, the Master of Balliol College, who was staying near Milton House; B is described as "perpetrating 'Hohenstiel Schwangau' at the rate of so many lines a day, neither more nor less" (quoted in McAleer, 366n.).

On the seventieth leaf of the Balliol MS (34a), near l. 2123 a few lines from the top of the page, B wrote in the R margin: "A few lines of the rough sketch written at Rome, 1860. Resumed, in the middle of August, and finished at Milton House, Glen Fincastle, Perthsh. Oct 7.71." This might suggest that B at one time considered ending his poem here, after the half-line "Feed on a lie." To stop here would distinctly be an artistically unsatisfactory conclusion, and there is immediate evidence that B did not consider this an end to *Prince Hohenstiel-Schwangau*. Had he finished at this point, most of the manuscript sheet would have remained for his concluding note; but instead of writing it below l. 2123, he had to shape it around the ends of ll. 2122-24. The remaining twenty-odd lines of the poem fill the rest of the sheet, right down to the bottom edge; the added l. 2145 occupies the middle of the R margin, and B's note is added above it, where some space remained when he completed his manuscript. The ink and handwriting of the note also suggest it was a later addition, and B's recollection was slightly in error: he left Milton House on 2 October for Loch Luichart, returning to London ten days later (P. Kelley and R. Hudson, comps., *The B's Correspondence: a Checklist* [N. Y., 1978], 496).

A few months later, writing to Edith Story, B described again the "little sketch" he worked from in composing *Prince Hohenstiel-Schwangau*. Having deprecated his subject ("What poetry can be in a sort of political satire?"), he recalled the old days with EBB in Rome:

> I really wrote—that is, conceived the poem, twelve years
> ago in the Via del Tritone—in a little handbreadth of
> prose,—now yellow with age and Italian ink,—which I
> breathed out into this full-blown bubble in a couple of
> months this autumn that is gone—thinking it fair to do so.
> (Hudson, 166, 167)

Prose, verse, monologue, or "rough sketch"—whatever the little document was, it is not known to have survived. By the time B sent the above account to Story, *Prince Hohenstiel-Schwangau* was in the shops, and he had begun writing *Fifine at the Fair.*

Text and Publication

The Balliol Manuscript The manuscript of *Prince Hohenstiel-Schwangau* preserved in the Balliol College Library consists of 70 leaves of lined paper. Though the binding of the MS has obscured the evidence, B apparently folded foolscap sheets into folios, composing on the resulting rectos and leaving the versos for additions, revisions, and trial readings. Such a practice would explain the page numbering of the Balliol MSS, in which alternating leaves (the first of each folio) bear numbers in B's hand. Whether this numbering was done as each fresh folio was begun or when the entire MS was completed is not obvious, but in doing it B seems to have skipped the fourteenth leaf (which should have borne the number 7), throwing off his sequence. He subsequently put the designation *6** on this page.

Overall the MS bears extensive revisions and a few sizeable insertions. Though it is usually apparent that the Browning MSS now at Balliol College were used as printers' copy, the matter is less clear in the case of *Prince Hohenstiel-Schwangau*. There are take-marks, used to estimate the printing job, on the opening leaves, but not throughout; no compositors' names or other typical printing-house marks appear either. In some of the heavily reworked passages, such as 551-55 and 2013-23, the MS would have presented serious difficulties to the compositors. Furthermore, there are enough differences between the MS and the first edition to hint at another stage of composition. It was not uncommon for B to add new lines and completely re-write others during proofing, but the amount of this sort of revision in *Prince Hohenstiel-Schwangau* is greater than normal. It may be that in this instance B (or his sister Sarianna) made a fair copy of the poem for the printers, and that further revisions were made on it. In any case, the Balliol MS is the record of the poem's composition, and it shows all the signs of the speed with which B worked.

The MS title-page leaf bears the epigraph from Euripides, and on the verso B wrote three and a half lines of Greek vertically at the L margin. The passage, undoubtedly an alternative candidate for the epigraph to *Prince Hohenstiel-Schwangau*, is a quotation from Pindar's second Olympian Ode, ll. 15-18 (Greek text and translation from W. H. Race, ed. and tr., *Pindar* [London, 1997], 64-65.):

τῶν δὲ πεπραγμένων
ἐν δίκᾳ τε καὶ παρὰ δίκαν ἀποίητον οὐδ᾽ ἂν Χρόνος ὁ πάντων
πατὴρ δύναιτο θέμεν ἔργων τέλος.
λάθα δὲ πότμῳ σὺν εὐδαίμονι γένοιτ᾽ ἄν.

Once deeds are done,
whether in justice or contrary to it, not even
Time, the father of all, could undo their outcome.
But with a fortunate destiny forgetfulness may result.

In revising, B added paragraph breaks at many points throughout the MS where the lines as composed ran continuously. With a horizontal line and/or a marginal note, B called for paragraphs at ll. 111, 230, 253, 287, 376, 390, 432, 440, 555, 613, 649, 706, 806, 902, 935, 1112, 1162, 1200, 1214, 1231, 1232, 1410, 1413, 1475, 1597, 1731, 1853, 1908, 2033, 2043, 2072, and 2123. All but seven of these (at ll. 432, 649, 902, 935, 1112, and 1475, 2033) appeared in the copy-text, and only the latter, being genuine variants, are recorded in the variant listings.

At the end of the MS appear the four letters that become a regular feature in the Balliol MSS: "L. D. I. E.," standing for *Laus Deo in excelsis*, "Praise God in the highest," the poet's expression of thanks that his labor is completed.

The First English Edition (1871b)   Either the Balliol MS or a fair copy made from it (see above) was used to set up the first English edition of *Prince Hohenstiel-Schwangau* in late 1871; on 8 November B wrote to Isa Blagden that he had finished proofing and would that day deliver the MS to Smith, Elder (McAleer, 369). The book was advertised in the *Athenaeum* on 2 December as "nearly ready" and on the 16th as available on the following Monday, 18 December 1871. Between the surviving MS and the first publication, B expanded his poem by sixteen lines, most of them in the last quarter of the work. The 2146 lines in the first edition were leaded out generously—to 15 lines in the page—to make up a volume of 148 pages.

The poem was met by a burst of hostile criticism, much of it betraying the reviewers' bafflement at the multiple narrative voices and the dreaming-and-waking frame story. Many commentators fell back on their own or their publications' political views, and condemned *Prince Hohenstiel-Schwangau* accordingly. It was "an offensive impertinence" to the *Illustrated London News* (13 January 1872, 35), a "glorification of Napoleon III" to the *Edinburgh Review* (135 [January-

April 1872]: 113), and a "frightful absurdity" to *The Times* (2 January 1872, 5). Rejecting all criticism, B thought it was "just what I thought the man might, if he pleased, say for himself" (McAleer, 372). He also took some pride in the initial success of the new volume with buyers: 1400 copies were sold in the first five days (McAleer, 371). The topical nature of the subject had something to do with this, as did the surprising public enthusiasm for *Balaustion's Adventure* in the autumn of 1871.

It is probable that the first edition consisted of about 1500 copies, some of which were still available seventeen years later, listed in the advertisements at the back of several volumes of 1888-89. There was no announced second edition or impression, and none has been detected through collation. By the summer of 1872, B and his audience had moved on to *Fifine at the Fair*.

Collected Editions   The preparation of the eleventh volume of the 1888-89 *Poetical Works* offered B his sole occasion to revise and correct *Prince Hohenstiel-Schwangau*. He made one major change, adding nine lines near the end (ll. 2135-43) to clear up an erroneous allusion the Prince had created in ll. 1986-2019. See ll. 1986-2019n., 2002-6n., and 2141n. Beyond this, B made several dozen small but careful revisions in spelling, punctuation, and word choice.

Title]   P-C and others propose that *Hohenstiel-Schwangau* derives from the name of Hohenschwangau castle in Bavaria, a famous fantasy of a romantic fortress built by King Ludwig II of Bavaria. DeVane (*Hbk.*, 359) reports a possibility that the title was suggested by William Cartwright, an old friend of B's from his days in Rome in the 1850s and 1860s. But *Hohenstiel-Schwangau* may also glance at related (and similarly tongue-twisting) German names, such as Hohenlohe-Schillings-fürst, the Bavarian prime minister who repelled attempts by Napoleon III to form an alliance against Prussia; Leopold of Hohenzollern-Sigmaringen, claimant to the Spanish throne; and the Schleswig-Holstein question, a much-vexed European territorial dispute which Napoleon III tried to influence.

Subtitle]   At the time of the coup d'etat in 1851, Louis Napoleon was hailed by his supporters as "the savior of society."

Epigraph]   The Greek epigraph quotes lines 1276-80 of Euripides' *Herakles* (sometimes titled *The Madness of Herakles*), from the hero's lamentation on waking from madness to find that he has killed his wife and children. The second of Herakles' twelve labors was to kill the *Hydra*, a multi-headed poisonous snake. B's rereading of Euripides in 1870-71 had already prompted him to write *Balaustion's Adventure* (1871), and this epigraph is freighted with ironic links to the character of Prince Hohenstiel-Schwangau and his original. Louis Napoleon had come to power by winning the confidence of the populace (figured as the slaying of the many-headed Hydra), pressed forward with numerous public works to enhance the technological, economic, and military standing of France ("tribes of labours"), but failed at last in his attempt to make imperial France the dominant power on the continent. Despite EBB's ardent admiration for Louis Napoleon, B always felt there was something false about the man, and suggesting that Prince Hohenstiel-Schwangau would portray himself as Herakles must be seen as pointedly sardonic. An additional ironic resonance issues from B's phrasing in the last line of his translation: in a speech to the Assembly in 1853, Napoleon III asserted that though repressive measures were necessary for the moment, soon liberty would "crown the edifice" of the new society he was building. In the British press, this became a jeering catchphrase used for years to mock Louis Napoleon's occasional gestures toward restoring personal liberties in France. See also *Text and Publication: The Balliol Manuscript* above for B's alternative epigraph.

1]   *better days, dear? So have I*   As we learn at the very end of his monologue (ll. 2072 ff.), Prince Hohenstiel-Schwangau has not yet suffered his fall. Though he was a ruthlessly practical politician and a lover of luxury, Napoleon III portrayed himself as an idealist and thinker on the grand scale. Correspondingly, B makes his Prince a dreamer whose fantasy consists of fleshly pleasures and an opportunity for self-justification. As Louis Napoleon maintained an enduring liason with the English courtesan Harriet Howard, so Prince Hohenstiel-Schwangau dreams of a pick-up in Leicester Square. (See J. Bierman, *Napoleon III and His Carnival Empire* [N. Y., 1988], 54-58.)

6-8]   *Oedipus . . . Sphynx*   In the myth of Oedipus, the monstrous Sphinx of Thebes killed all those she encountered who could not answer her riddle: "What walks on four legs in the morning, on two at noon, and on three in the evening?" Oedipus, traveling from Corinth, answered the riddle correctly ("a man"), upon which the Sphinx hurled herself off a cliff. Ocdipus went on to become the husband of Jocasta and king of Thebes; the best-known version of the myth is *Oedipus Tyrannus* by Sophocles. Albert Guerard notes of Louis Napoleon that "at the height of his power they called him the Sphinx of the Tuileries; when he failed, there were many to declare with Bismark that he was a sphinx without a secret" (*Napoleon III* [Cambridge, MA, 1943], xiv).

7]   *pork-pie hat and crinoline*   Assuming that the "present" of the poem is 1868 (see l. 21n. below), the Prince imagines his interlocutrix dressed in faded fashions. Pork-pie hats became popular in France in the 1850s and were the mode in England by the 1860s, but by 1868 womens' hats were becoming much more elaborate. The rage for crinolines peaked around 1860, and though the fashion continued through the decade, it came to a swift end with the fall of the Second Empire.

8]   *Leicester Square*   Setting the poem's frame-story in London's Leicester Square has two significances: the area around Leicester Square was long a refuge for foreign exiles, Louis Napoleon himself having been exiled in London in the 1840s; and Leicester Square was a likely place for the Prince to have picked up his companion for the evening.

11]   *riddle's proper rede*   Offering the meaning "solution," *OED* lists only this usage by B as sense 7.c of *rede*; it was used similarly in *The Ring and the Book*, 10.227 (see this edition, 9.80)

14]   *Home's . . . medium-ware*   This is, in B's lexicon, the utterly fraudulent. Daniel Dunglas Home was the spiritualist medium attacked as "Mr. Sludge, 'The Medium,'" in *Dramatis Personæ* (see this edition, 6.285ff. and nn.), and the poet contended that he had caught Home cheating in a seance. Mechanical devices, including *stilts and tongs*, were used by Victorian mediums to produce spiritualist phenomena such as levitation, hovering hands, floating objects, and moving tables.

16]   *sands*   The sand in the lower half of an hourglass.

19] *Bright . . . Laïs*   In ancient Greece, Corinth was the only rival to Athens in sophistication and taste; its name eventually became synonymous with luxury. Thebes, N of Athens in Boeotia, was more rustic; when Oedipus fled Corinth and became king of Thebes, he moved to a lesser place. Laïs was a name used by several celebrated courtesans in ancient Greece, and B had encountered references to the original Laïs (called "the Corinthian") in Plutarch and Pausanias when he was composing *Balaustion's Adventure*   (Plutarch, *Lives*, "Nicias," 15; "Alcibiades," 39; Pausanias, 2.2.4).

20]   *hardly grey . . . likes my nose*   Probably B knew that Louis Napleon's vanities included corsets, dyed hair, and facial cosmetics; the Emperor also had a large, Gallic nose, often exaggerated in Victorian cartoons of the emperor.

21]   *man of sixty*   Louis Napoleon was born in 1808 and came to power in 1848; if the Prince shares that birthday, he would be sixty years old in 1868, having ruled for twenty years, as he later states he has. Thus B has him dreaming of exile two years before the Second

Empire collapsed in 1870. Such a date is certainly appropriate, since most of the monologue is a dream-projection by the Prince of what life might be like if he fell from power (see ll. 474, 511, and 2072-2155, where the Prince wakes); but the time-line of the poem is less than exact, as possible allusions in ll. 137-38 and 2150-55 show.

40] *Fitter . . . let alone* Though B considered Napoleon III an inveterate meddler in European affairs, the emperor's admirers sometimes called him "Saint-Simon on horseback," alluding to the positivist philosopher Claude Henri Saint-Simon (1760-1825). Saint-Simon was a socialist who proposed vast public works projects; Napoleon III was politically conservative, but he initiated the construction of roads, railroads, canals, bridges, communications networks, and housing. See ll. 79-84 and 678-79 for other expressions of this view, and l. 1672 and n. for another allusion to the Emperor's projects..

44] *moustache* Napoleon III's mustache and beard were so distinctive as to generate their own name: the Imperial.

48-49] *Euclid . . . circle* In the geometry of the ancient Greek mathematician Euclid, manipulation and measurement of simple shapes is easily understood; however, it is impossible to draw a square and a circle with the exact same area (because pi is a transcendental number).

59] *quadrature* The squaring of the circle, as impossible as determining "'What the whole man meant'" (l. 60).

70] *mind's eye* From *Hamlet*, 1.1.112 and 1.2.185. The first of several references to the play; see also ll. 450, 1595 and nn.

74] *somebody in Thrace* Possibly the Greek philosopher Democritus (460-c.357 B. C.), who was born in Thrace (P-C). Democritus used his mind's eye to imagine the fine structure of nature in developing the atomic theory of matter.

133] *Residenz* The German term for the state home of a ruler or governor.

135] *Galvanically . . . play* A dead muscle can be made to contract by applying a small electric current to it; the effect is known as Galvanism (after Luigi Galvani [1737-98], who discovered it). Galvanism is often used to demonstrate to students the electrical component of neural activity and muscle action, and B may have seen a demonstration of it when he attended lectures on physiology in his youth (Maynard, 101).

137-38] *last July . . . Message for me* The specification of the month hints at a reference to the provocative exchanges between Napoleon III and King Wilhelm of Prussia in July, 1870, which culminated in the outbreak of the Franco-Prussian War. Such a date conflicts with other details in the poem (see l. 21n. above), yet a similar connection between the communiques of 1870 and Prince Hohenstiel-Schwangau's reverie (and its aftermath) is suggested in ll. 2150-55.

150-52] *Sticks to . . . wayside* The imaginary messenger's progress recalls that of Childe Roland; see this edition, 5.248, 1-16.

174] *Wreaking* Bestowing (*OED*, s.v. *wreak*, sense II.3.d); B had used the term similarly in *Sordello*, 6.493.

186] *Pradier Magdalen* The female nudes sculpted by Jean-Jacques Pradier (1790-1852) combine sensuality and modesty to achieve a distinctly 19th-century kind of eroticism. Pradier was very popular in his time, specializing in nudes on subjects from classical mythology. His work was frequently exhibited in Paris, where B could have seen it; a contemporary guide to the Louvre describes Pradier as "so very remarkable in the delineation of female beauty in the purely sensual charm of its attractions" (H. O'Shea, *Galleries of the Louvre* [Paris, 1874]). There is no record of a statue of Mary Magdalen by Pradier (contra P-C); what B suggests is that if Pradier had done a Magdalen (whom legend holds to be a reformed prostitute), the figure would display a mixture of piety and lubricity.

188] *owl's-wing aigrette* An owl's wing on her hat would befit the Prince's companion, since she too is a bird of the night.

196] *grim guardian* Policeman.

197] *quarter-day* The day beginning a quarter of the year, upon which accounts were settled and rents collected.

221] *fruits to judge* Alluding to Matt. 7:20, "by their fruits ye shall know them."

223] *Lives of me* From 1840 to 1870 nearly a hundred volumes about Louis Napoleon appeared in France and England.

280] *stabilify* "To make stable" (*OED*, the present instance being the only cited usage of the word).

308] *plaster-monarch on his steed* From 1747 until 1874, an equestrian statue of George I stood in the center of Leicester Square.

328] *leavening the lump* From 1 Cor. 5:6, "Know ye not that a little leaven leaveneth the whole lump?"

330-37] *Where winter . . . outburst* The idea that glaciation had produced extreme changes in the Earth's climate was proposed by Louis Agassiz in 1837 and was accepted as fact by the 1860s. With *star-change* B alludes to the theory that glaciation itself was the result of astronomical events, a hypothesis put forth in the 1860s by the geologist James Croll.

350-51] *dervish . . . lyrist* The list of heroic types is parallel to the figures in Carlyle's *On Heroes and Hero-Worship* (1841), the desert-spectre being Mohammed; the swordsman, Napoleon I; the saint, Luther or Knox; the law-giver, Cromwell; and the lyrist, Dante or Shakespeare.

B himself had created his own parallel (and less conventional) list of heroes: the arab leader Djabel in *Return of the Druses* (1843); the warriors Childe Roland and Saul in *Men and Women* (1855); St. John in "A Death in the Desert," in *Dramatis Personæ* (1864); the statesman Thomas Wentworth in *Strafford* (1837); and poets such as Sordello (1840) and David ("Saul," *Men and Women* [1855]).

384] *dabster* Normally the word means "expert"; perhaps by association with *dabbler*, B gives it a sarcastic reversal to "meddler." The *OED* cites this instance as a deprecatory use of the word.

399] *crooked . . . smooth* Adapted from Isaiah 40:4; in preparation for the Messiah, "the crooked shall be made straight, and the rough places plain."

439] *Fourier, Comte* François Fourier (1772-1837), an early socialist philosopher, proposed that nation-states should be broken up into self-sufficient, independent communal groups. The positivist philosopher Auguste Comte (1798-1857) influenced numerous social thinkers of the 19th century, including Taine, Renan, and Mill. Comte's advocacy of universal education, rights for women, and the redistribution of wealth could hardly be said to end in smoke; these ideas so disturbed the conservative Napoleon III that he had Comte removed from his position at the Institut Polytechnique in 1853.

450] *toe . . . kibe* Echoing Hamlet's "the toe of the peasant comes so near the heel of the courtier, he galls his kibe" (5.1.140-41).

510-11] *each adventurer / Upon this 'sixty, Anno Domini* The Prince at first appears to be giving the normal human life-span as sixty years, which happens to be his own age (see l. 21n. above). The apostrophe before *sixty* and the words *Anno Domini*, however, indicate a reference to the year 1860. The poem is set in 1868, but B had first sketched it out in 1860, and it is possible that the line is a survival from the first draft (see *Composition and Sources* above). If that is the case, the passage means not "everyone who lives" but "everyone who is alive now" (in 1860).

517-55] *"O littleness . . . done with!"* The target of this satire has been taken as Byron, because of a rhetorically similar passage in *Childe Harold's Pilgrimage* (4.175-184, ll. 1570-1656); but it would be more in character for Louis Napoleon to mock his old opponent Victor Hugo, as proposed by P-C. Hugo's "Song of the Ocean," in *Les Châtiments* (1853) is similar in tone and sentiment to the orations of the Prince's bard. B's pastiche also echoes the sort of moralizing about the pettiness of humanity that is plentiful in Pope's *Essay on Man* (1733-34); the fly and worm of l. 515 appear appropriately in Epistle I, and the "Middle State" of Epistle II may be alluded to in ll. 568-69.

539] *Bond Street* A synecdoche for the citified audience to whom the bard condescended in his preceding speech; London's Bond Street has long been the site of numerous expensive, sophisticated shops.

545-46] *Wake up . . . in England* Victor Hugo, A. C. Swinburne, and other poets dreamed of agitating the English into open hostility toward Napoleon III; but six Prime Ministers inclined toward Queen Victoria's policy of maintaining a wary amicability between England and France.

551] *mane* With pun on *main*, the ocean, and echoing Byron's image of the sea as a horse (*Childe Harold's Pilgrimage*, 4.184, l.1656)

568-69] *a little lower . . . glory-crowned* Adapted from Ps. 8:5

581-88] *earth's best . . . art Thou!"* The Prince seems to be confusing Euclid (see ll. 48-49 n. above), who collected the sum of plane geometry in his *Elements*, with Plato, who Plutarch says called God a geometer (*Moralia*, "Symposiacs," 8.2). In the *Timaeus* dialogue, Plato's account of creation (30-38) describes the original earth and cosmos in terms of perfect Euclidean shapes, lines, and angles. B had alluded to the remark in Plutarch in *Christmas-Eve and Easter-Day* (1850); see this edition, 5.85, l.1003; 5.99, ll. 91-92; and nn.

612] *save society* See *Subtitle* n. above.

629-31] *a chemist . . . white forsooth* The chemical metaphor is in character because Louis Napoleon was an enthusiastic amateur chemist.

678-79] *he has . . . worked well* An echo of Carlyle's language in the conclusion to *Sartor Resartus*.

698] *architect* The word was capitalized in the MS, making it plainer that the Prince views the existing social order as of divine origin.

715-21] *the mightier . . . Oeta's top* The eleventh labor of Herakles required the hero to retrieve the golden apples of the Hesperides, daughters of Atlas, the Titan who supports the sky. Atlas offered to get the golden apples if Herakles took his place for a day; on his return, Atlas refused to reassume his duty, but was tricked into it by Herakles. (The origin of the common belief that Atlas holds up the earth, not the sky, is uncertain.) As a Titan, Atlas is immortal, but Herakles died a painful death, consumed by his funeral pyre on top of Mt. Oeta.

740-45] *Oh those . . . only live* This image of the starving multitude haunts *Prince Hohenstiel-Schwangau*, appearing again in ll. 907-11, 971-73, and 1492. By granting his character such sympathy, B gives credit to Napoleon III for his dedication to improving the lot of France's farmers and peasants.

781] *the Rights of Man* The adoption of the Declaration of the Rights of Man and of the Citizen by the French National Assembly in

October, 1789, was a key event at the beginning of the French Revolution.

782]   *Proudhon*   Though he originated a famous slogan ("Property is theft!") immortalized by socialists and communists, Pierre Joseph Proudhon (1809-65) was a vocal supporter of private enterprise and individual capitalism, which the Prince takes as tending toward anarchy.

787]   *the Great Nation*   In French politics, *La Grande Nation* is an oratorical cliché for "France."

843]   *"Be Italy again"*   For Napoleon III and the cause of Italian liberation, see *Sources* above.

847]   *the greybeards*   That is, Pope Pius IX and the College of Cardinals. In the early 1840s, Pius IX allied himself with reform movements, but his deep conservatism came to the fore after the revolutions of 1848. The Roman Catholic Church was a reactionary force in Italian politics, as is indicated by Pius IX's 1864 encyclical *Quanta Cura*, which contained a "Syllabus of Errors" denouncing liberal ideas in politics, morals, and theology.

853]   *plaster-patch . . . adieu*   B refers to the vast series of seventeen frescoes on the walls of the Stanze della Segnatura in the Vatican Palace, executed between 1508 and 1511 by Raphael (Raffaello Sanzio, 1483-1520). These and many other famous Renaissance works of art were decaying in the 19th century, and B lamented this often (see "Old Pictures in Florence," in *Men and Women, Volume II*, this edition, 5.24-36 and nn.).

860]   *free Church . . . state*   "A free church in a free state" was a catchphrase used by Camillo Cavour (1810-61), prime minister of Piedmont and an architect of Italian unity. The phrase became a slogan for all who opposed Austrian control in Italy.

875]   *altogether . . . as you*   The Prince appropriates the reproving words of God to the Israelites in Ps. 50:21.

862-65]   *its embodiment . . . hearts*   In plan view, Bernini's colonnades on the east face of St. Peter's basilica in the Vatican look like pincers.

883-86]   *we find . . . greybeards*   A reference to the presence of French troops in Rome to protect the Pope from Italian nationalists. In 1849, Pius IX made a promise to Louis Napoleon to liberalize the governance of the papal states in central Italy, in exchange for which promise French troops were dispatched to defend Rome against the patriotic uprising led by Giuseppe Mazzini and Giuseppe Garibaldi. The Pope soon proved no liberal, but the French army stayed in Rome for decades, putting Napoleon III in the position of opposing the Italian patriots he claimed to favor.

887]   *Judas*   I. e., the Prince, taking Judas Iscariot as the emblem of treachery.

890-92]   *power to speak . . . cool Cayenne*   Napoleon III imposed strict censorship on the press for many years, and his enforcement methods were harsh. Between the coup of December, 1851, and February, 1852, some 8500 suspected enemies of the new regime were sent to penal colonies in Algeria, most without trials. More than 200 incorrigible opponents of Napoleon III were transported to Devil's Island, the torrid prison camp at Cayenne in French Guyana.

893-95]   *The universal vote . . . universal Prefect*   Having expanded the government bureaucracy to an unprecedented size, Louis Napoleon used it as an efficient means to mobilize popular opinion in his favor. French prefects supervised the plebiscites in Nice and Savoy of 1860, in which the citizens of the two districts voted themselves out of Italy and into France (see ll. 1892-1903 and nn.).

897-99]   *his soul . . . somewhere*   In Matt. 4:4 and Luke 4:4, Jesus says to the devil, "Man shall not live by bread alone," echoing Deut. 8:3.

922]   *baulk*   Deprive (*OED*, s.v. *balk*, sense 2.c).

934]   *Barabbas*   The agitator and murderer whom the mob asked Pilate to set free instead of Jesus (Matt. 27:16-22, Mark 15:6-13).

987-91]   *That mass . . . but one*   B's earliest use of this evolutionist transformation of the Great Chain of Being can be found in *Paracelsus* (1835). His thinking was as much influenced by pre-Darwinian writings such as the *Bridgewater Treatises* (1833-40), R. Chambers's *Vestiges of Creation* (1844), and W. Paley's *A View of the Evidences of Christianity* (1794) as by the *Origin of Species* (1859) itself. Similar uses of evolution-as-metaphor occur in "Caliban upon Setebos" and *Fifine at the Fair*, and the "Parleying with Francis Furini" contains a complex address to "evolutionists" (see this edition, 16.81-91 and nn.).

995]   *ruled the roast*   To *rule the roast* is to have complete control or authority; this version of the catchphrase precedes its common bucolic equivalent, "rule the roost," by several centuries and was the standard idiom in the 19th century.

998]   *Practice as exile*   Until Louis Napoleon was elected to the French Assembly in 1848, he spent much more time outside France than in it. A second sense of *practice*, to plot or scheme, has ironic application: while he was in exile, Louis Napoleon was usually planning some way of returning to France to seize power.

1004]   *embryo potentate*   The 19th century was fascinated by the embryological studies of Ernst Haeckel, which suggested that ontology (the development of an individual) recapitulates the stages of phylogeny (the evolution of the phylum). The Prince's notion of being educated as a ruler by rising through the social ranks owes something to this developmental hypothesis, but also harkens back to Shakespeare's Prince Hal (*1* and *2 Henry 4*) and beyond that to Thomas Aquinas's observations on kingship.

1022]   *mollusc*   Used figuratively to indicate an early phylogenetic stage on the evolutionary path toward mammals.

1029-35]   *the Persian . . . apparel*   The origin of this tale about the King of Persia and his admiration of a tree is in Herodotus (*Histories*, 7.31), but B's version is closer to that found in Daniello Bartoli's *De' Simboli Transportati al Morale* (1684). B knew Bartoli's book well in the edition of the *Simboli* published in 1830 by his Italian tutor, and he carried it with him on his journeys to Italy in 1838 and 1844 (Maynard, 304, 306; Irvine and Honan, 76; see also *Reconstruction*, A167, A168). Bartoli, giving his source for the anecdote as the Roman historian Aelian, specifies that Xerxes' army stopped for an entire day and provides details of the gold ornaments and jewels hung on the tree (Bartoli, *Opere* [Roma, 1684] 3.4, 760). The incident is also alluded to by John Donne in Elegy 15: "The Autumnal."

1056]   *height . . . breadth*   A curious (perhaps unconscious) echo of the second line of EBB's Sonnet XLIII in *Sonnets from the Portuguese*.

1108-11]   *Kant . . . Pure Reason*   Immanuel Kant (1724-1804), German idealist philosopher; his most famous work was *The Critique of Pure Reason* (1781). Both philosopher and book are used here as the epitome of abstract, impractical thought, of no use to *Hans Slouch*, whose name (like the English "Hodge") is emblematic of the peasantry. In the first MS version of l. 1108, B had the German poet Heinrich Heine (1797-1856) as the Prince's example of an intellectual.

1131-32]   *ignorance . . . uncharitableness*   Drawn from "The Litany" in the *Book of Common Prayer*.

1145]   *Terni*   A town in central Italy near the spectacular waterfalls of the Velino river, the Cascata delle Marmore. The Bs visited Terni on their way to Rome in November 1853.

1150]   *Kant understands . . . well*   Though Kant was not overtly hostile to religion, his philosophy implied a species of moral rationalism that outraged orthodox Christians. In 1792, the government of Frederick Wilhelm II attempted to block publication of Kant's book *On Religion within the Boundaries of Pure Reason*, extracting from him a promise that he would no longer lecture or write on religious subjects.

1157]   *time . . . long*   Prince Hohenstiel-Schwangau's ironic version of a proverb (familiar in the Latin tag, *ars longa, vita brevis*) with origins at least as old as the *Aphorisms* of Hippocrates (460-377 B. C.). A few years before *Prince Hohenstiel-Schwangau* B had used the proverb in *The Ring and the Book*, 9.1449 (see this edition, 9.63).

1184-89] *statue . . . Laocoön . . . gesture* Laocoön, a Trojan prince and priest of Apollo, warned the leaders of Troy not to bring the huge Greek wooden horse (inside which were hidden Odysseus and his warriors) into their city. After giving his warning, Laocoön and his sons were attacked and killed by two snakes, an event which prompted the Trojans to bring in the horse and thus engender their own destruction. The Prince refers to a famous statuary group in the Vatican that portrays Laocoön in his death agonies. This work, carved in Rhodes about 25 B. C., was deemed by Pliny the Elder to be the greatest work of art ever created; it was well-known to B. The Vatican Laocoön includes the sons and the snakes, and if B alludes to an actual veiling of the "accessories," the experiment seems to have gone unrecorded elsewhere.

1216] *ceiling-rose* A plaster medallion in the center of the ceiling.

1223] *Thiers . . . exercise* Both Adolphe Thiers (1797-1877) and Victor Hugo (1802-85) vehemently opposed Napoleon III, and both were exiled for their pains. Thiers made a reputation as a popular, if not particularly reliable, historian of the French Revolution and the Napoleonic era. Later, as a conservative member of the Assembly, Theirs supported Louis Napoleon in 1848; as the President made his ambitions to imperial power more evident, Thiers turned against him. He was escorted out of France after the coup of 1851, but soon he was back in the Assembly as the leader of a small anti-imperial faction. Prince Hohenstiel-Schwangau uses Thiers as the emblem of his critics on the political right. To represent the leftists he chooses Hugo, whose loyalty to the Bonaparte name had led him to support Louis Napoleon initially. As Louis Napoleon's policies became more authoritarian, Hugo reversed his position, finally fleeing the country at the time of the coup. Hugo took up residence on the isle of Guernsey, producing a stream of anti-Napoleonic poems and essays like *Napoleon le Petit* (1852) and *Histoire d'un Crime* (1877); he too returned to France as a hero after Napoleon III fell.

1234-39] *chose the Assembly . . . vacate his place* A description of Louis Napoleon's rise to power and his position in 1851, as his term as president neared its end.

1247-49] *not one minute . . . Head away* Louis Napoleon took as justification for his coup the widespread fear that anarchy and bloodshed would follow his departure from the Presidency. If he did not openly promote the public's fears, he also made no effort to counter them.

1254-59] *this to Pope . . . whole and sole*   A list of the factions in the French Assembly in 1851, including the Ultramontane clergy, the Royalists (both Bourbon and Orleanist), the Socialists, and the Bonapartists.

1262] *Hohenstiel-Schwangau*   As in l. 1233, the name here indicates the country, not the man.

1285] *crowned*   The word presents a double irony by referring both to the "crowning of the edifice" in the epigraph and to the crowning of Napoleon III as emperor.

1304] *anticize*   The *OED* cites only B's use of the word, defined as "To play antics, sport grotesquely."

1328] *Man's Adversary*   Satan, whose name in Hebrew means "the adversary"; see Job 1:7, 1 Peter 5:8.

1363] *unstridulosity*   Calm silence; *OED* lists only this instance.

1364] *stroke of state*   The literal translation of French *coup d'etat*.

1371-72] *Dock . . . at once*   In 1850, opponents of Louis Napoleon managed to pass a strict residency requirement for voters. They hoped that the resulting disenfranchisement of over three million citizens would weaken popular support for Louis Napoleon in future elections and plebiscites. The law was repealed by imperial order shortly after the coup of 1851.

1450] *Sagacity*   As B uses the word, it is stripped of the positive connotation "wisdom" and means "craftiness" or "shrewdness."

1558] *Brennus*   In 390 B. C., the military leader Brennus brought an army of Celtic Gauls to the walls of Rome, destroying a Roman army of 40,000 men along the way. Unable to take the fortified citadel on top of the Capitoline hill by direct assault, the Gauls tried to climb up the rocky cliffs at night. As they neared the top, the sacred geese in the temple of Juno awakened a Roman guard, who pushed the first of Brennus's men back over the edge. Many years earlier B had alluded to this story in *Sordello* (3.587-92; see this edition, 2.213); he probably found it in Livy's *History of Rome* (5.47-48).

1568] *try conclusions*   A Shakespearean locution meaning "make experiments"; see *Hamlet*, 3.4.195, *Merchant of Venice*, 2.2.37

1581] *free State . . . free Church*   See l. 860n. above.

1595] *compliance . . . teat*   Hamlet says that the loquacious courtier Osric "did comply, sir, with his dug before 'a suck'd it" (*Hamlet*, 5.2.187-88).

1604-5] *self-conceit . . . wing*   The image may look back to numerous cartoons in *Punch* which portrayed Napoleon III as a drunken cock.

1608-13] *champion-armour . . . fighter yet*   Napoleon III frequently resorted to military bluster in his dealings with other nations. Though he had little military experience, the Emperor was fond of appearing in a general's uniform, and he repeatedly unsettled European affairs by ordering new weapons and building gun ships.

1632-33]   *peace . . . new war*   This cynical commonplace appears in Machiavelli (*The Prince*, 14), Hobbes (*Leviathan*, 1.4), and Burke (*Vindication of Natural Society* 1.15), among others.

1672]   *boulevard-building . . . theatre*   Napoleon III ordered the rebuilding of much of Paris; under the direction of his master planner Georges Haussmann, thoroughfares were widened, new streets created, parks established, and government buildings erected. Among the grandest projects was the Paris Opera, begun in 1861 and still unfinished when Napoleon III fell from power.

1696]   *Terror on her vantage-coign*   A period (1793-94) of violent government repression in the latter stages of the French Revolution was known as the Reign of Terror. A *vantage-coign* is an elevated position useful for observation; the words mirror *Macbeth* 1.6.7, "coign of vantage."

1697]   *the powers of air*   Borrowing from the Bible and Milton, B habitually refers to Satan as "the prince of the powers of the air"; see also l. 2120. He had applied the phrase to Guido in *The Ring and the Book*, 1.561, 591 (this edition, 7.561, 591).

1730]   *Hohenstiel . . . peace*   Napoleon III often used the slogan "L'Empire, c'est la paix" ("The Empire is peace") in his speeches.

1759-68]   *Oh Glory,—gilded bubble . . . thou art*   The imagery and diction of this overdone speech closely parallel a passage on fame in *The Ring and the Book*, 12.636-41 (see this edition, 9.275-76). More distantly, the skepticism about military glory may echo Jacques' characterization of the soldier, "seeking the bubble reputation" (*As You Like It*, 2.7.152).

1841-42]   *build bridge . . . tunnel*   Among other reasons, Napoleon III wanted control over the Savoy district so that he could use French capital and French labor to build the Mont Cenis railroad tunnel between France and Italy. See also ll. 1892-1903 and nn.

1856-59]   *beat the sword . . . fig-tree*   Echoing Micah 4:3-4: "they shall beat their swords into ploughshares, and their spears into pruning hooks: nation shall not lift up a sword against nation, neither shall they learn war any more. / But they shall sit every man under his vine and his fig tree" (see also Isaiah 2:4 and Zech. 3:10).

1877-84]   *Austria's rule . . . bad day*   Control over Italy, particularly the northern states, was disputed among several nations and ruling houses for centuries. In the second half of the 19th century, Austria and France were the main contenders, with the Austrians gaining the upper hand during the French Revolution. Napoleon I set out to liberate Italy from the Austrians, taking over Genoa by political means and occupying Rome with troops. After the climactic battle of Marengo in 1800, Napoleon imposed a legal and political reorganization on Italy along French administrative lines. Eventually French control extended over much of the country, and many Italian men were conscripted into Napoleon's armies. But in 1813, as a consequence of their victory over Napoleon at Leipzig, the Austrians were able to recover their power in Italy, where they and their agents remained for decades.

1892-1903] *All for nought . . . marketable value* Napoleon III followed Sagacity's advice in the war of 1859 (see *Sources* above). He had long wanted control of Nice in order to fortify it, and the most favorable railroad route between Paris and Turin lay through Savoy; but Savoy and Nice were under Piedmontese dominion. In the summer of 1858, Napoleon III and Cavour, the Piedmontese prime minister, met secretly to plan a war and arrange the eventual concession of the two territories to France. The French military intervention in Italy the following year was cloaked in noble ideals, but its goals were strictly material and political. Less than three months after declaring war on Austria, despite two French victories in the field, the Emperor suddenly ended the war. The Treaty of Villafranca (11 July 1859) gave Lombardy to the Piedmont, and Nice and Savoy to France; the French paid off the Piedmontese war debts as well.

1904] *Metternich* The reference is probably to both Clemens Lothar Metternich (1773-1859) and his son Richard (1829-95), either of whom might stand figuratively for ruthless political cunning. The elder Metternich was chancellor of Austria during the reign of Napoleon I; he was responsible for the treaties of Vienna (1815), which consolidated Austrian power at France's expense. Richard Metternich was the Austrian ambassador to France from 1859 to 1870; he was a close friend of Napoleon III's wife, the Empress Eugenie.

1913-19] *The ball . . . the mountain* A version of the myth of Sisyphus, the king of Corinth who was condemned to roll a heavy stone up a hill in Hades only to have it roll down again.

1919-23] *he ruled . . . dice-throw* An indirect allusion to the tangled blood lines that allowed Louis Napoleon to assume the name Napoleon III. He was the son of Hortense de Beauharnais (daughter of the Empress Josephine) and Louis Bonaparte, a brother of Napoleon I. Speculation persisted that Louis Napoleon's biological father was the Comte de Flahaut, Hortense's lover; she admitted that another of her sons was sired by Flahaut. The matter was politically explosive because much of the Emperor's support was based on reverence for the name Napoleon. At his assumption of the name Napoleon

III, English journalists scoffed that his only claim to imperial power was "I am the nephew of my uncle." See also ll. 2020-71.

1923-53] *Oft Sagacity . . . free state* Here, as with the matter of Nice and Savoy, B has rendered what Napoleon III actually did through a speech of Sagacity. In 1852, desirous of founding a dynasty, the Emperor sought a mate. His advisers went in search of a candidate, approaching first Princess Caroline of Wasa and then Princess Adelaide of Hohenlohe; both women refused the offer. Meanwhile, Napoleon III had fallen in love with and proposed to Eugénie de Montijo, a well-born (but not royal) Spanish woman. Marrying a commoner later allowed the Emperor to characterize his family as a dynasty arising from the populace.

1959-64] *God drops . . . of rock* An adaptation of the parable of the sower, Matt. 13:4-6, Mark 4:5-6, Luke 8:5-6.

1975] *Salvatore's boy* B alludes to Salvatore Rosa (1615-73), a celebrated Neapolitan painter. Whether B refers to a particular anecdote is not known, but Rosa had several children, two of whom had some artistic skill. In 1656, at the age of fifteen, his elder son Rosalo was praised by his father for having a vigorous personality and a great talent for painting; the boy died in a plague a few months later. Rosa's last child, Augusto, was born in 1657; after Salvatore's death Augusto supported himself by making and selling copies of his father's works (J. Scott, *Salvatore Rosa: his life and times* [New Haven, 1995], 109, 220).

1986-2019] *wayside temple . . . Clitumnian god . . . willow shade* By conflating two distinct legends, B throws the Prince into a confusion he will have to clear up later, in ll. 2135-43. There is no traditional connection between the Italian river Clitumnis, reputed to turn sacred cattle white, and a temple whose chief priest gained his position by murdering his predecessor. The sources for B's tale are all Latin: Virgil (*Georgics*, 2.146-48) mentions the ox-whitening; Strabo (*Geography*, 5.239-40) tells of the murderous priesthood; Propertius (*Elegies*, 2.19, 25-26) repeats Virgil; and Pliny the Younger (*Epistles*, 8.8) describes a temple near the Clitumnis. According to Orr (170n.), B had visited the Clitumnis, a small stream in Umbria, N of Rome; the so-called temple there is in fact an ancient tomb converted into a Christian church.

1994] *Land of the Ox* Some etymologists speculate that Italia is a Greek form of the Italic word *Vitelia*, which means "calf-land."

2002-6] *Each priest . . . murder* Strabo locates the particular cult of Diana which got its priest this way at Aricia, on the shore of Lake Nemi, in Latium SE of Rome (*Geography*, 5.239-40). Though fairly obscure in B's day, the cult has become well-known since. Sir James Frazer gave it a prominent place in *The Golden Bough*.

2066] *legitimate blockhead* Another reference to the rumors about Louis Napoleon's parentage; see l. 1919-23n.

2073] *pendule* French for "timepiece."

2080-81] *A nod . . . Homer* Thus Horace, in *The Art of Poetry*, 358-60: "I am indignant when good Homer nods; but truly in a long work it is permissible to sleep."

2084] *Thiers* See l. 1223n.

2090] *if one . . . the tongue* Louis Napoleon was a poor public speaker, having a weak voice and a habit of speaking into the lectern.

2108] *famed cave-fish* Catfish of the species *amblyopsidae*, native to North and Central America, live in caves and underground rivers and have underdeveloped, functionless eye structures. This modification caused the *amblyopsidae* to become an oft-cited example in debates about evolution and natural selection.

2118-19] *lust o' the flesh . . . pride of life* From 1 John 2:16.

2120] *prince . . . air* Satan, as denominated in Eph. 2:2; see l. 1697n. above.

2130-31] *gorget . . . spurs* Referring to the weaponry of fighting cocks, and perhaps distantly to the English cartoonists' image of Napoleon III as a strutting rooster (see l. 1604-5n.).

2141] *Nemi was the true lake's style* See ll. 1986-2019, 2002-6, and nn.

2144] *Residenz . . . Leicester Square* See ll. 133, 8, and nn.

2150-55] *My Cousin-Duke . . . or quits!* Perhaps B alludes to Napoleon Joseph Bonaparte, called Prince Napoleon (1822-91), Napoleon III's only cousin of serious political importance. Married to the daughter of King Victor Emmanuel of Italy, he was devoted to liberal causes and attempted to restrain French military control in Tuscany; he must have been the recipient of any number of significant letters from the Emperor. It is also possible that the Cousin-Duke and the letter to him are entirely imaginary, or that B glances here at the high-stakes gambles that Napoleon III took in the diplomatic maneuverings preceding the Franco-Prussian War (see ll. 137-38n. above). For the importance of those communiques, see J. Bierman, *Napoleon III and His Carnival Empire* (N. Y., 1988), 324-29.